The Torture Memos

ALSO BY DAVID COLE

Enemy Aliens:
Double Standards and Constitutional Freedoms in the War on Terrorism

Justice at War: The Men and Ideas that Shape America's War in Terror

Less Safe, Less Free: Why America Is Losing the War on Terror

No Equal Justice:
Race and Class in the American Criminal Justice System

Terrorism and the Constitution:
Sacrificing Civil Liberties for National Security

The Torture Memos

Rationalizing the Unthinkable

EDITED
AND WITH INTRODUCTORY
COMMENTARY BY DAVID COLE

ONEWORLD
OXFORD

A Oneworld Book

First published in Great Britain and the Commonwealth by
Oneworld Publications 2009
Published by arrangement with The New Press, New York

ISBN 978–1–85168–735–0

Cover design designedbydavid.co.uk
Printed and bound in Great Britain by Bell & Bain, Glasgow

Oneworld Publications
UK: 185 Banbury Road, Oxford, OX2 7AR, England
USA: 38 Greene Street, 4th Floor, New York, NY 10013, USA
www.oneworld-publications.com

Contents

Foreword
by Philippe Sands
vii

Introductory Commentary: Torture Law
1

August 1, 2002, Memorandum for Alberto R. Gonzales
Re: Standards of Conduct for Interrogation
under 18 U.S.C. §§ 2340-2340A
41

August 1, 2002, Memorandum for John Rizzo
Interrogation of al Qaeda Operative
106

December 30, 2004, Memorandum for James B. Comey
Re: Legal Standards Applicable Under 18 U.S.C. §§ 2340-2340A
128

May 10, 2005, Memorandum for John A. Rizzo
Re: Application of 18 U.S.C. §§ 2340-2340A
to Certain Techniques That May Be Used
in the Interrogation of a High Value al Qaeda Detainee
152

May 10, 2005, Memorandum for John A. Rizzo
Re: Application of 18 U.S.C. §§ 2340-2340A
to the Combined Use of Certain Techniques
in the Interrogation of High Value al Qaeda Detainees
199

May 30, 2005, Memorandum for John A. Rizzo
Re: Application of United States Obligations Under Article 16
of the Convention Against Torture to Certain Techniques That
May Be Used in the Interrogation of High Value al Qaeda Detainees
225

April 22, 2009 Release of Declassified Narrative Describing
the Department of Justice Office of Legal Counsel's Opinions
on the CIA's Detention and Interrogation Program
275

Foreword

The world is watching the United States' efforts to come to terms with the abuse unleashed in the aftermath of 9/11. On the heels of a potentially far-reaching Spanish criminal investigation, in April 2009 the Barack Obama Administration declassified more legal memos. This important volume brings together the newly released documents, together with some released in the summer of 2004, in the aftermath of the publication of the Abu Ghraib photographs. Whether these new documents allow the country to "move forward," as President Obama intends, is unclear. The documents set out in meticulous detail the full extent of the cruelty: who, how, and what has been starkly revealed, from the legal deliberations to the number of times waterboarding was used. As David Cole notes here, these documents "are the 'smoking guns' in the torture controversy." That controversy has crossed the Atlantic, as reports circulate about the involvement of British intelligence officers – duly authorized by the government – to contribute to the interview of detainees who had been (or were to be) tortured in circumstances in which the legal memos set out in this book may have played a role.

When President Obama took office, the evidence of torture was strong. Susan Crawford, appointed by President George W. Bush to head the Guantánamo military commission process, confirmed that the use of stress positions, sleep deprivation, dogs, and forced grooming on Mohammed al-Qahtani, a Guantánamo detainee, was torture. The Obama Administration agrees that waterboarding is torture. The issue was not how to characterize these international crimes, but what to do about them. News of a Spanish investigation by Judge Baltasar Garzon appears to have catalyzed debate on what to do about the Department of Justice (DOJ) and other senior lawyers and officials known as the Bush Six (Alberto Gonzales, David Addington, Jim Haynes, John Yoo, Jay Bybee, and Doug Feith), as well as others closely associated with the embrace of cruelty. Particular attention may focus on those present in the meeting at CIA offices on July 13, 2002, when it seems that the decision was taken to approve an interrogation plan that included waterboarding.[1]

President Obama has assured CIA officers that "those who carried out their duties relying in good faith upon legal advice from the Department of Justice" would not be prosecuted. Using careful words, however, he did not exclude all prosecutions. "With respect to those who formulated those legal decisions," he added, "that is going to be more of a decision for the attorney general . . . and I don't want to prejudge that." Further investigation is inevitable. And it is required, by the 1984 Convention against Torture.

Five years have passed since the release of a one-page memo written by Jim Haynes, Donald Rumsfeld's lawyer at the U.S. Department of Defense, in November 2002. In plain violation of international law, the Rumsfeld memo provided blanket authorization for the use of stress positions, sleep deprivation, dogs, and nudity. It left open the use of waterboarding. This memo secretly relied on the August 1, 2002, DOJ memos and caused the torture of Mohammed al-Qahtani, at Guantánamo. The techniques later migrated to Afghanistan, Iraq, and Abu Ghraib.

It is difficult to understand how the senior lawyers involved—trained at Harvard and other fine law schools—could have autho-

---

1. See memo drafted by Senator John D. Rockefeller, chairman of the Senate Committee on Intelligence, April 19, 2009, reprinted in this volume at page 275.

rized torture. I spent eighteen months trekking around the U.S. to write *Torture Team*, meeting many of the officials involved. For the most part, these were ordinary, decent people. Some spoke openly and, I thought, honestly. Others didn't; the higher up the political chain, the greater the hubris.

Early on, the idea of criminal investigations against the senior lawyers and officials seemed almost preposterous. Yet as the ideas got off the ground, they developed a life of their own. A seed was sown and, in the background, a seething, broad discontent. In the summer of 2008, fifty-four members of the U.S. House of Repre-sentatives called for the appointment of a special prosecutor. Hear-ings before the U.S. Congress produced thousands of pages of new documents; the story firmed up; the central, dastardly role of the lawyers became ever clearer as a common plan to get around the laws came into sight. Laws didn't apply, or they created no rights for detainees. Established definitions of torture were ditched. Ob-jections from lawyers with knowledge—in the military or State Department—were cast aside.

As security and national interest trumped all else, the circle of complicity and weakness grew in size. Some I spoke with told me categorically that they had no involvement in early decisions, even if their names appeared in publicly available memos. Others dis-sembled, misled, and lied. Some claims just collapsed. Before the House Judiciary Committee, a Republican congressman reported information that waterboarding was used on only three men for a grand total of three minutes. What's all the fuss about, the con-gressman seemed to be saying. Then President Obama released these new memos and we learned that two men were waterboarded a total of 266 times in a limited period of time.

The torture has deeply damaged the reputation of the U.S., a country that has done more than any other to promote the idea of the rule of international law. Such harm cannot be repaired merely by putting out the documents. Accountability is needed. An in-vestigation is inevitable, to get to the full facts, but what sort? In theory, a criminal investigation and an independent or congressional inquiry are not mutually exclusive. In reality, it is difficult for them to go hand in hand. Criminal proceedings will halt the flow of information, as those who fear prosecution clam up. Yet serious crimes have been committed, and as a nation of laws, the U.S. is bound to investigate criminal wrongdoing. This is a difficult balance to strike, as other countries, like South Africa and Chile, have found. The way forward may be to begin with the fullest possible investigation by a blue-chip independent commission, as David Cole suggests, with the power to compel the production of documents and witness testimony. This will only be a temporary reprieve of the inevitable criminal inquiry, however, whether in the U.S., Spain, or elsewhere.

Yet it is testament to America's remarkable powers of reinvention that so spirited a debate could take place so soon after the "dark and painful chapter." Eventually the system worked, sort of, as ever more documents emerged. The body politic and the media finally got their act together, sort of. The U.S. Attorney General appointed a special prosecutor to investigate the allegations and the role of the legal memos, sort of. The Supreme Court gave decisive rulings, sort of. And it's hard to imagine many other countries allowing so much material to become available so quickly. The difference of approach in Britain, where the culture of secrecy remains dominant, is stark, to say the least. In the meantime, and for the foreseeable future, the eyes of the world are on the U.S. The Bush Six and their cohorts remain in a deep, legal black hole of their own making. As this book spreads the facts, that hole can only get deeper.

Philippe Sands QC
Professor of Law, University College London
Barrister, Matrix Chambers

Introductory Commentary: Torture Law

"Those methods, read on a bright, sunny, safe day in April 2009, appear graphic and disturbing." So stated Dennis Blair, President Barack Obama's director of national intelligence, as he sought to downplay the horror of CIA interrogation techniques described and sanctioned in four previously secret Justice Department memos disclosed on April 16, 2009. The techniques, he suggested, would have looked very different in August 2002, when they were first authorized.[1]

"It was a bright cold day in April, and the clocks were striking thirteen." So begins *1984*, the classic novel of the security state by George Orwell. It's unlikely that Blair intended the allusion, but the reference could not have been more apt. The Justice Department memos do precisely what Orwell foretold: twist language and the law in order to rationalize the unthinkable.

A Note on Pagination
Because page numbers of memoranda reprinted in the current book do not match page numbers of the original memoranda, the author provides both page references in footnotes. Page numbers as found in the original memos are referenced without brackets; the equivalent page number in the current book follows within brackets.

1. Statement by the Director of National Intelligence, Dennis C. Blair, April 16, 2009, available at http://www.dni.gov/press_releases/20090416_1_release .pdf.

The interrogation techniques used by the CIA against al Qaeda suspects have inspired two competing narratives. Many have argued that the techniques were patently illegal, and surely would have been viewed as such had an enemy of the United States used them against American soldiers—in August 2002 or April 2009. No good-faith legal argument could possibly give a green light to stripping a suspect naked, slamming him repeatedly into a wall, dousing him with cold water, slapping his face, depriving him of any sleep for eleven days straight, forcing him into stress positions and small dark boxes for hours at a time, and waterboarding him repeatedly—183 times in the case of Khalid Sheikh Mohammed, and 83 times in the case of Abu Zubaydah, two al Qaeda detainees.[2]

Others, however, such as Dennis Blair and former attorney general Michael Mukasey, point to the overwhelming panic and fear that pervaded the United States in the wake of the terrorist attacks of September 11, 2001; note the ambiguity of the laws governing torture and cruel, inhuman, and degrading treatment; and insist that government officials sought only to approach, not to cross, the line of illegality. Cabinet officials directed that the CIA be permitted to use only lawful interrogation tactics, and in the legal memos reproduced here, U.S. Justice Department lawyers engaged in a good-faith effort to draw a difficult line. One might disagree with that line with the benefit of hindsight, they would say, but surely no crimes were intentionally committed.[3]

---

2. *See, e.g.,* Jane Mayer, *The Dark Side: The Inside Story of How the War on Terror Turned into a War on American Ideals* (Doubleday: 2008); Jamie Mayerfeld, "Playing by Our Own Rules: How U.S. Marginalization of International Human Rights Law Led to Torture," 20 Harv. Hum. Rts. J. 89 (2007): 103–04; David Luban, "Liberalism, Torture, and the Ticking Bomb," 91 Va. L. Rev. 1425 (2005).

3. *See* Michael B. Mukasey, "National Security and the Rule of Law," 32 Harv. J. of L. & Pub. Pol'y 831 (2009); David Rivkin and Lee Casey, "The Memos Prove We Didn't Torture," *Wall Street Journal* (April 19, 2009); Neil A. Lewis, "Official Defends Signing Interrogation Memos," *New York Times* (April 29, 2009): p. A12 (reporting that Jay Bybee, who signed the first two memos approving CIA interrogation tactics, defended the memos as "a good-faith analysis of the law" of the "thin line between harsh treatment of a high-ranking

The release of the previously secret Justice Department memos in April 2009 allows us to go beneath the surface of these competing claims and examine how George W. Bush's administration actually sought to justify its actions. This volume reproduces, for the first time, all of the principal memos drafted by the U.S. Justice Department's Office of Legal Counsel (OLC) on the CIA's interrogation program. The first two were issued in secret on August 1, 2002; the third was issued publicly on December 30, 2004; the last three were issued secretly in May 2005. The memos have been edited only to eliminate unnecessary repetition. (Some sections remain blacked out because they are still classified.) The final document in the book, drafted by the office of Senator John D. Rockefeller IV, chairman of the Select Committee on Intelligence, provides a valuable official overview of the process that led to the OLC memos.[4]

Analysis of all six memos taken together tells a more complicated story than the two competing narratives that have thus far dominated public debate. The memos show that there were indeed many close and difficult questions of judgment to be made, upon which reasonable lawyers could disagree. Not all physically coercive interrogation, for example, is torture. And determining whether tactics rise to the level of torture requires difficult distinctions between "severe" and less-than-severe pain and suffering, and between "prolonged" and temporary mental harm.

Al Qaeda terrorist that is not torture and harsh treatment that is"); John Yoo, *War by Other Means* (Atlantic Monthly Press: 2008): 168–87 (former OLC lawyer who authored the August 2002 memos defending the memos as justified in the name of national defense and legally sound); "What Went Wrong?: Torture and the Office of Legal Counsel in the Bush Administration," Hearing Before the Senate Judiciary Committee, Subcommittee on Administrative Oversight and the Courts (May 13, 2009) (testimony of Michael Stokes Paulsen, Robert Turner, and Jeffrey F. Addicott).

4. Other legal memos, some secret and some now public, are relevant to a number of the broader issues presented, including the status of al Qaeda and Taliban detainees under the Geneva Conventions, the scope of presidential power, and the law governing military interrogations. This volume focuses on the CIA interrogation policies, however, and provides all of the memos authorizing that policy.

Precisely because the questions were so difficult, however, one would expect a good-faith analysis to reach a nuanced conclusion, perhaps approving some measures while definitely prohibiting others. Yet on *every* question, no matter how much the law had to be stretched, the OLC lawyers reached the same result—the CIA could do whatever it had proposed to do.

Most tellingly, the lawyers secretly preserved that bottom line even as the law in public appeared to tighten its standards to prohibit these tactics. Thus, when its initial August 2002 memo was leaked to the press and widely condemned, the OLC publicly issued a replacement memo, dated December 30, 2004, which pointedly rejected several arguments and interpretations advanced in its prior memo. But the secret memos now disclosed reveal that even as the OLC sought to convince the public that it had changed its view, behind the scenes it continued to approve all the same interrogation tactics. And when, in 2005, Congress threatened to tighten the law further by confirming that every person in U.S. custody was protected against not only torture, but all cruel, inhuman, and degrading treatment, the Bush lawyers drafted yet another secret opinion, concluding that none of the CIA's tactics could even be considered cruel, inhuman, or degrading. The latter memos were issued years after the panic induced by the 9/11 attacks had begun to fade. When considered as a whole, the memos read not as an objective assessment of what the law permits or precludes, but as a strained effort to rationalize a predetermined—and illegal—result. Rather than demand that the CIA conform its conduct to the law, the lawyers contorted the law to conform it to the CIA's desires.

The memos reproduced here, even more than the photographs from Abu Ghraib or interrogation records from Guantánamo, are the "smoking guns" in the torture controversy. They show that abusive tactics were the deliberately considered official policy of the executive branch, not the isolated misdeeds of a few "bad apples" or rogue agents. They reveal a concerted effort over many years to maintain the program, even as the law changed in order to prohibit it more clearly. And they provide an object lesson in the limits of law when employed by those who seek not to uphold legal principle and protect the vulnerable, but to facilitate the wishes of the powerful and minimize the possibility of accountability.

To understand what this meant on the ground, one need go no further than the following account, told to the International Committee of the Red Cross by Abu Zubaydah, the first person subjected to the CIA's "enhanced interrogation techniques":

> About two or three months after I arrived in this place, the interrogation began again, but with more intensity than before. Then the real torturing started. Two black wooden boxes were brought into the room outside my cell. One was tall, slightly higher than me and narrow. Measuring perhaps in area 1m × 0.75m and 2m in height. The other was shorter, perhaps only 1m in height. I was taken out of my cell and one of the interrogators wrapped a towel around my neck, then they used it to swing me around and smash me repeatedly against the hard walls of the room. I was also repeatedly slapped in the face. As I was still shackled, the pushing and pulling around meant that the shackles pulled painfully on my ankles. . . .
>
> After the beating I was then placed in the small box. They placed a cloth or cover over the box to cut out all light and restrict my air supply. As it was not high enough even to sit upright, I had to crouch down. It was very difficult because of my wounds. The stress on my legs held in this position meant my wounds both in the leg and stomach became very painful. . . . It was always cold in the room, but when the cover was placed over the box it made it hot and sweaty inside. The wound on my leg began to open and started to bleed. I don't know how long I remained in the small box, I think I may have slept or maybe fainted.
>
> I was then dragged from the small box, unable to walk properly and put on what looked like a hospital bed, and strapped down very tightly with belts. A black cloth was

then placed over my face and the interrogators used a mineral water bottle to pour water on the cloth so that I could not breathe. After a few minutes the cloth was removed and the bed was rotated into an upright position. The pressure of the straps on my wounds was very painful. I vomited. The bed was then again lowered to a horizontal position and the same torture carried out again with the black cloth over my face and water poured on from a bottle. On this occasion my head was in a more backward, downwards position and the water was poured on for a longer time. I struggled against the straps, trying to breathe, but it was hopeless. I thought I was going to die. I lost control of my urine. Since then I still lose control of my urine when under stress.[5]

How did it become official U.S. policy to treat human beings in United States' custody in this manner? What rationales could possibly justify such conduct? And what is to be done now to correct the wrongs? These are the critical questions posed by the Bush administration's foray into "enhanced interrogation techniques." The Justice Department memos reproduced here shed important and disturbing new light on these questions, and show that at the core of the problem was the failure of some of the nation's most powerful lawyers to live up to their ethical and legal responsibilities.

The Legal Background

The law recognizes few absolutes. Virtually all of the law's highest principles acknowledge exceptions. Thou shalt not kill—except in self-defense, or if the target is a military opponent during wartime,

---

5. International Committee of the Red Cross, *ICRC Report on the Treatment of Fourteen "High Value Detainees"* in CIA Custody (February 2007). The report was leaked to Mark Danner and first published on the *New York Review of Books* website, at http://www.nybooks.com/icrc-report.pdf.

or, in the United States, if a jury issues a death sentence after a fair trial. Even innocent civilians may be killed when their deaths are a foreseeable but unavoidable and proportionate collateral consequence of a legitimate attack on a military target. Race discrimination triggers the U.S. Constitution's most skeptical scrutiny, yet it is permissible with a sufficiently compelling justification, as in some affirmative action programs. The First Amendment commands that "Congress shall make no law" abridging free speech, but, in fact, Congress may do so for sufficiently important reasons, such as preventing imminent crime, protecting children from sexual exploitation, or regulating fraudulent business transactions.

Torture is different. International and U.S. law provide that torture is never justifiable, under any circumstances, for any reason, in war or peace. The absolute character of this ban has spawned countless debates. Wouldn't torturing one individual be justifiable, the British philosopher Jeremy Bentham asked, if doing so could save 100 others from being tortured themselves? In modern parlance, the question often takes the form of the "ticking time bomb" hypothetical; if torturing an individual who has planted a ticking time bomb were the only way to find and defuse the bomb and save the lives of thousands, shouldn't the prohibition give way? The fact that the prohibition is absolute means that the answer to such questions must always be no. Whatever benefit torture might conceivably bring, or more to the point, no matter what disaster it might help prevent, the prohibition must hold. (In practice, this does not mean that a U.S. state official will never torture, but only that if he does, his actions will be deemed illegal and he will face appropriate consequences.)

In the United States, such discussions were generally confined to philosophy classrooms before the terrorist attacks of September 11, 2001. As the world now knows only too well, however, after 9/11 the issue was no longer academic. Some commentators, invoking the specter of nuclear, chemical, or biological weapons, suggested that to prevent another terrorist attack, torture would be warranted.[6] The administration spoke less explicitly. Cofer Black, director of the CIA's Counterterrorism Center, told Congress in 2002 that "after 9/11, the gloves came off."[7] President Bush ultimately admitted that he had authorized the CIA to use what he called "enhanced interrogation techniques." But Bush insisted that the United States did not engage in torture, and adhered to all its legal obligations in its treatment of detainees.

What became increasingly clear over time, however, and is now confirmed in chilling detail by the memos reproduced here, is that the Bush administration "adhered" to the law only by twisting its meaning in extraordinary ways. Once the lawyers were done, laws designed to prohibit absolutely all forms of torture and cruel, inhuman, and degrading treatment were read instead to *permit* exactly that.

The Convention Against Torture, which the United States championed and has ratified, and which has now been signed by more than 150 other nations, was adopted precisely because we know that government officials will feel tempted to employ harsh and coercive interrogation tactics when they feel threatened—whether to deter dissent, to terrorize opposition, or to obtain information from suspects. History has shown that even officials acting with the best intentions may come to feel, especially in times of crisis, that the end justifies the means, and that the greater good of national security makes it permissible to inflict physical or psychological pain on a resisting suspect in order to break his will and make him talk. History has also shown that taking that route—no matter how "well-intentioned"—dehumanizes both the suspect and his interrogator, deeply corrodes the system of justice, makes a fair trial

---

6. "Dershowitz: Torture Could Be Justified," interview conducted March 4, 2003, available at http://edition.cnn.com/2003/LAW/03/03/cnna.Dershowitz; Charles Krauthammer, "The Truth About Torture," *Weekly Standard*, Vol. 11, Issue 12 (December 5, 2005).

7. Joint Investigation Into September 11th: Fifth Public Hearing, September 26, 2002—Joint House/Senate Intelligence Committee Hearing, statement of Cofer Black, former chief, CIA Counterterrorism Center.

virtually impossible, and often fuels the very threat to the nation's security that was said to warrant the interrogation tactics in the first place. Knowing that history, the world's lawyers and statesmen sought to place torture off-limits forever, forbidding it in absolute terms in a series of international treaties, culminating in the Convention Against Torture itself, which provides that "[n]o exceptional circumstances whatsoever, whether a state of war or a threat of war, internal political instability or any other public emergency, may be invoked as a justification of torture."[8]

If laws such as the Torture Convention are to work, however, lawyers must be willing to stand up for them. That means being willing to say no when asked whether it is permissible to treat a prisoner as Abu Zubaydah was treated. In the memos reproduced here, Justice Department lawyers said yes—again and again and again. The fact that it took them nearly two hundred pages to do so is itself a sign of how much effort it required to say yes in the face of an international treaty barring both torture and "cruel, inhuman, and degrading treatment." To conclude, as the memos did, that waterboarding not only does not amount to torture, but is not even cruel, inhuman, or degrading, takes not only a lot of work, but an affirmative suspension of disbelief.

This is not to deny that some of the questions addressed in the memos were difficult ones without obvious answers. Neither "torture" nor "cruel, inhuman, or degrading treatment" is defined in crystal-clear terms. The federal statute making torture a crime, 18 U.S.C. § 2340, requires an assessment of whether conduct is intended to inflict "severe" pain or suffering or "prolonged" mental harm, and there is no objective benchmark for when pain becomes "severe" or how long mental harm must last to be "prolonged." To judge whether the CIA's techniques were "cruel, inhuman, or degrading" required an assessment of whether they "shock the conscience"—but how do we know what the collective conscience

---

8. Convention Against Torture and Other Cruel, Inhuman or Degrading Treatment or Punishment (CAT), art. 2 ¶ 2, 1465 UNTS 85 (June 26, 1987).

is, much less when it has been shocked? Without a doubt, reasonable people could reach different conclusions on many (although not all) of the questions addressed in the memos.

Yet no matter how hard or simple the questions presented, the OLC lawyers always said yes. The six OLC memos included here offer, for the first time, the opportunity to assess the OLC's legal reasoning in reaching that result. The first two memos, dated August 1, 2002, set forth a general interpretation of the federal torture statute (August 2002 Torture Memo for Alberto R. Gonzales), and apply that standard to a proposed interrogation plan for Abu Zubaydah (August 2002 Interrogation Memo for John Rizzo). Both memos were issued in secret, but the memo interpreting the torture statute was leaked to the public in 2004. The third memo, dated December 30, 2004, was issued publicly as a replacement for the August 2002 Torture Memo. The last three memos were issued in secret in May 2005. Two, dated May 10 (May 2005 Techniques Memo and May 2005 Combined Use Memo), address whether the CIA's interrogation techniques, used individually or in combination, violate the torture statute under the new interpretation in the December 30, 2004, memo. The third, dated May 30 (May 2005 CID Memo), asks whether the CIA's program constitutes "cruel, inhuman, or degrading treatment." With the exception of the August 2002 Torture Memo and the December 30, 2004, memo, all of these opinions were kept secret until President Obama ordered their disclosure in April 2009.

On the surface, the law governing interrogation evolved over the period in which the memos were in effect. The publicly released December 2004 memo disagreed with many of the August 2002 Torture Memo's arguments, and opened with the proclamation that "Torture is abhorrent both to American law and values and to international norms." When the public learned in January 2005 that the Justice Department had secretly taken the position that the ban on cruel, inhuman, and degrading treatment did not protect foreign nationals held by the CIA abroad, Congress, led by Senator John McCain, sought to reverse that position. Again, it appeared that the law governing interrogations had changed. But the memos reveal that no matter how much the law changed on the surface, the Justice Department's lawyers' secret bottom line never changed. Despite the very public repudiation of the August 2002 Torture Memo, despite the passage of the "McCain amendment," and despite repeated assurances that the U.S. "does not torture," official U.S. policy, as reflected in the secret memos, continued to authorize the CIA to strip suspects naked, deprive them of sleep for seven to eleven days straight, slam them into walls, slap them, douse them with cold water, force them into painful stress positions and cramped boxes for hours, and waterboard them repeatedly.

The Office of Legal Counsel

In any context, such lawyering would be troubling. But it is especially disturbing given the role of the Office of Legal Counsel that issued them. That office is designed to serve as the "constitutional conscience" of the Justice Department. Its responsibility is to provide authoritative interpretations on questions of federal constitutional and statutory law for the executive branch. It typically attracts some of the United States' best lawyers, and its alumni include former chief justice William Rehnquist, Justice Antonin Scalia, former solicitors general Theodore Olson and Walter Dellinger, former attorneys general Nicholas Katzenbach and William Barr, State Department Legal Adviser (and former Yale Law School dean) Harold Koh, Georgetown Law dean Alex Aleinikoff, Harvard law professor Cass Sunstein, and federal appellate judges Malcolm Wilkey, Jay Bybee, Tim Dyk, and Michael Luttig. Unlike the White House Counsel's office, whose lawyers serve the president as an individual, OLC lawyers are said to represent the long-term institutional interests of the executive branch, and are supposed to exercise judgment independent of the political will of the president.[9]

---

9. Cornelia T. Pillard, "The Unfulfilled Promise of the Constitution in Executive Hands," 103 Mich. L. Rev. 676 (2005).

When it comes to covert activities such as the CIA interrogation program, judgments of legality are often uniquely in executive hands, as the judiciary and Congress often will not even learn of the activities' existence. Under settled practice, the president relies on his attorney general for advice about the legality of such programs. It is the OLC, in turn, that actually researches and drafts such advice in the form of an "opinion" or memorandum, as the attorney general has formally delegated his authority to render legal opinions to that office. While the attorney general and president are free to reject the OLC's advice, as a matter of custom and practice they almost never do.[10] As Jack Goldsmith, one of the heads of the OLC under President Bush, has said, "OLC is, and views itself as, the frontline institution responsible for ensuring that the executive branch charged with executing the law is itself bound by law."[11]

The role of the OLC lawyer gives rise to special professional and constitutional obligations. Private lawyers are sometimes considered "hired guns," whose obligation is to do their client's bidding—within the law, of course. A private lawyer acting for a criminal defendant, for example, knows that his job is simply to make the best case he can for his client's innocence. In that setting, the defense lawyer is playing a very particular role in an adversarial system, where the prosecutor will in turn present the strongest arguments in favor of conviction, and the judge or jury will render an objective decision only after hearing both sides in a public trial.

---

10. *See, e.g.,* Dawn E. Johnsen, "Faithfully Executing the Laws: Internal Legal Constraints on Executive Power," 54 UCLA L. Rev. 1559, 1577 (2007) ("By virtue of regulation and tradition, OLC's legal opinions are considered binding within the executive branch, unless overruled by the attorney general or the president, an exceedingly rare occurrence."); Randolph D. Moss, "Executive Branch Legal Interpretation: A Perspective from the Office of Legal Counsel," 52 Admin. L. Rev. 1303, 1320 (2000) ("We've been able to go for over 200 years without conclusively determining whether the law demands adherence to [OLC opinions], because agencies have in practice treated these opinions as binding.")

11. Jack Goldsmith, *The Terror Presidency* (W.W. Norton: 2007): p. 33.

The lawyers writing the memos for the Office of Legal Counsel, by contrast, were operating in a setting that permitted no adversarial presentation or public scrutiny. In that context, the lawyer's obligation is to provide objective advice as an "honest broker," not to act as an advocate or a hired gun. And because of the covert nature of the program, the OLC lawyers were the only line of defense for individuals who had been "disappeared" into secret CIA prisons and had no recourse to any court, lawyer, or human rights monitor. The OLC lawyers had the opportunity, and the *responsibility*, to prevent illegal conduct *before* it occurred. The lawyers involved in drafting the "torture memos"—Jay Bybee, John Yoo, Daniel Levin, and Stephen Bradbury—failed to live up to these obligations. In their hands, law became not a constraint on power, but the handmaiden of unconscionable abuse.

The Memos in Context

To appreciate what is most troubling about the torture memos, it helps to understand their provenance and purpose. In the months immediately following 9/11, the administration, understandably concerned about the possibility of further attacks, grew increasingly frustrated about the paucity of intelligence it had obtained on al Qaeda, and began to consider more aggressive interrogation tactics. Military and CIA officials consulted psychologists and trainers involved in the U.S. military's Survival, Evasion, Resistance, Escape (SERE) training, which seeks to prepare members of the U.S. military to resist abuse and torture if captured. SERE training was modeled on illegal interrogation and torture tactics used by the United States' enemies, including the Chinese during the Korean War. According to the Senate Armed Services Committee, SERE training includes "stripping students of their clothing, placing them in stress positions, putting hoods over their heads, disrupting their sleep, treating them like animals, subjecting them to loud music and flashing lights, and exposing them to extreme temperatures. It can also include face and body slaps and until recently . . . waterboarding."[12] Despite the fact that these measures were designed to replicate illegal interrogation tactics used against American soldiers, both the military and the CIA, after 9/11, undertook to "reverse engineer" them for use not as defensive training measures, but as affirmative techniques for questioning al Qaeda detainees.[13]

In late March 2002, U.S. officials captured Abu Zubaydah, a senior al Qaeda operative, and transferred him to a secret CIA prison. A seasoned FBI interrogator, Ali Soufan, was immediately dispatched to interrogate him. Soufan later testified in Congress that Abu Zubaydah was responsive to traditional noncoercive interrogation methods, and provided important intelligence, including details about Khalid Sheikh Mohammed's role in 9/11, and Jose Padilla's plans to engage in terrorism in the United States.[14] CIA officials were nonetheless convinced that Abu Zubaydah was not being sufficiently forthcoming, and in April and May 2002, CIA lawyers met with Justice Department and White House officials and lawyers to discuss "alternative interrogation methods."

Nervous about their vulnerability to prosecution or other sanction, the CIA sought explicit legal blessing from the Justice Department's Office of Legal Counsel for its proposed interrogation plan. As Jack Goldsmith has explained, a legal opinion from the OLC stating that the CIA's tactics were legal was for all practical purposes a "get out of jail free" card.[15] Whether or not the advice was a correct statement of the law, it would be virtually impossible for the Justice Department to prosecute someone for authorizing or undertaking conduct that the Justice Department itself had officially advised was lawful.

---

12. SASC Inquiry Into the Treatment of Detainees in U.S. Custody, Executive Summary, p. xiv.

13. *Id.* at xiv (quoting Richard Shiffrin, deputy general counsel, Department of Defense).

14. Statement of Ali Soufan Before the Senate Committee on the Judiciary, May 13, 2009, pp. 4–5.

15. Jack Goldsmith, *The Terror Presidency, supra* at 9.

If OLC lawyers had exercised independent judgment and said no, as they should have, that might well have been the end of the Bush administration's experiment with torture. Vice President Dick Cheney and his chief counsel, David Addington, would undoubtedly have put tremendous pressure on the OLC to change its views. Had the OLC stood firm, however, it is difficult to imagine even the Bush-Cheney White House going forward with a program that the OLC said was illegal. But in what might be called the "original sin" in this narrative, the office said yes. In two memos issued August 1, 2002, the OLC gave the green light to every tactic the CIA had proposed.[16]

The CIA, acting on the authority of the August 2002 memos, and reportedly with the specific approval of high-level administration officials, including Vice President Dick Cheney, Attorney General John Ashcroft, White House Counsel Alberto Gonzales, Defense Secretary Donald Rumsfeld, National Security Adviser Condoleezza Rice, Director of Central Intelligence George Tenet, and Secretary of State Colin Powell, then applied the measures to Abu Zubaydah and at least 27 other so-called "high-valued detainees" held incommunicado in CIA secret prisons.

The August 2002 decision had widespread effects, eventually reaching Abu Ghraib.[17] In March 2003, the OLC delivered a memo

---

16. In fact, the CIA was given the go-ahead even before that. On July 17, National national Security security Adviser Condoleezza Rice, with the apparent concurrence of her legal counsel, John Bellinger, authorized the proposed interrogation of Abu Zubaydah to proceed, subject to the OLC's determination of legality. On July 24 and 26, OLC lawyers orally advised the CIA that Attorney General John Ashcroft had determined that the proposed interrogation tactics were legal. The August 1 memos put that advice in writing. *See* OLC Opinions of the Detention and Interrogation Program, Submitted by John D. Rockefeller IV for Classification Review (Rockefeller Narrative), April 22, 2009, pp. 2–5 [pp. 277–280].

17. Except where otherwise indicated, the facts in this and the following two paragraphs regarding military interrogation policy are based on the report of the Senate Armed Services Committee. *Inquiry Into the Treatment of Detainees in U.S. Custody,* Report of the Committee on Armed Services, U.S. Senate, Nov. 20, 2008 (SASC Report), available at http://graphics8.nytimes.com/packages/images/nytint/docs/report-by-the-senate-armed-services-

on interrogation to the Department of Defense repeating the interpretation it had adopted for the CIA.[18] But even before that formal opinion was delivered, beginning in September 2002, the military proceeded as if it knew that SERE tactics had already been given the OLC's legal blessing. In September 2002, Guantánamo interrogators traveled to Fort Bragg, North Carolina, for training from SERE instructors. The same month, David Addington, the CIA's John Rizzo, and Defense Department general counsel William J. Haynes traveled together to Guantánamo. One week later, two Guantánamo behavioral scientists who had attended the Fort Bragg training drafted a memo proposing tougher interrogation techniques for Guantánamo. In October, Jonathan Fredman, chief counsel to the CIA's Counterterrorism Center, flew to Guantánamo to discuss interrogation techniques, "including sleep deprivation, death threats, and waterboarding, which was discussed in relation to its use in SERE training."[19]

By December, Defense Secretary Donald Rumsfeld had personally signed an order authorizing similar coercive interrogation tactics for use at Guantánamo. That order was then used to justify a lengthy interrogation of Mohammed al-Qahtani, who was thought to be the would-be 20th hijacker on 9/11. Al-Qahtani's interrogation was so brutal that Susan Crawford, head of military prosecutions at Guantánamo, concluded in May 2008 that she had to drop all war crimes charges against al-Qahtani because the case against him was tainted by the fact that he had been tortured.[20]

---

committee-on-detainee-treatment/original.pdf.

18. U.S. Dept of Justice, Office of Legal Counsel, Memorandum for William J. Haynes II, General Counsel of the Department of Defense, Re: Military Interrogation of Alien Unlawful Combatants Held Outside the United States, March 14, 2003, available at http://fas.org/irp/agency/doj/olc-interrogation.pdf. This memo is not reproduced in this volume because it addresses military interrogation, not CIA interrogation, and is in large part duplicative of the August 2002 Torture Memo.

19. SASC Report, *supra* at xvii.

20. Bob Woodward, "Detainee Tortured, Says U.S. Official," *Washington Post* (January 14, 2009), at A1. For an excellent in-depth account of the devel-

After Navy general counsel Alberto Mora objected that the tactics authorized by Rumsfeld "could rise to the level of torture" and threatened to issue a memo to that effect, Rumsfeld rescinded his order on January 15, 2003. However, even though Rumsfeld's order was in effect for only six weeks and was allegedly restricted to Guantánamo, a copy was sent to Afghanistan, where it continued to influence military interrogation practices long after it had been rescinded at Guantánamo. From there, the techniques made their way to Iraq via the Special Mission Unit Task Force, and then became "Standard Operating Procedures (SOPs) for all U.S. forces in Iraq."[21] Moreover, once the line of physical coercion was officially breached, a culture quickly developed that fostered unauthorized abuse. The results were broadcast to the world in June 2004 in a series of photographs of deeply degrading and depraved mistreatment of prisoners at Abu Ghraib.

Around the time that the Abu Ghraib photos emerged, someone leaked the August 2002 Torture Memo to the *Washington Post*, which published the memo on its website. The leaked memo did not address any specific techniques, but offered a perversely narrow definition of torture, limiting it to acts specifically intended to inflict pain of the severity associated with organ failure or death. Once subject to public scrutiny, the memo was widely condemned, and on December 30, 2004, the OLC issued a replacement. As noted above, the new memo struck a more acceptable tone, and rejected several aspects of the August 2002 Torture Memo's reasoning. But its single most important line was buried in a footnote, stating that "while we have identified various disagreements with the August 2002 Memorandum, we have reviewed this Office's prior opinions addressing issues involving treatment of detainees and *do not believe that any of their conclusions would be different* un-

---

opment of the Rumsfeld order, see Philippe Sands, *Torture Team* (Palgrave Macmillan: rev. paperback ed. 2009).

21. SASC Report, *supra* at xxiii.

der the standard set forth in this memorandum."[22] In other words, without the OLC's expressly saying so in public, waterboarding, body slamming, head- and abdomen-slapping, sleep deprivation, stress positions, and all the other tactics approved in August 2002 were still fully legal.

On May 10, 2005, the OLC issued two more secret memos on the CIA's interrogation program, confirming that the CIA's interrogation tactics remained legal under the December 30, 2004, memo. The new memos authorized every one of the CIA's tactics.[23] The second of the two memos concluded that even when all the tactics were applied in combination, they did not constitute torture.

The OLC's final memo, issued May 30, 2005, addresses the much broader ban on cruel, inhuman, and degrading treatment contained in the Torture Convention. As noted above, Congress, having learned that the Bush administration had sought to evade that ban by treating it as categorically inapplicable to foreigners held overseas, was threatening to adopt legislation to reaffirm that the ban applied to all persons in U.S. custody. The administration aggressively and publicly opposed any such legislation. But at the same time, it secretly asked the OLC to determine whether its tactics would be legal if the ban *did* apply to overseas foreign nationals. In December 2005, Congress finally succeeded in enacting a law that could no longer be "interpreted" not to protect foreign nationals abroad. But by that time, the OLC had issued its secret May 30, 2005, memo, concluding that, in any event, none of the CIA's tactics even rose to the level of cruel, inhuman, or degrading treatment.

---

22. Dept of Justice, Office of Legal Counsel, Memorandum for James B. Comey, Deputy Attorney General, Re: Legal Standards Applicable Under 18 U.S.C. §§ 2340–2340A, December 30, 2004, at 2 n.8 [p. 130] (emphasis added).

23. The CIA had since altered its sleep deprivation policy, adopting a ceiling of seven, rather than eleven, days. And it abandoned its proposal to put insects into cramped boxes with detainees, a proposal apparently adopted to exploit Abu Zubaydah's specific fear of insects. Thus, the May 2005 memos did not address insects, and only addressed seven days of sleep deprivation.

What Was Wrong With the Torture Memos?

There is certainly much about the OLC memos that is reasonable. They are premised, for example, on the unobjectionable claim that torture, both as a criminal and international law matter, is limited to a subset of all cruel, inhuman, and degrading treatment. While there are certainly good reasons to question whether the distinction really makes sense,[24] the Convention Against Torture expressly acknowledges such a distinction. For example, it requires states to seek to prevent "acts of cruel, inhuman or degrading treatment or punishment *which do not amount to torture*," and imposes different obligations on states vis-à-vis torture and cruel, inhuman, and degrading treatment.[25]

Similarly, the memos reasonably maintain that in order for conduct to qualify as torture under the federal statute making torture a crime, it must be intended to inflict "severe physical pain or suffering" or "prolonged mental harm."[26] Those terms appear in the statute's definition of torture, and thus any assessment of whether a given course of conduct violates the statute must assess the intent of the actor, the severity of any physical pain or suffering, and the

---

24. See Jessica Wolfendale, "The Myth of 'Torture Lite,'" Ethics & Intl Affairs 47 (2009) (arguing that "lesser" forms of torture are easier for government officials to justify, but can impose just as serious harm); Metin Basoglu, Maria Livanou, and Cvetana Crnoharic, "Torture vs. Other Cruel, Inhuman, and Degrading Treatment: Is the Distinction Real or Apparent?," 64 Arch. of Gen. Psychiatry 277 (2007) (finding that ill treatment short of torture is not significantly different from torture in terms of the severity of mental suffering they cause, the underlying mechanism of traumatic stress, or their long-term psychological effects); Seth F. Kreimer, "'Torture Lite,' 'Full Bodied' Torture, and the Insulation of Legal Conscience," 1 J. Nat'l Sec. L. & Pol'y 187 (2005) (arguing that both torture and cruelty short of torture are constitutionally prohibited).

25. CAT, *supra* note 8, art. 16 (emphasis added). The Reagan administration, when it presented the treaty to the Senate for ratification, explained that "torture is at the extreme end of cruel, inhuman and degrading treatment or punishment." S. Treaty Doc. No. 100-20, at 3; *see also id.* at 4 ("rough treatment as generally falls into the category of 'police brutality,' while deplorable, does not amount to 'torture.'").

26. 18 U.S.C. § 2340.

duration of any mental harm. And the last of the memos, the May 2005 CID Memo, correctly notes that under the terms of a reservation made by the Senate in adopting the Torture Convention, the prohibition on "cruel, inhuman, and degrading treatment" has been effectively redefined for purposes of U.S. obligations to match constitutional standards under the Fifth, Eighth, and Fourteenth Amendments.

Moreover, on many of the specific questions the memos address, there is undoubtedly a range of plausible interpretations. What is most telling in the end, however, is that at every juncture, the memos choose the interpretation most likely to foreclose any possibility of criminal responsibility for the CIA interrogators—regardless of how strained the interpretation is. It is this consistent pattern of result-oriented reasoning, insistently maintained in secret over several years and by multiple lawyers—even as both the statutory law and the administration's own public statements seemed to become more restrictive—that is ultimately the most compelling evidence of bad-faith lawyering.

The August 2002 Memos—Twisting Law and Language

Because it all began with the two August 2002 memos, they warrant a particularly close reading. The August 2002 Torture Memo interpreting the torture statute has been public since 2004. The April 2009 release of the simultaneous memo approving specific CIA interrogation techniques (August 2002 Interrogation Memo), however, reveals in chilling detail the driving force behind both memos. Rather than offer a nuanced evaluation of competing claims about the legality of the methods in question, every argument was clearly motivated by the desire to protect Cabinet-level officials and CIA agents from prosecution if they subjected Abu Zubaydah to a series of increasingly brutal interrogation techniques.

Other OLC memos had already ruled that the Geneva Conventions, which prohibit any cruel or humiliating treatment of detainees, did not apply to al Qaeda detainees. (That interpretation, beyond the scope of this essay, was rejected by the Supreme Court in 2006.)[27] And the OLC had also concluded that the treaty's prohibition on cruel, inhuman, and degrading treatment simply did not apply to foreigners held in CIA custody abroad. The August 2002 Torture Memo therefore addressed the sole remaining legal obstacle to harsh interrogation tactics—the federal statute making torture a crime.

The memo begins by focusing on the critical statutory terms "severe pain and suffering" and "prolonged mental harm." In the absence of controlling legal precedent further defining these terms, the OLC looked first to the dictionary. They cited Webster's New International Dictionary, which defines "severe" as "distressing," among other things, and the Oxford English Dictionary, which defines it as "hard to sustain or endure." Both definitions might bar the CIA's tactics in their entirety. The pain inflicted by any of the CIA's proposed techniques could certainly be described as "distressing," and the whole point of the CIA's interrogation tactics was to inflict pain that was "hard to endure" in order to compel the suspect to talk. But the memo passes over both dictionary definitions for one drawn from an entirely inapposite federal health benefits statute defining an "emergency medical condition," and concludes that in order to be "severe," pain must be "equivalent in intensity to the pain accompanying organ failure, impairment of bodily function, or even death."[28] The decision to disregard basic dictionary definitions and instead invoke an arcane and irrelevant source having nothing to do with torture cannot be explained by anything other than a desire to ensure that the law would pose no conceivable obstacle to the CIA's program.

The memo offers a similarly restrictive reading of "prolonged mental harm." It cites dictionary definitions providing that to "prolong" means simply to "lengthen in time." But it then arbitrarily concludes that in order to be prolonged, the harm must last

---

27. *Hamdan v. Rumsfeld*, 548 U.S. 557, 631 (2006) (holding that Common Article 3 of the Geneva Conventions applies to the conflict with al Qaeda).

28. August 2002 Torture Memo for Alberto R. Gonzales at 1, 6 [p. 41, 47].

"months or years," as in post-traumatic stress disorder.[29] It offers no authority whatsoever for limiting "prolonged" harm in this way.

To make doubly sure that no criminal liability could come to the CIA interrogators, the August 2002 Torture Memo also maintains that, even if an interrogator's conduct amounts to torture, no criminal penalties would apply if the interrogator acted at the behest of the president. Echoing President Richard Nixon's infamous (and erroneous) claim that "if the president does it, that means it's not illegal,"[30] the memo reasons that, because the Constitution makes the president the commander in chief, it would be unconstitutional for Congress to restrict in any way the president's decisions about how to engage the enemy—including a decision that enemy fighters should be tortured.

This argument flies in the face of history and precedent. The Supreme Court has ruled that when the president acts contrary to Congress's express or implied will, his power is at its "lowest ebb," and his actions can be upheld only if Congress has no authority to regulate in the area in question.[31] Thus, in 1804, the Supreme Court ruled that President John Adams, during a military conflict with France, could not order the seizure of merchant ships coming *from* France where Congress had authorized the seizure only of ships going *to* France.[32] And during the Korean War, the Court held, in what is unquestionably its most important case ever on presidential power, that President Harry S. Truman could not seize a steel mill to avert a national strike where Congress had declined to give him such authority, even though Truman had argued that he needed to keep the mills running specifically to support the war effort.[33] The

---

29. *Id.* at 7 [p. 51].

30. David Cole, "Reviving the Nixon Doctrine: NSA Spying, the Commander-in-Chief, and Executive Power in the War on Terror," 13 Wash. & Lee J. of Civ. Rts. & Soc. Justice 1 (2006).

31. *Youngstown Sheet and Tube Co. v. Sawyer*, 343 U.S. 579, 637 (1952) (Jackson, J., concurring).

32. *Little v. Barreme*, 6 U.S. (2 Cranch) 170 (1804), 177–78.

33. *Youngstown Sheet and Tube Co. v. Sawyer*, 343 U.S. 579 (1952).

August 2002 memo did not seek to distinguish these contrary precedents, as any basic legal memo should do. It simply disregarded
them altogether, thereby violating the lawyer's ethical obligation
when acting in an advisory capacity to present objective advice that
accounts for contrary as well as supporting precedent.[34]

The August 2002 Torture Memo concludes by opining that an
interrogator who tortured could also avoid liability by relying on
"necessity" or "self defense." These doctrines, both of which favor
criminal defendants, are typically construed very narrowly by the
Justice Department, which is charged with prosecuting crime, not
concocting expansive theories for would-be criminals to escape liability. But in this setting, the OLC adopted a more liberal interpretation of these defenses than even a zealous defense lawyer would
have the temerity to advance. The OLC argued that the "necessity" defense, which excuses a crime if necessary to avert a greater
harm, might be applicable, not merely in a ticking time bomb situation, but where a detainee "may possess information that could
enable the United States to prevent [future] attacks" in general.[35]
The OLC declined to mention a Supreme Court case questioning
whether any necessity defense can be recognized to a federal criminal statute unless the statute explicitly sets one forth.[36] The torture
statute recognizes no such defense. It was enacted to enforce the
Convention Against Torture, which, as a separate part of the August 2002 Torture Memo concedes, precludes a necessity defense
by providing that "no exceptional circumstances" justify torture.[37]

---

34. *See* "What Went Wrong?: Torture and the Office of Legal Counsel in the
    Bush Administration," Hearing Before the Senate Judiciary Committee,
    Subcommittee on Administrative Oversight and the Courts (May 13, 2009)
    (testimony of David Luban).

35. August 2002 Torture Memo for Alberto R. Gonzales at 41 [p. 92].

36. *United States v. Oakland Cannabis Buyers Coop.*, 532 U.S. 483, 490 (2001).

37. August 2002 Torture Memo at 31 [p. 79]. In this section of the memo, the
    OLC argues that Israel's Supreme Court had treated physically coercive
    interrogation as less than torture, and cites that as support for its view, that
    similar methods used by the CIA would not constitute torture. The Israeli
    Supreme Court did not expressly address whether the coercive techniques

The memo's treatment of "self defense" is no less strained. The self-defense doctrine typically allows an individual to use force against an assailant only as a last resort, when absolutely necessary to forestall an immediate threat of bodily harm to himself or another. The memo stretches the doctrine far beyond anything remotely recognizable in precedent. It argues that the requirement of imminent harm can be relaxed where the threat is of an al Qaeda attack; that the doctrine can be applied not only to a would-be assailant but to someone who may merely have knowledge regarding a possible attack; and that the doctrine can be invoked not only to defend oneself or another person, but "the nation" as a whole. No cases are cited to support any of these novel and sweeping contentions, because there are none.

Once the OLC had set the bar so high in the August 2002 Torture Memo, it concluded in short order, in the separate August 2002 Interrogation Memo, that all of the CIA's proposed tactics were permissible: specifically, "(1) attention grasp, (2) walling, (3) facial hold, (4) facial slap (insult slap), (5) cramped confinement, (6) wall standing, (7) stress position, (8) sleep deprivation, (9) insects placed in a confinement box, and (10) the waterboard."[38] None of the techniques, the OLC insisted, inflicted pain of a severity associated with organ failure or death, or were even difficult to endure.[39] While being slammed into a wall repeatedly "may

---

were torture, but because the Court recognized a necessity defense, and the OLC memo argues that "had the court been of the view that the [Israeli security service interrogation] methods constituted torture, the Court could not permit this affirmative defense under the [Convention Against Torture]." *Id.* Yet when it turns to addressing a necessity defense for CIA agents, the memo concludes that necessity could be a defense even against full-fledged torture.

38. August 2002 Interrogation Memo at 2 [p. 107].

39. *See, e.g.,* Aug. 2002 Interrogation Memo at 10 [p. 117] ("Any pain associated with muscle fatigue [caused by wall standing] is not of the intensity sufficient to amount to 'severe physical pain or suffering' under the statute, nor despite its discomfort, can it be said to be difficult to endure.").

hurt . . . any pain experienced is not of the intensity associated with serious physical injury."[40]

What was the basis for these OLC conclusions? The CIA itself. With respect to waterboarding, for example, "you have informed us that this procedure does not inflict actual physical harm," and therefore the waterboard "inflicts no pain or actual harm whatsoever," much less severe pain or suffering.[41] It cannot cause any long-term suffering, the OLC determined, because it "is simply a controlled acute episode."[42] (Many classic forms of torture, including electric shocks and whipping, are also "controlled acute episodes," but the OLC did not mention these.)

The Cover-Up—The 2004 and 2005 Memos

If an argument cannot be sustained in the light of day, it is probably not a valid argument. As soon as the August 2002 Torture Memo became public, the Bush administration was forced to rescind it (although, tellingly, the August 2002 Interrogation Memo, which remained secret, was left in force, and continued to sanction all of the CIA's tactics). The OLC's December 30, 2004, replacement memo made a public show of departing from the August 2002 Torture Memo on a number of specific points. But as the May 2005 memos now show, these disagreements were purely cosmetic; behind closed doors, issuance of the ostensibly contrite replacement memo did not change *anything* with respect to the bottom line. The December 2004 memo was more an exercise in public relations than in law.

For example, the December 2004 memo rejected the earlier definition of "severe" as limited to pain associated with organ failure or death, correctly noting that there was absolutely no justification for relying on a federal health benefit statute. But it offered no specific alternative definition. Instead, it repeatedly characterized "severe"

---

40. *Id.* at 11 [p. 118].
41. *Id.*
42. *Id.*

as "extreme and outrageous;"; offered examples of torture such as electric shock to the testicles, Russian roulette, cutting off fingers, and pulling out fingernails, as if to imply that torture might be limited to such egregious acts; and argued that beatings and death threats were not necessarily torture.[43] When it applied this "new" definition of "severe" to the CIA's proposed techniques in the May 2005 memos, the OLC reached the same conclusions that it had in August 2002. What seems clear is that having approved the techniques in the first place, the OLC was not going to reach any legal conclusion that called into question its prior authorization.

On the one hand, the May 2005 memos sound more reasonable than the August 2002 memos. They acknowledge more contrary authority, and occasionally even express doubt. They were written with acute awareness of the widespread public criticism of the August 2002 Torture Memo. On the other hand, the May 2005 memos, all signed by Stephen Bradbury, are in a fundamental sense the worst of the lot. They use less incendiary language, but they ultimately reach even more unreasonable positions than the initial memos.

By the time the May 2005 memos were written, the administration had not only been forced to retract its August 2002 Torture Memo, but had been confronted with a May 2004 CIA inspector general's report revealing that the CIA had applied the techniques in abusive ways, and that the CIA's own medical office had contended that there was no basis for believing that waterboarding as it had been applied was "either efficacious or medically safe."[44] By then OLC lawyers knew that waterboarding had been used 183 times against Khalid Sheikh Mohammed and 83 times against Abu Zubaydah. And by then, Congress had learned of—and shown serious signs of intending to overrule—the administration's evasion of the ban on "cruel, inhuman and degrading treatment." Yet none of

---

43. Dec. 2004 Memo at 5–10 [p. 133–141].

44. May 10 Techniques Memo at 41 n. 51 [p. 191] (quoting CIA Office of Medical Services).

these factors changed the bottom line. The new memos once again approved the CIA's techniques in full. Indeed, it appears that the memos' main purpose was to reassure the CIA that nothing had changed about U.S. law and policy—even as the administration worked to make it appear to the public that things *had* changed.

The May 2005 Techniques Memo assessed whether each of the CIA techniques, standing alone, constituted torture under the OLC's revised interpretation of the federal torture statute. Like the August 2002 Interrogation Memo, it concluded that none of the techniques inflicts severe pain or suffering or prolonged mental harm. While it eschewed the "organ failure" and "months or years" thresholds, it employed a vague "extreme and outrageous" standard that achieved the same result.

The central factual predicate for the May 2005 Techniques Memo's conclusions was the fact that American soldiers subjected to many of these techniques in SERE counter-torture training reportedly had not exhibited signs of severe physical pain or suffering or prolonged mental harm.[45] The memo admits that being subjected to these techniques in SERE training is not the same as being subjected to them by hostile forces.[46] But it never explores the legal significance of that difference. A soldier who chooses to subject himself to these techniques in SERE training does so voluntarily, knows that the whole scenario is constructed, and is given a code word that he can use at any time to halt the process. To be

---

45. May 10 Techniques Memo at 15 [p. 171] ("in SERE training, the waterboard technique (although used in a substantially more limited way) has not resulted in any cases of serious physical pain or prolonged mental harm"); *id.* at 29 n. 33 [p. 174] (noting absence of evidence that any of the techniques have caused severe pain in SERE training); *id.* at 35 [p. 183] (dousing with cold water does not inflict severe pain because there is no evidence that it caused severe pain in SERE training). The other memos also rely on the SERE experience. *See* August 2002 Interrogation Memo at 4–6, 15 [p. 110–113, 123] (relying on evidence from SERE training to conclude that CIA techniques will not inflict severe pain or suffering); May 30 CID Memo at 32, 37–38 [p. 263, 270–271] (relying on SERE training to support conclusion that CIA techniques are not cruel, inhuman, or degrading).

46. May 10 Techniques Memo at 6 [p. 159].

waterboarded in such a voluntary setting by someone you know is on your side, playacting, and has no intention of harming you, simply cannot be analogized in any way to being subjected to such treatment by the enemy in a secret prison, where you have no recourse whatsoever and the fear of death is perfectly reasonable. The fact that consensual sex does not inflict severe physical or mental pain or suffering does not mean that rape has no such effects.

Indeed, the May 2005 memo admits, albeit in a footnote, that the CIA's inspector general reported that "the SERE waterboard experience is so different from the subsequent Agency usage as to make it almost irrelevant."[47] Yet the same memo relies on the absence of evidence that SERE trainees experienced severe or prolonged pain or suffering to support its conclusion that the "panic brought on by the waterboarding" causes neither prolonged mental harm nor severe physical pain or suffering.[48]

Whenever the May 2005 Techniques Memo acknowledges the possibility that a given technique might cause severe pain or prolonged mental harm, it finds fully sufficient assurance in the fact that medical experts with SERE experience will be present and will stop the procedures "if deemed medically necessary to prevent severe mental or physical harm."[49] Notably, the medical profes-

---

47. May 10 Techniques Memo at 41 n. 51 [p. 191].

48. May 10 Techniques Memo at 43 [p. 194].

49. May 10 Techniques Memo at 6 [p. 158] ("medical personnel watch for signs of physical distress or mental harm so significant as possibly to amount to the 'severe physical or mental pain or suffering' that is prohibited"); id. at 15 [p. 172] (same); id. at 29 [p. 174] (involvement of medical personnel "is particularly noteworthy for purposes of our analysis"); id. at 32 [p. 179] (noting presence of doctors to check on pain caused by slamming suspects into walls); id. at 38–39 [p. 187–188] (relying on doctors to ensure that sleep deprivation does not inflict severe pain or suffering); id. at 41 n. 51 [p. 191] (citing presence of doctors at waterboarding as assurance that it will not inflict severe pain or suffering); id. at 45 [p. 197] ("our conclusion is based on the assumption . . . that [the medical] personnel . . . will stop the use of a technique at any time if they believe . . . that a detainee may be at risk of suffering severe physical or mental pain or suffering."); see also August 2002 Interrogation Memo at 3–4, 11 [p. 109–111, 118].

sional's role is not to prevent the infliction of all pain, but only of "pain that is severe or lasting."[50]

How exactly is a medical expert supposed to assess whether a given technique is imposing severe versus less-than-severe pain, or might give rise to prolonged versus temporary psychological harm? There is no universal sign, much less medical definition, of "severe" pain or "prolonged mental harm." No doctor could assess these things on the spot. Indeed, at one point the December 2004 memo seems to admit this, quoting a medical journal to the effect that *"pain is a subjective experience and there is no way to objectively quantify it."*[51]

Furthermore experts with SERE experience are likely to be especially insensitive to the risks involved, because the effects are so muted in the voluntary staged setting to which they are accustomed. They are the last persons one should rely on as watchdogs—unless one is less interested in checking abuse than in the *appearance* of checking abuse. The better approach would conclude that any interrogation technique requiring a doctor in the room to monitor (or launder) its application should not be permitted in the first place.

In short, despite its qualifications and reservations, the May 2005 Techniques Memo is every bit as unreasonable as the August 2002 Interrogation Memo that it replaced. And, tellingly, it achieves precisely the same result.

Still, it is the second and third May memos that most strongly confirm that the OLC was engaged in a process of intellectual cover-up and rationalization, not objective, good-faith lawyering. The second memo, also dated May 10, 2005, concludes that even when all of the techniques are applied to a single suspect in combi-

---

50. May 10 Techniques Memo at 30 [p. 176–177] (quoting OMS Guidelines at 8–9).
51. December 2004 Memo at 8 n. 18 [p. 138], quoting Dennis C. Turk, "Assess the Person, Not Just the Pain," Pain: Clinical Updates, September 1993 (emphasis added by OLC).

nation, they do not rise to the level of torture. This is more a leap of (bad) faith than an exercise in careful analysis. Surely *some* combination of the techniques would constitute torture even under the OLC's definition, and therefore it makes no sense even to try to grant advance approval—unless, that is, one's purpose is to provide the "get out of jail free" card that Jack Goldsmith described.

The final memo, issued May 30, 2005 (CID Memo), is the most disingenuous of all. It concludes that the CIA's techniques do not even constitute cruel, inhuman, and degrading treatment. This conclusion is reached despite the fact that in the May 2005 Techniques Memo, the OLC on several occasions virtually concedes that many of the tactics are degrading. It described forced nudity, for example, as humiliating, and as intended to cause "psychological discomfort, particularly if a detainee, for cultural or other reasons is especially modest."[52] Forcing someone to violate his own sense of modesty in order to humiliate him is precisely what it means to degrade. Facial slapping is similarly described as humiliating in the May 2005 Techniques Memo, but found not to be cruel, inhuman, or degrading in the CID Memo. And even if one might argue about whether depriving someone of sleep for a week straight, forcing him into cramped boxes for hours, and repeatedly waterboarding him are torture, can there be any doubt that these tactics are, at a minimum, cruel? How could the OLC possibly conclude that *none* of the CIA's tactics was cruel, inhuman, or degrading?

Prior to this memo, as we have seen, the Bush administration had evaded the "cruel, inhuman, or degrading treatment" standard altogether by secretly maintaining that it simply did not apply to foreign nationals held outside U.S. borders. But when that interpretation was publicly disclosed, Congress undertook to reject it by confirming that the prohibition on cruel, inhuman, or degrading treatment applied to all persons held in U.S. custody, wherever they

---

52. May 2005 Techniques Memo at 7, 32 [p. 160, 177].

were held and whatever their nationality.[53] The Bush administration did all it could to fend off Congress's efforts. It took several iterations for Congress to get it right, but in the Detainee Treatment Act, enacted in December 2005, Congress expressly prohibited cruel, inhuman, or degrading treatment of any person in U.S. custody.[54]

While the Bush administration was doing all it could to forestall application of the cruel, inhuman, and degrading treatment standard, it was also working behind closed doors to ensure that, even if Congress prevailed, the legal change would have no effect on the CIA's program. The May 30, 2005, memo accordingly argues that, even if foreign nationals in CIA custody are protected by the prohibition on cruel, inhuman, and degrading treatment, none of the CIA's techniques violate that prohibition.

The memo reasons correctly that the relevant standard under U.S. law is whether government conduct "shocks the conscience," a due process test, because the Senate had said as much in approving the treaty. But the OLC then concluded—entirely unreasonably—that the CIA tactics would not shock the conscience, for two reasons. First, CIA interrogators inflicted pain not arbitrarily, but for a good end—to gather intelligence about terrorism. Citing Supreme Court language stating that "the official conduct 'most likely to rise to the conscience-shocking level,' is the 'conduct intended to injure in some way unjustifiable by any government interest,'"[55] the memo then treats that standard as if it is the *only* standard for conscience-shocking behaviour. Second, the techniques were not arbitrary because the government sought to "minimize the risk of

---

53. *See* Jamie Mayerfeld, *Playing by Our Own Rules: How U.S. Marginalization of International Human Rights Law Led to Torture*, 20 Harv. Hum. Rts. J. 89, 103–04 (2007).

54. Detainee Treatment Act of 2005, Pub. L. No. 109-148, § 1003, 119 Stat. 2739.

55. *Chavez v. Martinez*, 538 U.S. 760, 775 (1994) (quoting *County of Sacramento v. Lewis*, 523 U.S. 833, 849 (1998)).

injury or any suffering that does not further the Government's interest in obtaining actionable intelligence."[56]

Significantly, however, the memo did not claim that the CIA's techniques sought to minimize the risk of *all* injury or suffering, but only of injury or suffering *"that does not further the Government's interest."*

The case law is clear that *any* intentional infliction of pain for interrogation purposes violates due process. And the Court has recognized no sliding scale that would permit the infliction of pain if the government's reason is good enough. Injurious conduct that is "unjustifiable by any government interest" is the easiest case, to be sure, but the Court has repeatedly found its conscience shocked where the government acted with wholly legitimate interests.

The Court ruled, for example, that pumping a man's stomach in a hospital after seeing him swallow what appeared to be drugs shocked the conscience, even though the procedure was carried out in a hospital pursuant to safe procedures, and for a wholly legitimate purpose—to gather evidence of crime.[57] The Court has repeatedly held that *any* use or threat of force to coerce a confession violates due process—even where employed to solve a murder.[58] And it has stated that government conduct that contravenes "the decencies of civilized conduct" or that is "so 'brutal' and 'offensive' that it [does] not comport with traditional ideas of fair play and decency' would violate due process." [59] All of these decisions point to the same conclusion—that the deliberate infliction of pain to compel a suspect to talk against his will shocks the conscience

In the single case perhaps most on point, the Supreme Court, in 2002, addressed whether the interrogation of a man while he was hospitalized and suffering substantial pain from a police shooting

---

56. May 2005 CID Memo at 31 [p. 262].

57. *Rochin v. California*, 342 U.S. 165, 172 (1952).

58. *See, e.g., Rogers v. Richmond*, 365 U.S. 534 (1961); *Ashcraft v. Tennessee*, 322 U.S. 143 (1944).

59. *Rochin*, 342 U.S. at 172–73; *Breithaupt v. Abram*, 352 U.S. 432, 435 (1957).

violated the Constitution—even though the statements were never used in a prosecution. In *Chavez v. Martinez*, the officers themselves did not inflict pain for the purpose of questioning, but did continue the interrogation despite the man's cries of pain. They argued that his testimony was critical to investigating the encounter, and that they feared that he might die, so that this may have been their only opportunity to obtain his version of events. The Court remanded the case to the court of appeals to consider whether the questioning violated substantive due process. While the justices disagreed about the specific conclusions to be drawn from the facts at hand, both Justice Anthony Kennedy, who concluded that due process had been violated, and Justice Clarence Thomas, who concluded that it had not, agreed that the *deliberate* infliction of pain on an individual to compel him to talk *would* shock the conscience. Justice Kennedy reasoned that police "may not prolong or increase a suspect's suffering against the suspect's will," or even give him "the impression that severe pain will be alleviated only if [he] cooperates."[60] Under this standard, likely to be the majority view given Justice Kennedy's central role on the Court, any use of pain to compel a suspect to talk violates due process. Justice Thomas found that due process had not been violated, but only because he found "no evidence that Chavez acted with a purpose to harm Martinez," or that "Chavez's conduct exacerbated Martinez's injuries."[61] Under either approach, then, a purpose to harm violates due process. The court of appeals on remand in *Chavez* unanimously held that the alleged conduct indeed shocked the conscience, a fact not even acknowledged by the OLC memo.[62]

The OLC memo cites *Chavez*, but concludes, incredibly, that "the CIA program is considerably less invasive or extreme than

---

60. *Chavez*, 538 U.S. at 797 (Kennedy, J., dissenting) (joined by Justices Ginsburg and Stevens).

61. *Id.* at 775 (Thomas, J.) (joined by Chief Justice Rehnquist and Justice Scalia).

62. *Martinez v. City of Oxnard*, 337 F.3d 1091 (9th Cir. 2003).

much of the conduct at issue in" *Chavez*.[63] In fact, just the opposite is true. The officers in *Chavez* inflicted no pain for purposes of in-terrogation—yet three members of the Supreme Court found their conduct conscience-shocking nonetheless, as did the unanimous court of appeals on remand. The CIA's entire program, by contrast, is based on the deliberate infliction of pain and humiliation to com-pel recalcitrant suspects to talk against their will.

At the very end of its memo, the OLC candidly admits that "we cannot predict with confidence that a court would agree with our conclusion."[64] This caveat might well be worrying, except that the OLC goes on to reassure the CIA that there is no need to worry, because the question "is unlikely to be subject to judicial inquiry."[65] Congress specified that the Convention Against Torture is "non-self-executing," the memo explains, meaning that even if it is vio-lated, "the courts have nothing to do and can give no redress."[66] In other words, when it comes to the ban on cruel, inhuman, or degrading treatment, the CIA operates for all practical purposes in a "law-free zone," or at least a zone where the law is what the executive says it is—in secret—and no court will ever have the op-portunity to disagree.

As the above discussion makes clear, OLC lawyers engaged in substantial and sometimes complex legal analysis, including a de-tailed assessment of whether each of the CIA's techniques, singly or in combination, violated the federal torture statute or the treaty prohibition on "cruel, inhuman, and degrading treatment." It took almost two hundred pages and several years to get there, but from all appearances, the destination was never in doubt. The August 2002 memos exploited every loophole they could find, and created new loopholes when they did not exist, no matter how far-fetched.

---

63. May 30 CID Memo at 33 [p. 264].
64. May 30 CID Memo at 38 [p. 274].
65. *Id.*
66. *Id.* at 39 [p. 274] (quoting *Head Money Cases*, 112 U.S. 580, 598 (1884)).

And once the August 2002 memos cleared the way for the CIA to waterboard Abu Zubaydah 83 times, there was no question what the lawyers would conclude. The December 2004 memo was a public relations ploy, not a bona fide legal undertaking. And the secret May 2005 memos assured that the CIA could continue its practices even after Congress enacted an unambiguous prohibition expressly designed to halt all cruel, inhuman, and degrading treatment. Considered as a whole, the memos read not as a good-faith effort to apply the law to regulate a proposed course of conduct, but as a calculated conspiracy to give legal cover to conduct that on its face violated federal criminal law, international treaties, and basic human decency.

On Accountability

Law at its best is about seeking justice, resolving disputes pursuant to principle and reasoned judgment, regulating state power, respecting human dignity, and protecting the vulnerable. Law at its worst treats legal doctrine as infinitely manipulable, capable of being twisted cynically in whatever direction serves the client's desires. Had the OLC lawyers adopted the former view, they very likely could have stopped the CIA abuses in their tracks. Instead, they used law not as a check on power, but as a facilitator of brutality, deployed against captive human beings who had absolutely no other recourse.

Official repudiation of the CIA tactics, and of the actions of those who authorized them, is essential if the United States is to hold fast to a better vision of what the law can and should be. Official repudiation is critical if the rule of law in the United States is to be restored, and respect regained around the world for the United States as a law-abiding nation. And official repudiation is necessary if the United States hopes to build meaningful safeguards against this kind of descent into cruelty happening again. History, it seems plain, will judge the Bush administration harshly on this subject; indeed, it already has. But history's judgment is not sufficient. Some form of official acknowledgment of wrongdoing is essential.

President Obama has sent decidedly mixed messages on the subject of accountability. He ended these interrogation tactics in no uncertain terms, and released the previously secret OLC memos reproduced here—both of which are critical steps in the direction of accountability. But he has said that he favors looking forward, not backward, and has resisted proposals to create a blue-ribbon, nonpartisan commission to study the problem. He has said that the decision whether to prosecute is his attorney general's to make, and that existing proceedings in the courts and Congress offer opportunities for accountability. But he has already advanced claims of "state secrets" in lawsuits seeking accountability that, if accepted, would be a roadblock to public accountability in almost any forum.

What should be done? Some, including former attorney general Michael Mukasey and former OLC head Jack Goldsmith, have argued that no further investigations, much less prosecutions, are needed. Mukasey insists that everyone acted in good faith, trying to draw difficult lines in trying times. Goldsmith maintains that we already know what happened, and that any further inquiry will render CIA agents too cautious and risk-averse in fighting terrorism and other threats in the future. But the analysis above suggests that, while there were difficult judgments to be made, the desired result drove the legal analysis, rather than vice versa—and that is the very definition of bad faith. We certainly don't know everything; Goldsmith's role as head of OLC while the CIA's tactics remained authorized is itself unclear, as are the roles of many who are likely to have been involved but did not sign the actual memos in question. And if an inquiry deters CIA agents from experimenting with brutality in the future, we should celebrate that, not bemoan it.

Others, including many human rights groups, have advocated criminal prosecution. Torture is a crime, and both Attorney General Eric Holder and President Obama have stated that waterboarding is torture. The Convention Against Torture obligates its signatories to investigate and refer for prosecution all cases of torture by persons within their jurisdiction. Moreover, the crime of torture supports "universal jurisdiction," meaning that any nation may undertake to prosecute it. Two judges in Spain are currently investigating whether to prosecute U.S. officials and lawyers for their part in authorizing torture at Guantánamo and elsewhere. Those important investigations may put pressure on the United States to take action of its own, as the universal jurisdiction principle requires cessation of the foreign prosecution if the home country takes responsible action for its own wrongdoing.

All of the facts are not yet known, but criminal prosecution within or outside the United States at this point seems unlikely. As noted above, the OLC's memos would make prosecution of anyone other than the lawyers themselves extremely difficult. The Cabinet officers who authorized the program will argue that they never intended to inflict torture, but did feel obliged to do everything they could within the law to obtain information that might prevent another attack. They therefore referred the matter to the lawyers. The lawyers returned with a lengthy analysis, citing many cases and precedents, and concluding that the tactics the CIA proposed to employ did not rise to the level of torture. Both the Cabinet officers who approved the CIA's program and the CIA agents who carried it out relied on that legal advice. Thus, the nonlawyers will claim that they went ahead only because the lawyers told them the techniques were not torture, and not illegal.

The criminal law recognizes a "reasonable reliance" defense, which provides that individuals cannot be held criminally responsible when they take action in reasonable reliance on an official statement that the conduct is lawful by the government body or official charged with interpreting the law.[67] And even if that defense were

---

67. See Model Penal Code § 2.04(3)(9b)(rev. ed. 1985). This defense is to be distinguished from "following orders," which would not excuse torture. In a "following orders" case, a soldier seeks to avoid responsibility for criminal conduct because his commanding officer ordered him to commit the crime. The "reasonable reliance" defense, by contrast, asserts that the individual engaged in the conduct in question not because he was ordered to commit a

held inapplicable, the existence of the OLC memos would still be a powerful argument to the jury that the defendants lacked the intent necessary for a criminal conviction. As if that were not enough, Congress, in the Military Commissions Act of 2006, granted retrospective immunity to officials involved in the interrogation of al Qaeda suspects in the wake of September 11.[68]

The lawyers may be more vulnerable to criminal prosecution, especially if further evidence supports the conclusion that they acted in bad faith, knowing that what they authorized was in fact forbidden. But such a showing would be extremely difficult to make; this area of the law was so sufficiently uncharted that the lawyers are likely to be able to raise reasonable questions as to whether they were knowingly authorizing torture, and a criminal conviction requires proof beyond a reasonable doubt.

Accountability, however, need not take the form of a criminal prosecution. Consider two examples of noncriminal accountability. In World War II, the United States military interned approximately 120,000 people simply because they were Japanese or Japanese Americans. At the time, the Supreme Court upheld the internment. But Japanese American and other groups never gave up fighting to right that wrong. And in 1988, more than forty years later, President Reagan signed the Civil Liberties Act, officially apologizing for the Japanese internment and paying reparations to the internees and their survivors. No one was prosecuted, but that (admittedly belated) legislation marks a formal repudiation of the United States' past acts, and provides an important cultural bulwark against something similar happening again.

Or consider how Canada responded when Maher Arar came home to Canada in 2003. Arar is a Canadian citizen who U.S.

---

crime, but because he reasonably relied on official advice that the conduct in question was *not* criminal, provided by the government body charged with interpreting the law in question.

68. Military Commissions Act of 2006, §§ 6(b), 8(b), 1 U.S.C. § 2441 (d)(1) (2009).

agents rendered to Syria, where he was locked up without charges for a year and tortured. The U.S. agents acted in part based on erroneous information provided by the Canadians. Upon Arar's return, Canada established a commission of inquiry headed by a prominent appellate judge, which conducted a serious investigation and issued an 1,100-page report, fully exonerating Arar and criticizing the Canadian authorities. Canada's Parliament unanimously issued a formal apology to Arar, and the Canadian government paid him $10 million in damages for the injuries he endured in part due to sloppy Canadian intelligence. Again, no one was prosecuted. But that official repudiation is likely to have a substantial deterrent effect on similar wrongs being perpetrated in the future.

We have seen nothing of this kind with respect to the United States' recent acts of torture. None of the lawyers or officials responsible for authorizing torture has even apologized. There has been no payment of compensation to victims, no disbarment proceedings against the lawyers responsible, and most disturbingly, no official acknowledgment that what was done was not only morally despicable, but *illegal*.

The United States cannot move forward in reforming the law effectively unless it is willing to account for what it did wrong in the past. Otherwise, the state of the matter in the United States is that, when it has a president who does not believe in torture, it won't torture, but when it has a president who does believe in it, it will. Torture becomes a question of policy, not law. But torture must not be a policy option.

The first step, therefore, should be appointment of an independent, nonpartisan, high-caliber commission, along the lines of the 9/11 Commission, to investigate and assess responsibility for the United States' adoption of coercive interrogation policies. Only such a commission has the possibility of rising above the partisan wrangling that any attempt to hold accountable high-level officials of the prior administration is certain to trigger. Congressional hearings risk devolving into a partisan battle. If an independent commission is to be effective, moreover, it must have subpoena power, sufficient funding, security clearances, access to all the relevant evidence, and, most importantly, a charge to assess responsibility, not just to look forward. Depending on the facts that emerge, disbarment proceedings, civil damages actions, or criminal prosecution may also be warranted. But we already know more than enough to know that some form of official accountability is absolutely essential. Absent a reckoning for those responsible for making torture and cruel, inhuman, and degrading treatment official U.S. policy, the United States' commitment to the rule of law appears to be a hollow shell.

U.S. Department of Justice

Office of Legal Counsel

Office of the Assistant Attorney General   *Washington, D.C. 20530*

August 1, 2002

Memorandum for Alberto R. Gonzales
Counsel to the President

*Re: Standards of Conduct for Interrogation
under 18 U.S.C. §§ 2340-2340A*

You have asked for our Office's views regarding the standards of conduct under the Convention Against Torture and Other Cruel, Inhuman and Degrading Treatment or Punishment as implemented by Sections 2340-2340A of title 18 of the United States Code. As we understand it, this question has arisen in the context of the conduct of interrogations outside of the United States. We conclude below that Section 2340A proscribes acts inflicting, and that are specifically intended to inflict, severe pain or suffering, whether mental or physical. Those acts must be of an extreme nature to rise to the level of torture within the meaning of Section 2340A and the Convention. We further conclude that certain acts may be cruel, inhuman, or degrading, but still not produce pain and suffering of the requisite intensity to fall within Section 2340A's proscription against torture. We conclude by examining possible defenses that would negate any claim that certain interrogation methods violate the statute.

In Part I, we examine the criminal statute's text and history. We conclude that for an act to constitute torture as defined in Section 2340, it must inflict pain that is difficult to endure. Physical pain amounting to torture must be equivalent in intensity to the pain accompanying serious physical injury, such as organ failure, impairment of bodily function, or even death. For purely mental pain or suffering to amount to torture under Section 2340, it must result in significant psychological harm of significant duration, e.g., lasting for months or even years. We conclude that the mental harm also must result from one of the predicate acts listed in the statute, namely: threats of imminent death; threats of infliction of the kind of pain that would amount to physical torture; infliction of such physical

pain as a means of psychological torture; use of drugs or other procedures designed to deeply disrupt the senses, or fundamentally alter an
individual's personality; or threatening to do any of these things to a third
party. The legislative history simply reveals that Congress intended for the
statute's definition to track the Convention's definition of torture and the
reservations, understandings, and declarations that the United States submitted with its ratification. We conclude that the statute, taken as a whole,
makes plain that it prohibits only extreme acts.

In Part II, we examine the text, ratification history, and negotiating
history of the Torture Convention. We conclude that the treaty's text prohibits only the most extreme acts by reserving criminal penalties solely for
torture and declining to require such penalties for "cruel, inhuman, or degrading treatment or punishment." This confirms our view that the criminal statute penalizes only the most egregious conduct. Executive branch
interpretations and representations to the Senate at the time of ratification
further confirm that the treaty was intended to reach only the most extreme conduct.

In Part III, we analyze the jurisprudence of the Torture Victims Protection Act, 28 U.S.C. § 1350 note (2000), which provides civil remedies
for torture victims, to predict the standards that courts might follow in
determining what actions reach the threshold of torture in the criminal
context. We conclude from these cases that courts are likely to take a totality-of-the-circumstances approach, and will look to an entire course of
conduct, to determine whether certain acts will violate Section 2340A.
Moreover, these cases demonstrate that most often torture involves cruel
and extreme physical pain. In Part IV, we examine international decisions
regarding the use of sensory deprivation techniques. These cases make
clear that while many of these techniques may amount to cruel, inhuman
or degrading treatment, they do not produce pain or suffering of the necessary intensity to meet the definition of torture. From these decisions, we
conclude that there is a wide range of such techniques that will not rise to
the level of torture.

In Part V, we discuss whether Section 2340A may be unconstitutional if applied to interrogations undertaken of enemy combatants pursuant to the President's Commander-in-Chief powers. We find that in the
circumstances of the current war against al Qaeda and its allies, prosecution under Section 2340A may be barred because enforcement of the statute would represent an unconstitutional infringement of the President's
authority to conduct war. In Part VI, we discuss defenses to an allegation
that an interrogation method might violate the statute. We conclude that,

under the current circumstances, necessity or self-defense may justify interrogation methods that might violate Section 2340A.

I.   18 U.S.C. §§ 2340-2340A

Section 2340A makes it a criminal offense for any person "outside the United States [to] commit[] or attempt[] to commit torture."[1] Section 2340 defines the act of torture as an:

> act committed by a person acting under the color of law specifically intended to inflict severe physical or mental pain or suffering (other than pain or suffering incidental to lawful sanctions) upon another person within his custody or physical control.

18 U.S.C.A. § 2340(1); *see id.* § 2340A. Thus, to convict a defendant of torture, the prosecution must establish that: (1) the torture occurred outside the United States; (2) the defendant acted under the color of law; (3) the victim was within the defendant's custody or physical control; (4) the defendant specifically intended to cause severe physical or mental pain or suffering; and (5) that the act inflicted severe physical or mental pain or suffering. *See also* S. Exec. Rep. No. 101-30, at 6 (1990) ("For an act to be

---

[1] If convicted of torture, a defendant faces a fine or up to twenty years' imprisonment or both. If, however, the act resulted in the victim's death, a defendant may be sentenced to life imprisonment or to death. *See 18 U.S.C.A.* § 2340A(a). Whether death results from the act also affects the applicable statute of limitations. Where death does not result, the statute of limitations is eight years; if death results, there is no statute of limitations. *See* 18 U.S.C.A. § 3286(b) (West Supp. 2002); *id.* § 2332b(g)(5)(B) (West Supp. 2002). Section 2340A as originally enacted did not provide for the death penalty as a punishment. *See* Omnibus Crime Bill, Pub. L. No. 103-322, Title VI, Section 60020, 108 Stat. 1979 (1994) (amending section 2340A to provide for the death penalty); H. R. Conf. Rep. No. 103-711, at 388 (1994) (noting that the act added the death penalty as a penalty for torture).

Most recently, the USA Patriot Act, Pub. L. No. 107-56, 115 Stat. 272 (2001), amended section 2340A to expressly codify the offense of conspiracy to commit torture. Congress enacted this amendment as part of a broader effort to ensure that individuals engaged in the planning of terrorist activities could be prosecuted irrespective of where the activities took place. *See* H. R. Rep. No. 107-236, at 70 (2001) (discussing the addition of "conspiracy" as a separate offense for a variety of "Federal terrorism offense[s]").

'torture,' it must . . . cause severe pain and suffering, and be intended to cause severe pain and suffering."). You have asked us to address only the elements of specific intent and the infliction of severe pain or suffering. As such, we have not addressed the elements of "outside the United States," "color of law," and "custody or control"[2] At your request, we would be happy to address these elements in a separate memorandum.

A. "Specifically Intended"

To violate Section 2340A, the statute requires that severe pain and suffering must be inflicted with specific intent. *See* 18 U.S.C. § 2340(1). In order for a defendant to have acted with specific intent, he must expressly intend to achieve the forbidden act. *See United States v. Carter,* 530 U.S. 255, 269 (2000); Black's Law Dictionary at 814 (7th ed. 1999) (defining specific intent as "[t]he intent to accomplish the precise criminal act that one is later charged with"). For example, in *Ratzlaf v. United States,* 510 U.S. 135, 141 (1994), the statute at issue was construed to require that the defendant act with the "specific intent to commit the crime." (Internal quotation marks and citation omitted). As a result, the defendant had to act with the express "purpose to disobey the law" in order for the *mens rea* element to be satisfied. *Ibid.* (internal quotation marks and citation omitted)

Here, because Section 2340 requires that a defendant act with the specific intent to inflict severe pain, the infliction of such pain must be the defendant's precise objective. If the statute had required only general intent, it would be sufficient to establish guilt by showing that the defendant "possessed knowledge with respect to the *actus reus* of the crime." *Carter,* 530 U.S. at 268. If the defendant acted knowing that severe pain or suffering was reasonably likely to result from his actions, but no more, he would have acted only with general intent. *See id,* at 269; Black's Law Dictionary 813 (7th ed. 1999) (explaining that general intent "usu[ally] takes the

---

[2] We note, however, that 18 U.S.C. § 2340(3) supplies a definition of the term "United States." It defines it as "all areas under the jurisdiction of the United States including any of the places described in" 18 U.S.C. §§ 5 and 7, and in 49 U.S.C. § 46501(2). Section 5 provides that United States "includes all places and waters, continental or insular, subject to the jurisdiction of the United States." By including the definition set out in Section 7, the term "United States" as used in Section 2340(3) includes the "special maritime and territorial jurisdiction of the United States." Moreover, the incorporation by reference to Section 46501(2) extends the definition of the "United States" to "special aircraft jurisdiction of the United States."

form of recklessness (involving actual awareness of a risk and the culpable taking of that risk) or negligence (involving blameworthy inadvertence)"). The Supreme Court has used the following example to illustrate the difference between these two mental states:

> [A] person entered a bank and took money from a teller at gunpoint, but deliberately failed to make a quick getaway from the bank in the hope of being arrested so that he would be returned to prison and treated for alcoholism. Though this defendant knowingly engaged in the acts of using force and taking money (satisfying "general intent"), he did not intend permanently to deprive the bank of its possession of the money (failing to satisfy "specific intent").

Carter, 530 U.S. at 268 (citing 1 W. LaFave & A. Scott, Substantive Criminal Law § 3.5, at 315 (1986)).

As a theoretical matter, therefore, knowledge alone that a particular result is certain to occur does not constitute specific intent. As the Supreme Court explained in the context of murder, "the . . . common law of homicide distinguishes . . . between a person who knows that another person will be killed as a result of his conduct and a person who acts with the specific purpose of taking another's life[.]" *United States v. Bailey,* 444 U.S. 394, 405 (1980). "Put differently, the law distinguishes actions taken 'because of' a given end from actions taken 'in spite of their unintended but foreseen consequences." *Vacco v. Quill,* 521 U.S. 793, 802-03 (1997). Thus, even if the defendant knows that severe pain will result from his actions, if causing such harm is not his objective, he lacks the requisite specific intent even though the defendant did not act in good faith. Instead, a defendant is guilty of torture only if he acts with the express purpose of inflicting severe pain or suffering on a person within his custody or physical control. While as a theoretical matter such knowledge does not constitute specific intent, juries are permitted to infer from the factual circumstances that such intent is present. *See, e.g., United States v. Godwin,* 272 F.3d 659, 666 (4th Cir. 2001); *United States v. Karro,* 257 F.3d 112, 118 (2d Cir. 2001); *United States v. Wood,* 207 F.3d 1222, 1232 (10th Cir. 2000); *Henderson v. United States,* 202 F.2d 400, 403 (6th Cir. 1953). Therefore, when a defendant knows that his actions will produce the prohibited result, a jury will in all likelihood conclude that the defendant acted with specific intent.

Further, a showing that an individual acted with a good faith belief that his conduct would not produce the result that the law prohibits negates specific intent. *See, e.g., South Atl. Lmtd. Ptrshp. of Tenn. v. Reise*, 218 F.3d 518, 531 (4th Cir. 2002). Where a defendant acts in good faith, he acts with an honest belief that he has not engaged in the proscribed conduct. *See Cheek v. United States*, 498 U.S. 192, 202 (1991); *United States v. Mancuso*, 42 F.3d 836, 837 (4th Cir. 1994). For example, in the context of mail fraud, if an individual honestly believes that the material transmitted is truthful, he has not acted with the required intent to deceive or mislead. *See, e.g., United States v. Sayakhom*, 186 F.3d 928, 939-40 (9th Cir. 1999). A good faith belief need not be a reasonable one. *See Cheek*, 498 U.S. at 202.

Although a defendant theoretically could hold an unreasonable belief that his acts would not constitute the actions prohibited by the statute, even though they would as a certainty produce the prohibited effects, as a matter of practice in the federal criminal justice system it is highly unlikely that a jury would acquit in such a situation. Where a defendant holds an unreasonable belief, he will confront the problem of proving to the jury that he actually held that belief. As the Supreme Court noted in *Cheek*, "the more unreasonable the asserted beliefs or misunderstandings are, the more likely the jury . . . will find that the Government has carried its burden of proving" intent. *Id.* at 203-04. As we explained above, a jury will be permitted to infer that the defendant held the requisite specific intent. As a matter of proof, therefore, a good faith defense will prove more compelling when a reasonable basis exists for the defendant's belief.

B.   "Severe Pain or Suffering"

The key statutory phrase in the definition of torture is the statement that acts amount to torture if they cause "severe physical or mental pain or suffering." In examining the meaning of a statute, its text must be the starting point. *See INS v. Phinpathya*, 464 U.S. 183, 189 (1984) ("This Court has noted on numerous occasions that in all cases involving statutory construction, our starting point must be the language employed by Congress, . . . and we assume that the legislative purpose is expressed by the ordinary meaning of the words used.") (internal quotations and citations omitted). Section 2340 makes plain that the infliction of pain or suffering per se, whether it is physical or mental, is insufficient to amount to torture. Instead, the text provides that pain or suffering must be "severe." The statute does not, however, define the term "severe." "In the absence of such a definition, we construe a statutory term in accordance with its ordinary or natural meaning." *FDIC v. Meyer*, 510 U.S. 471, 476 (1994). The dictionary defines "severe" as "[u]nsparing in exaction, punishment,

or censure" or "[I]nflicting discomfort or pain hard to endure; sharp; af-
flictive; distressing; violent; extreme; as *severe* pain, anguish, torture."
Webster's New International Dictionary 2295 (2d ed. 1935); *see* American Heritage Dictionary of the English Language 1653 (3d ed. 1992) ("extremely violent or grievous: *severe* pain") (emphasis in original); IX The
Oxford English Dictionary 572 (1978) ("Of pain, suffering, loss, or the
like: Grievous, extreme" and "of circumstances . . . : hard to sustain or
endure"). Thus, the adjective "severe" conveys that the pain or suffering
must be of such a high level of intensity that the pain is difficult for the
subject to endure.

Congress's use of the phrase "severe pain" elsewhere in the United
States Code can shed more light on its meaning. *See, e.g., West Va. Univ.
Hosps., Inc.* v. *Casey*, 499 U.S. 83, 100 (1991) ("[W]e construe [a statutory
term] to contain that permissible meaning which fits most logically and
comfortably into the body of both previously and subsequently enacted
law."). Significantly, the phrase "severe pain" appears in statutes defining an emergency medical condition for the purpose of providing health
benefits. *See, e.g.*, 8 U.S.C. § 1369 (2000); 42 U.S.C § 1395w-22 (2000);
id. § 1395x (2000); *id.* § 1395dd (2000); *id.* § 1396b (2000); *id.* § 1396u-2
(2000). These statutes define an emergency condition as one "manifesting
itself by acute symptoms of sufficient severity (including *severe pain*) such
that a prudent lay person, who possesses an average knowledge of health
and medicine, could reasonably expect the absence of immediate medical
attention to result in—placing the health of the individual . . . (i) in serious
jeopardy, (ii) serious impairment to bodily functions, or (iii) serious dys-
function of any bodily organ or part." *Id.* § 1395w-22(d)(3)(B) (emphasis
added). Although these statutes address a substantially different subject
from Section 2340, they are nonetheless helpful for understanding what
constitutes severe physical pain. They treat severe pain as an indicator of
ailments that are likely to result in permanent and serious physical damage in the absence of immediate medical treatment. Such damage must
rise to the level of death, organ failure, or the permanent impairment of
a significant body function. These statutes suggest that "severe pain," as
used in Section 2340, must rise to a similarly high level—the level that
would ordinarily be associated with a sufficiently serious physical condition or injury such as death, organ failure, or serious impairment of body
functions—in order to constitute torture.[3]

---

[3] One might argue that because the statute uses "or" rather than "and" in the
phrase "pain or suffering" that "severe physical suffering" is a concept distinct

C.   "Severe mental pain or suffering"

Section 2340 gives further guidance as to the meaning of "severe mental pain or suffering," as distinguished from severe physical pain and suffering. The statute defines "severe mental pain or suffering" as:

> the prolonged mental harm caused by or resulting from—
> (A) the intentional infliction or threatened infliction of severe physical pain or suffering;
> (B) the administration or application, or threatened administration or application, of mind-altering substances or other procedures calculated to disrupt profoundly the senses or the personality;
> (C) the threat of imminent death; or
> (D) the threat that another person will imminently be subjected to death, severe physical pain or suffering, or the administration or application of mind-altering substances or other procedures calculated to disrupt profoundly the senses or personality.

18 U.S.C. § 2340(2). In order to prove "severe mental pain or suffering," the statute requires proof of "prolonged mental harm" that was caused by

---

from "severe physical pain." We believe the better view of the statutory text is, however, that they are not distinct concepts. The statute does not define "severe mental pain" and "severe mental suffering" separately. Instead, it gives the phrase "severe mental pain or suffering" a single definition. Because "pain or suffering" is [a] single concept for the purposes of "severe mental pain or suffering," it should likewise be read as a single concept for the purposes of severe physical pain or suffering. Moreover, dictionaries define the words "pain" and "suffering" in terms of each other. *Compare, e.g.*, Webster's Third New International Dictionary 2284 (1993) (defining suffering as "the endurance of . . . pain" or "a pain endured"); Webster's Third New International Dictionary 2284 (1986) (same); XVII The Oxford English Dictionary 125 (2d ed. 1989) (defining suffering as "the bearing or undergoing of pain"); *with, e.g.*, Random House Webster's Unabridged Dictionary 1394 (2d ed. 1999) (defining "pain" as "physical suffering"); The American Heritage Dictionary of the English Language 942 (College ed. 1976) (defining pain as "suffering or distress"). Further, even if we were to read the infliction of severe physical suffering as distinct from severe physical pain, it is difficult to conceive of such suffering that would not involve severe physical pain. Accordingly, we conclude that "pain or suffering" is a single concept within the definition of Section 2340.

or resulted from one of four enumerated acts. We consider each of these elements.

1.   "Prolonged Mental Harm"

As an initial matter, Section 2340(2) requires that the severe mental pain must be evidenced by "prolonged mental harm." To prolong is to "lengthen in time" or to "extend the duration of, to draw out." Webster's Third New International Dictionary 1815 (1988); Webster's New International Dictionary 1980 (2d ed. 1935). Accordingly, "prolong" adds a temporal dimension to the harm to the individual, namely, that the harm must be one that is endured over some period of time. Put another way, the acts giving rise to the harm must cause some lasting, though not necessarily permanent, damage. For example, the mental strain experienced by an individual during a lengthy and intense interrogation—such as one that state or local police might conduct upon a criminal suspect—would not violate Section 2340(2). On the other hand, the development of a mental disorder such as posttraumatic stress disorder, which can last months or even years, or even chronic depression, which also can last for a considerable period of time if untreated, might satisfy the prolonged harm requirement. *See* American Psychiatric Association, *Diagnostic and Statistical Manual of Mental Disorders* 426, 439-45 (4th ed. 1994) ("DSM-IV"). *See also* Craig Haney & Mona Lynch, *Regulating Prisons of the Future: A Psychological Analysis of Supermax and Solitary Confinement*, 23 N.Y.U. Rev. L. & Soc. Change 477, 509 (1997) (noting that posttraumatic stress disorder is frequently found in torture victims); *cf.* Sana Loue, *Immigration Law and Health* § 10:46 (2001) (recommending evaluating for post-traumatic stress disorder immigrant-client who has experienced torture).[4] By contrast to

---

[4] The DSM-IV explains that posttraumatic disorder ("PTSD") is brought on by exposure to traumatic events, such as serious physical injury or witnessing the deaths of others and during those events the individual felt "intense fear" or "horror." *Id.* at 424. Those suffering from this disorder reexperience the trauma through, *inter alia*, "recurrent and intrusive distressing recollections of the event," "recurrent distressing dreams of the event," or "intense psychological distress at exposure to internal or external cues that symbolize or resemble an aspect of the traumatic event." *Id.* at 428. Additionally, a person with PTSD "[p]ersistent[ly]" avoids stimuli associated with the trauma, including avoiding conversations about the trauma, places that stimulate recollections about the trauma; and they experience a numbing of general responsiveness, such as a "restricted range of affect (e.g., unable to have loving feelings)," and "the feeling of detachment or estrangement from others." *Ibid.* Finally, an individual with PTSD

"severe pain," the phrase "prolonged mental harm" appears nowhere else in the U.S. Code nor does it appear in relevant medical literature or international human rights reports.

Not only must the mental harm be prolonged to amount to severe mental pain and suffering, but also it must be caused by or result from one of the acts listed in the statute. In the absence of a catchall provision, the most natural reading of the predicate acts listed in Section 2340(2) (A)-(D) is that Congress intended it to be exhaustive. In other words, other acts not included within Section 2340(2)'s enumeration are not within the statutory prohibition. *See Leatherman v. Tarrant County Narcotics Intelligence & Coordination Unit*, 507 U.S. 163, 168 (1993) (*"Expressio unius est exclusio alterius."*); Norman Singer, 2A Sutherland on Statutory Construction § 47.23 (6th ed. 2000) ("[W]here a form of conduct, the manner of its performance and operation, and the persons and things to which it refers are designated, there is an inference that all omissions should be understood as exclusions.") (footnotes omitted). We conclude that torture within the meaning of the statute requires the specific intent to cause prolonged mental harm by one of the acts listed in Section 2340(2).

A defendant must specifically intend to cause prolonged mental harm for the defendant to have committed torture. It could be argued that a defendant needs to have specific intent only to commit the predicate acts that give rise to prolonged mental harm. Under that view, so long as the defendant specifically intended to, for example, threaten a victim with imminent death, he would have had sufficient *mens rea* for a conviction. According to this view, it would be further necessary for a conviction to show only that the victim factually suffered prolonged mental harm, rather than that the defendant intended to cause it. We believe that this approach is contrary to the text of the statute. The statute requires that the defendant specifically intend to inflict severe mental pain or suffering. Because the statute requires this mental state with respect to the infliction of severe mental pain, and because it expressly defines severe mental pain in terms of prolonged mental harm, that mental state must be present with respect to prolonged mental harm. To read the statute otherwise would read the phrase "the prolonged mental harm caused by or resulting from" out of the definition of "severe mental pain or suffering."

---

has "[p]ersistent symptoms of increased arousal," as evidenced by "irritability or outbursts of anger," "hypervigilance," "exaggerated startle response," and difficulty sleeping or concentrating. *Ibid.*

A defendant could negate a showing of specific intent to cause severe mental pain or suffering by showing that he had acted in good faith that his conduct would not amount to the acts prohibited by the statute. Thus, if a defendant has a good faith belief that his actions will not result in prolonged mental harm, he lacks the mental state necessary for his actions to constitute torture. A defendant could show that he acted in good faith by taking such steps as surveying professional literature, consulting with experts, or reviewing evidence gained from past experience. *See, e.g., Ratlzlaf*, 510 U.S. at 142 n.10 (noting that where the statute required that the defendant act with the specific intent to violate the law, the specific intent element "might be negated by, e.g., proof that defendant relied in good faith on advice of counsel.") (citations omitted). All of these steps would show that he has drawn on the relevant body of knowledge concerning the result proscribed that the statute, namely prolonged mental harm. Because the presence of good faith would negate the specific intent element of torture, it is a complete defense to such a charge. *See, e.g., United States v. Wall*, 130 F.3d 739, 746 (6th Cir. 1997); *United States v. Casperson*, 773 F.2d 216, 222-23 (8th Cir. 1985).

2.   Harm Caused By Or Resulting From Predicate Acts

Section 2340(2) sets forth four basic categories of predicate acts. First in the list is the "intentional infliction or threatened infliction of severe physical pain or suffering." This might at first appear superfluous because the statute already provides that the infliction of severe physical pain or suffering can amount to torture. This provision, however, actually captures the infliction of physical pain or suffering when the defendant inflicts physical pain or suffering with general intent rather than the specific intent that is required where severe physical pain or suffering alone is the basis for the charge. Hence, this subsection reaches the infliction of severe physical pain or suffering when it is but the means of causing prolonged mental harm. Or put another way, a defendant has committed torture when he intentionally inflicts severe physical pain or suffering with the specific intent of causing prolonged mental harm. As for the acts themselves, acts that cause "severe physical pain or suffering" can satisfy this provision.

Additionally, the threat of inflicting such pain is a predicate act under the statute. A threat may be implicit or explicit. *See, e.g., United States v. Sachdev*, 279 F.3d 25, 29 (1st Cir. 2002). In criminal law, courts generally determine whether an individual's words or actions constitute a threat by examining whether a reasonable person in the same circumstances would conclude that a threat had been made. *See, e.g., Watts v. United*

States, 394 U.S. 705, 708 (1969) (holding that whether a statement constituted a threat against the president's life had to be determined in light of all the surrounding circumstances); *Sachdev*, 279 F.3d at 29 ("a reasonable person in defendant's position would perceive there to be a threat, explicit, or implicit, of physical injury"); *United States v. Khorrami*, 895 F.2d 1186, 1190 (7th Cir. 1990) (to establish that a threat was made, the statement must be made "in a context or under such circumstances wherein a reasonable person would foresee that the statement would be interpreted by those to whom the maker communicates a statement as a serious expression of an intention to inflict bodily harm upon [another individual]") (citation and internal quotation marks omitted); *United States v. Peterson*, 483 F.2d 1222, 1230 (D.C. Cir. 1973) (perception of threat of imminent harm necessary to establish self-defense had to be "objectively reasonable in light of the surrounding circumstances"). Based on this common approach, we believe that the existence of a threat of severe pain or suffering should be assessed from the standpoint of a reasonable person in the same circumstances.

Second, Section 2340(2)(B) provides that prolonged mental harm, constituting torture, can be caused by "the administration or application or threatened administration or application, of mind-altering substances or other procedures calculated to disrupt profoundly the senses or the personality." The statute provides no further definition of what constitutes a mind-altering substance. The phrase "mind-altering substances" is found nowhere else in the U.S. Code nor is it found in dictionaries. It is, however, a commonly used synonym for drugs. *See, e.g., United States v. Kingsley*, 241 F.3d 828, 834 (6th Cir.) (referring to controlled substances as "mind-altering substance[s]") *cert. denied*, 122 S. Ct. 137 (2001); *Hogue v. Johnson*, 131 F.3d 466, 501 (5th Cir. 1997) (referring to drugs and alcohol as "mind-altering substance[s]"), *cert. denied*, 523 U.S. 1014 (1998). In addition, the phrase appears in a number of state statutes, and the context in which it appears confirms this understanding of the phrase. *See, e.g.*, Cal. Penal Code § 3500(c) (West Supp. 2000) ("Psychotropic drugs also include mind-altering . . . drugs . . . ."); Minn. Stat. Ann. § 260B.201(b) (West Supp. 2002) ("'chemical dependency treatment'" define as programs designed to "reduc[e] the risk of the use of alcohol, drugs, or other mind-altering substances").

This subparagraph, however, does not preclude any and all use of drugs. Instead, it prohibits the use of drugs that "disrupt profoundly the senses or the personality." To be sure, one could argue that this phrase applies only to "other procedures," not the application of mind-altering substances. We reject this interpretation because the terms of Section 2340(2) expressly indicate that the qualifying phrase applies to both "other procedures" *and* the "application of mind-altering substances." The word "other" modifies "procedures calculated to disrupt profoundly the senses." As an adjective, "other" indicates that the term or phrase it modifies is the remainder of several things. *See* Webster's Third New International Dictionary 1598 (1986) (defining "other" as "the one that remains of two or more"); Webster's Ninth New Collegiate Dictionary 835 (1985) (defining "other" as "being the one (as of two or more) remaining or not included"). Or put another way, "other" signals that the words to which it attaches are of the same kind, type, or class as the more specific item previously listed. Moreover, where statutes couple words or phrases together, it "denotes an intention that they should be understood in the same general sense." Norman Singer, 2A Sutherland on Statutory Construction § 47:16 (6th ed. 2000); *see also Beecham v. United States*, 511 U.S. 368, 371 (1994) ("That several items in a list share an attribute counsels in favor of interpreting the other items as possessing that attribute as well."). Thus, the pairing of mind-altering substances with procedures calculated to disrupt profoundly the senses or personality and the use of "other" to modify "procedures" shows that the use of such substances must also cause a profound disruption of the senses or personality.

For drugs or procedures to rise to the level of "disrupt[ing] profoundly the senses or personality," they must produce an extreme effect. And by requiring that they be "calculated" to produce such an effect, the statute requires for liability the defendant has consciously designed the acts to produce such an effect. 28 U.S.C. § 2340(2)(B). The word "disrupt" is defined as "to break asunder; to part forcibly; rend," imbuing the verb with a connotation of violence. Webster's New International Dictionary 753 (2d ed. 1935); *see* Webster's Third New International Dictionary 656 (1986) (defining disrupt as "to break apart: Rupture" or "destroy the unity or wholeness of"); IV The Oxford English Dictionary 832 (1989) (defining disrupt as "[t]o break or burst asunder; to break in pieces; to separate forcibly"). Moreover, disruption of the senses or personality alone is insufficient to fall within the scope of this subsection; instead, that disruption must be profound. The word "profound" has a number of meanings, all of which convey a significant depth. Webster's New International Dictionary 1977 (2d ed. 1935) defines profound as: "Of very great depth; extending far below the surface or top; unfathomable[;] . . . [c]oming from, reaching to, or situated at a depth or more than ordinary depth; not superficial; deep-seated; chiefly with reference to the body; as a *profound* sigh, wound, or pain[;] . . . [c]haracterized by intensity, as of feeling or quality; deeply felt or realized; as, *profound* respect, fear, or melancholy; hence, encompass-

ing; thoroughgoing; complete; as, *profound* sleep, silence, or ignorance."
See Webster's Third New International Dictionary 1812 (1986) ("having
very great depth: extending far below the surface . . . not superficial").
Random House Webster's Unabridged Dictionary 1545 (2d ed. 1999) also
defines profound as "originating in or penetrating to the depths of one's
being" or "pervasive or intense; thorough; complete" or "extending, situated, or originating far down, or far beneath the surface." By requiring
that the procedures and the drugs create a *profound* disruption, the statute
requires more than that the acts "forcibly separate" or "rend" the senses or
personality. Those acts must penetrate to the core of an individual's ability
to perceive the world around him, substantially interfering with his cognitive abilities, or fundamentally alter his personality.

The phrase "disrupt profoundly the senses or personality" is not
used in mental health literature nor is it derived from elsewhere in U.S.
law. Nonetheless, we think the following examples would constitute a profound disruption of the senses or personality. Such an effect might be seen
in a drug-induced dementia. In such a state, the individual suffers from
significant memory impairment, such as the inability to retain any new
information or recall information about things previously of interest to
the individual. *See* DSM-IV at 134.[5] This impairment is accompanied by
one or more of the following: deterioration of language function, e.g., repeating sounds or words over and over again; impaired ability to execute
simple motor activities, e.g., inability to dress or wave goodbye; "[in]abil-
ity to recognize [and identify] objects such as chairs or pencils" despite
normal visual functioning; or "[d]isturbances in executive level functioning," i.e., serious impairment of abstract thinking. *Id.* at 134-35. Similarly,
we think that the onset of "brief psychotic disorder" would satisfy this
standard. *See id.* at 302-03. In this disorder, the individual suffers psychotic symptoms, including among other things, delusions, hallucinations,
or even a catatonic state. This can last for one day or even one month.
See id. We likewise think that the onset of obsessive-compulsive disor-

---

[5] Published by the American Psychiatric Association, and written as a collabo-
ration of over a thousand psychiatrists, the DSM-IV is commonly used in U.S.
courts as a source of information regarding mental health issues and is likely to
be used in trial should charges be brought that allege this predicate act. *See, e.g.,*
Atkins v. Virginia, 122 S. Ct. 2242, 2245 n.3 (2002); *Kansas v. Crane,* 122 S. Ct.
867, 871 (2002); *Kansas v. Hendricks,* 521 U.S. 346, 359–60 (1997); *McClean v.
Merrifield,* No. 00–CV–0120E(SC), 2002 WL 1477607 at *2 n.7 (W.D.N.Y. June
28, 2002); *Peeples v. Coastal Office Prods.,* 203 F. Supp. 2d. 432, 439 (D. Md.
2002); *Lassiegne v. Taco Bell Corp.,* 202 F. Supp. 2d 512, 519 (E.D. La. 2002).

der behaviors would rise to this level. Obsessions are intrusive thoughts unrelated to reality. They are not simple worries, but are repeated doubts or even "aggressive or horrific impulses." *See id.* at 418. The DSM-IV further explains that compulsions include "repetitive behaviors (e.g., hand washing, ordering, checking)" and that "[b]y definition, [they] are either clearly excessive or are not connected in a realistic way with what they are designed to neutralize or prevent." *See id.* Such compulsions or obsessions must be "time-consuming." *See id.* at 419. Moreover, we think that pushing someone to the brink of suicide, particularly where the person comes from a culture with strong taboos against suicide, and it is evidenced by acts of self-mutilation, would be a sufficient disruption of the personality to constitute a "profound disruption." These examples, of course, are in no way intended to be [an] exhaustive list. Instead, they are merely intended to illustrate the sort of mental health effects that we believe would accompany an action severe enough to amount to one that "disrupt[s] profoundly the senses or the personality."

The third predicate act listed in Section 2340(2) is threatening a prisoner with "imminent death." 18 U.S.C. § 2340(2)(C). The plain text makes clear that a threat of death alone is insufficient; the threat must indicate that death is "imminent." The "threat of imminent death" is found in the common law as an element of the defense of duress. *See Bailey,* 444 U.S. at 409. "[W]here Congress borrows terms of art in which are accumulated the legal tradition and meaning of centuries of practice, it presumably knows and adopts the cluster of ideas that were attached to each borrowed word in the body of learning from which it was taken and the meaning its use will convey to the judicial mind unless otherwise instructed. In such case, absence of contrary direction may be taken as satisfaction with widely accepted definitions, not as a departure from them." *Morissette v. United States,* 342 U.S. 246, 263 (1952). Common law cases and legislation generally define imminence as requiring that the threat be almost immediately forthcoming. 1 Wayne R. LaFave & Austin W. Scott, Jr., Substantive Criminal Law § 5.7, at 655 (1986). By contrast, threats referring vaguely to things that might happen in the future do not satisfy this immediacy requirement. *See United States v. Fiore,* 178 F.3d 917, 923 (7th Cir. 1999). Such a threat fails to satisfy this requirement not because it is too remote in time but because there is a lack of certainty that it will occur. Indeed, timing is an indicator of certainty that the harm *will* befall the defendant. Thus, a vague threat that someday the prisoner *might* be killed would not suffice. Instead, subjecting a prisoner to mock executions or playing Russian roulette with him would have sufficient immediacy to constitute a threat of imminent death. Additionally, as discussed earlier, we believe that the existence of a threat must be assessed from the perspective of a reasonable person in the same circumstances.

Fourth, if the official threatens to do anything previously described to a third party, or commits such an act against a third party, that threat or action can serve as the necessary predicate for prolonged mental harm. *See* 18 U.S.C. § 2340(2)(D). The statute does not require any relationship between the prisoner and the third party.

3.   Legislative History

The legislative history of Sections 2340-2340A is scant. Neither the definition of torture nor these sections as a whole sparked any debate. Congress criminalized this conduct to fulfill U.S. obligations under the U.N. Convention Against Torture and Other Cruel, Inhuman or Degrading Treatment or Punishment ("CAT"), adopted Dec. 10, 1984, S. Treaty Doc. No. 100-20 (1988), 1465 U.N.T.S. 85 (entered into force June 26, 1987), which requires signatories to "ensure that all acts of torture are offenses under its criminal law." CAT art. 4. These sections appeared only in the Senate version of the Foreign Affairs Authorization Act, and the conference bill adopted them without amendment. *See* H. R. Conf. Rep. No. 103-482, at 229 (1994). The only light that the legislative history sheds reinforces what is already obvious from the texts of Section 2340 and CAT: Congress intended Section 2340's definition of torture to track the definition set forth in CAT, as elucidated by the United States' reservations, understandings, and declarations submitted as part of its ratification. *See* S. Rep. No. 103-107, at 58 (1993) ("The definition of torture emanates directly from article 1 of the Convention."); *id.* at 58-59 ("The definition for 'severe mental pain and suffering' incorporates the understanding made by the Senate concerning this term.").

4.   Summary

Section 2340's definition of torture must be read as a sum of these component parts. *See Argentine Rep. v. Amerada Hess Shipping Corp.*, 488 U.S. 428, 434-35 (1989) (reading two provisions together to determine statute's meaning); *Bethesda Hosp. Ass'n v. Bowen*, 485 U.S. 399, 405 (1988) (looking to "the language and design of the statute as a whole" to ascertain a statute's meaning). Each component of the definition emphasizes that torture is not the mere infliction of pain or suffering on another, but is instead a step well removed. The victim must experience intense pain or suffering of the kind that is equivalent to the pain that would be associated with serious physical injury so severe that death, organ failure, or permanent damage resulting in a loss of significant body function will likely result. If that pain or suffering is psychological, that suffering must result from one of the acts set forth in the statute. In addition, these acts must cause long-term mental harm. Indeed, this view of the criminal act of torture is consistent with the term's common meaning. Torture is generally understood to involve "intense pain" or "excruciating pain," or put another way, "extreme anguish of body or mind." Black's Law Dictionary at 1498 (7th Ed. 1999); Random House Webster's Unabridged Dictionary 1999 (1999); Webster's New International Dictionary 2674 (2d ed. 1935). In short, reading the definition of torture as a whole, it is plain that the term encompasses only extreme acts.[6]

---

[6] Torture is a term also found in state law. Some states expressly proscribe "murder by torture." *See, e.g.*, Idaho Code § 18-4001 (Michie 1997); N.C. Gen. Stat. Ann. § 14-17 (1999); *see also* Me. Rev. Stat. Ann. tit. 17-A, § 152–A (West Supp. 2001) (aggravated attempted murder is "[t]he attempted murder . . . accompanied by torture, sexual assault or other extreme cruelty inflicted upon the victim"). Other states have made torture an aggravating factor supporting imposition of the death penalty. *See, e.g.*, Ark. Code Ann. § 5-4-604(8)(B); Del. Code Ann. tit. 11, § 4209(e)(1)(*l*) (1995); Ga. Code Ann. § 17-10-30(b)(7) (1997); ; 720 Ill. Comp. Stat. Ann. 5/9-1(b)(14) (West Supp. 2002); Mass. Ann. Laws ch. 279, § 69(a) (Law. Co-op. 1992); Mo. Ann. Stat. § 565.032(2)(7) (West 1999); Nev. Rev. Stat. Ann. 200-033(8) (Michie 2001); N.J. Stat. Ann. § 2C:11-3 (West Supp. 2002) (same); Tenn. Code Ann. § 39-13-204(i)(5) (Supp. 2001); *see also* Alaska Stat. § 12.55.125(a)(3) (2000) (term of 99 years' imprisonment mandatory where defendant subjected victim to "substantial physical torture"). *All of these laws support the conclusion that torture is generally an extreme act far beyond the infliction of pain or suffering alone.*

California law is illustrative on this point. The California Penal Code not only makes torture itself an offense, see Cal. Penal Code § 206 (West Supp. 2002), it also prohibits murder by torture, see Cal. Penal Code § 189 (West Supp. 2002), and provides that torture is an aggravating circumstance supporting the imposition of the death penalty, see Cal. Penal Code § 190.2 (West Supp. 2002). California's definitions of torture demonstrate that the term is reserved for especially cruel acts inflicting serious injury. Designed to "fill[] a gap in existing law dealing with extremely violent and callous criminal conduct[,]" *People v. Hale,* 88 Cal. Rptr. 2d 904, 913 (1999) (internal quotation marks and citation omitted), Section 206 defines the offense of torture as:

> [e]very person who, with the intent to cause *cruel* or *extreme* pain and suffering for the purpose of revenge, extortion, persuasion, or for any sadistic purpose, inflicts great bodily injury . . . upon the person of another, is guilty of torture. The crime of torture does not require any proof that the victim suffered pain.

(Emphasis added). With respect to sections 190.2 and 189, neither of which are

II. U.N. Convention Against Torture and Other Cruel Inhuman or Degrading Treatment or Punishment.

Because Congress enacted the criminal prohibition against torture to implement CAT, we also examine the treaty's text and history to develop a fuller understanding of the context of Sections 2340-2340A. As with the statute, we begin our analysis with the treaty's text. *See Eastern Airlines Inc. v. Floyd*, 499 U.S. 530, 534-35 (1991) ("When interpreting a treaty, we begin with the text of the treaty and the context in which the written words are used.) (quotation marks and citations omitted). CAT defines torture as:

> any act by which *severe* pain or suffering, whether physical
> or mental, is intentionally inflicted on a person for such pur-
> poses as obtaining from him or a third person information or
> a confession, punishing him for an act he or a third person has
> committed or is suspected of having committed, or intimidat-
> ing or coercing him or a third person, or for any reason based
> on discrimination of any kind, when such pain or suffering
> is inflicted by or at the instigation of or with the consent or

---

statutorily defined, California courts have recognized that torture generally means an "[a]ct or process of inflicting severe pain, esp[ecially] as a punishment to extort confession, or in revenge. ... Implicit in that definition is the requirement of an intent to cause pain and suffering in addition to death." *People v. Barrera*, 18 Cal. Rptr. 2d 395, 399 (Ct. App. 1993) (quotation marks and citation omitted). Further, "murder by torture was and is considered among the most reprehensible types of murder because of the calculated nature of the acts causing death." *Id.* at 403 (quoting *People v. Wiley*, 133 Cal. Rptr. 135, 138 (1976) (in bank)). The definition of murder by torture special circumstance, proscribed under Cal. Penal Code § 190.2, likewise shows an attempt to reach the most heinous acts imposing pain beyond that which a victim suffers through death alone. To establish murder by torture special circumstance, the "intent to kill, intent to torture, and infliction of an extremely painful act upon a living victim" must be present. *People v. Bemore*, 94 Cal. Rptr. 2d 840, 861 (2000). The intent to torture is characterized by a " 'sadistic intent to cause the victim to suffer pain in addition to the pain of death.'" *Id.* at 862 (quoting *People v. Davenport*, 221 Cal. Rptr. 794, 875 (1985)). Like the Torture Victims Protection Act and the Convention Against Torture, discussed *infra* at Parts II and III, each of these California prohibitions against torture require an evil intent—such as cruelty, revenge or even sadism. Section 2340 does not require this additional intent, but as discussed *supra* pp. 2-3, requires that the individual specifically intended to cause severe pain or suffering. Furthermore, unlike Section 2340, neither section 189 nor section 206 appear to require proof of actual pain to establish torture.

acquiescence of a public official or other person acting in an official capacity.

Article 1(1) (emphasis added). Unlike Section 2340, this definition includes a list of purposes for which such pain and suffering is inflicted. The prefatory phrase "such purposes as" makes clear that this list is, however, illustrative rather than exhaustive. Accordingly, severe pain or suffering need not be inflicted for those specific purposes to constitute torture; instead, the perpetrator must simply have a purpose of the same kind. More importantly, like Section 2340, the pain and suffering must be severe to reach the threshold of torture. Thus, the text of CAT reinforces our reading of Section 2340 that torture must be an extreme act.[7]

CAT also distinguishes between torture and other acts of cruel, inhuman, or degrading treatment or punishment.[8] Article 16 of CAT requires

---

[7] To be sure, the text of the treaty requires that an individual act "intentionally." This language might be read to require only general intent for violations of the Torture Convention. We believe, however, that the better interpretation is that that the use of the phrase "intentionally" also created a specific intent-type standard. In that event, the Bush administration's understanding represents only an explanation of how the United States intended to implement the vague language of the Torture Convention. If, however, the Convention established a general intent standard, then the Bush understanding represents a modification of the obligation undertaken by the United States.

[8] Common article 3 of Geneva Convention on prisoners of war, Convention Relative to the Treatment of Prisoners of War, 6 U.S.T. 3517 ("Geneva Convention III") contains somewhat similar language. Article 3(1)(a) prohibits "violence to life and person, in particular murder of all kinds, mutilation, *cruel treatment and torture*." (Emphasis added). Article 3(1)(c) additionally prohibits "outrages upon personal dignity, in particular, humiliating and degrading treatment." Subsection (c) must forbid more conduct than that already covered in subsection (a) otherwise subsection (c) would be superfluous. Common article 3 does not, however, define either of the phrases "outrages upon personal dignity" or "humiliating and degrading treatment." International criminal tribunals, such as those respecting Rwanda and former Yugoslavia have used common article 3 to try individuals for committing inhuman acts lacking any military necessity whatsoever. Based on our review of the case law, however, these tribunals have not yet articulated the full scope of conduct prohibited by common article 3. Memorandum for John C. Yoo, Deputy Assistant Attorney General, Office of Legal Counsel, from James C. Ho, Attorney-Advisor, Office of Legal Counsel, *Re: Possible Interpretations of Common Article 3 of the 1949 Geneva Convention Relative to the Treatment of Prisoners of War* (Feb. 1, 2002).

We note that Section 2340A and CAT protect any individual from torture. By contrast, the standards of conduct established by common article 3 of Convention III, do not apply to "an armed conflict between a nation-state and state parties to "undertake to prevent . . . other acts of cruel, inhuman or degrading treatment or punishment *which do not amount to torture* as defined in article 1." (Emphasis added). CAT thus establishes a category of acts that are not to be committed and that states must endeavor to prevent, but that states need not criminalize, leaving those acts without the stigma of criminal penalties. CAT reserves criminal penalties and the stigma attached to those penalties for torture alone. In so doing, CAT makes clear that torture is at the farthest end of impermissible actions, and that it is distinct and separate from the lower level of "cruel, inhuman, or degrading treatment or punishment." This approach is in keeping with CAT's predecessor, the U.N. Declaration on the Protection from Torture. That declaration defines torture as "an aggravated and deliberate form of cruel, inhuman or degrading treatment or punishment." Declaration on Protection from Torture, UN Res. 3452, Art. 1(2) (Dec. 9, 1975).

A.   Ratification History

Executive branch interpretation of CAT further supports our conclusion that the treaty, and thus Section 2340A, prohibits only the most extreme forms of physical or mental harm. As we have previously noted, the "division of treaty-making responsibility between the Senate and the President is essentially the reverse of the division of law-making authority, with the President being the draftsman of the treaty and the Senate holding the authority to grant or deny approval." *Relevance of Senate Ratification History to Treaty Interpretation,* 11 Op. O.L.C. 28, 31 (Apr. 9, 1987) ("Sofaer Memorandum"). Treaties are negotiated by the President in his capacity as the "sole organ of the federal government in the field of international relations." *United States v. Curtiss-Wright Export Corp.,* 299 U.S. 304, 320 (1936). Moreover, the President is responsible for the day-to-day interpretation of a treaty and retains the power to unilaterally terminate a treaty. *See Goldwater v. Carter,* 617 F.2d 697, 707-08 (D.C. Cir.) (en banc) *vacated and remanded with instructions to dismiss on other grounds,* 444 U.S. 996 (1979). The Executive's interpretation is to be accorded the greatest weight in ascertaining a treaty's intent and meaning. *See, e.g., United States v. Stuart,* 489 U.S. 353, 369 (1989) ("'the meaning attributed to

---

a transnational terrorist organization." Memorandum for Alberto R. Gonzales, Counsel to the President, and William J. Haynes, II, General Counsel, Department of Defense, from Jay S. Bybee, Assistant Attorney General, Office of Legal Counsel, *Re: Application of Treaties and Laws to al Qaeda and Taliban Detainees* at 8 (Jan. 22, 2002).

treaty provisions by the Government agencies charged with their negotiation and enforcement is entitled to great weight'") (quoting *Sumitomo
Shoji America, Inc. v. Avagliano*, 457 U.S. 176, 184-85 (1982)); *Kolovrat
v. Oregon*, 366 U.S. 187, 194 (1961) ("While courts interpret treaties for
themselves, the meaning given them by the department of government
particularly charged with their negotiation and enforcement is given great
weight."); *Charlton v. Kelly*, 229 U.S. 447, 468 (1913) ("A construction of
a treaty by the political departments of the government, while not conclusive upon a court . . . , is nevertheless of much weight.").

A review of the Executive branch's interpretation and understanding of CAT reveals that Congress codified the view that torture included
only the most extreme forms of physical or mental harm. When it submitted the Convention to the Senate, the Reagan administration took the
position that CAT reached only the most heinous acts. The Reagan administration included the following understanding:

> The United States understands that, in order to constitute tor-
> ture, an act must be a deliberate and calculated act of an ex-
> tremely cruel and inhuman nature, specifically intended to
> inflict excruciating and agonizing physical or mental pain or
> suffering.

S. Treaty Doc. No. 100-20, at 4-5. Focusing on the treaty's requirement of
"severity," the Reagan administration concluded, "The extreme nature of
torture is further emphasized in [this] requirement." S. Treaty Doc. No.
100-20, at 3 (1988); S. Exec. Rep. 101-30, at 13 (1990). The Reagan administration also determined that CAT's definition of torture fell in line with
"United States and international usage, [where it] is usually reserved for
extreme deliberate and unusually cruel practices, for example, sustained
systematic beatings, application of electric currents to sensitive parts of
the body and tying up or hanging in positions that cause extreme pain."
S. Exec. Rep. No. 101-30, at 14 (1990). In interpreting CAT's definition
of torture as reaching only such extreme acts, the Reagan administration
underscored the distinction between torture and other cruel, inhuman, or
degrading treatment or punishment. In particular, the administration declared that article l's definition of torture ought to be construed in light of
article 16. *See* S. Treaty Doc. No. 100-20, at 3. Based on this distinction,
the administration concluded that: "'Torture' is thus to be distinguished
from lesser forms of cruel, inhuman, or degrading treatment or punishment, which are to be deplored and prevented, but are not so universally
and categorically condemned as to warrant the severe legal consequences

that the Convention provides in case of torture." S. Treaty Doc. 100-20, at 3. Moreover, this distinction was "adopted in order to emphasize that torture is at the extreme end of cruel, inhuman and degrading treatment or punishment." S. Treaty Doc. No. 100-20, at 3. Given the extreme nature of torture, the administration concluded that "rough treatment as generally falls into the category of 'police brutality,' while deplorable, does not amount to 'torture.'" S. Treaty Doc. No. 100-20, at 4.

Although the Reagan administration relied on CAT's distinction between torture and "cruel, inhuman, or degrading treatment or punishment," it viewed the phrase "cruel, inhuman, or degrading treatment or punishment" as vague and lacking in a universally accepted meaning. Of even greater concern to the Reagan administration was that because of its vagueness this phrase could be construed to bar acts not prohibited by the U.S. Constitution. The administration pointed to *Case of X v. Federal Republic of Germany* as the basis for this concern. In that case, the European Court of Human Rights determined that the prison officials' refusal to recognize a prisoner's sex change might constitute degrading treatment. *See* S. Treaty Doc. No. 100-20, at 15 (citing European Commission on Human Rights, *Dec. on Adm.*, Dec. 15, 1977, *Case of X v. Federal Republic of Germany* (No. 6694/74), 11 Dec. & Rep. 16)). As a result of this concern, the Administration added the following understanding:

> The United States understands the term, 'cruel, inhuman or degrading treatment or punishment,' as used in Article 16 of the Convention, to mean the cruel, unusual, and inhumane treatment or punishment prohibited by the Fifth, Eighth and/ or Fourteenth Amendments to the Constitution of the United States."

S. Treaty Doc. No. 100-20, at 15-16. Treatment or punishment must therefore rise to the level of action that U.S. courts have found to be in violation of the U.S. Constitution in order to constitute cruel, inhuman, or degrading treatment or punishment. That which fails to rise to this level must fail, *a fortiori*, to constitute torture under Section 2340.[9]

---

[9] The vagueness of "cruel, inhuman and degrading treatment" enables the term to have a far-ranging reach. Article 3 of the European Convention on Human Rights similarly prohibits such treatment. The European Court of Human Rights has construed this phrase broadly, even assessing whether such treatment has occurred from the subjective stand point of the victim. *See* Memorandum from James C. Ho, Attorney-Advisor to John C. Yoo, Deputy Assistant Attorney

The Senate did not give its advice and consent to the Convention until the first Bush administration. Although using less vigorous rhetoric, the Bush administration joined the Reagan administration in interpreting torture as only reaching extreme acts. To ensure that the Convention's reach remained limited, the Bush administration submitted the following understanding:

> The United States understands that, in order to constitute torture, an act must be specifically intended to inflict severe physical or mental pain or suffering and that mental pain or suffering refers to prolonged mental pain caused by or resulting from (1) the intentional infliction or threatened infliction of severe physical pain or suffering; (2) administration or application, or threatened administration or application, of mind altering substances or other procedures calculated to disrupt profoundly the senses or the personality; (3) the threat of imminent death; or (4) the threat that another person will imminently be subjected to death, severe physical pain or suffering, or the administration or application of mind-altering substances or other procedures calculated to disrupt profoundly the senses or personality.

S. Exec. Rep. No. 101-30, at 36. This understanding accomplished two things. First, it ensured that the term "intentionally" would be understood as requiring specific intent. Second, it added form and substance to the otherwise amorphous concept of *mental* pain or suffering. In so doing, this understanding ensured that mental torture would rise to a severity seen in the context of physical torture. The Senate ratified CAT with this

---

General, *Re: Possible Interpretations of Common Article 3 of the 1949 Geneva Convention Relative to the Treatment of Prisoners of War* (Feb. 1, 2002) (finding that European Court of Human Right's construction of inhuman or degrading treatment "is broad enough to arguably forbid even standard U.S. law enforcement interrogation techniques, which endeavor to break down a detainee's 'moral resistance' to answering questions.").

Moreover, despite the Reagan and Bush administrations' efforts to limit the reach of the cruel, inhuman and degrading treatment language, it appears to still have a rather limitless reach. *See id.* (describing how the Eighth Amendment ban on "cruel and unusual punishment" has been used by courts to, *inter alia*, "engage in detailed regulation of prison conductions, including the exact size cells, exercise, and recreational activities, quality of food, access to cable television, internet, and law libraries.")

understanding, and as is obvious from the text, Congress codified this understanding almost verbatim in the criminal statute.

To be sure, it might be thought significant that the Bush administration's language differs from the Reagan administration understanding. The Bush administration said that it had altered the CAT understanding in response to criticism that the Reagan administration's original formulation had raised the bar for the level of pain necessary for the act or acts to constitute torture. *See* Convention Against Torture: Hearing Before the Senate Comm. On Foreign Relations, 101st Cong. 9-10 (1990) ("1990 Hearing") (prepared statement of Hon. Abraham D. Sofaer, Legal Adviser, Department of State). While it is true that there are rhetorical differences between the understandings, both administrations consistently emphasize the extraordinary or extreme acts required to constitute torture. As we have seen, the Bush understanding as codified in Section 2340 reaches only extreme acts. The Reagan understanding, like the Bush understanding, ensured that "intentionally" would be understood as a specific intent requirement. Though the Reagan administration required that the "act be deliberate and calculated" *and* that it be inflicted with specific intent, in operation there is little difference between requiring specific intent alone and requiring that the act be deliberate and calculated. The Reagan understanding's also made express what is obvious from the plain text of CAT: torture is an extreme form of cruel and inhuman treatment. The Reagan administration's understanding that the pain be "excruciating and agonizing" is in substance not different from the Bush administration's proposal that the pain must be severe.

The Bush understanding simply took a rather abstract concept—excruciating and agonizing mental pain—and gave it a more concrete form. Executive branch representations made to the Senate support our view that there was little difference between these two understandings and that the further definition of mental pain or suffering merely sought [to] remove the vagueness created by [the] concept of "agonizing and excruciating" mental pain. *See* 1990 Hearing, at 10 (prepared statement of Hon. Abraham D. Sofaer, Legal Adviser, Department of State) ("no higher standard was intended" by the Reagan administration understanding than was present in the Convention or the Bush understanding); *id.* at 13-14 (statement of Mark Richard, Deputy Assistant Attorney General, Criminal Division, Department of Justice) ("In an effort to overcome this unacceptable element of vagueness [in the term "mental pain"], we have proposed an understanding which defines severe mental pain constituting torture with sufficient specificity . . . to protect innocent persons and meet constitutional due process requirements.") Accordingly, we believe that the two definitions submitted by the Reagan and Bush administrations had the same purpose in terms of articulating a legal standard, namely, ensuring that the prohibition against torture reaches only the most extreme acts. Ultimately, whether the Reagan standard would have been even higher is a purely academic question because the Bush understanding clearly established a very high standard.

Executive branch representations made to the Senate confirm that the Bush administration maintained the view that torture encompassed only the most extreme acts. Although the ratification record, i.e., testimony, hearings, and the like, is generally not accorded great weight in interpreting treaties, authoritative statements made by representatives of the Executive Branch are accorded the most interpretive value. *See* Sofaer Memorandum, at 35-36. Hence, the testimony of the executive branch witnesses defining torture, in addition to the reservations, understandings and declarations that were submitted to the Senate by the Executive branch, should carry the highest interpretive value of any of the statements in the ratification record. At the Senate hearing on CAT, Mark Richard, Deputy Assistant Attorney General, Criminal Division, Department of Justice, offered extensive testimony as to the meaning of torture. Echoing the analysis submitted by the Reagan administration, he testified that "[t]orture is understood to be that barbaric cruelty which lies at the top of the pyramid of human rights misconduct." 1990 Hearing, at 16 (prepared statement of Mark Richard). He further explained, "As applied to physical torture, there appears to be some degree of consensus that the concept involves conduct, the mere mention of which sends chills down one's spine[.]" *Id.* Richard gave the following examples of conduct satisfying this standard: "the needle under the fingernail, the application of electrical shock to the genital area, the piercing of eyeballs, etc." *Id.* In short, repeating virtually verbatim the terms used in the Reagan understanding, Richard explained that under the Bush administration's submissions with the treaty "the essence of torture" is treatment that inflicts "excruciating and agonizing physical pain." *Id.* (emphasis added).

As to mental torture, Richard testified that "no international consensus had emerged [as to] what degree of mental suffering is required to constitute torture[,]" but that it was nonetheless clear that severe mental pain or suffering "does not encompass the normal legal compulsions which are properly a part of the criminal justice system[:] interrogation, incarceration, prosecution, compelled testimony against a friend, etc,— notwithstanding the fact that they may have the incidental effect of producing mental strain." *Id.* at 17. According to Richard, CAT was intended to "condemn as torture intentional acts such as those designed to damage and destroy the human personality." *Id.* at 14. This description of mental suffering emphasizes the requirement that any mental harm be of significant duration and lends further support for our conclusion that mind-altering substances must have a profoundly disruptive effect to serve as a predicate act.

Apart from statements from Executive branch officials, the rest of a ratification record is of little weight in interpreting a treaty. *See generally* Sofaer Memorandum. Nonetheless, the Senate understanding of the definition of torture largely echoes the administrations' views. The Senate Foreign Relations Committee Report on CAT opined: "[f]or an act to be 'torture' it must be an *extreme* form of cruel and inhuman treatment, cause *severe* pain and suffering and be *intended to cause severe* pain and suffering." S. Exec. Rep. No. 101-30, at 6 (emphasis added). Moreover, like both the Reagan and Bush administrations, the Senate drew upon the distinction between torture and cruel, inhuman or degrading treatment or punishment in reaching its view that torture was extreme.[10] Finally, the Senate concurred with the administrations' concern that "cruel, inhuman, or degrading treatment or punishment" could be construed to establish a new standard above and beyond that which the Constitution mandates and supported the inclusion of the reservation establishing the Constitution as the baseline for determining whether conduct amounted to cruel, inhuman, degrading treatment or punishment. *See* 136 Cong. Rec. 36,192 (1990); S. Exec. Rep. 101-30, at 39.

B.   Negotiating History

CAT's negotiating history also indicates that its definition of torture supports our reading of Section 2340. The state parties endeavored to craft a definition of torture that reflected the term's gravity. During the negotiations, state parties offered various formulations of the definition of torture to the working group, which then proposed a definition based

---

[10] Hearing testimony, though the least weighty evidence of meaning of all of the ratification record, is not to the contrary. Other examples of torture mentioned in testimony similarly reflect acts resulting in intense pain: the "gouging out of childrens' [sic] eyes, the torture death by molten rubber, the use of electric shocks," cigarette burns, hanging by hands or feet. 1990 Hearing at 45 (Statement of Winston Nagan, Chairman, Board of Directors, Amnesty International USA); *id.* at 79 (Statement of David Weissbrodt, Professor of Law, University of Minnesota, on behalf of the Center for Victims of Torture, the Minnesota Lawyers International Human Rights Committee).

on those formulations. Almost all of these suggested definitions illustrate the consensus that torture is an extreme act designed to cause agonizing pain. For example, the United States proposed that torture be defined as "includ[ing] any act by which extremely severe pain or suffering . . . is deliberately and maliciously inflicted on a person." J. Herman Burgers & Hans Danelius, *The United Nations Convention Against Torture: A Handbook on the Convention Against Torture and Other Cruel Inhuman and Degrading Treatment or Punishment* 41 (1988) ("CAT Handbook"). The United Kingdom suggested an even more restrictive definition, i.e., that torture be defined as the "*systematic and intentional* infliction of *extreme* pain or suffering rather than *intentional* infliction of *severe* pain or suffering." *Id.* at 45 (emphasis in original). Ultimately, in choosing the phrase "severe pain," the parties concluded that this phrase "sufficient[ly] . . . convey[ed] the idea that only acts of a certain gravity shall . . . constitute torture." *Id.* at 117.

In crafting such a definition, the state parties also were acutely aware of the distinction they drew between torture and cruel, inhuman, or degrading treatment or punishment. The state parties considered and rejected a proposal that would have defined torture merely as cruel, inhuman or degrading treatment or punishment. *See id.* at 42. Mirroring the Declaration on Protection From Torture, which expressly defined torture as an "aggravated and deliberate form of cruel, inhuman or degrading treatment or punishment," some state parties proposed that in addition to the definition of torture set out in paragraph 2 of article 1, a paragraph defining torture as "an aggravated and deliberate form of cruel, inhuman or degrading treatment or punishment" should be included. *See id.* at 41; *see also* S. Treaty Doc. No. 100-20, at 2 (the U.N. Declaration on Protection from Torture (1975) served as "a point of departure for the drafting of [CAT]"). In the end, the parties concluded that the addition of such a paragraph was superfluous because Article 16 "impl[ies] that torture is the gravest form of such treatment or punishment." *CAT Handbook* at 80; *see* S. Exec. Rep. No. 101-30, at 13 ("The negotiating history indicates that [the phrase 'which do not amount to torture'] was adopted in order to emphasize that torture is at the extreme end of cruel, inhuman and degrading treatment or punishment and that Article 1 should be construed with this in mind.").

Additionally, the parties could not reach a consensus about the meaning of "cruel, inhuman, or degrading treatment or punishment." *See CAT Handbook* at 47. Without a consensus, the parties viewed the term as simply "'too vague to be included in a convention which was to form the basis for criminal legislation in the Contracting States.'" *Id.* This view evinced by the parties reaffirms the interpretation of CAT as purposely reserving criminal penalties for torture alone.

CAT's negotiating history offers more than just support for the view that pain or suffering must be extreme to amount to torture. First, the negotiating history suggests that the harm sustained from the acts of torture need not be permanent. In fact, "the United States considered that it might be useful to develop the negotiating history which indicates that although conduct resulting in permanent impairment of physical or mental faculties is indicative of torture, it is not an essential element of the offence." *Id.* at 44. Second, the state parties to CAT rejected a proposal to include in CAT's definition of torture the use of truth drugs, where no physical harm or mental suffering was apparent. This rejection at least suggests that such drugs were not viewed as amounting to torture per se. *See id.* at 42.

C. Summary

The text of CAT confirms our conclusion that Section 2340A was intended to proscribe only the most egregious conduct. CAT not only defines torture as involving severe pain and suffering, but also it makes clear that such pain and suffering is at the extreme end of the spectrum of acts by reserving criminal penalties solely for torture. Executive interpretations confirm our view that the treaty (and hence the statute) prohibits only the worst forms of cruel, inhuman, or degrading treatment or punishment. The ratification history further substantiates this interpretation. Even the negotiating history displays a recognition that torture is a step far-removed from other cruel, inhuman or degrading treatment or punishment. In sum, CAT's text, ratification history and negotiating history all confirm that Section 2340A reaches only the most heinous acts.

III. U.S. Judicial Interpretation

There are no reported cases of prosecutions under Section 2340A. *See* Beth Stephens, *Corporate Liability: Enforcing Human Rights Through Domestic Litigation*, 24 Hastings Int'l & Comp. L. Rev. 401, 408 & n.29 (2001); Beth Van Schaack, *In Defense of Civil Redress: The Domestic Enforcement of Human Rights Norms in the Context of the Proposed Hague Judgments Convention*, 42 Harv. Int'l L. J. 141, 148-49 (2001); Curtis A. Bradley, *Universal Jurisdiction and U.S. Law*, 2001 U. Chi. Legal F. 323, 327-28. Nonetheless, we are not without guidance as to how United States courts would approach the question of what conduct constitutes torture. Civil suits filed under the Torture Victims Protection Act ("TVPA"), 28

U.S.C. § 1350 note (2000), which supplies a tort remedy for victims of torture, provide insight into what acts U.S. courts would conclude constitute torture under the criminal statute.

The TVPA contains a definition similar in some key respects to the one set forth in Section 2340. Moreover, as with Section 2340, Congress intended for the TVPA's definition of torture to follow closely the definition found in CAT. *See Xuncax v. Gramajo,* 886 F. Supp. 162, 176 n.12 (D. Mass 1995) (noting that the definition of torture in the TVPA tracks the definitions in Section 2340 and CAT).[11] The TVPA defines torture as:

> (1) . . . any act, directed against an individual in the offender's custody or physical control, by which severe pain or suffering (other than pain or suffering arising only from or inherent in, or incidental to, lawful sanctions), whether physical or mental, is intentionally inflicted on that individual for such purposes as obtaining from that individual or a third person information or a confession, punishing that individual for an act that individual or a third person has committed or is suspected of having committed, intimidating or coercing that individual or a third person, or for any reason based on discrimination of any kind; and
> (2) mental pain or suffering refers to prolonged mental harm caused by or resulting from—
> (A) the intentional infliction or threatened infliction of severe physical pain or suffering;
> (B) the administration or application, or threatened administration or application, of mind altering substances or other procedures calculated to disrupt profoundly the senses or the personality;
> (C) the threat of imminent death; or
> (D) the threat that another individual will imminently be subjected to death, severe physical pain or suffering, or the

---

[11] *See also* 137 Cong. Rec. 34,785 (statement of Rep. Mazzoli) ("Torture is defined in accordance with the definition contained in [CAT]"); *see also* Torture Victims Protection Act: Hearing and Markup on H.R. 1417 Before the Subcomm. On Human Rights and International Organizations of the House Comm. on Foreign Affairs, 100th Cong. 38 (1988) (Prepared Statement of the Association of the Bar of the City of New York, Committee on International Human Rights) ("This language essentially tracks the definition of 'torture' adopted in the Torture Convention.").

administration or application of mind altering substances or other procedures calculated to disrupt profoundly the senses or personality.

28 U.S.C. § 1350 note § 3(b). This definition differs from Section 2340's definition in two respects. First, the TVPA definition contains an illustrative list of purposes for which such pain may have been inflicted. *See id.* Second, the TVPA includes the phrase "arising only from or inherent in, or incidental to lawful sanctions"; by contrast, Section 2340 refers only to pain or suffering "incidental to lawful sanctions." *Id.* Because the purpose of our analysis here is to ascertain acts that would cross the threshold of producing "severe physical or mental pain or suffering," the list of illustrative purposes for which it is inflicted, generally would not affect this analysis.[12] Similarly, to the extent that the absence of the phrase "arising only from or inherent in" from Section 2340 might affect the question of whether pain or suffering was part of lawful sanctions and thus not torture, the circumstances with which we are concerned here are solely that of interrogations, not the imposition of punishment subsequent to judgment. These differences between the TVPA and Section 2340 are therefore not sufficiently significant to undermine the usefulness of TVPA cases here.[13]

In suits brought under the TVPA, courts have not engaged in any lengthy analysis of what acts constitute torture. In part, this is due to the nature of the acts alleged. Almost all of the cases involve physical torture, some of which is of an especially cruel and even sadistic nature. Nonetheless, courts appear to look at the entire course of conduct rather than any one act, making it somewhat akin to a totality-of-the-circumstances analysis. Because of this approach, it is difficult to take a specific act out of context and conclude that the act in isolation would constitute torture.

---

[12] This list of purposes is illustrative only. Nevertheless, demonstrating that a defendant harbored any of these purposes "may prove valuable in assisting in the establishment of intent at trial." Matthew Lippman, *The Development and Drafting of the United Nations Convention Against Torture and Other Cruel Inhuman or Degrading Treatment or Punishment*, 17 B.C. Int'l & Comp. L. Rev. 275, 314 (1994).

[13] The TVPA also requires that an individual act "intentionally." As we noted with respect to the text of CAT, see *supra* n. 7, this language might be construed as requiring general intent. It is not clear that this is so. We need not resolve that question, however, because we review the TVPA cases solely to address the acts that would satisfy the threshold of inflicting "severe physical or mental pain or suffering."

Certain acts do, however, consistently reappear in these cases or are of such a barbaric nature, that it is likely a court would find that allegations of such treatment would constitute torture: (1) severe beatings using instruments such as iron barks, truncheons, and clubs; (2) threats of imminent death, such as mock executions; (3) threats of removing extremities; (4) burning, especially burning with cigarettes; (5) electric shocks to genitalia or threats to do so; (6) rape or sexual assault, or injury to an individual's sexual organs, or threatening to do any of these sorts of acts; and (7) forcing the prisoner to watch the torture of others. Given the highly contextual nature of whether a set of acts constitutes torture, we have set forth in the attached appendix the circumstances in which courts have determined that the plaintiff has suffered torture, which include the cases from which these seven acts are drawn. While we cannot say with certainty that acts falling short of these seven would *not* constitute torture under Section 2340, we believe that interrogation techniques would have to be similar to these in their extreme nature and in the type of harm caused to violate the law.

Despite the limited analysis engaged in by courts, a recent district court opinion provides some assistance in predicting how future courts might address this issue. In *Mehinovic v. Vuckovic,* 198 F. Supp. 2d 1322, (N.D. Ga. 2002), the plaintiffs, Bosnian Muslims, sued a Bosnian Serb, Nikola Vuckovic, for, among other things, torture and cruel and inhumane treatment. The court described in vivid detail the treatment the plaintiffs endured. Specifically, the plaintiffs experienced the following:

Vuckovic repeatedly beat Kemal Mehinovic with a variety of blunt objects and boots, intentionally delivering blows to areas he knew to already be badly injured, including Mehinovic's genitals. *Id.* at 1333-34. On some occasions he was tied up and hung against windows during beatings. *Id.* Mehinovic, was subjected to the game of "Russian roulette" *See id.* Vuckovic, along with other guards, also forced Mehinovic to run in a circle while the guards swung wooden planks at him. *Id.*

Like Mehinovic, Muhamed Bicic was beaten repeatedly with blunt objects, to the point of loss of consciousness. *See Id* at 1335. He witnessed the severe beatings of other prisoners, including his own brother. "On one occasion, Vuckovic ordered Bicic to get on all fours while another soldier stood or rode on his back and beat him with a baton—a game the soldiers called 'horse.'" *Id.* Bicic, like Mehinovic, was subjected to the game of Russian roulette. Additionally, Vuckovic and the other guards forcibly extracted a number of Bicic's teeth. *Id.* at 1336.

Safet Hadzialijagic was subjected to daily beatings with "metal pipes, bats, sticks, and weapons." *Id.* at 1337. He was also subjected to

Russian roulette *See id.* at 1336-37. Hadzialijagic also frequently saw other prisoners being beaten or heard their screams as they were beaten. Like Bicic, he was subjected to the teeth extraction incident. On one occasion, Vuckovic rode Hadzialijagic like a horse, simultaneously hitting him in the head and body with a knife handle. During this time, other soldiers kicked and hit him. He fell down during this episode and was forced to get up and continue carrying Vuckovic. *See id.* "Vuckovic and the other soldiers [then] tied Hadzialijagic with a rope, hung him upside down, and beat him. When they noticed that Hadzialijagic was losing consciousness, they dunked his head in a bowl used as a toilet." *Id.* Vuckovic then forced Hadzialijagic to lick the blood off of Vuckovic's boots and kicked Hadzialijagic as he tried to do so. Vuckovic then used his knife to carve a semi-circle in Hadzialijagic's forehead. Hadzialijagic went into cardiac arrest just after this incident and was saved by one of the other plaintiffs. *See id.*

Hasan Subasic was brutally beaten and witnessed the beatings of other prisoners, including the beating and death of one of his fellow prisoners and the beating of Hadzialijagic in which he was tied upside down and beaten. *See id.* at 1338-39. *Id.* at 1338. Subasic also was subjected to the teeth pulling incident. Vuckovic personally beat Subasic two times, punching him and kicking him with his military boots. In one of these beatings, "Subasic had been forced into a kneeling position when Vuckovic kicked him in the stomach." *Id.*

The district court concluded that the plaintiffs suffered both physical and mental torture at the hands of Vuckovic.[14] With respect to physical torture, the court broadly outlined with respect to each plaintiff the acts in which Vuckovic had been at least complicit and that it found rose to the level of torture. Regarding Mehinovic, the court determined that Vuckovic's beatings of Mehinovic in which he kicked and delivered other blows

---

[14] The court also found that a number of acts perpetrated against the plaintiffs constituted cruel, inhuman, or degrading treatment but not torture. In its analysis, the court appeared to fold into cruel, inhuman, or degrading treatment two distinct categories. First, cruel, inhuman, or degrading treatment includes acts that "do not rise to the level of 'torture.'" *Id.* at 1348. Second, cruel, inhuman, or degrading treatment includes acts that "do not have the same purposes as 'torture.'" *Id.* By including this latter set of treatment as cruel, inhuman or degrading, the court appeared to take the view that acts that would otherwise constitute torture fall outside that definition because of the absence of the particular purposes listed in the TVPA and the treaty. Regardless of the relevance of this concept to the TVPA or CAT, the purposes listed in the TVPA are not an element of torture for purposes of sections 2340-2340A.

to Mehinovic's face, genitals, and others body parts, constituted torture. The court noted that these beatings left Mehinovic disfigured, may have broken ribs, almost caused Mehinovic to lose consciousness, and rendered him unable to eat for a period of time. As to Bicic, the court found that Bicic had suffered severe physical pain and suffering as a result of Vuckovic's repeated beatings of him in which Vuckovic used various instruments to inflict blows, the "horse" game, and the teeth pulling incident. *See id.* at 1346. In finding that Vuckovic inflicted severe physical pain on Hadzialijagic, the court unsurprisingly focused on the beating in which Vuckovic tied Hadzialijagic upside down and beat him. *See id.* The court pointed out that in this incident, Vuckovic almost killed Hadzialijagic. *See id.* The court further concluded that Subasic experienced severe physical pain and thus was tortured based on the beating in which Vuckovic kicked Subasic in the stomach. *See id.*

The court also found that the plaintiffs had suffered severe mental pain. In reaching this conclusion, the court relied on the plaintiffs' testimony that they feared they would be killed during beatings by Vuckovic or during the "game" of Russian roulette. Although the court did not specify the predicate acts that caused the prolonged mental harm, it is plain that both the threat of severe physical pain and the threat of imminent death were present and persistent. The court also found that the plaintiffs established the existence of prolonged mental harm as each plaintiff *"continues* to suffer long-term psychological harm as a result of [their] ordeals." *Id.* (emphasis added). In concluding that the plaintiffs had demonstrated the necessary "prolonged mental harm," the court's description of that harm as ongoing and "long-term" confirms that, to satisfy the prolonged mental harm requirement, the harm must be of a substantial duration.

The court did not, however, delve into the nature of psychological harm in reaching its conclusion. Nonetheless, the symptoms that the plaintiffs suffered and continue to suffer are worth noting as illustrative of what might in future cases be held to constitute mental harm. Mehinovic had "anxiety, flashbacks, and nightmares and has difficulty sleeping." *Id.* at 1334. Similarly, Bicic, "suffers from anxiety, sleeps very little, and has frequent nightmares" and experiences frustration at not being able to work due to the physical and mental pain he suffers. *Id.* at 1336. Hadzialijagic experienced nightmares, at times required medication to help him sleep, suffered from depression, and had become reclusive as a result of his ordeal. *See id.* at 1337-38. Subasic, like the others, had nightmares and flashbacks, but also suffered from nervousness, irritability, and experienced difficulty trusting people. The combined effect of these symptoms impaired Subasic's ability to work. *See id.* at 1340. Each of these plaintiffs suffered from mental harm that destroyed his ability to function normally, on a daily basis, and would continue to do so into the future.

In general, several guiding principles can be drawn from this case. First, this case illustrates that a single incident can constitute torture. The above recitation of the case's facts shows that Subasic was clearly subjected to torture in a number of instances, e.g., the teeth pulling incident, which the court finds to constitute torture in discussing Bicic. The court nevertheless found that the beating in which Vuckovic delivered a blow to Subasic's stomach while he was on his knees sufficed to establish that Subasic had been tortured. Indeed, the court stated that this incident "caus[ed] Subasic to suffer severe pain." *Id.* at 1346. The court's focus on this incident, despite the obvious context of a course of torturous conduct, suggests that a course of conduct is unnecessary to establish that an individual engaged in torture. It bears noting, however, that there are no decisions that have found an example of torture on facts that show the action was isolated, rather than part of a systematic course of conduct. Moreover, we believe that had this been an isolated instance, the court's conclusion that this act constituted torture would have been in error, because this single blow does not reach the requisite level of severity.

Second, the case demonstrates that courts may be willing to find that a wide range of physical pain can rise to the necessary level of "severe pain or suffering." At one end of the spectrum is what the court calls the "nightmarish beating" in which Vuckovic hung Hadzialijagic upside down and beat him, culminating in Hadzialijagic going into cardiac arrest and narrowly escaping death. *Id.* It takes little analysis or insight to conclude that this incident constitutes torture. At the other end of the spectrum, is the court's determination that a beating in which "Vuckovic hit plaintiff Subasic and kicked him in the stomach with his military boots while Subasic was forced into a kneeling position[]" constituted torture. *Id.* To be sure, this beating caused Subasic substantial pain. But that pain pales in comparison to the other acts described in this case. Again, to the extent the opinion can be read to endorse the view that this single act and the attendant pain, considered in isolation, rose to the level of "severe pain or suffering," we would disagree with such a view based on our interpretation of the criminal statute.

The district court did not attempt to delineate the meaning of torture. It engaged in no statutory analysis. Instead, the court merely recited the definition and described the acts that it concluded constituted torture. This approach is representative of the approach most often taken in TVPA cases. The adoption of such an approach suggests that torture generally is of such an extreme nature—namely, the nature of acts are so shocking and obviously incredibly painful—that courts will more likely examine the totality of the circumstances, rather than engage in a careful parsing of the statute. A broad view of this case, and of the TVPA cases more generally, shows that only acts of an extreme nature have been redressed under the TVPA's civil remedy for torture. We note, however, that *Mehinovic* presents, with the exception of the single blow to Subasic, facts that are well over the line of what constitutes torture. While there are cases that fall far short of torture, see *infra* app., there are no cases that analyze what the lowest boundary of what constitutes torture. Nonetheless, while this case and the other TVPA cases generally do not approach that boundary, they are in keeping with the general notion that the term "torture" is reserved for acts of the most extreme nature.

IV.   International Decisions

International decisions can prove of some value in assessing what conduct might rise to the level of severe mental pain or suffering. Although decisions by foreign or international bodies are in no way binding authority upon the United States, they provide guidance about how other nations will likely react to our interpretation of the CAT and Section 2340. As this Part will discuss, other Western nations have generally used a high standard in determining whether interrogation techniques violate the international prohibition on torture. In fact, these decisions have found various aggressive interrogation methods to, at worst, constitute cruel, inhuman, and degrading treatment, but not torture. These decisions only reinforce our view that there is a clear distinction between the two standards and that only extreme conduct, resulting in pain that is of an intensity often accompanying serious physical injury, will violate the latter.

A.   European Court of Human Rights

An analogue to CAT's provisions can be found in the European Convention on Human Rights and Fundamental Freedoms (the "European Convention"). This convention prohibits torture, though it offers no definition of it. It also prohibits cruel, inhuman, or degrading treatment or punishment. By barring both types of acts, the European Convention implicitly distinguishes between them and further suggests that torture is a grave act beyond cruel, inhuman, or degrading treatment or punishment. Thus, while neither the European Convention nor the European Court of Human Rights decisions interpreting that convention would be authority for the interpretation of Sections 2340-2340A, the European Convention decisions concerning torture nonetheless provide a useful barometer of the international view of what actions amount to torture.

The leading European Court of Human Rights case explicating the differences between torture and cruel, inhuman, or degrading treatment or punishment is *Ireland v. the United Kingdom* (1978).[15] In that case, the European Court of Human Rights examined interrogation techniques somewhat more sophisticated than the rather rudimentary and frequently obviously cruel acts described in the TVPA cases. Careful attention to this case is worthwhile not just because it examines methods not used in the TVPA cases, but also because the Reagan administration relied on this case in reaching the conclusion that the term torture is reserved in international usage for "extreme, deliberate, and unusually cruel practices." S. Treaty Doc. 100-20, at 4.

The methods at issue in *Ireland* were:

(1) Wall Standing. The prisoner stands spread eagle against the wall, with fingers high above his head, and feet back so that he is standing on his toes such that all of his weight falls on his fingers.

(2) Hooding. A black or navy hood is placed over the prisoner's head and kept there except during the interrogation.

(3) Subjection to Noise. Pending interrogation, the prisoner is kept in a room with a loud and continuous hissing noise.

---

[15] According to one commentator, the Inter-American Court of Human Rights has also followed this decision. *See* Julie Lantrip, *Torture and Cruel, Inhuman and Degrading Treatment in the Jurisprudence of the Inter-American Court of Human Rights*, 5 ILSA J. Int'l & Comp. L. 551, 560-61 (1999). The Inter-American Convention to Prevent and Punish Torture, however, defines torture much differently than it is defined in CAT or U.S. law. *See* Inter-American Convention to Prevent and Punish Torture, opened for signature Dec. 9, 1985, art. 2, OAS T.S. No. 67 (entered into force Feb. 28, 1987 but the United States has never signed or ratified it). It defines torture as "any act intentionally performed whereby physical or mental pain or suffering is inflicted on a person for purposes of criminal investigation, as a means of intimidation, as personal punishment, as a preventive measure, as a penalty or for any other purpose. Torture shall also be understood to be the use of methods upon a person intended to obliterate the personality of the victim or to diminish his physical or mental capacities, even if they do not cause physical pain or mental anguish." Art. 2. While the Inter-American Convention to Prevent and Punish Torture does not require signatories to criminalize cruel, inhuman, or degrading treatment or punishment, the textual differences in the definition of torture are so great that it would be difficult to draw from that jurisprudence anything more than the general trend of its agreement with the *Ireland* decision.

(4) Sleep Deprivation. Prisoners are deprived of sleep pending interrogation.

(5) Deprivation of Food and Drink. Prisoners receive a reduced diet during detention and pending interrogation.

The European Court of Human Rights concluded that these techniques used in combination, and applied for hours at a time, were inhuman and degrading but did not amount to torture. In analyzing whether these methods constituted torture, the court treated them as part of a single program. *See Ireland.* ¶ 104. The court found that this program caused "if not actual bodily injury, at least intense physical and mental suffering to the person subjected thereto and also led to acute psychiatric disturbances during the interrogation." *Id.* ¶ 167. Thus, this program "fell into the category of inhuman treatment[.]" *Id.* The court further found that "[t]he techniques were also degrading since they were such as to arouse in their victims feeling of fear, anguish and inferiority capable of humiliating and debasing them and possible [sic] breaking their physical or moral resistance." *Id.* Yet, the court ultimately concluded:

> Although the five techniques, as applied in combination, undoubtedly amounted to inhuman and degrading treatment, although their object was the extraction of confession, the naming of others and/or information and although they were used systematically, they did not occasion suffering of the particular *intensity* and *cruelty* implied by the word torture . . .

Id. (emphasis added). Thus, even though the court had concluded that the techniques produce "intense physical and mental suffering" and "acute psychiatric disturbances," they were not sufficient intensity or cruelty to amount to torture.

The court reached this conclusion based on the distinction the European Convention drew between torture and cruel, inhuman, or degrading treatment or punishment. The court reasoned that by expressly distinguishing between these two categories of treatment, the European Convention sought to "attach a special stigma to deliberate inhuman treatment causing very serious and cruel suffering." *Id.* ¶ 167. According to the court, "this distinction derives principally from a difference in the intensity of the suffering inflicted." *Id.* The court further noted that this distinction paralleled the one drawn in the U.N. Declaration on the Protection From Torture, which specifically defines torture as "'an aggravated and deliberate form of cruel, inhuman or degrading treatment or punishment.'" *Id.* (quoting U.N. Declaration on the Protection From Torture).

The court relied on this same "intensity/cruelty" distinction to conclude that some physical maltreatment fails to amount to torture. For example, four detainees were severely beaten and forced to stand spread eagle up against a wall. *See id.* ¶ 110. Other detainees were forced to stand spread eagle while an interrogator kicked them "continuously on the inside of the legs." *Id.* ¶ 111. Those detainees were beaten, some receiving injuries that were "substantial" and, others received "massive" injuries. *See id.* Another detainee was "subjected to . . . 'comparatively trivial' beatings" that resulted in a perforation of the detainee's eardrum and some "minor bruising." *Id.* ¶ 115. The court concluded that none of these situations "attain[ed] the particular level [of severity] inherent in the notion of torture." *Id.* ¶ 174.

B.   Israeli Supreme Court

The European Court of Human Rights is not the only other court to consider whether such a program of interrogation techniques was permissible. In *Public Committee Against Torture in Israel v. Israel*, 38 I.L.M. 1471 (1999), the Supreme Court of Israel reviewed a challenge brought against the General Security Service ("GSS") for its use of five techniques. At issue in *Public Committee Against Torture In Israel* were: (1) shaking, (2) the Shabach, (3) the Frog Crouch, (4) the excessive tightening of handcuffs, and (5) sleep deprivation. "Shaking" is "the forceful shaking of the suspect's upper torso, back and forth, repeatedly, in a manner which causes the neck and head to dangle and vacillate rapidly." *Id.* ¶ 9. The "Shabach" is actually a combination of methods wherein the detainee

> is seated on a small and low chair, whose seat is tilted forward, towards the ground. One hand is tied behind the suspect, and placed inside the gap between the chair's seat and back support. His second hand is tied behind the chair, against its back support. The suspect's head is covered by an opaque sack, falling down to his shoulders. Powerfully loud music is played in the room.

Id. ¶ 10.

The "frog crouch" consists of "consecutive, periodical crouches on the tips of one's toes, each lasting for five minute intervals." *Id.* ¶ 11. The excessive tightening of handcuffs simply referred to the use handcuffs that were too small for the suspects' wrists. *See id.* ¶ 12. Sleep deprivation occurred when the Shabach was used during "intense non-stop interrogations."[16] *Id.* ¶ 13.

While the Israeli Supreme Court concluded that these acts amounted to cruel, and inhuman treatment, the court did not expressly find that they amounted to torture. To be sure, such a conclusion was unnecessary because even if the acts amounted only to cruel and inhuman treatment the GSS lacked authority to use the five methods. Nonetheless, the decision is still best read as indicating that the acts at issue did not constitute torture. The court's descriptions of and conclusions about each method indicate that the court viewed them as merely cruel, inhuman or degrading but not of the sufficient severity to reach the threshold of torture. While its descriptions discuss necessity, dignity, degradation, and pain, the court carefully avoided describing any of these acts as having the severity of pain or suffering indicative of torture. *See id.* at ¶¶ 24-29. Indeed, in assessing the *Shabach* as a whole, the court even relied upon the European Court of Human Rights' *Ireland* decision for support and it did not evince disagreement with that decision's conclusion that the acts considered therein did not constitute torture. *See id.* ¶ 30.

Moreover, the Israeli Supreme Court concluded that in certain circumstances GSS officers could assert a necessity defense.[17] CAT, however, expressly provides that "[n]o exceptional circumstance whatsoever, whether a state of war or a threat of war, internal political instability or any other public emergency may be invoked as a justification of torture." Art. 2(2). Had the court been of the view that the GSS methods constituted torture, the Court could not permit this affirmative defense under CAT.

---

[16] The court did, however, distinguish between this sleep deprivation and that which occurred as part of routine interrogation, noting that some degree of interference with the suspect's regular sleep habits was to be expected. *Public Committee Against Torture in Israel* ¶ 23.

[17] In permitting a necessity defense, the court drew upon the ticking time bomb hypothetical proffered by the GSS as a basis for asserting a necessity defense. In that hypothetical, the GSS has arrested a suspect, who holds information about the location of a bomb and the time at which it is set to explode. The suspect is the only source of this information, and without that information the bomb will surely explode, killing many people. Under those circumstances, the court agreed that the necessity defense's requirement of imminence, which the court construed as the "imminent nature of the act rather than that of danger," would be satisfied. *Id.* ¶ 34. It further agreed "that in appropriate circumstances" this defense would be available to GSS investigators. *Id.* ¶ 35.

Accordingly, the court's decision is best read as concluding that these methods amounted to cruel and inhuman treatment, but not torture.

In sum, both the European Court on Human Rights and the Israeli Supreme Court have recognized a wide array of acts that constitute cruel, inhuman, or degrading treatment or punishment, but do not amount to torture. Thus, they appear to permit, under international law, an aggressive interpretation as to what amounts to torture, leaving that label to be applied only where extreme circumstances exist.

V.   The President's Commander-in-Chief Power

Even if an interrogation method arguably were to violate Section 2340A, the statute would be unconstitutional if it impermissibly encroached on the President's constitutional power to conduct a military campaign. As Commander-in-Chief, the President has the constitutional authority to order interrogations of enemy combatants to gain intelligence information concerning the military plans of the enemy. The demands of the Commander-in-Chief power are especially pronounced in the middle of a war in which the nation has already suffered a direct attack. In such a case, the information gained from interrogations may prevent future attacks by foreign enemies. Any effort to apply Section 2340A in a manner that interferes with the President's direction of such core war matters as the detention and interrogation of enemy combatants thus would be unconstitutional.

A.   The War with Al Qaeda

At the outset, we should make clear the nature of the threat presently posed to the nation. While your request for legal advice is not specifically limited to the current circumstances, we think it is useful to discuss this question in the context of the current war against the al Qaeda terrorist network. The situation in which these issues arise is unprecedented in recent American history. Four coordinated terrorist attacks, using hijacked commercial airliners as guided missiles, took place in rapid succession on the morning of September 11, 2001. These attacks were aimed at critical government buildings in the Nation's capital and landmark buildings in its financial center. These events reach a different scale of destructiveness than earlier terrorist episodes, such as the destruction of the Murrah Building in Oklahoma City in 1994. They caused thousands of deaths. Air traffic and communications within the United States were disrupted; national stock exchanges were shut for several days; and damage from the attack has been estimated to run into the tens of billions of dollars. More-over, these attacks are part of a violent campaign against the United States that is believed to include an unsuccessful attempt to destroy an airliner in December 2001; a suicide bombing attack in Yemen on the *U.S.S. Cole* in 2000; the bombings of the United States Embassies in Kenya and in Tanzania in 1998; a truck bomb attack on a U.S. military housing complex in Saudi Arabia in 1996; an unsuccessful attempt to destroy the World Trade Center in 1993; and the ambush of U.S. servicemen in Somalia in 1993. The United States and its overseas personnel and installations have been attacked as a result of Usama Bin Laden's call for a "jihad against the U.S. government, because the U.S. government is unjust, criminal and tyrannical."[18]

In response, the Government has engaged in a broad effort at home and abroad to counter terrorism. Pursuant to his authorities as Com-mander-in-Chief, the President in October, 2001, ordered the Armed Forces to attack al Qaeda personnel and assets in Afghanistan, and the Taliban militia that harbored them. That military campaign appears to be nearing its close with the retreat of al Qaeda and Taliban forces from their strongholds and the installation of a friendly provisional government in Afghanistan. Congress has provided its support for the use of forces against those linked to the September 11 attacks, and has recognized the President's constitutional power to use force to prevent and deter future attacks both within and outside the United States. S. J. Res. 23, Pub. L. No. 107-40, 115 Stat. 224 (2001). We have reviewed the President's constitu-tional power to use force abroad in response to the September 11 attacks in a separate memorandum. *See* Memorandum for Timothy E. Flanigan, Deputy Counsel to the President, from John C. Yoo, Deputy Assistant Attorney General, Office of Legal Counsel, *Re: The President's Consti-tutional Authority to Conduct Military Operations Against Terrorists and Nations Supporting Them* (Sept. 25, 2001) ("September 11 War Powers Memorandum"). We have also discussed the President's constitutional au-thority to deploy the armed forces domestically to protect against foreign terrorist attack in a separate memorandum. *See* Memorandum for Alberto R. Gonzales, Counsel to the President and William J. Haynes, II, General Counsel, Department of Defense, from John C. Yoo, Deputy Assistant Attorney General and Robert J. Delahunty, Special Counsel, Office of Le-

---

[18] *See Osama Bin Laden v. The U.S.: Edicts and Statements*, CNN Interview with Osama bin Laden, March 1997, *available at* http://www.pbs.org/wgbh/pages/frontline/shows/binladen/who/edicts.html.

gal Counsel, *Re: Authority for Use of Military Force to Combat Terrorist Activities Within the United States* at 2-3 (Oct. 17, 2001). The Justice Department and the FBI have launched a sweeping investigation in response to the September 11 attacks, and last fall Congress enacted legislation to expand the Justice Department's powers of surveillance against terrorists. *See* The USA Patriot Act, Pub. L. No. 107-56, 115 Stat. 272 (Oct. 26, 2001). This spring, the President proposed the creation of a new cabinet department for homeland security to implement a coordinated domestic program against terrorism.

Despite these efforts, numerous upper echelon leaders of al Qaeda and the Taliban, with access to active terrorist cells and other resources, remain at large. It has been reported that the al Qaeda fighters are already drawing on a fresh flow of cash to rebuild their forces. *See* Paul Haven, *U.S.: al-Qaida Trying to Regroup*, Associated Press, Mar. 20, 2002. As the Director of the Central Intelligence Agency has recently testified before Congress, "Al-Qa'ida and other terrorist groups will continue to plan to attack this country and its interests abroad. Their modus operandi is to have multiple attack plans in the works simultaneously, and to have al-Qa'ida cells in place to conduct them." Testimony of George J. Tenet, Director of Central Intelligence, Before the Senate Armed Services Committee at 2 (Mar. 19, 2002). Nor is the threat contained to Afghanistan. "Operations against US targets could be launched by al-Qa'ida cells already in place in major cities in Europe and the Middle East. Al-Qa'ida can also exploit its presence or connections to other groups in such countries as Somalia, Yemen, Indonesia, and the Philippines." *Id.* at 3. It appears that al Qaeda continues to enjoy information and resources that allow it to organize and direct active hostile forces against this country, both domestically and abroad.

Al Qaeda continues to plan further attacks, such as destroying American civilian airliners and killing American troops, which have fortunately been prevented. It is clear that bin Laden and his organization have conducted several violent attacks on the United States and its nationals, and that they seek to continue to do so. Thus, the capture and interrogation of such individuals is clearly imperative to our national security and defense. Interrogation of captured al Qaeda operatives may provide information concerning the nature of al Qaeda plans and the identities of its personnel, which may prove invaluable in preventing further direct attacks on the United States and its citizens. Given the massive destruction and loss of life caused by the September 11 attacks, it is reasonable to believe that information gained from al Qaeda personnel could prevent attacks of a similar (if not greater) magnitude from occurring in the United

States. The case of Jose Padilla, a.k.a. Abdullah Al Mujahir, illustrates the importance of such information. Padilla allegedly had journeyed to Afghanistan and Pakistan, met with senior al Qaeda leaders, and hatched a plot to construct and detonate a radioactive dispersal device in the United States. After allegedly receiving training in wiring explosives and with a substantial amount of currency in his position, Padilla attempted in May, 2002, to enter the United States to further his scheme. Interrogation of captured al Qaeda operatives allegedly allowed U.S. intelligence and law enforcement agencies to track Padilla and to detain him upon his entry into the United States.

B.   Interpretation to Avoid Constitutional Problems

As the Supreme Court has recognized, and as we will explain further below, the President enjoys complete discretion in the exercise of his Commander-in-Chief authority and in conducting operations against hostile forces. Because both "[t]he executive power and the command of the military and naval forces is vested in the President," the Supreme Court has unanimously stated that it is *the President alone* [] who is constitutionally invested with the *entire charge of hostile operations*." *Hamilton v. Dillin*, 88 U.S. (21 Wall.) 73, 87 (1874) (emphasis added). That authority is at its height in the middle of a war.

In light of the President's complete authority over the conduct of war, without a clear statement otherwise, we will not read a criminal statute as infringing on the President's ultimate authority in these areas. We have long recognized, and the Supreme Court has established a canon of statutory construction that statutes are to be construed in a manner that avoids constitutional difficulties so long as a reasonable alternative construction is available. *See, e.g., Edward J. DeBartolo Corp. v. Florida Gulf Coast Bldg. & Constr. Trades Council*, 485 U.S. 568, 575 (1988) (citing *NLRB v. Catholic Bishop of Chicago*, 440 U.S. 490, 499-501, 504 (1979)) ("[W]here an otherwise acceptable construction of a statute would raise serious constitutional problems, [courts] will construe [a] statute to avoid such problems unless such construction is plainly contrary to the intent of Congress."). This canon of construction applies especially where an act of Congress could be read to encroach upon powers constitutionally committed to a coordinate branch of government. *See, e.g., Franklin v. Massachusetts*, 505 U.S. 788, 800-1 (1992) (citation omitted) ("Out of respect for the separation of powers and the unique constitutional position of the President, we find that textual silence is not enough to subject the President to the provisions of the [Administrative Procedure Act]. We would require an express statement by Congress before assuming it intended the President's performance of his statutory duties to be reviewed for abuse of discretion."); *Public Citizen v. United States Dep't of Justice*, 491 U.S. 440, 465-67 (1989) (construing Federal Advisory Committee Act not to apply to advice given by American Bar Association to the President on judicial nominations, to avoid potential constitutional question regarding encroachment on Presidential power to appoint judges).

In the area of foreign affairs, and war powers in particular, the avoidance canon has special force. *See, e.g., Dep't of Navy v. Egan*, 484 U.S. 518, 530 (1988) ("unless Congress specifically has provided otherwise, courts traditionally have been reluctant to intrude upon the authority of the Executive in military and national security affairs."); *Japan Whaling Ass'n v. American Cetacean Soc'y*, 478 U.S. 221, 232-33 (1986) (construing federal statutes to avoid curtailment of traditional presidential prerogatives in foreign affairs). We do not lightly assume that Congress has acted to interfere with the President's constitutionally superior position as Chief Executive and Commander in Chief in the area of military operations. *See Egan*, 484 U.S. at 529 (quoting *Haig v. Agee*, 453 U.S. 280, 293-94 (1981)). *See also Agee*, 453 U.S. at 291 (deference to Executive Branch is "especially" appropriate "in the area . . . of . . . national security").

In order to respect the President's inherent constitutional authority to manage a military campaign against al Qaeda and its allies, Section 2340A must be construed as not applying to interrogations undertaken pursuant to his Commander-in-Chief authority. As our Office has consistently held during this Administration and previous Administrations, Congress lacks authority under Article I to set the terms and conditions under which the President may exercise his authority as Commander in Chief to control the conduct of operations during a war. *See, e.g.,* Memorandum for Daniel J. Bryant, Assistant Attorney General, Office of Legislative Affairs, from Patrick F. Philbin, Deputy Assistant Attorney General, Office of Legal Counsel, *Re: Swift Justice Authorization Act* (Apr. 8, 2002); Memorandum for Timothy E. Flanigan, Deputy Counsel to the President, from John C. Yoo, Deputy Assistant Attorney General, Office of Legal Counsel, *Re: The President's Constitutional Authority to Conduct Military Operations Against Terrorists and Nations Supporting Them* (Sep. 25, 2001) ("Flanigan Memorandum"); Memorandum for Andrew Fois, Assistant Attorney General, Office of Legislative Affairs, from Richard L. Shiffrin, Deputy Assistant Attorney General, Office of Legal Counsel, *Re: Defense Authorization Act* (Sep. 15, 1995). As we discuss below, the President's power to detain and interrogate enemy combatants arises out of his constitutional authority as Commander in Chief. A construction of

Section 2340A that applied the provision to regulate the President's authority as Commander-in-Chief to determine the interrogation and treatment of enemy combatants would raise serious constitutional questions. Congress may no more regulate the President's ability to detain and interrogate enemy combatants than it may regulate his ability to direct troop movements on the battlefield. Accordingly, we would construe Section 2340A to avoid this constitutional difficulty, and conclude that it does not apply to the President's detention and interrogation of enemy combatants pursuant to his Commander-in-Chief authority.

This approach is consistent with previous decisions of our Office involving the application of federal criminal law. For example, we have previously construed the congressional contempt statute not to apply to executive branch officials who refuse to comply with congressional subpoenas because of an assertion of executive privilege. In a published 1984 opinion, we concluded that

> if executive officials were subject to prosecution for criminal contempt whenever they carried out the President's claim of executive privilege, it would significantly burden and immeasurably impair the President's ability to fulfill his constitutional duties. Therefore, the separation of powers principles that underlie the doctrine of executive privilege also would preclude an application of the contempt of Congress statute to punish officials for aiding the President in asserting his constitutional privilege.

Prosecution for Contempt of Congress of an Executive Branch Official Who Has Asserted A Claim of Executive Privilege, 8 Op. O.L.C. 101, 134 (May 30, 1984). Likewise, we believe that, if executive officials were subject to prosecution for conducting interrogations when they were carrying out the President's Commander-in-Chief powers, "it would significantly burden and immeasurably impair the President's ability to fulfill his constitutional duties." These constitutional principles preclude an application of Section 2340A to punish officials for aiding the President in exercising his exclusive constitutional authorities. *Id.*

C.   The Commander-in-Chief Power

It could be argued that Congress enacted 18 U.S.C. § 2340A with full knowledge and consideration of the President's Commander-in-Chief power, and that Congress intended to restrict his discretion in the interrogation of enemy combatants. Even were we to accept this argument, however, we conclude that the Department of Justice could not enforce Section 2340A against federal officials acting pursuant to the President's constitutional authority to wage a military campaign.

Indeed, in a different context, we have concluded that both courts and prosecutors should reject prosecutions that apply federal criminal laws to activity that is authorized pursuant to one of the President's constitutional powers. This Office, for example, has previously concluded that Congress could not constitutionally extend the congressional contempt statute to executive branch officials who refuse to comply with congressional subpoenas because of an assertion of executive privilege. We opined that "courts . . . would surely conclude that a criminal prosecution for the exercise of a presumptively valid, constitutionally based privilege is not consistent with the Constitution." 8 Op. O.L.C. at 141. Further, we concluded that the Department of Justice could not bring a criminal prosecution against a defendant who had acted pursuant to an exercise of the President's constitutional power. "The President, through a United States Attorney, need not, indeed may not, prosecute criminally a subordinate for asserting on his behalf a claim of executive privilege. Nor could the Legislative Branch or the courts require or implement the prosecution of such an individual." *Id.* Although Congress may define federal crimes that the President, through the Take Care Clause, should prosecute, Congress cannot compel the President to prosecute outcomes taken pursuant to the President's own constitutional authority. If Congress could do so, it could control the President's authority through the manipulation of federal criminal law.

We have even greater concerns with respect to prosecutions arising out of the exercise of the President's express authority as Commander in Chief than we do with prosecutions arising out of the assertion of executive privilege. In a series of opinions examining various legal questions arising after September 11, we have explained the scope of the President's Commander-in-Chief power.[19] We briefly summarize the findings of those opinions here. The President's constitutional power to protect the security of the United States and the lives and safety of its people must be understood in light of the Founders' intention to create a federal govern-

---

[19] *See, e.g.*, September 11 War Powers Memorandum; Memorandum for Alberto R. Gonzales, Counsel to the President, from Patrick F. Philbin, Deputy Assistant Attorney General, Office of Legal Counsel, *Re: Legality of the Use of Military Commissions to Try Terrorists* (Nov. 6, 2001).

ment "cloathed with all the powers requisite to the complete execution of its trust." *The Federalist* No. 23, at 147 (Alexander Hamilton) (Jacob E. Cooke ed. 1961). Foremost among the objectives committed to that trust by the Constitution is the security of the nation. As Hamilton explained in arguing for the Constitution's adoption, because "the circumstances which may affect the public safety" are not "reducible within certain determinate limits,"

> it must be admitted, as a necessary consequence, that there can be no limitation of that authority, which is to provide for the defence and protection of the community, in any matter essential to its efficacy.

Id. at 147-48. Within the limits that the Constitution itself imposes, the scope and distribution of the powers to protect national security must be construed to authorize the most efficacious defense of the nation and its interests in accordance "with the realistic purposes of the entire instrument." *Lichter v. United States*, 334 U.S. 742, 782 (1948).

The text, structure and history of the Constitution establish that the Founders entrusted the President with the primary responsibility, and therefore the power, to ensure the security of the United States in situations of grave and unforeseen emergencies. The decision to deploy military force in the defense of United States interests is expressly placed under Presidential authority by the Vesting Clause, U.S. Const. Art. I, § 1, cl. 1, and by the Commander-in-Chief Clause, *id.*, § 2, cl. 1.[20] This Office

---

[20] *See Johnson v. Eisentrager*, 339 U.S. 763, 789 (1950) (President has authority to deploy United States armed forces "abroad or to any particular region"); *Fleming v. Page*, 50 U.S. (9 How.) 603, 614-15 (1850) ("As commander-in-chief, [the President] is authorized to direct the movements of the naval and military forces placed by law at his command, and to employ them in the manner he may deem most effectual") *Loving v. United States*, 517 U.S. 748, 776 (1996) (Scalia, J., concurring in part and concurring in judgment) (The "inherent powers" of the Commander in Chief "are clearly extensive."); *Maul v. United States*, 274 U.S. 501, 515-16 (1927) (Brandeis & Holmes, JJ., concurring) (President "may direct any revenue cutter to cruise in any waters in order to perform any duty of the service"); *Commonwealth of Massachusetts v. Laird*, 451 F.2d 26, 32 (1st Cir. 1971) (the President has "power as Commander-in-Chief to station forces abroad"); *Ex parte Vallandigham*, 28 F. Cas. 874, 922 (C.C.S.D. Ohio 1863) (No. 16,816) (in acting "under this power where there is no express legislative declaration, the president is guided solely by his own judgment and discretion"); *Authority to Use United States Military Forces in Somalia*, 16 Op. O.L.C. 6, 6 (Dec. 4, 1992) (Barr, Attorney General).

has long understood the Commander-in-Chief Clause in particular as an affirmative grant of authority to the President. *See, e.g.*, Memorandum for Charles W. Colson, Special Counsel to the President, from William H. Rehnquist, Assistant Attorney General, Office of Legal Counsel, *Re: The President and the War Power: South Vietnam and the Cambodian Sanctuaries* (May 22, 1970) ("Rehnquist Memorandum"). The Framers understood the Clause as investing the President with the fullest range of power understood at the time of the ratification of the Constitution as belonging to the military commander. In addition, the structure of the Constitution demonstrates that any power traditionally understood as pertaining to the executive—which includes the conduct of warfare and the defense of the nation—unless expressly assigned in the Constitution to Congress, is vested in the President. Article II, Section 1 makes this clear by stating that the "executive Power shall be vested in a President of the United States of America." That sweeping grant vests in the President an unenumerated "executive power" and contrasts with the specific enumeration of the powers—those "herein"—granted to Congress in Article I. The implications of constitutional text and structure are confirmed by the practical consideration that national security decisions require the unity in purpose and energy in action that characterize the Presidency rather than Congress.[21]

---

[21] Judicial decisions since the beginning of the Republic confirm the President's constitutional power and duty to repel military action against the United States and to take measures to prevent the recurrence of an attack. As Justice Joseph Story said long ago, "[i]t may be fit and proper for the government, in the exercise of the high discretion confided to the executive, for great public purposes, to act on a sudden emergency, or to prevent an irreparable mischief, by summary measures, which are not found in the text of the laws." *The Apollon*, 22 U.S. (9 Wheat.) 362, 366–67 (1824). If the President is confronted with an unforeseen attack on the territory and people of the United States, or other immediate, dangerous threat to American interests and security, it is his constitutional responsibility to respond to that threat with whatever means are necessary. *See, e.g., The Prize Cases*, 67 U.S. (2 Black) 635, 668 (1862) ("If a war be made by invasion of a foreign nation, the President is not only authorized but bound to resist force by force . . . without waiting for any special legislative authority."); *United States v. Smith*, 27 F. Cas. 1192, 1229-30 (C.C.D.N.Y. 1806) (No. 16,342) (Paterson, Circuit Justice) (regardless of statutory authorization, it is "the duty . . . of the executive magistrate . . . to repel an invading foe"); *see also* 3 Story, *Commentaries* § 1485 ("[t]he command and application of the public force . . . to maintain peace, and to resist foreign invasion" are executive powers).

As the Supreme Court has recognized, the Commander-in-Chief power and the President's obligation to protect the nation imply the ancillary powers necessary to their successful exercise. "The first of the enumerated powers of the President is that he shall be Commander-in-Chief of the Army and Navy of the United States. And, of course, the grant of war power includes all that is necessary and proper for carrying those powers into execution." *Johnson v. Eisentrager*, 339 U.S. 763, 788 (1950). In wartime, it is for the President alone to decide what methods to use to best prevail against the enemy. *See, e.g.*, Rehnquist Memorandum; Flanigan Memorandum at 3. The President's complete discretion in exercising the Commander-in-Chief power has been recognized by the courts. In the *Prize Cases*, 67 U.S. (2 Black) 635, 670 (1862), for example, the Court explained that whether the President "in fulfilling his duties as Commander in Chief" had appropriately responded to the rebellion of the southern states was a question "to be *decided by him*" and which the Court could not question, but must leave to "the political department of the Government to which this power was entrusted."

One of the core functions of the Commander in Chief is that of capturing, detaining, and interrogating members of the enemy. *See, e.g.*, Memorandum for William J. Haynes, II, General Counsel, Department of Defense, from Jay S. Bybee, Assistant Attorney General, Office of Legal Counsel, *Re: The President's Power as Commander in Chief to Transfer Captured Terrorists to the Control and Custody of Foreign Nations* at 3 (March 13, 2002) ("the Commander-in-Chief Clause constitutes an independent grant of substantive authority to engage in the detention and transfer of prisoners captured in armed conflicts"). It is well settled that the President may seize and detain enemy combatants, at least for the duration of the conflict, and the laws of war make clear that prisoners may be interrogated for information concerning the enemy, its strength, and its plans.[22]

---

[22] The practice of capturing and detaining enemy combatants is as old as war itself. *See* Allan Rosas, The Legal Status of Prisoners of War 44-45 (1976). In modern conflicts, the practice of detaining enemy combatants and hostile civilians generally has been designed to balance the humanitarian purpose of sparing lives with the military necessity of defeating the enemy on the battlefield. *Id.* at 59-80. While Article 17 of the Geneva Convention Relative to the Treatment of Prisoners of War, Aug. 12, 1949, 6 U.S.T. 3517, places restrictions on interrogation of enemy combatants, members of al Qaeda and the Taliban militia are not legally entitled to the status of prisoners of war as defined in the Convention. *See* Memorandum for Alberto R. Gonzales, Counsel to the President and William J. Haynes, II, General Counsel, Department of Defense, from Jay S. Bybee, Assis-

Numerous Presidents have ordered the capture, detention, and questioning of enemy combatants during virtually every major conflict in the Nation's history, including recent conflicts such as the Gulf, Vietnam, and Korean wars. Recognizing this authority, Congress has never attempted to restrict or interfere with the President's authority on this score. *Id.*

Any effort by Congress to regulate the interrogation of battlefield combatants would violate the Constitution's sole vesting of the Commander-in-Chief authority in the President. There can be little doubt that intelligence operations, such as the detention and interrogation of enemy combatants and leaders, are both necessary and proper for the effective conduct of a military campaign. Indeed, such operations may be of more importance in a war with an international terrorist organization than one with the conventional armed forces of a nation-state, due to the former's emphasis on secret operations and surprise attacks against civilians. It may be the case that only successful interrogations can provide the information necessary to prevent the success of covert terrorist attacks upon the United States and its citizens. Congress can no more interfere with the President's conduct of the interrogation of enemy combatants than it can dictate strategic or tactical decisions on the battlefield. Just as statutes that order the President to conduct warfare in a certain manner or for specific goals would be unconstitutional, so too are laws that seek to prevent the President from gaining the intelligence he believes necessary to prevent attacks upon the United States.

VI.   Defenses

In the foregoing parts of this memorandum, we have demonstrated that the ban on torture in Section 2340A is limited to only the most extreme forms of physical and mental harm. We have also demonstrated that Section 2340A, as applied to interrogations of enemy combatants ordered by the President pursuant to his Commander-in-Chief power would be unconstitutional. Even if an interrogation method, however, might arguably cross the line drawn in Section 2340, and application of the statute was not held to be an unconstitutional infringement of the President's Commander-in-Chief authority, we believe that under the current circumstances certain justification defenses might be available that would po-

---

tant Attorney General, Office of Legal Counsel, *Re: Application of Treaties and Laws to al Qaeda and Taliban Detainees* (Jan. 22, 2002).

tentially eliminate criminal liability. Standard criminal law defenses of necessity and self-defense could justify interrogation methods needed to elicit information to prevent a direct and imminent threat to the United States and its citizens.

A. Necessity

We believe that a defense of necessity could be raised, under the current circumstances, to an allegation of a Section 2340A violation. Often referred to as the "choice of evils" defense, necessity has been defined as follows:

> Conduct that the actor believes to be necessary to avoid a harm or evil to himself or to another is justifiable, provided that:
> (a) the harm or evil sought to be avoided by such conduct is greater than that sought to be prevented by the law defining the offense charged; and
> (b) neither the Code nor other law defining the offense provides exceptions or defenses dealing with the specific situation involved; and
> (c) a legislative purpose to exclude the justification claimed does not otherwise plainly appear.

Model Penal Code § 3.02. *See also* Wayne R. LaFave & Austin W. Scott, 1 Substantive Criminal Law § 5.4 at 627 (1986 & 2002 supp.) ("LaFave & Scott"). Although there is no federal statute that generally establishes necessity or other justifications as defenses to federal criminal laws, the Supreme Court has recognized the defense. *See United States v. Bailey*, 444 U.S. 394, 410 (1980) (relying on LaFave & Scott and Model Penal Code definitions of necessity defense).

The necessity defense may prove especially relevant in the current circumstances. As it has been described in the case law and literature, the purpose behind necessity is one of public policy. According to LaFave and Scott, "the law ought to promote the achievement of higher values at the expense of lesser values, and sometimes the greater good for society will be accomplished by violating the literal language of the criminal law." LaFave & Scott, at 629. In particular, the necessity defense can justify the intentional killing of one person to save two others because "it is better that two lives be saved and one lost than that two be lost and one saved." *Id.* Or, put in the language of a choice of evils, "the evil involved in violating the terms of the criminal law (. . . even taking another's life) may be less than that which would result from literal compliance with the law (. . . two lives lost)." *Id.*

Additional elements of the necessity defense are worth noting here. First, the defense is not limited to certain types of harms. Therefore, the harm inflicted by necessity may include intentional homicide, so long as the harm avoided is greater (i.e., preventing more deaths). *Id.* at 634. Second, it must actually be the defendant's intention to avoid the greater harm; intending to commit murder and then learning only later that the death had the fortuitous result of saving other lives will not support a necessity defense. *Id.* at 635. Third, if the defendant reasonably believed that the lesser harm was necessary, even if, unknown to him, it was not, he may still avail himself of the defense. As LaFave and Scott explain, "if A kills B reasonably believing it to be necessary to save C and D, he is not guilty of murder even though, unknown to A, C and D could have been rescued without the necessity of killing B." *Id.* Fourth, it is for the court, and not the defendant to judge whether the harm avoided outweighed the harm done. *Id.* at 636. Fifth, the defendant cannot rely upon the necessity defense if a third alternative is open and known to him that will cause less harm.

It appears to us that under the current circumstances the necessity defense could be successfully maintained in response to an allegation of a Section 2340A violation. On September 11, 2001, al Qaeda launched a surprise covert attack on civilian targets in the United States that led to the deaths of thousands and losses in the billions of dollars. According to public and governmental reports, al Qaeda has other sleeper cells within the United States that may be planning similar attacks. Indeed, al Qaeda plans apparently include efforts to develop and deploy chemical, biological and nuclear weapons of mass destruction. Under these circumstances, a detainee may possess information that could enable the United States to prevent attacks that potentially could equal or surpass the September 11 attacks in their magnitude. Clearly, any harm that might occur during an interrogation would pale to insignificance compared to the harm avoided by preventing such an attack, which could take hundreds or thousands of lives.

Under this calculus, two factors will help indicate when the necessity defense could appropriately be invoked. First, the more certain that government officials are that a particular individual has information needed to prevent an attack, the more necessary interrogation will be. Second, the more likely it appears to be that a terrorist attack is likely to occur, and the greater the amount of damage expected from such an attack, the more that an interrogation to get information would become necessary. Of course, the strength of the necessity defense depends on the circumstances that prevail, and the knowledge of the government actors involved, when the interrogation is conducted. While every interrogation that might violate Section 2340A does not trigger a necessity defense, we can say that certain circumstances could support such a defense.

Legal authorities identify an important exception to the necessity defense. The defense is available "only in situations wherein the legislature has not itself, in its criminal statute, made a determination of values." *Id.* at 629. Thus, if Congress explicitly has made clear that violation of a statute cannot be outweighed by the harm avoided, courts cannot recognize the necessity defense. LaFave and Israel provide as an example an abortion statute that made clear that abortions even to save the life of the mother would still be a crime; in such cases the necessity defense would be unavailable. *Id.* at 630. Here, however, Congress has not explicitly made a determination of values vis-à-vis torture. In fact, Congress explicitly removed efforts to remove torture from the weighing of values permitted by the necessity defense.[23]

B.   Self-Defense

Even if a court were to find that a violation of Section 2340A was not justified by necessity, a defendant could still appropriately raise a claim of self-defense. The right to self-defense, even when it involves deadly force,

---

[23] In the CAT, torture is defined as the intentional infliction of severe pain or suffering "for such purpose[] as obtaining from him or a third person information or a confession." CAT art. 1.1. One could argue that such a definition represented an attempt to indicate that the good of obtaining information—no matter what the circumstances—could not justify an act of torture. In other words, necessity would not be a defense. In enacting Section 2340, however, Congress removed the purpose element in the definition of torture, evidencing an intention to remove any fixing of values by statute. By leaving Section 2340 silent as to the harm done by torture in comparison to other harms, Congress allowed the necessity defense to apply when appropriate.

Further, the CAT contains an additional provision that "no exceptional circumstances whatsoever, whether a state of war or a threat of war, internal political instability or any other public emergency, may be invoked as a justification of torture." CAT art. 2.2. Aware of this provision of the treaty, and of the definition of the necessity defense that allows the legislature to provide for an exception to the defense, see Model Penal Code § 3.02(b), Congress did not incorporate CAT article 2.2 into Section 2340. Given that Congress omitted CAT's effort to bar a necessity or wartime defense, we read Section 2340 as permitting the defense.

is deeply embedded in our law, both as to individuals and as to the nation as a whole. As the Court of Appeals for the D.C. Circuit has explained:

> More than two centuries ago, Blackstone, best known of the expositors of the English common law, taught that "all homicide is malicious, and of course amounts to murder, unless . . . excused on the account of accident or self-preservation. . . . " Self-defense, as a doctrine legally exonerating the taking of human life, is as viable now as it was in Blackstone's time.

United States v. Peterson, 483 F.2d 1222, 1228-29 (D.C. Cir. 1973). Self-defense is a common-law defense to federal criminal law offenses, and nothing in the text, structure or history of Section 2340A precludes its application to a charge of torture. In the absence of any textual provision to the contrary, we assume self-defense can be an appropriate defense to an allegation of torture.

The doctrine of self-defense permits the use of force to prevent harm to another person. As LaFave and Scott explain, "one is justified in using reasonable force in defense of another person, even a stranger, when he reasonably believes that the other is in immediate danger of unlawful bodily harm from his adversary and that the use of such force is necessary to avoid this danger." *Id.* at 663-64. Ultimately, even deadly force is permissible, but "only when the attack of the adversary upon the other person reasonably appears to the defender to be a deadly attack." *Id.* at 664. As with our discussion of necessity, we will review the significant elements of this defense.[24] According to LaFave and Scott, the elements of the defense of others are the same as those that apply to individual self-defense.

First, self-defense requires that the use of force be *necessary* to avoid the danger of unlawful bodily harm. *Id.* at 649. A defender may justifiably use deadly force if he reasonably believes that the other person is about to inflict unlawful death or serious bodily harm upon another, and that it is necessary to use such force to prevent it. *Id.* at 652. Looked at from the opposite perspective, the defender may not use force when the force would be as equally effective at a later time and the defender suffers no harm or risk by waiting. *See* Paul H. Robinson, 2 Criminal Law De-

---

[24] Early cases had suggested that in order to be eligible for defense of another, one should have some personal relationship with the one in need of protection. That view has been discarded. LaFave & Scott at 664.

fenses § 131(c) at 77 (1984). If, however, other options permit the defender to retreat safely from a confrontation without having to resort to deadly force, the use of force may not be necessary in the first place. LaFave and Scott at 659-60.

Second, self-defense requires that the defendant's belief in the necessity of using force be reasonable. If a defendant honestly but unreasonably believed force was necessary, he will not be able to make out a successful claim of self-defense. *Id.* at 654. Conversely, if a defendant reasonably believed an attack was to occur, but the facts subsequently showed no attack was threatened, he may still raise self-defense. As LaFave and Scott explain, "one may be justified in shooting to death an adversary who, having threatened to kill him, reaches for his pocket as if for a gun, though it later appears that he had no gun and that he was only reaching for his handkerchief." *Id.* Some authorities, such as the Model Penal Code, even eliminate the reasonability element, and require only that the defender honestly believed—regardless of its unreasonableness—that the use of force was necessary.

Third, many legal authorities include the requirement that a defender must reasonably believe that the unlawful violence is "imminent" before he can use force in his defense. It would be a mistake, however, to equate imminence necessarily with timing—that an attack is immediately about to occur. Rather, as the Model Penal Code explains, what is essential is that, the defensive *response* must be "immediately necessary." Model Penal Code § 3.04(1). Indeed, imminence may be merely another way of expressing the requirement of necessity. Robinson at 78. LaFave and Scott, for example, believe that the imminence requirement makes sense as part of a necessity defense because if an attack is not immediately upon the defender, the defender has other options available to avoid the attack that do not involve the use of force. LaFave and Scott at 656. If, however, the fact of the attack becomes certain and no other options remain, the use of force may be justified. To use a well-known hypothetical, if A were to kidnap and confine B, and then tell B he would kill B one week later, B would be justified in using force in self-defense, even if the opportunity arose before the week had passed. *Id.* at 656; *see also* Robinson at § 131(c) (1) at 78. In this hypothetical, while the attack itself is not imminent, B's use of force becomes immediately necessary whenever he has an opportunity to save himself from A.

Fourth, the amount of force should be proportional to the threat. As LaFave and Scott explain, "the amount of force which [the defender] may justifiably use must be reasonably related to the threatened harm which he seeks to avoid." LaFave and Scott at 651. Thus, one may not use deadly force in response to a threat that does not rise to death or serious bodily harm. If such harm may result, however, deadly force is appropriate. As the Model Penal Code § 3.04(2)(b) states, "[t]he use of deadly force is not justifiable . . . unless the actor believes that such force is necessary to protect himself against death, serious bodily injury, kidnapping or sexual intercourse compelled by force or threat."

Under the current circumstances, we believe that a defendant accused of violating Section 2340A could have, in certain circumstances, grounds to properly claim the defense of another. The threat of an impending terrorist attack threatens the lives of hundreds if not thousands of American citizens. Whether such a defense will be upheld depends on the specific context within which the interrogation decision is made. If an attack appears increasingly likely, but our intelligence services and armed forces cannot prevent it without the information from the interrogation of a specific individual, then the more likely it will appear that the conduct in question will be seen as necessary. If intelligence and other information support the conclusion that an attack is increasingly certain, then the necessity for the interrogation will be reasonable. The increasing certainty of an attack will also satisfy the imminence requirement. Finally, the fact that previous al Qaeda attacks have had as their aim the deaths of American citizens, and that evidence of other plots have had a similar goal in mind, would justify proportionality of interrogation methods designed to elicit information to prevent such deaths.

To be sure, this situation is different from the usual self-defense justification, and, indeed, it overlaps with elements of the necessity defense. Self-defense as usually discussed involves using force against an individual who is about to conduct the attack. In the current circumstances, however, an enemy combatant in detention does not himself present a threat of harm. He is not actually carrying out the attack; rather, he has participated in the planning and preparation for the attack, or merely has knowledge of the attack through his membership in the terrorist organization. Nonetheless, leading scholarly commentators believe that interrogation of such individuals using methods that might violate Section 2340A would be justified under the doctrine of self-defense, because the combatant by aiding and promoting the terrorist plot "has culpably caused the situation where someone might get hurt. If hurting him is the only means to prevent the death or injury of others put at risk by his actions, such torture should be permissible, and on the same basis that self-defense is permissible." Michael S. Moore, *Torture and the Balance of Evils*, 23 Israel L. Rev. 280,

323 (1989) (symposium on Israel's Landau Commission Report).[25] Thus, some commentators believe that by helping to create the threat of loss of life, terrorists become culpable for the threat even though they do not actually carry out the attack itself. They may be hurt in an interrogation because they are part of the mechanism that has set the attack in motion, *id.* at 323, just as is someone who feeds ammunition or targeting information to an attacker. Under the present circumstances, therefore, even though a detained enemy combatant may not be the exact attacker—he is not planting the bomb, or piloting a hijacked plane to kill civilians—he still may be harmed in self-defense if he has knowledge of future attacks because he has assisted in their planning and execution.

Further, we believe that a claim by an individual of the defense of another would be further supported by the fact that, in this case, the nation itself is under attack and has the right to self-defense. This fact can bolster and support an individual claim of self-defense in a prosecution, according to the teaching of the Supreme Court in *In re Neagle*, 135 U.S. 1 (1890). In that case, the State of California arrested and held deputy U.S. Marshal Neagle for shooting and killing the assailant of Supreme Court Justice Field. In granting the writ of habeas corpus for Neagle's release, the Supreme Court did not rely alone upon the marshal's right to defend another or his right to self-defense. Rather, the Court found that Neagle, as an agent of the United States and of the executive branch, was justified in the killing because, in protecting Justice Field, he was acting pursuant to the executive branch's inherent constitutional authority to protect the United States government. *Id.* at 67 ("We cannot doubt the power of the president to take measures for the protection of a judge of one of the courts of the United States who, while in the discharge of the duties of his office, is threatened with a personal attack which may probably result in his death."). That authority derives, according to the Court, from the President's power under Article II to take care that the laws are faithfully executed. In other words, Neagle as a federal officer not only could raise self-defense or defense of another, but also could defend his actions on

---

[25] Moore distinguishes that case from one in which a person has information that could stop a terrorist attack, but who does not take a hand in the terrorist activity itself, such as an innocent person who learns of the attack from her spouse. Moore, 23 Israel L. Rev. at 324. Such individuals, Moore finds, would not be subject to the use of force in self-defense, although they might be under the doctrine of necessity.

the ground that he was implementing the Executive Branch's authority to protect the United States government.

If the right to defend the national government can be raised as a defense in an individual prosecution, as *Neagle* suggests, then a government defendant, acting in his official capacity, should be able to argue that any conduct that arguably violated Section 2340A was undertaken pursuant to more than just individual self-defense or defense of another. In addition, the defendant could claim that he was fulfilling the Executive Branch's authority to protect the federal government, and the nation, from attack. The September 11 attacks have already triggered that authority, as recognized both under domestic and international law. Following the example of *In re Neagle*, we conclude that a government defendant may also argue that his conduct of an interrogation, if properly authorized, is justified on the basis of protecting the nation from attack.

There can be little doubt that the nation's right to self-defense has been triggered under our law. The Constitution announces that one of its purposes is "to provide for the common defense." U.S. Const., Preamble. Article I, § 8 declares that Congress is to exercise its powers to "provide for the common Defence." *See also* 2 Pub. Papers of Ronald Reagan 920, 921 (1988-89) (right of self-defense recognized by Article 51 of the U.N. Charter). The President has a particular responsibility and power to take steps to defend the nation and its people. *In re Neagle*, 135 U.S. at 64. *See also* U.S. Const., art. IV, § 4 ("The United States shall . . . protect [each of the States] against Invasion"). As Commander-in-Chief and Chief Executive, he may use the armed forces to protect the nation and its people. *See, e.g., United States v. Verdugo-Urquidez*, 494 U.S. 259, 273 (1990). And he may employ secret agents to aid in his work as Commander-in-Chief. *Totten v. United States*, 92 U.S. 105, 106 (1876). As the Supreme Court observed in *The Prize Cases*, 67 U.S. (2 Black) 635 (1862), in response to an armed attack on the United States "the President is not only authorized but bound to resist force by force . . . without waiting for any special legislative authority." *Id.* at 668. The September 11 events were a direct attack on the United States, and as we have explained above, the President has authorized the use of military force with the support of Congress.[26]

---

[26] While the President's constitutional determination alone is sufficient to justify the nation's resort to self-defense, it also bears noting that the right to self-defense is further recognized under international law. Article 51 of the U.N. Charter declares that "[n]othing in the present Charter shall impair the inherent right of individual or collective self-defense if an armed attack occurs against a Member of the United Nations until the Security Council has taken the measures

As we have made clear in other opinions involving the war against al Qaeda, the nation's right to self-defense has been triggered by the events of September 11. If a government defendant were to harm an enemy combatant during an interrogation in a manner that might arguably violate Section 2340A, he would be doing so in order to prevent further attacks on the United States by the al Qaeda terrorist network. In that case, we believe that he could argue that his actions were justified by the executive branch's constitutional authority to protect the nation from attack. This national and international version of the right to self-defense could supplement and bolster the government defendant's individual right.

Conclusion

For the foregoing reasons, we conclude that torture as defined in and proscribed by Sections 2340-2340A, covers only extreme acts. Severe pain is generally of the kind difficult for the victim to endure. Where the pain is physical, it must be of an intensity akin to that which accompanies serious physical injury such as death or organ failure. Severe mental pain requires suffering not just at the moment of infliction but it also requires lasting psychological harm, such as seen in mental disorders like posttraumatic stress disorder. Additionally, such severe mental pain can arise only from the predicate acts listed in Section 2340. Because the acts inflicting torture are extreme, there is significant range of acts that though they might constitute cruel, inhuman, or degrading treatment or punishment fail to rise to the level of torture.

---

necessary to maintain international peace and security." The attacks of September 11, 2001 clearly constitute an armed attack against the United States, and indeed were the latest in a long history of al Qaeda sponsored attacks against the United States. This conclusion was acknowledged by the United Nations Security Council on September 28, 2001, when it unanimously adopted Resolution 1373 explicitly "reaffirming the inherent right of individual and collective self-defence as recognized by the charter of the United Nations." This right of self-defense is a right to effective self-defense. In other words, the victim state has the right to use force against the aggressor who has initiated an "armed attack" until the threat has abated. The United States, through its military and intelligence personnel, has a right recognized by Article 51 to continue using force until such time as the threat posed by al Qaeda and other terrorist groups connected to the September 11th attacks is completely ended." Other treaties re-affirm the right of the United States to use force in its self-defense. See, e.g., Inter-American Treaty of Reciprocal Assistance, art. 3, Sept. 2, 1947, T.I.A.S. No. 1838, 21 U.N.T.S. 77 (Rio Treaty); North Atlantic Treaty, art. 5, Apr. 4, 1949, 63 Stat. 2241, 34 U.N.T.S. 243.

Further, we conclude that under the circumstances of the current war against al Qaeda and its allies, application of Section 2340A to interrogations undertaken pursuant to the President's Commander-in-Chief powers may be unconstitutional. Finally, even if an interrogation method might violate Section 2340A, necessity or self-defense could provide justifications that would eliminate any criminal liability.

Please let us know if we can be of further assistance.

Jay S. Bybee
Assistant Attorney General

APPENDIX

Cases in which U.S. courts have concluded the defendant tortured the plaintiff:

- Plaintiff was beaten and shot by government troops while protesting the destruction of her property. *See Wiwa v. Royal Dutch Petroleum*, 2002 WL 319887 at *7 (S.D.N.Y. Feb. 28, 2002).

- Plaintiff was removed from ship, interrogated, and held incommunicado for months. Representatives of defendant threatened her with death if she attempted to move from quarters where she was held. She was forcibly separated from her husband and unable to learn of his welfare or whereabouts. *See Simpson v. Socialist People's Libyan Arab Jamahiriya*, 180 F. Supp. 2d 78, 88 (D.D.C. 2001) (Rule 12(b)(6) motion).

- Plaintiff was held captive for five days in a small cell that had no lights, no window, no water, and no toilet. During the remainder of his captivity, he was frequently denied food and water and given only limited access to the toilet. He was held at gunpoint, with his captors threatening to kill him if he did not confess to espionage. His captors threatened to cut off his fingers, pull out his fingernails, and shock his testicles. *See Daliberti v. Republic of Iraq*, 146 F. Supp. 2d 19, 22-23, 25 (D.D.C. 2001) (default judgment).

- Plaintiff was imprisoned for 205 days. He was confined in a car park that had been converted into a prison. His cell had no water or toilet and had only a steel cot for a bed. He was convicted of illegal entry into Iraq and transferred to another facility, where he was placed in a cell infested with vermin. He shared a single toilet with 200 other prisoners. While imprisoned he had a heart attack but was denied adequate medical attention and medication. *See Daliberti v. Republic of Iraq*, 146 F. Supp. 2d 19, 22-23 (D.D.C. 2001) (default judgment).

- Plaintiff was imprisoned for 126 days. At one point, a guard attempted to execute him, but another guard intervened. A truck transporting the plaintiff ran over pedestrian at full speed without stopping. He heard other prisoners being beaten and he feared being

beaten. He had serious medical conditions that were not promptly
or adequately treated. He was not given sufficient food or water.
See Daliberti v. Republic of Iraq, 146 F. Supp. 2d 19, 22-23 (D.D.C.
2001) (default judgment).

- Allegations that guards beat, clubbed, and kicked the plaintiff and
  that the plaintiff was interrogated and subjected to physical and verbal abuse sufficiently stated a claim for torture so as to survive Rule
  12(b)(6) motion. *See Price v. Socialist People's Libyan Arab Jamahiriya*, 110 F. Supp. 2d 10 (D.D.C. 2000).

- Plaintiffs alleged that they were blindfolded, interrogated and subjected to physical, mental, and verbal abuse while they were held
  captive. Furthermore, one plaintiff was held eleven days without
  food, water, or bed. Another plaintiff was held for four days without food, water, or a bed, and was also stripped naked, blindfolded,
  and threatened with electrocution of his testicles. The other two remaining plaintiffs alleged that they were not provided adequate or
  proper medical care for conditions that were life threatening. The
  court concluded that these allegations sufficiently stated a claim for
  torture and denied defendants Rule 12(b)(6) motion. *See Daliberti
  v. Republic v. Iraq,* 97 F. Supp. 2d 38, 45 (D.D.C. 2000) (finding that
  these allegations were "more than enough to meet the definition of
  torture in the [TVPA]").

- Plaintiff's kidnappers pistol-whipped him until he lost consciousness. They then stripped him and gave him only a robe to wear and
  left him bleeding, dizzy, and in severe pain. He was then imprisoned for 1,908 days. During his imprisonment, his captors sought to
  force a confession from him by playing Russian Roulette with him
  and threatening him with castration. He was randomly beaten and
  forced to watch the beatings of others. Additionally, he was confined in a rodent and scorpion infested cell. He was bound in chains
  almost the entire time of his confinement. One night during the win-
  ter, his captors chained him to an upper floor balcony, leaving him
  exposed to the elements. Consequently, he developed frostbite on
  his hands and feet. He was also subjected to a surgical procedure for
  an unidentified abdominal problem. *See Cicippio v. Islamic Republic of Iran*, 18 F. Supp. 2d 62 (D.D.C. 1998).

- Plaintiff was kidnapped at gunpoint. He was beaten for several days after his kidnapping. He was subjected to daily torture and threats of death. He was kept in solitary confinement for two years. During that time, he was blindfolded and chained to the wall in a six-foot by six-foot room infested with rodents. He was shackled in a stooped position for 44 months and he developed eye infections as a result of the blindfolds. Additionally, his captors did the following: forced him to kneel on spikes, administered electric shocks to his hands; battered his feet with iron bars and struck him in the kidneys with a rifle; struck him on the side of his head with a hand grenade, breaking his nose and jaw; placed boiling tea kettles on his shoulders; and they laced his food with arsenic. *See Cicippio v. Islamic Republic of Iran*, 18 F. Supp. 2d 62 (D.D.C. 1998).

- Plaintiff was pistol-whipped, bound and gagged, held captive in darkness or blindfold for 18 months. He was kept chained at either his ankles or wrists, wearing nothing but his undershorts and a t-shirt. As for his meals, his captors gave him pita bread and dry cheese for breakfast, rice with dehydrated soup for lunch, and a piece of bread for dinner. Sometimes the guards would spit into his food. He was regularly beaten and incessantly interrogated; he overheard the deaths and beatings of other prisoners. *See Cicippio v. Islamic Republic of Iran*, 18 F. Supp. 2d 62, (D.D.C. 1998).

- Plaintiff spent eight years in solitary or near solitary confinement. He was threatened with death, blindfolded and beaten while handcuffed and fettered. He was denied sleep and repeatedly threatened him with death. At one point, while he was shackled to a cot, the guards placed a towel over his nose and mouth and then poured water down his nostrils. They did this for six hours. During this incident, the guards threatened him with death and electric shock. Afterwards, they left him shackled to his cot for six days. For the next seven months, he was imprisoned in a hot, unlit cell that measured 2.5 square meters. During this seven-month period, he was shackled to his cot—at first by all his limbs and later by one hand or one foot. He remained shackled in this manner except for the briefest moments, such as when his captors permitted him to use the bathroom. The handcuffs cut into his flesh. *See Hilao v. Estate of Marcos*, 103 F.3d 789, 790 (9th Cir. 1996). The court did not, however, appear to consider the solitary confinement per se to constitute torture. *See id.* at 795 (stating that to the extent that [the plaintiff's] years in solitary confinement do not constitute torture, they clearly meet the definition of prolonged arbitrary detention.").

- High-ranking military officers interrogated the plaintiff and subjected him to mock executions. He was also threatened with death. *See Hilao v. Estate of Marcos*, 103 F.3d 789, 795 (9th Cir. 1996).

- Plaintiff, a nun, received anonymous threats warning her to leave Guatemala. Later, two men with a gun kidnapped her. They blindfolded her and locked her in an unlit room for hours. The guards interrogated her and regardless of the answers she gave to their questions, they burned her with cigarettes. The guards then showed her surveillance photographs of herself. They blindfolded her again, stripped her, and raped her repeatedly. *See Xuncax v. Gramajo*, 886 F. Supp. 162, 176 (1995).

- Plaintiffs were beaten with truncheons, boots, and guns and threatened with death. Nightsticks were used to beat their backs, kidneys, and the soles of their feet. The soldiers pulled and squeezed their testicles. When they fainted from the pain, the soldiers revived them by singeing their nose hair with a cigarette lighter. They were interrogated as they were beaten with iron barks, rifle butts, helmets, and fists. One plaintiff was placed in the "djak" position, *i.e.*, with hands and feet bound and suspended from a pole. Medical treatment was withheld for one week and then was sporadic and inadequate. *See Paul v. Avril*, 901 F. Supp. 330, 332 (S.D. Fla. 1994).

- Alien subjected to sustained beatings for the month following his first arrest. After his second arrest, suffered severe beatings and was burned with cigarettes over the course of an eight-day period. *Al-Saher v. INS*, 268 F.3d 1143, 1147 (9th Cir. 2001) (deportation case).

- Decedent was attacked with knifes and sticks, and repeatedly hit in the head with the butt of a gun as he remained trapped in his truck by his attackers. The attackers then doused the vehicle with gasoline. Although he managed to get out of the truck, he nonetheless burned to death. *Tachiona v. Mugabe*, No. 00 Civ. 6666VMJCF, 2002 WL 1424598 at *1 (S.D.N.Y. July 1, 2002).

• Decedent was attacked by spear, stick, and stone wielding support-
ers of defendant. He was carried off by the attackers and "was found
dead the next day, naked and lying in the middle of the road[.]" From
the physical injuries, it was determined that he had been severely
beaten. According to his death certificate, he died from "massive
brain injury from trauma; [] assault; and [] laceration of the right
lung." *Tachiona v. Mugabe*, No. 00 Civ. 6666VMJCF, 2002 WL
1424598 at *2 (S.D.N.Y. July 1, 2002).

• Decedent was abducted, along with five others. He and the others were severely beaten and he was forced to drink diesel oil. He
was then summarily executed. *Tachiona v. Mugabe*, No. 00 Civ.
6666VMJCF, 2002 WL 1424598 at *4 (S.D.N.Y. July 1, 2002).

• Forced sterilization constitutes torture. *Bi Zhu Lin v. Ashcroft*, 183
F. Supp. 2d 551 (D. Conn. 2002) (noting determination by immigration judge that such conduct constitutes torture).

There are two cases in which U.S. courts have rejected torture
claims on the ground that the alleged conduct did not rise to the level of
torture. In *Faulder v. Johnson*, 99 F. Supp. 2d 774 (S.D. Tex. 1999), the district court rejected a death row inmate's claim that psychological trauma
resulting from repeated stays of his execution and his 22-year-wait for that
execution was torture under CAT. The court rejected this contention because of the United States' express death penalty reservation to CAT. *See
id.* In *Eastman Kodak v. Kavlin*, 978 F. Supp. 1078, 1093 (S.D. Fla. 1997),
the plaintiff was held for eight days in a filthy cell with drug dealers and
an AIDS patient. He received no food, no blanket and no protection from
other inmates. Prisoners murdered one another in front of the plaintiff. *Id.*
The court flatly rejected the plaintiff's claim that this constituted torture.

U.S. Department of Justice

Office of Legal Counsel

Office of the Assistant Attorney General   *Washington, D.C. 20530*

August 1, 2002

Memorandum for John Rizzo
Acting General Counsel of the Central Intelligence Agency

Interrogation of al Qaeda Operative

You have asked for this Office's views on whether certain proposed conduct would violate the prohibition against torture found at Section 2340A of title 18 of the United States Code. You have asked for this advice in the course of conducting interrogations of Abu Zubaydah. As we understand it, Zubaydah is one of the highest ranking members of the al Qaeda terrorist organization, with which the United States is currently engaged in an international armed conflict following the attacks on the World Trade Center and the Pentagon on September 11, 2001. This letter memorializes our previous oral advice, given on July 24, 2002 and July 26, 2002, that the proposed conduct would not violate this prohibition.

I.

Our advice is based upon the following facts, which you have provided to us. We also understand that you do not have any facts in your possession contrary to the facts outlined here, and this opinion is limited to these facts. If these facts were to change, this advice would not necessarily apply. Zubaydah is currently being held by the United States. The interrogation team is certain that he has additional information that he refuses to divulge. Specifically, he is withholding information regarding terrorist networks in the United States or in Saudi Arabia and information regarding plans to conduct attacks within the United States or against our interests overseas. Zubaydah has become accustomed to a certain level of treatment and displays no signs of willingness to disclose further information. Moreover, your intelligence indicates that there is currently a level of "chatter" equal to that which preceded the September 11 attacks. In light of the information you believe Zubaydah has and the high level of threat you believe now exists, you wish to move the interrogations into what you have described as an "increased pressure phase."

As part of this increased pressure phase, Zubaydah will have contact only with a new interrogation specialist, whom he has not met previously, and the Survival, Evasion, Resistance, Escape ("SERE") training psychologist, who has been involved with the interrogations since they began. This phase will likely last no more than several days but could last up to thirty days. In this phase, you would like to employ ten techniques that you believe will dislocate his expectations regarding the treatment he believes he will receive and encourage him to disclose the crucial information mentioned above. These ten techniques are: (1) attention grasp, (2) walling, (3) facial hold, (4) facial slap (insult slap), (5) cramped confinement, (6) wall standing, (7) stress positions, (8) sleep deprivation, (9) insects placed in a confinement box, and (10) the waterboard. You have informed us that the use of these techniques would be on an as-needed basis and that not all of the techniques will necessarily be used. The interrogation team would use these techniques in some combination to convince Zubaydah that the only way he can influence his surrounding environment is through cooperation. You have, however, informed us that you expect these techniques to be used in some sort of escalating fashion, culminating with the waterboard, though not necessarily ending with this technique. Moreover, you have also orally informed us that although some of these techniques may be used with [sic] more than once, that repetition will not be substantial because the techniques generally lose their effectiveness after several repetitions. You have also informed us that Zubaydah sustained a wound during his capture, which is being treated.

Based on the facts you have given us, we understand each of these techniques to be as follows. The attention grasp consists of grasping the individual with both hands, one hand on each side of the collar opening, in a controlled and quick motion. In the same motion as the grasp, the individual is drawn toward the interrogator.

For walling, a flexible false wall will be constructed. The individual is placed with his heels touching the wall. The interrogator pulls the individual forward and then quickly and firmly pushes the individual into the wall. It is the individual's shoulder blades that hit the wall. During this motion, the head and neck are supported with a rolled hood or towel that provides a c-collar effect to help prevent whiplash. To further reduce the probability of injury, the individual is allowed to rebound from the flexible wall. You have orally informed us that the false wall is in part constructed to create a loud sound when the individual hits it, which will further shock or surprise in [sic] the individual. In part, the idea is to create a sound that will make the impact seem far worse than it is and that will be far worse than any injury that might result from the action.

The facial hold is used to hold the head immobile. One open palm is placed on either side of the individual's face. The fingertips are kept well away from the individual's eyes.

With the facial slap or insult slap, the interrogator slaps the individual's face with fingers slightly spread. The hand makes contact with the area directly between the tip of the individual's chin and the bottom of the corresponding earlobe. The interrogator invades the individual's personal space. The goal of the facial slap is not to inflict physical pain that is severe or lasting. Instead, the purpose of the facial slap is to induce shock, surprise, and/or humiliation.

Cramped confinement involves the placement of the individual in a confined space, the dimensions of which restrict the individual's movement. The confined space is usually dark. The duration of confinement varies based upon the size of the container. For the larger confined space, the individual can stand up or sit down; the smaller space is large enough for the subject to sit down. Containment in the larger space can last up to eighteen hours; for the smaller space, confinement lasts for no more than two hours.

Wall standing is used to induce muscle fatigue. The individual stands about four to five feet from a wall, with his feet spread approximately to shoulder width. His arms are stretched out in front of him, with his fingers resting on the wall. His fingers support all of his body weight. The individual is not permitted to move or reposition his hands or feet.

A variety of stress positions may be used. You have informed us that these positions are not designed to produce the pain associated with contortions or twisting of the body. Rather, somewhat like walling, they are designed to produce the physical discomfort associated with muscle fatigue. Two particular stress positions are likely to be used on Zubaydah: (1) sitting on the floor with legs extended straight out in front of him with his arms raised above his head; and (2) kneeling on the floor while leaning back at a 45 degree angle. You have also orally informed us that through observing Zubaydah in captivity, you have noted that he appears to be quite flexible despite his wound.

Sleep deprivation may be used. You have indicated that your purpose in using this technique is to reduce the individual's ability to think on his feet and, through the discomfort associated with lack of sleep, to motivate him to cooperate. The effect of such sleep deprivation will generally remit after one or two nights of uninterrupted sleep. You have informed us that your research has revealed that, in rare instances, some individuals who are already predisposed to psychological problems may experience abnormal reactions to sleep deprivation. Even in those cases, however, reactions abate after the individual is permitted to sleep. Moreover, personnel with medical training are available to and will intervene in the unlikely event of an abnormal reaction. You have orally informed us that you would not deprive Zubaydah of sleep for more than eleven days at a time and that you have previously kept him awake for 72 hours, from which no mental or physical harm resulted.

You would like to place Zubaydah in a cramped confinement box with an insect. You have informed us that he appears to have a fear of insects. In particular, you would like to tell Zubaydah that you intend to place a stinging insect into the box with him. You would, however, place a harmless insect in the box. You have orally informed us that you would in fact place a harmless insect such as a caterpillar in the box with him.

Finally, you would like to use a technique called the "waterboard." In this procedure, the individual is bound securely to an inclined bench, which is approximately four feet by seven feet. The individual's feet are generally elevated. A cloth is placed over the forehead and eyes. Water is then applied to the cloth in a controlled manner. As this is done, the cloth is lowered until it covers both the nose and mouth. Once the cloth is saturated and completely covers the mouth and nose, air flow is slightly restricted for 20 to 40 seconds due to the presence of the cloth. This causes an increase in carbon dioxide level in the individual's blood. This increase in the carbon dioxide level stimulates increased effort to breathe. This effort plus the cloth produces the perception of "suffocation and incipient panic," i.e., the perception of drowning. The individual does not breathe any water into his lungs. During those 20 to 40 seconds, water is continuously applied from a height of twelve to twenty-four inches. After this period, the cloth is lifted, and the individual is allowed to breathe unimpeded for three or four full breaths. The sensation of drowning is immediately relieved by the removal of the cloth. The procedure may then be repeated. The water is usually applied from a canteen cup or small watering can with a spout. You have orally informed us that this procedure triggers an automatic physiological sensation of drowning that the individual cannot control even though he may be aware that he is in fact not drowning. You have also orally informed us that it is likely that this procedure would not last more than 20 minutes in any one application.

We also understand that a medical expert with SERE experience will be present throughout this phase and that the procedures will be stopped if deemed medically necessary to prevent severe mental or physical harm to Zubaydah. As mentioned above, Zubaydah suffered an injury during his capture. You have informed us that steps will be taken to ensure that this injury is not in any way exacerbated by the use of these methods and that adequate clinical attention will be given to ensure that it will heal properly.

II.

In this part, we review the context within which these procedures will be applied. You have infomed us that you have taken various steps to ascertain what effect, if any, these techniques would have on Zubaydah's mental health. These same techniques, with the exception of the insect in the cramped confined space, have been used and continue to be used on some members of our military personnel during their SERE training. Because of the use of these procedures in training our own military personnel to resist interrogations, you have consulted with various individuals who have extensive experience in the use of these techniques. You have done so in order to ensure that no prolonged mental harm would result from the use of these proposed procedures.

Through your consultation with various individuals responsible for such training, you have learned that these techniques have been used as elements of a course of conduct without any reported incident of prolonged mental harm. ███████████████████████ of the SERE school, ████████████ has reported that, during the seven-year period that he spent in those positions, there were two requests from Congress for information concerning alleged injuries resulting from the training. One of these inquiries was prompted by the temporary physical injury a trainee sustained as result of being placed in a confinement box. The other inquiry involved claims that the SERE training caused two individuals to engage in criminal behavior, namely, felony shoplifting and downloading child pornography onto a military computer. According to this official, these claims were found to be baseless. Moreover, he has indicated that during the three and a half years he spent as ████████████████ of the SERE program, he trained 10,000 students. Of those students, only two dropped out of the training following the use of these techniques. Although on rare occasions some students temporarily postponed the remainder of their training and received psychological counseling, those students were able to finish the program without any indication of subsequent mental health effects.

You have informed us that you have consulted with ███████ ███ who has ten years of experience with SERE training ███████ He stated that, during those ten years, insofar as he is aware, none of the individuals who completed the program suffered any adverse mental health effects. He informed you that there was one person who did not complete the training. That person experienced an adverse mental health reaction that lasted only two hours. After those two hours, the individual's symptoms spontaneously dissipated without requiring treatment or counseling and no other symptoms were ever reported by this individual. According to the information you have provided to us, this assessment of the use of these procedures includes the use of the waterboard.

Additionally, you received a memorandum from the ███████ ███████ which you supplied to us. ███████ has experience with the use of all of these procedures in a course of conduct, with the exception of the insect in the confinement box and the waterboard. This memorandum confirms that the use of these procedures has not resulted in any reported instances of prolonged mental harm, and very few instances of immediate and temporary adverse psychological responses to the training. ███████ reported that a small minority of students have had temporary adverse psychological reactions during training. Of the 26,829 students trained from 1992 through 2001 in the Air Force SERE training, 4.3 percent of those students had contact with psychology services. Of those 4.3 percent, only 3.2 percent were pulled from the program for psychological reasons. Thus, out of the students trained overall, only 0.14 percent were pulled from the program for psychological reasons. Furthermore, although ███████ indicated that surveys of students having completed this training are not done, he expressed confidence that the training did not cause any long-term psychological impact. He based his conclusion on the debriefing of students that is done after the training. More importantly, he based this assessment on the fact that although training is required to be extremely stressful in order to be effective, very few complaints have been made regarding the training. During his tenure, in which 10,000 students were trained, no congressional complaints have been made. While there was one Inspector General complaint, it was not due to psychological concerns. Moreover, he was aware of only one letter inquiring about the long-term impact of these techniques from an individual trained over twenty years ago. He found that it was impossible to attribute this individual's symptoms to his training. ████████████████ concluded that if there are any long-term psychological effects of the United States Air Force training using the procedures outlined above they "are certainly minimal."

With respect to the waterboard, you have also orally informed us that the Navy continues to use it in training. You have informed us that your on-site psychologists, who have extensive experience with the use of the waterboard in Navy training, have not encountered any significant long-term mental health consequences from its use. Your on-site psychologists have also indicated that JPRA has likewise not reported any significant long-term mental health consequences from the use of the waterboard. You have informed us that other services ceased use of the waterboard because it was so successful as an interrogation technique, but not because of any concerns over any harm, physical or mental, caused by it. It was also reported to be almost 100 percent effective in producing cooperation among the trainees. ████████████████ also indicated that he had observed the use of the waterboard in Navy training some ten to twelve times. Each time it resulted in cooperation but it did not result in any physical harm to the student.

You have also reviewed the relevant literature and found no empirical data on the effect of these techniques, with the exception of sleep deprivation. With respect to sleep deprivation, you have informed us that it is not uncommon for someone to be deprived of sleep for 72 hours and still perform excellently on visual-spatial motor tasks and short-term memory tests. Although some individuals may experience hallucinations, according to the literature you surveyed, those who experience such psychotic symptoms have almost always had such episodes prior to the sleep deprivation. You have indicated the studies of lengthy sleep deprivation showed no psychosis, loosening of thoughts, flattening of emotions, delusions, or paranoid ideas. In one case, even after eleven days of deprivation, no psychosis or permanent brain damage occurred. In fact the individual reported feeling almost back to normal after one night's sleep. Further, based on the experiences with its use in military training (where it is induced for up to 48 hours), you found that rarely, if ever, will the individual suffer harm after the sleep deprivation is discontinued. Instead, the effects remit after a few good nights of sleep.

You have taken the additional step of consulting with U.S. interrogations experts, and other individuals with oversight over the SERE training process. None of these individuals was aware of any prolonged psychological effect caused by the use of any of the above techniques either separately or as a course of conduct. Moreover, you consulted with outside psychologists who reported that they were unaware of any cases where long-term problems have occurred as a result of these techniques.

Moreover, in consulting with a number of mental health experts, you have learned that the effect of any of these procedures will be dependent on the individual's personal history, cultural history and psychological tendencies. To that end, you have informed us that you have completed a psychological assessment of Zubadyah. This assessment is based on interviews with Zubaydah, observations of him, and information collected from other sources such as intelligence and press reports. Our understanding of Zubaydah's psychological profile, which we set forth below, is based on that assessment.

According to this assessment, Zubaydah, though only 31, rose quickly from very low level mujahedin to third or fourth man in al Qaeda. He has served as Usama Bin Laden's senior lieutenant. In that capacity, he has managed a network of training camps. He has been instrumental in the training of operatives for al Qaeda, the Egyptian Islamic Jihad, and other terrorist elements inside Pakistan and Afghanistan. He acted as the Deputy Camp Commander for al Qaeda training camp in Afghanistan, personally approving entry and graduation of all trainees during 1999-2000. From 1996 until 1999, he approved all individuals going in and out of Afghanistan to the training camps. Further no one went in and out of Peshawar, Pakistan without his knowledge and approval. He also acted as al Qaeda's coordinator of external contacts and foreign communications. Additionally, he has acted as al Qaeda's counterintelligence officer and has been trusted to find spies within the organization.

Zubaydah has been involved in every major terrorist operation carried out by al Qaeda. He was a planner for the Millennium plot to attack U.S. and Israeli targets during the Millennium celebrations in Jordan. Two of the central figures in this plot who were arrested have identified Zubaydah as the supporter of their cell and the plot. He also served as a planner for the Paris Embassy plot in 2001. Moreover, he was one of the planners of the September 11 attacks. Prior to his capture, he was engaged in planning future terrorist attacks against U.S. interests.

Your psychological assessment indicates that it is believed Zubaydah wrote al Qaeda's manual on resistance techniques. You also believe that his experiences in al Qaeda make him well-acquainted with and well-versed in such techniques. As part of his role in al Qaeda, Zubaydah visited individuals in prison and helped them upon their release. Through this contact and activities with other al Qaeda mujahedin, you believe that he knows many stories of capture, interrogation, and resistance to such interrogation. Additionally, he has spoken with Ayman al-Zawahiri, and you believe it is likely that the two discussed Zawahiri's experiences as a prisoner of the Russians and the Egyptians.

Zubaydah stated during interviews that he thinks of any activity outside of jihad as "silly." He has indicated that his heart and mind are devoted to serving Allah and Islam through jihad and he has stated that he has no doubts or regrets about committing himself to jihad. Zubaydah believes that the global victory of Islam is inevitable. You have informed us that he continues to express his unabated desire to kill Americans and Jews.

Your psychological assessment describes his personality as follows. He is "a highly self-directed individual who prizes his independence." He has "narcissistic features," which are evidenced in the attention be pays to his personal appearance and his "obvious 'efforts' to demonstrate that he is really a rather 'humble and regular guy.'" He is "somewhat compulsive" in how he organizes his environment and business. He is confident, self-assured, and possesses an air of authority. While he admits to at times wrestling with how to determine who is an "innocent," he has acknowledged celebrating the destruction of the World Trade Center. He is intelligent and intellectually curious. He displays "excellent self-discipline." The assessment describes him as a perfectionist, persistent, private, and highly capable in his social interactions. He is very guarded about opening up to others and your assessment repeatedly emphasizes that he tends not to trust others easily. He is also "quick to recognize and assess the moods and motivations of others." Furthermore, he is proud of his ability to lie and deceive others successfully. Through his deception he has, among other things, prevented the location of al Qaeda safehouses and even acquired a United Nations refugee identification card.

According to your reports, Zubaydah does not have any pre-existing mental conditions or problems that would make him likely to suffer prolonged mental harm from your proposed interrogation methods. Through reading his diaries and interviewing him, you have found no history of "mood disturbance or other psychiatric pathology[,]" "thought disorder[,] . . . enduring mood or mental health problems." He is in fact "remarkably resilient and confident that he can overcome adversity." When he encounters stress or low mood, this appears to last only for a short time. He deals with stress by assessing its source, evaluating the coping resources available to him, and then taking action. Your assessment notes that he is "generally self-sufficient and relies on his understanding and application of religious and psychological principles, intelligence and discipline to avoid and overcome problems." Moreover, you have found that he has a "reliable and durable support system" in his faith, "the blessings of religious leaders, and camaraderie of like-minded mujahedin brothers." During detention, Zubaydah has managed his mood, remaining at most points "circumspect, calm, controlled, and deliberate." He has maintained this demeanor during aggressive interrogations and reductions in sleep. You describe that in an initial confrontational incident, Zubaydah showed signs of sympathetic nervous system arousal, which you think was possibly fear. Although this incident led him to disclose intelligence information, he was able to quickly regain his composure, his air of confidence, and his "strong resolve" not to reveal any information.

Overall, you summarize his primary strengths as the following: ability to focus, goal-directed discipline, intelligence, emotional resilience, street savvy, ability to organize and manage people, keen observation skills, fluid adaptability (can anticipate and adapt under duress and with minimal resources), capacity to assess and exploit the needs of others, and ability to adjust goals to emerging opportunities.

You anticipate that he will draw upon his vast knowledge of interrogation techniques to cope with the interrogation. Your assessment indicates that Zubaydah may be willing to die to protect the most important information that he holds. Nonetheless, you are of the view that his belief that Islam will ultimately dominate the world and that this victory is inevitable may provide the chance that Zubaydah will give information and rationalize it solely as a temporary setback. Additionally, you believe he may be willing to disclose some information, particularly information he deems to not be critical, but which may ultimately be useful to us when pieced together with other intelligence information you have gained.

III.

Section 2340A makes it a criminal offense for any person "outside of the United States [to] commit[] or attempt[] to commit torture." Section 2340(1) defines torture as:

> an act committed by a person acting under the color of law specifically intended to inflict severe physical or mental pain or suffering (other than pain or suffering incidental to law-

ful sanctions) upon another person within his custody of [*sic*] physical control.

18 U.S.C. § 2340(1). As we outlined in our opinion on standards of conduct under Section 2340A, a violation of 2340A requires a showing that: (1) the torture occurred outside the United States; (2) the defendant acted under the color of law; (3) the victim was within the defendant's custody or control; (4) the defendant specifically intended to inflict severe pain or suffering; and (5) that the acted [*sic*] inflicted severe pain or suffering. *See* Memorandum for John Rizzo, Acting General Counsel for the Central Intelligence Agency, from Jay S. Bybee, Assistant Attorney General, Office of Legal Counsel, *Re: Standards of Conduct for Interrogation under* 18 *U.S.C.* §§ *2340-2340A* at 3 (August 1, 2002) ("Section 2340A Memorandum"). You have asked us to assume that Zubaydah is being held outside the United States, Zubaydah is within U.S. custody, and the interrogators are acting under the color of law. At issue is whether the last two elements would be met by the use of the proposed procedures, namely, whether those using these procedures would have the requisite mental state and whether these procedures would inflict severe pain or suffering within the meaning of the statute.

Severe Pain or Suffering. In order for pain or suffering to rise to the level of torture, the statute requires that it be severe. As we have previously explained, this reaches only extreme acts. *See id.* at 13. Nonetheless, drawing upon cases under the Torture Victim Protection Act (TVPA), which has a definition of torture that is similar to Section 2340's definition, we found that a single event of sufficiently intense pain may fall within this prohibition. *See id.* at 26. As a result, we have analyzed each of these techniques separately. Further drawing upon those cases, we also have found that courts tend to take a totality-of-the-circumstances approach and consider an entire course of conduct to determine whether torture has occurred. *See id* at 27. Therefore, in addition to considering each technique separately, we consider them together as a course of conduct.

Section 2340 defines torture as the infliction of severe physical or mental pain or suffering. We will consider physical pain and mental pain separately. *See* 18 U.S.C. § 2340(1). With respect to *physical* pain, we previously concluded that "severe pain" within the meaning of Section 2340 is pain that is difficult for the individual to endure and is of an intensity akin to the pain accompanying serious physical injury. *See* Section 2340A

Memorandum at 6. Drawing upon the TVPA precedent, we have noted that examples of acts inflicting severe pain that typify torture are, among other things, severe beatings with weapons such as clubs, and the burning of prisoners. *See id.* at 24. We conclude below that none of the proposed techniques inflicts such pain.

The facial hold and the attention grasp involve no physical pain. In the absence of such pain it is obvious that they cannot be said to inflict severe physical pain or suffering. The stress positions and wall standing both may result in muscle fatigue. Each involves the sustained holding of a position. In wall standing, it will be holding a position in which all of the individual's body weight is placed on his finger tips. The stress positions will likely include sitting on the floor with legs extended straight out in front and arms raised above the head, and kneeling on the floor and leaning back at a 45 degree angle. Any pain associated with muscle fatigue is not of the intensity sufficient to amount to "severe physical pain or suffering" under the statute, nor, despite its discomfort, can it be said to be difficult to endure. Moreover, you have orally informed us that no stress position will be used that could interfere with the healing of Zubaydah's wound. Therefore, we conclude that these techniques involve discomfort that falls far below the threshold of severe physical pain.

Similarly, although the confinement boxes (both small and large) are physically uncomfortable because their size restricts movement, they are not so small as to require the individual to contort his body to sit (small box) or stand (large box). You have also orally informed us that despite his wound, Zubaydah remains quite flexible, which would substantially reduce any pain associated with being placed in the box. We have no information from the medical experts you have consulted that the limited duration for which the individual is kept in the boxes causes any substantial physical pain. As a result, we do not think the use of these boxes can be said to cause pain that is of the intensity associated with serious physical injury.

The use of one of these boxes with the introduction of an insect does not alter this assessment. As we understand it, no actually harmful insect will be placed in the box. Thus, although the introduction of an insect may produce trepidation in Zubaydah (which we discuss below), it certainly does not cause physical pain.

As for sleep deprivation, it is clear that depriving someone of sleep does not involve severe physical pain within the meaning of the statute. While sleep deprivation may involve some physical discomfort, such as the fatigue or the discomfort experienced in the difficulty of keeping one's eyes open, these effects remit after the individual is permitted to sleep. Based on the facts you have provided us, we are not aware of any evidence that sleep deprivation results in severe physical pain or suffering. As a result, its use does not violate Section 2340A.

Even those techniques that involve physical contact between the interrogator and the individual do not result in severe pain. The facial slap and walling contain precautions to ensure that no pain even approaching this level results. The slap is delivered with fingers slightly spread, which you have explained to us is designed to be less painful than a closed-hand slap. The slap is also delivered to the fleshy part of the face, further reducing any risk of physical damage or serious pain. The facial slap does not produce pain that is difficult to endure. Likewise, walling involves quickly pulling the person forward and then thrusting him against a flexible false wall. You have informed us that the sound of hitting the wall will actually be far worse than any possible injury to the individual. The use of the rolled towel around the neck also reduces any risk of injury. While it may hurt to be pushed against the wall, any pain experienced is not of the intensity associated with serious physical injury.

As we understand it, when the waterboard is used, the subject's body responds as if the subject were drowning—even though the subject may be well aware that he is in fact not drowning. You have informed us that this procedure does not inflict actual physical harm. Thus, although the subject may experience the fear or panic associated with the feeling of drowning, the waterboard does not inflict physical pain. As we explained in the Section 2340A Memorandum, "pain and suffering" as used in Section 2340 is best understood as a single concept, not distinct concepts of "pain" as distinguished from "suffering." *See* Section 2340A Memorandum at 6 n.3. The waterboard, which inflicts no pain or actual harm whatsoever, does not, in our view inflict "severe pain or suffering." Even if one were to parse the statute more finely to attempt to treat "suffering" as a distinct concept, the waterboard could not be said to inflict severe suffering. The waterboard is simply a controlled acute episode, lacking the connotation of a protracted period of time generally given to suffering.

Finally, as we discussed above, you have informed us that in determining which procedures to use and how you will use them, you have selected techniques that will not harm Zubaydah's wound. You have also indicated that numerous steps will be taken to ensure that none of these procedures in any way interferes with the proper healing of Zubaydah's wound. You have also indicated that, should it appear at any time that Zubaydah is experiencing severe pain or suffering, the medical personnel on hand will stop the use of any technique.

Even when all of these methods are considered combined in an overall course of conduct, they still would not inflict severe physical pain or suffering. As discussed above, a number of these acts result in no physical pain, others produce only physical discomfort. You have indicated that these acts will not be used with substantial repetition, so that there is no possibility that severe physical pain could arise from such repetition. Accordingly, we conclude that these acts neither separately nor as part of a course of conduct would inflict severe physical pain or suffering within the meaning or the statute.

We next consider whether the use of these techniques would inflict severe *mental* pain or suffering within the meaning of Section 2340. Section 2340 defines severe mental pain or suffering as "the prolonged mental harm caused by or resulting from" one of several predicate acts. 18 U.S.C. § 2340(2). Those predicate acts are: (1) the intentional infliction or threatened infliction of severe physical pain or suffering; (2) the administration or application, or threatened administration or application of mind-altering substances or other procedures calculated to disrupt profoundly the senses or the personality; (3) the threat of imminent death; or (4) the threat that any the preceding acts will be done to another person. *See* 18 U.S.C. § 2340(2)(A)-(D). As we have explained, this list of predicate acts is exclusive. *See* Section 2340A Memorandum at 8. No other acts can support a charge under Section 2340A based on the infliction of severe mental pain or suffering. *See id.* Thus, if the methods that you have described do not either in and of themselves constitute one of these acts or as a course of conduct fulfill the predicate act requirement, the prohibition has not been violated. *See id.* Before addressing these techniques, we note that it is plain that none of these procedures involves a threat to any third party, the use of any kind of drugs, or for the reasons described above, the infliction of severe physical pain. Thus, the question is whether any of these acts, separately or as a course of conduct, constitutes a threat of severe physical pain or suffering, a procedure designed to disrupt profoundly the senses, or a threat of imminent death. As we previously explained, whether an action constitutes a threat must be assessed from the standpoint of a reasonable person in the subject's position. *See id* at 9.

No argument can be made that the attention grasp or the facial hold constitute threats of imminent death or are procedures designed to disrupt profoundly the senses or personality. In general the grasp and the facial hold will startle the subject, produce fear, or even insult him. As you have informed us, the use of these techniques is not accompanied by a specific verbal threat of severe physical pain or suffering. To the extent that these techniques could be considered a threat of severe physical pain or suffering, such a threat would have to be inferred from the acts themselves. Because these actions themselves involve no pain, neither could be interpreted by a reasonable person in Zubaydah's position to constitute a threat of severe pain or suffering. Accordingly, these two techniques are not predicate acts within the meaning of Section 2340.

The facial slap likewise falls outside the set of predicate acts. It plainly is not a threat of imminent death, under Section 2340(2)(C), or a procedure designed to disrupt profoundly the senses or personality, under Section 2340(2)(B). Though it may hurt, as discussed above, the effect is one of smarting or stinging and surprise or humiliation, but not severe pain. Nor does it alone constitute a threat of severe pain or suffering, under Section 2340(2)(A). Like the facial hold and the attention grasp, the use of this slap is not accompanied by a specific verbal threat of further escalating violence. Additionally, you have informed us that in one use this technique will typically involve at most two slaps. Certainly, the use of this slap may dislodge any expectation that Zubaydah had that he would not be touched in a physically aggressive manner. Nonetheless, this alteration in his expectations could hardly be construed by a reasonable person in his situation to be tantamount to a threat of severe physical pain or suffering. At most, this technique suggests that the circumstances of his confinement and interrogation have changed. Therefore, the facial slap is not within the statute's exclusive list of predicate acts.

Walling plainly is not a procedure calculated to disrupt profoundly the senses or personality. While walling involves what might be characterized as rough handling, it does not involve the threat of imminent death or, as discussed above, the infliction of severe physical pain. Moreover, once again we understand that use of this technique will not be accompanied by any specific verbal threat that violence will ensue absent cooperation. Thus, like the facial slap, walling can only constitute a threat of severe physical pain if a reasonable person would infer such a threat from the use of the technique itself. Walling does not in and of itself inflict severe pain or suffering. Like the facial slap, walling may alter the subject's expectations as to the treatment he believes he will receive. Nonetheless, the character of the action falls so far short of inflicting severe pain or suffering within the meaning of the statute that even if he inferred that greater aggressiveness was to follow, the type of actions that could be reasonably be anticipated would still fall below anything sufficient to inflict severe physical pain or suffering under the statute. Thus, we conclude that this technique falls outside the proscribed predicate acts.

Like walling, stress positions and wall-standing are not procedures calculated to disrupt profoundly the senses, nor are they threats of imminent death. These procedures, as discussed above, involve the use of muscle fatigue to encourage cooperation and do not themselves constitute the infliction of severe physical pain or suffering. Moreover, there is no aspect of violence to either technique that remotely suggests future severe pain or suffering from which such a threat of future harm could be inferred. They simply involve forcing the subject to remain in uncomfortable positions. While these acts may indicate to the subject that he may be placed in these positions again if he does not disclose information, the use of these techniques would not suggest to a reasonable person in the subject's position that he is being threatened with severe pain or suffering. Accordingly, we conclude that these two procedures do not constitute any of the predicate acts set forth in Section 2340(2).

As with the other techniques discussed so far, cramped confinement is not a threat of imminent death. It may be argued that, focusing in part on the fact that the boxes will be without light, placement in these boxes would constitute a procedure designed to disrupt profoundly the senses. As we explained in our recent opinion, however, to "disrupt profoundly the senses" a technique must produce an extreme effect in the subject. *See* Section 2340A Memorandum at 10-12. We have previously concluded that this requires that the procedure cause substantial interference with the individual's cognitive abilities or fundamentally alter his personality. *See id.* at 11. Moreover, the statute requires that such procedures must be calculated to produce this effect. *See id* at 10; §18 U.S.C. 2340(2)(B).

With respect to the small confinement box, you have informed us that he would spend at most two hours in this box. You have informed us that your purpose in using these boxes is not to interfere with his senses or his personality, but to cause him physical discomfort that will encourage him to disclose critical information. Moreover, your imposition of time limitations on the use of either of the boxes also indicates that the use of these boxes is not designed or calculated to disrupt profoundly the senses or personality. For the larger box, in which he can both stand and sit, he may be placed in this box for up to eighteen hours at a time, while you have informed us that he will never spend more than an hour at time in the smaller box. These time limits further ensure that no profound disruption of the senses or personality, were it even possible, would result. As such, the use of the confinement boxes does not constitute a procedure calculated to disrupt profoundly the senses or personality.

Nor does the use of the boxes threaten Zubaydah with severe physical pain or suffering. While additional time spent in the boxes may be threatened, their use is not accompanied by any express threats of severe physical pain or suffering. Like the stress positions and walling, placement in the boxes is physically uncomfortable but any such discomfort does not rise to the level of severe physical pain or suffering. Accordingly, a reasonable person in the subject's position would not infer from the use of this technique that severe physical pain is the next step in his interrogator's treatment of him. Therefore, we conclude that the use of the confinement boxes does not fall within the statute's required predicate acts.

In addition to using the confinement boxes alone, you also would like to introduce an insect into one of the boxes with Zubaydah. As we understand it, you plan to inform Zubaydah that you are going to place a stinging insect into the box, but you will actually place a harmless insect in the box, such as a caterpillar. If you do so, to ensure that you are outside the predicate act requirement, you must inform him that the insects will not have a sting that would produce death or severe pain. If, however, you were to place the insect in the box without informing him that you are doing so, then, in order to not commit a predicate act, you should not affirmatively lead him to believe that any insect is present which has a sting that could produce severe pain or suffering or even cause his death. ███ ███████████████████████████████████████ so long as you take either of the approaches we have described, the insect's placement in the box would not constitute a threat of severe physical pain or suffering to a reasonable person in his position. An individual placed in a box, even an individual with a fear of insects, would not reasonably feel threatened with severe physical pain or suffering if a caterpillar was placed in the box. Further, you have informed us that you are not aware that Zubaydah has any allergies to insects, and you have not informed us of any other factors that would cause a reasonable person in that same situation to believe that an unknown insect would cause him severe physical pain or death. Thus, we conclude that the placement of the insect in the confinement box with Zubaydah would not constitute a predicate act.

Sleep deprivation also clearly does not involve a threat of imminent death. Although it produces physical discomfort, it cannot be said to constitute a threat of severe physical pain or suffering from the perspective of a reasonable person in Zubaydah's position. Nor could sleep deprivation constitute a procedure calculated to disrupt profoundly the senses, so long as sleep deprivation (as you have informed us is your intent) is used for limited periods, before hallucinations or other profound disruptions of the senses would occur. To be sure, sleep deprivation may reduce the subject's ability to think on his feet. Indeed, you indicate that this is the intended result. His mere reduced ability to evade your questions and resist answering does not, however, rise to the level of disruption required by the statute. As we explained above, a disruption within the meaning of the statute is an extreme one, substantially interfering with an individual's cognitive abilities, for example, inducing hallucinations, or driving him to engage in uncharacteristic self-destructive behavior. *See infra* 13; Section 2340A Memorandum at 11. Therefore, the limited use of sleep deprivation does not constitute one of the required predicate acts.

We find that the use of the waterboard constitutes a threat of imminent death. As you have explained the waterboard procedure to us, it creates in the subject the uncontrollable physiological sensation that the subject is drowning. Although the procedure will be monitored by personnel with medical training and extensive SERE school experience with this procedure who will ensure the subject's mental and physical safety, the subject is not aware of any of these precautions. From the vantage point of any reasonable person undergoing this procedure in such circumstances, he would feel as if he is drowning at [the] very moment of the procedure due to the uncontrollable physiological sense he is experiencing. Thus, this procedure cannot be viewed as too uncertain to satisfy the imminence requirement. Accordingly, it constitutes a threat of imminent death and fulfills the predicate act requirement under the statute.

Although the waterboard constitutes a threat of imminent death, prolonged mental harm must nonetheless result to violate the statutory prohibition on infliction of severe mental pain or suffering. *See* Section 2340A Memorandum at 7. We have previously concluded that prolonged mental harm is mental harm of some lasting duration, e.g., mental harm lasting months or years. *See id.* Prolonged mental harm is not simply the stress experienced in, for example, an interrogation by state police. *See id.* Based on your research into the use of these methods at the SERE school and consultation with others with expertise in the field of psychology and interrogation, you do not anticipate that any prolonged mental harm would result from the use of the waterboard. Indeed, you have advised us that the relief is almost immediate when the cloth is removed from the nose and mouth. In the absence of prolonged mental harm, no severe mental pain or suffering would have been inflicted, and the use of these procedures would not constitute torture within the meaning of the statute.

When these acts are considered as a course of conduct, we are unsure whether these acts may constitute a threat of severe physical pain or suffering. You have indicated to us that you have not determined either the order or the precise timing for implementing these procedures. It is conceivable that these procedures could be used in a course of escalating conduct, moving incrementally and rapidly from least physically intrusive, e.g., facial hold, to the most physical contact, e.g., walling or the waterboard. As we understand it, based on his treatment so far, Zubaydah has come to expect that no physical harm will be done to him. By using these techniques in increasing intensity and in rapid succession, the goal would be to dislodge this expectation. Based on the facts you have provided to us, we cannot say definitively that the entire course of conduct would cause a reasonable person to believe that he is being threatened with severe pain or suffering within the meaning of section 2340. On the other hand, however, under certain circumstances—for example, rapid escalation in the use of these techniques culminating in the waterboard (which we acknowledge constitutes a threat of imminent death) accompanied by verbal or other suggestions that physical violence will follow—might cause a reasonable person to believe that they are faced with such a threat. Without more information, we are uncertain whether the course of conduct would constitute a predicate act under Section 2340(2).

Even if the course of conduct were thought to pose a threat of physical pain or suffering, it would nevertheless—on the facts before us—not constitute a violation of Section 2340A. Not only must the course of conduct be a predicate act, but also those who use the procedure must actually cause prolonged mental harm, Based on the information that you have provided to us, indicating that no evidence exists that this course of conduct produces any prolonged mental harm, we conclude that a course of conduct using these procedures and culminating in the waterboard would not violate Section 2340A.

Specific Intent. To violate the statute, an individual must have the specific intent to inflict severe pain or suffering. Because specific intent is an element of the offense, the absence of specific intent negates the charge of torture. As we previously opined, to have the required specific intent, an individual must expressly intend to cause such severe pain or suffering. *See* Section 2340A Memorandum at 3 *citing Carter v. United States*, 530 U.S. 255, 267 (2000). We have further found that if a defendant acts with the good faith belief that his actions will not cause such suffering, he has not acted with specific intent. *See id.* at 4 *citing South Atl. Lmtd. Ptrshp. of Tenn. v. Reise*, 218 F.3d 518, 531 (4th Cir. 2002). A defendant acts in good faith when he has an honest belief that his actions will not result in severe pain or suffering. *See id. citing Cheek v. United States*, 498 U.S. 192, 202 (1991). Although an honest belief need not be reasonable, such a belief is easier to establish where there is a reasonable basis for it. *See id.* at 5. Good faith may be established by, among other things, the reliance on the advice of experts. *See id.* at 8.

Based on the information you have provided us, we believe that those carrying out these procedures would not have the specific intent to inflict severe physical pain or suffering. The objective of these techniques is not to cause severe physical pain. First, the constant presence of personnel with medical training who have the authority to stop the interrogation should it appear it is medically necessary indicates that it is not your intent to cause severe physical pain. The personnel on site have extensive experience with these specific techniques as they are used in SERE school training. Second, you have informed us that you are taking steps to ensure that Zubaydah's injury is not worsened or his recovery impeded by the use of these techniques.

Third, as you have described them to us, the proposed techniques involving physical contact between the interrogator and Zubaydah actually contain precautions to prevent any serious physical harm to Zubaydah. In "walling," a rolled hood or towel will be used to prevent whiplash and he will be permitted to rebound from the flexible wall to reduce the likelihood of injury. Similarly, in the "facial hold," the fingertips will be kept well away from the his [sic] eyes to ensure that there is no injury to them. The purpose of that facial hold is not injure him but to hold the head immobile. Additionally, while the stress positions and wall standing will undoubtedly result in physical discomfort by tiring the muscles, it is obvious that these positions are not intended to produce the kind of extreme pain required by the statute.

Furthermore, no specific intent to cause severe mental pain or suffering appears to be present. As we explained in our recent opinion, an individual must have the specific intent to cause prolonged mental harm in order to have the specific intent to inflict severe mental pain or suffering. *See* Section 2340A Memorandum at 8. Prolonged mental harm is substantial mental harm of a sustained duration, e.g., harm lasting months or even years after the acts were inflicted upon the prisoner. As we indicated above, a good faith belief can negate this element. Accordingly, if an individual conducting the interrogation has a good faith belief that the procedures he will apply, separately or together, would not result in prolonged mental harm, that individual lacks the requisite specific intent. This conclusion concerning specific intent is further bolstered by the due diligence that has been conducted concerning the effects of these interrogation procedures.

The mental health experts that you have consulted have indicated that the psychological impact of a course of conduct must be assessed with reference to the subject's psychological history and mental health status.

The healthier the individual, the less likely that the use of any one procedure or set of procedures as a course of conduct will result in prolonged
mental harm. A comprehensive psychological profile of Zubaydah has been
created. In creating this profile, your personnel drew on direct interviews,
Zubaydah's diaries, observation of Zubaydah since his capture, and information from other sources such as other intelligence and press reports.

As we indicated above, you have informed us that your proposed
interrogation methods have been used and continue to be used in SERE
training. It is our understanding that these techniques are not used one by
one in isolation, but as a full course of conduct to resemble a real interrogation. Thus, the information derived from SERE training bears both
upon the impact of the use of the individual techniques and upon their use
as a course of conduct. You have found that the use of these methods together or separately, including the use of the waterboard, has not resulted
in any negative long-term mental health consequences. The continued
use of these methods without mental health consequences to the trainees indicates that it is highly improbable that such consequences would
result here. Because you have conducted the due diligence to determine
that these procedures, either alone or in combination, do not produce prolonged mental harm, we believe that you do not meet the specific intent
requirement necessary to violate Section 2340A.

You have also informed us that you have reviewed the relevant literature on the subject, and consulted with outside psychologists. Your review of the literature uncovered no empirical data on the use of these
procedures, with the exception of sleep deprivation for which no long-
term health consequences resulted. The outside psychologists with whom
you consulted indicated [that they] were unaware of any cases where long-
term problems have occurred as a result of these techniques.

As described above, it appears you have conducted an extensive inquiry to ascertain what impact, if any, these procedures individually and as a course of conduct would have on Zubaydah. You have consulted with interrogation experts, including those with substantial SERE school experience, consulted with outside psychologists, completed a psychological assessment and reviewed the relevant literature on this topic. Based on this inquiry, you believe that the use of the procedures, including the waterboard, and as a course of conduct would not result in prolonged mental harm. Reliance on this information about Zubaydah and about the effect of the use of these techniques more generally demonstrates the presence of a good faith belief that no prolonged mental harm will result from using these methods in the interrogation of Zubaydah. Moreover, we think that this represents not only an honest belief but also a reasonable belief based on the information that you have supplied to us. Thus, we believe that the specific intent to inflict prolonged mental [harm] is not present, and consequently, there is no specific intent to inflict severe mental pain or suffering. Accordingly, we conclude that on the facts in this case the use of these methods separately or [as] a course of conduct would not violate Section 2340A.

Based on the foregoing, and based on the facts that you have provided, we conclude that the interrogation procedures that you propose would not violate Section 2340A. We wish to emphasize that this is our best reading of the law; however, you should be aware that there are no cases construing this statute, just as there have been no prosecutions brought under it.

Please let us know if we can be of further assistance.

Jay S. Bybee
Assistant Attorney General

U.S. Department of Justice

Office of Legal Counsel

Office of the Assistant Attorney General   *Washington, D.C. 20530*

December 30, 2004

MEMORANDUM FOR JAMES B. COMEY
DEPUTY ATTORNEY GENERAL

Re: Legal Standards Applicable Under 18 U.S.C. §§ 2340-2340A

Torture is abhorrent both to American law and values and to international norms. This universal repudiation of torture is reflected in our criminal law, for example, 18 U.S.C. §§ 2340-2340A; international agreements, exemplified by the United Nations Convention Against Torture (the "CAT")[1]; customary international law[2]; centuries of Anglo-American law[3]; and the longstanding policy of the United States, repeatedly and recently reaffirmed by the President.[4]

---

[1] Convention Against Torture and Other Cruel, Inhuman or Degrading Treatment or Punishment, Dec. 10, 1984, S. Treaty Doc. No. 100-20, 1465 U.N.T.S. 85. *See also, e.g.*, International Covenant on Civil and Political Rights, Dec. 16, 1966, 999 U.N.T.S. 171.

[2] It has been suggested that the prohibition against torture has achieved the status of *jus cogens* (i.e., a peremptory norm) under international law. *See, e.g., Siderman de Blake v. Republic of Argentina*, 965 F.2d 699, 714 (9th Cir. 1992); *Regina v. Bow Street Metro. Stipendiary Magistrate Ex Parte Pinochet Ugarte (No. 3)*, [2000] 1 AC 147, 198; *see also* Restatement (Third) of Foreign Relations Law of the United States § 702 reporters' note 5.

[3] *See generally* John H. Langbein, *Torture and the Law of Proof: Europe and England in the Ancien Régime* (1977).

[4] *See, e.g.*, Statement on United Nations International Day in Support of Victims of Torture, 40 Weekly Comp. Pres. Doc. 1167 (July 5, 2004) ("Freedom from torture is an inalienable human right . . . ."); Statement on United Nations International Day in Support of Victims of Torture, 39 Weekly Comp. Pres. Doc. 824 (June 30, 2003) ("Torture anywhere is an affront to human dignity everywhere."); *see also Letter of Transmittal from President Ronald Reagan to the*

This Office interpreted the federal criminal prohibition against torture—codified at 18 U.S.C. §§ 2340-2340A—in *Standards of Conduct for Interrogation under 18 U.S.C. §§ 2340-2340A* (Aug. 1, 2002) ("August 2002 Memorandum"). The August 2002 Memorandum also addressed a number of issues beyond interpretation of those statutory provisions, including the President's Commander-in-Chief power, and various defenses that might be asserted to avoid potential liability under sections 2340-2340A. *See id.* at 31-46.

Questions have since been raised, both by this Office and by others, about the appropriateness and relevance of the non-statutory discussion in the August 2002 Memorandum, and also about various aspects of the statutory analysis, in particular the statement that "severe" pain under the statute was limited to pain "equivalent in intensity to the pain accompanying serious physical injury, such as organ failure, impairment of bodily function, or even death." *Id.* at 1.[5] We decided to withdraw the August 2002 Memorandum, a decision you announced in June 2004. At that time, you directed this Office to prepare a replacement memorandum. Because of the importance of—and public interest in—these issues, you asked that this memorandum be prepared in a form that could be released to the public so that interested parties could understand our analysis of the statute.

This memorandum supersedes the August 2002 Memorandum in its entirety.[6] Because the discussion in that memorandum concerning the

---

Senate (May 20, 1988), *in Message from the President of the United States Transmitting the Convention Against Torture and Other Cruel, Inhuman or Degrading Treatment or Punishment*, S. Treaty Doc. No. 100-20, at iii (1988) ("Ratification of the Convention by the United States will clearly express United States opposition to torture, an abhorrent practice unfortunately still prevalent in the world today.").

[5] *See, e.g.*, Anthony Lewis, *Making Torture Legal*, N.Y. Rev. of Books, July 15, 2004; R. Jeffrey Smith, *Slim Legal Grounds for Torture Memos*, Wash. Post, July 4, 2004, at A12; Kathleen Clark & Julie Mertus, *Torturing the Law; the Justice Department's Legal Contortions on Interrogation*, Wash. Post, June 20, 2004, at B3; Derek Jinks & David Sloss, *Is the President Bound by the Geneva Conventions?*, 90 Cornell L. Rev. 97 (2004).

[6] This memorandum necessarily discusses the prohibition against torture in sections 2340-2340A in somewhat abstract and general terms. In applying this criminal prohibition to particular circumstances, great care must be taken to avoid approving as lawful any conduct that might constitute torture. In addition, this memorandum does not address the many other sources of law that may apply, depending on the circumstances, to the detention or interrogation of detainees (for example, the Geneva Conventions; the Uniform Code of Military

President's Commander-in-Chief power and the potential defenses to liability was—and remains—unnecessary, it has been eliminated from the analysis that follows. Consideration of the bounds of any such authority would be inconsistent with the President's unequivocal directive that United States personnel not engage in torture.[7]

We have also modified in some important respects our analysis of the legal standards applicable under 18 U.S.C. §§ 2340-2340A. For example, we disagree with statements in the August 2002 Memorandum limiting "severe" pain under the statute to "excruciating and agonizing" pain, *id.* at 19, or to pain "equivalent in intensity to the pain accompanying serious physical injury, such as organ failure, impairment of bodily function, or even death," *id.* at 1. There are additional areas where we disagree with or modify the analysis in the August 2002 Memorandum, as identified in the discussion below.[8]

The Criminal Division of the Department of Justice has reviewed this memorandum and concurs in the analysis set forth below.

I.

Section 2340A provides that "[w]hoever outside the United States commits or attempts to commit torture shall be fined under this title or imprisoned not more than 20 years, or both, and if death results to any person from conduct prohibited by this subsection, shall be punished by death or imprisoned for any term of years or for life."[9] Section 2340(1) defines

---

Justice, 10 U.S.C. § 801 et seq.; the Military Extraterritorial Jurisdiction Act, 18 U.S.C. §§ 3261-3267; and the War Crimes Act, 18 U.S.C. § 2441, among others). Any analysis of particular facts must, of course, ensure that the United States complies with all applicable legal obligations.

[7] *See, e.g.,* Statement on United Nations International Day in Support of Victims of Torture, 40 Weekly Comp. Pres. Doc. 1167-68 (July 5, 2004) ("America stands against and will not tolerate torture. We will investigate and prosecute all acts of torture . . . in all territory under our jurisdiction. . . . Torture is wrong no matter where it occurs, and the United States will continue to lead the fight to eliminate it everywhere.").

[8] While we have identified various disagreements with the August 2002 Memorandum, we have reviewed this Office's prior opinions addressing issues involving treatment of detainees and do not believe that any of their conclusions would be different under the standards set forth in this memorandum.

[9] Section 2340A provides in full:

"torture" as "an act committed by a person acting under the color of law specifically intended to inflict severe physical or mental pain or suffering (other than pain or suffering incidental to lawful sanctions) upon another person within his custody or physical control." [10]

     (a) Offense.—Whoever outside the United States commits or attempts to commit torture shall be fined under this title or imprisoned not more than 20 years, or both, and if death results to any person from conduct prohibited by this subsection, shall be punished by death or imprisoned for any term of years or for life.

     (b) Jurisdiction.—There is jurisdiction over the activity prohibited in subsection (a) if—
         (1) the alleged offender is a national of the United States; or
         (2) the alleged offender is present in the United States, irrespective of the nationality of the victim or alleged offender.

     (c) Conspiracy.—A person who conspires to commit an offense under this section shall be subject to the same penalties (other than the penalty of death) as the penalties prescribed for the offense, the commission of which was the object of the conspiracy.

18 U.S.C. § 2340A (2000).

[10] Section 2340 provides in full:

     As used in this chapter—

     (1) "torture" means an act committed by a person acting under color of law specifically intended to inflict severe physical or mental pain or suffering (other than pain or suffering incidental to lawful sanctions) upon another person within his custody or physical control;

     (2) "severe mental pain or suffering" means the prolonged mental harm caused by or resulting from—
         (A) the intentional infliction or threatened infliction of severe physical pain or suffering;
         (B) the administration or application, or threatened administration or application, of mind-altering substances or other procedures calculated to disrupt profoundly the senses or the personality;
         (C) the threat of imminent death; or
         (D) the threat that another person will imminently be subjected to death, severe physical pain or suffering, or the administration or application of mind-altering substances or other procedures calculated to disrupt profoundly the senses or personality; and

     (3) "United States" means the several States of the United

In interpreting these provisions, we note that Congress may have adopted a statutory definition of "torture" that differs from certain colloquial uses of the term. *Cf. Cadet v. Bulger*, 377 F.3d 1173, 1194 (11th Cir. 2004) ("[I]n other contexts and under other definitions [the conditions] might be described as torturous. The fact remains, however, that the only relevant definition of 'torture' is the definition contained in [the] CAT. . . ."). We must, of course, give effect to the statute as enacted by Congress.[11]

Congress enacted sections 2340-2340A to carry out the United States' obligations under the CAT. *See* H.R. Conf. Rep. No. 103-482, at 229 (1994). The CAT, among other things, obligates state parties to take effective measures to prevent acts of torture in any territory under their jurisdiction, and requires the United States, as a state party, to ensure that acts of torture, along with attempts and complicity to commit such acts, are crimes under U.S. law. *See* CAT arts. 2, 4-5. Sections 2340-2340A satisfy that requirement with respect to acts committed outside the United States.[12] Conduct constituting "torture" occurring within the United States was—and remains—prohibited by various other federal and state criminal statutes that we do not discuss here.

The CAT defines "torture" so as to require the intentional infliction of "severe pain or suffering, whether physical or mental." Article 1(1) of the CAT provides:

> For the purposes of this Convention, the term "torture" means any act by which severe pain or suffering, whether physical or mental, is intentionally inflicted on a person for such purposes as obtaining from him or a third person information or

---

States, the District of Columbia, and the commonwealths, territories, and possessions of the United States.

18 U.S.C. § 2340 (as amended by Pub. L. No. 108-375, 118 Stat. 1811 (2004)).

[11] Our task is only to offer guidance on the meaning of the statute, not to comment on policy. It is of course open to policymakers to determine that conduct that might not be prohibited by the statute is nevertheless contrary to the interests or policy of the United States.

[12] Congress limited the territorial reach of the federal torture statute, providing that the prohibition applies only to conduct occurring "outside the United States," 18 U.S.C. § 2340A(a), which is currently defined in the statute to mean outside "the several States of the United States, the District of Columbia, and the commonwealths, territories, and possessions of the United States." *Id.* § 2340(3).

a confession, punishing him for an act he or a third person has
committed or is suspected of having committed, or intimidat-
ing or coercing him or a third person, or for any reason based
on discrimination of any kind, when such pain or suffering
is inflicted by or at the instigation of or with the consent or
acquiescence of a public official or other person acting in an
official capacity. It does not include pain or suffering arising
only from, inherent in or incidental to lawful sanctions.

The Senate attached the following understanding to its resolution of
advice and consent to ratification of the CAT:

The United States understands that, in order to constitute
torture, an act must be specifically intended to inflict severe
physical or mental pain or suffering and that mental pain or
suffering refers to prolonged mental harm caused by or resulting from (1) the intentional infliction or threatened infliction
of severe physical pain or suffering; (2) the administration
or application, or threatened administration or application,
of mind altering substances or other procedures calculated
to disrupt profoundly the senses or the personality; (3) the
threat of imminent death; or (4) the threat that another person
will imminently be subjected to death, severe physical pain
or suffering, or the administration or application of mind altering substances or other procedures calculated to disrupt
profoundly the senses or personality.

S. Exec. Rep. No. 101-30, at 36 (1990). This understanding was deposited with the U.S. instrument of ratification, *see* 1830 U.N.T.S. 320 (Oct.
21, 1994), and thus defines the scope of the United States' obligations
under the treaty. *See Relevance of Senate Ratification History to Treaty
Interpretation*, 11 Op. O.L.C. 28, 32-33 (1987). The criminal prohibition
against torture that Congress codified in 18 U.S.C. §§ 2340-2340A generally tracks the prohibition in the CAT, subject to the U.S. understanding.

II.

Under the language adopted by Congress in sections 2340-2340A,
to constitute "torture," the conduct in question must have been "specifically intended to inflict severe physical or mental pain or suffering." In the
discussion that follows, we will separately consider each of the principal

components of this key phrase: (1) the meaning of "severe"; (2) the meaning of "severe physical pain or suffering"; (3) the meaning of "severe mental pain or suffering"; and (4) the meaning of "specifically intended."

(1) The meaning of "severe."

Because the statute does not define "severe," "we construe [the] term in accordance with its ordinary or natural meaning." *FDIC v. Meyer*, 510 U.S. 471, 476 (1994). The common understanding of the term "torture" and the context in which the statute was enacted also inform our analysis.

Dictionaries define "severe" (often conjoined with "pain") to mean "extremely violent or intense: severe pain." *American Heritage Dictionary of the English Language* 1653 (3d ed. 1992); *see also* XV *Oxford English Dictionary* 101 (2d ed. 1989) ("Of pain, suffering, loss, or the like: Grievous, extreme" and "Of circumstances . . . : Hard to sustain or endure").[13]

The statute, moreover, was intended to implement the United States' obligations under the CAT, which, as quoted above, defines as "torture" acts that inflict "severe pain or suffering" on a person. CAT art. 1(1). As the Senate Foreign Relations Committee explained in its report recommending that the Senate consent to ratification of the CAT:

---

[13] Common dictionary definitions of "torture" further support the statutory concept that the pain or suffering must be severe. *See Black's Law Dictionary* 1528 (8th ed. 2004) (defining "torture" as "[t]he infliction of *intense pain* to the body or mind to punish, to extract a confession or information, or to obtain sadistic pleasure") (emphasis added); *Webster's Third New International Dictionary of the English Language Unabridged* 2414 (2002) (defining "torture" as "the infliction of *intense pain* (as from burning, crushing, wounding) to punish or coerce someone") (emphasis added); *Oxford American Dictionary and Language Guide* 1064 (1999) (defining "torture" as "the infliction of *severe bodily pain*, esp. as a punishment or a means of persuasion") (emphasis added).

This interpretation is also consistent with the history of torture. *See generally* the descriptions in Lord Hope's lecture, *Torture*, University of Essex/ Clifford Chance Lecture 7-8 (Jan. 28, 2004), and in Professor Langbein's book, *Torture and the Law of Proof: Europe and England in the Ancien Régime*. We emphatically are not saying that only such historical techniques—or similar ones—can constitute "torture" under sections 2340-2340A. But the historical understanding of "torture" is relevant to interpreting Congress's intent. *Cf. Morissette v. United States*, 342 U.S. 246, 263 (1952).

> The [CAT] seeks to define "torture" in a relatively limited fash-
> ion, corresponding to the common understanding of torture
> as an extreme practice which is universally condemned. . . .
>
> . . . .
>
> . . . The term "torture," in United States and interna-
> tional usage, is usually reserved for extreme, deliberate and
> unusually cruel practices, for example, sustained systematic
> beating, application of electric currents to sensitive parts of
> the body, and tying up or hanging in positions that cause ex-
> treme pain.

S. Exec. Rep. No. 101-30 at 13-14. *See also* David P. Stewart, *The Torture
Convention and the Reception of International Criminal Law Within the
United States*, 15 Nova L. Rev. 449, 455 (1991) ("By stressing the extreme
nature of torture, . . . [the] definition [of torture in the CAT] describes a
relatively limited set of circumstances likely to be illegal under most, if
not all, domestic legal systems.").

Further, the CAT distinguishes between torture and "other acts
of cruel, inhuman or degrading treatment or punishment which do not
amount to torture as defined in article 1." CAT art. 16. The CAT thus treats
torture as an "extreme form" of cruel, inhuman, or degrading treatment.
See S. Exec. Rep. No. 101-30 at 6, 13; *see also* J. Herman Burgers & Hans
Danelius, *The United Nations Convention Against Torture: A Handbook
on the Convention Against Torture and Other Cruel, Inhuman or Degrading Treatment or Punishment* 80 (1988) ("*CAT Handbook*") (noting that
Article 16 implies "that torture is the *gravest form* of [cruel, inhuman,
or degrading] treatment [or] punishment") (emphasis added); Malcolm D.
Evans, *Getting to Grips with Torture*, 51 Int'l & Comp. L.Q. 365, 369
(2002) (The CAT "formalises a distinction between torture on the one
hand and inhuman and degrading treatment on the other by attributing
different legal consequences to them.").[14] The Senate Foreign Relations

---

[14] This approach—distinguishing torture from lesser forms of cruel,
inhuman, or degrading treatment—is consistent with other international law
sources. The CAT's predecessor, the U.N. Torture Declaration, defined torture as
"an *aggravated* and deliberate form of cruel, inhuman or degrading treatment or
punishment." Declaration on the Protection of All Persons from Being Subjected
to Torture and Other Cruel, Inhuman or Degrading Treatment or Punishment,
U.N. Res. 3452, art. 1(2) (Dec. 9, 1975) (emphasis added); *see also* S. Treaty Doc.
No. 100-20 at 2 (The U.N. Torture Declaration was "a point of departure for the
drafting of the [CAT]."). Other treaties also distinguish torture from lesser forms
of cruel, inhuman, or degrading treatment. *See, e.g.,* European Convention for

Committee emphasized this point in its report recommending that the Senate consent to ratification of the CAT. *See* S. Exec. Rep, No. 101-30 at 13 ("'Torture' is thus to be distinguished from lesser forms of cruel, inhuman, or degrading treatment or punishment, which are to be deplored and prevented, but are not so universally and categorically condemned as to warrant the severe legal consequences that the Convention provides in the case of torture. . . . The requirement that torture be an extreme form of cruel and inhuman treatment is expressed in Article 16, which refers to 'other acts of cruel, inhuman or degrading treatment or punishment *which do not amount to torture* . . . .' "). *See also Cadet*, 377 F.3d at 1194 ("The definition in CAT draws a critical distinction between 'torture' and 'other acts of cruel, inhuman, or degrading punishment or treatment.' ").

---

the Protection of Human Rights and Fundamental Freedoms, art. 3, 213 U.N.T.S. 221 (Nov. 4, 1950) ("European Convention") ("No one shall be subjected to torture or to inhuman or degrading treatment or punishment."); Evans, *Getting to Grips with Torture*, 51 Int'l & Comp. L.Q. at 370 ("[T]he ECHR organs have adopted . . . a 'vertical' approach . . . , which is seen as comprising three separate elements, each representing a progression of seriousness, in which one moves progressively from forms of ill-treatment which are 'degrading' to those which are 'inhuman' and then to 'torture'. The distinctions between them is [*sic*] based on the severity of suffering involved, with 'torture' at the apex."); Debra Long, Association for the Prevention of Torture, *Guide to Jurisprudence on Torture and Ill-Treatment: Article 3 of the European Convention for the Protection of Human Rights* 13 (2002) (The approach of distinguishing between "torture," "in-human" acts, and "degrading" acts has "remained the standard approach taken by the European judicial bodies. Within this approach torture has been singled out as carrying a special stigma, which distinguishes it from other forms of ill-treatment."). *See also CAT Handbook* at 115-17 (discussing the European Court of Human Rights ("ECHR") decision in *Ireland v. United Kingdom*, 25 Eur. Ct. H.R. (ser. A) (1978) (concluding that the combined use of wall-standing, hood-ing, subjection to noise, deprivation of sleep, and deprivation of food and drink constituted inhuman or degrading treatment but not torture under the European Convention)). Cases decided by the ECHR subsequent to *Ireland* have continued to view torture as an aggravated form of inhuman treatment. *See, e.g., Aktas v. Turkey*, No. 24351/94 ¶ 313 (E.C.H.R. 2003); *Akkoc v. Turkey*, Nos. 22947/93 & 22948/93 ¶ 115 (E.C.H.R. 2000); *Kaya v. Turkey*, No. 22535/93 ¶ 117 (E.C.H.R. 2000).

The International Criminal Tribunal for the Former Yugoslavia ("ICTY") likewise considers "torture" as a category of conduct more severe than "inhuman treatment." *See, e.g., Prosecutor v. Delalic*, IT-96-21, Trial Chamber Judgment ¶ 542 (ICTY Nov. 16, 1998) ("[I]nhuman treatment is treatment which deliberately causes serious mental and physical suffering that falls short of the severe mental and physical suffering required for the offence of torture.").

Representations made to the Senate by Executive Branch officials when the Senate was considering the CAT are also relevant in interpreting the CAT's torture prohibition—which sections 2340-2340A implement. Mark Richard, a Deputy Assistant Attorney General in the Criminal Division, testified that "[t]orture is understood to be that barbaric cruelty which lies at the top of the pyramid of human rights misconduct." *Convention Against Torture: Hearing Before the Senate Comm. on Foreign Relations*, 101st Cong. 16 (1990) (*"CAT Hearing"*) (prepared statement). The Senate Foreign Relations Committee also understood torture to be limited in just this way. *See* S. Exec. Rep. No. 101-30 at 6 (noting that "[f]or an act to be 'torture,' it must be an extreme form of cruel and inhuman treatment, causing severe pain and suffering, and be intended to cause severe pain and suffering"). Both the Executive Branch and the Senate acknowledged the efforts of the United States during the negotiating process to strengthen the effectiveness of the treaty and to gain wide adherence thereto by focusing the Convention "on torture rather than on other relatively less abhorrent practices." *Letter of Submittal from George P. Shultz, Secretary of State, to President Ronald Reagan* (May 10, 1988), *in* S. Treaty Doc. No. 100-20 at v; *see also* S. Exec. Rep. No. 101-30 at 2-3 ("The United States" helped to focus the Convention "on torture rather than other less abhorrent practices."). Such statements are probative of a treaty's meaning. *See* 11 Op. O.L.C. at 35-36.

Although Congress defined "torture" under sections 2340-2340A to require conduct specifically intended to cause "severe" pain or suffering, we do not believe Congress intended to reach only conduct involving "excruciating and agonizing" pain or suffering. Although there is some support for this formulation in the ratification history of the CAT,[15] a proposed express understanding to that effect[16] was "criticized for setting too high a threshold of pain," S. Exec. Rep. No. 101-30 at 9, and was not adopted. We are not aware of any evidence suggesting that the standard was raised in the statute and we do not believe that it was.[17]

---

[15] Deputy Assistant Attorney General Mark Richard testified: "[T]he essence of torture" is treatment that inflicts "excruciating and agonizing physical pain." *CAT Hearing* at 16 (prepared statement).

[16] *See* S. Treaty Doc. No. 100-20 at 4-5 ("The United States understands that, in order to constitute torture, an act must be a deliberate and calculated act of an extremely cruel and inhuman nature, specifically intended to inflict excruciating and agonizing physical or mental pain or suffering.").

[17] Thus, we do not agree with the statement in the August 2002 Memo-

Drawing distinctions among gradations of pain (for example, severe, mild, moderate, substantial, extreme, intense, excruciating, or agonizing) is obviously not an easy task, especially given the lack of any precise, objective scientific criteria for measuring pain.[18] We are, however,

---

randum that "[t]he Reagan administration's understanding that the pain be 'excruciating and agonizing' is in substance not different from the Bush administration's proposal that the pain must be severe." August 2002 Memorandum at 19. Although the terms are concededly imprecise, and whatever the intent of the Reagan Administration's understanding, we believe that in common usage "excruciating and agonizing" pain is understood to be more intense than "severe" pain.

The August 2002 Memorandum also looked to the use of "severe pain" in certain other statutes, and concluded that to satisfy the definition in section 2340, pain "must be equivalent in intensity to the pain accompanying serious physical injury, such as organ failure, impairment of bodily function, or even death." *Id.* at 1; *see also id.* at 5-6, 13, 46. We do not agree with those statements. Those other statutes define an "emergency medical condition," for purposes of providing health benefits, as "a condition manifesting itself by acute symptoms of sufficient severity (including severe pain)" such that one could reasonably expect that the absence of immediate medical care might result in death, organ failure or impairment of bodily function. *See, e.g.,* 8 U.S.C. § 1369 (2000); 42 U.S.C. § 1395w-22(d)(3)(B) (2000); *id.* § 1395dd(e) (2000). They do not define "severe pain" even in that very different context (rather, they use it as an indication of an "emergency medical condition"), and they do not state that death, organ failure, or impairment of bodily function cause "severe pain," but rather that "severe pain" may indicate a condition that, if untreated, could cause one of those results. We do not believe that they provide a proper guide for interpreting "severe pain" in the very different context of the prohibition against torture in sections 2340-2340A. *Cf. United States v. Cleveland Indians Baseball Co.,* 532 U.S. 200, 213 (2001) (phrase "wages paid" has different meaning in different parts of Title 26); *Robinson v. Shell Oil Co.,* 519 U.S. 337, 343-44 (1997) (term "employee" has different meanings in different parts of Title VII).

[18] Despite extensive efforts to develop objective criteria for measuring pain, there is no clear, objective, consistent measurement. As one publication explains:

> Pain is a complex, subjective, perceptual phenomenon with a number of dimensions—intensity, quality, time course, impact, and personal meaning—that are uniquely experienced by each individual and, thus, can only be assessed indirectly. *Pain is a subjective experience and there is no way to objectively quantify it.* Consequently, assessment of a patient's pain depends on the patient's overt communications, both verbal and behavioral. Given pain's complexity, one must assess not only its somatic (sensory) component but also patients' moods, attitudes, coping efforts, resources, responses of family members, and the impact of pain on their lives.

aided in this task by judicial interpretations of the Torture Victims Protection Act ("TVPA"), 28 U.S.C. § 1350 note (2000). The TVPA, also enacted to implement the CAT, provides a civil remedy to victims of torture. The TVPA defines "torture" to include:

> any act, directed against an individual in the offender's custody or physical control, by which *severe pain or suffering* (other than pain or suffering arising only from or inherent in, or incidental to, lawful sanctions), *whether physical or mental*, is intentionally inflicted on that individual for such purposes as obtaining from that individual or a third person information or a confession, punishing that individual for an act that individual or a third person has committed or is suspected of having committed, intimidating or coercing that individual or a third person, or for any reason based on discrimination of any kind . . . .

28 U.S.C. § 1350 note, § 3(b)(l) (emphases added). The emphasized language is similar to section 2340's "severe physical or mental pain or suffering."[19] As the Court of Appeals for the District of Columbia Circuit has explained:

> The severity requirement is crucial to ensuring that the conduct proscribed by the [CAT] and the TVPA is sufficiently extreme and outrageous to warrant the universal condemnation that the term "torture" both connotes and invokes. The drafters of the [CAT], as well as the Reagan Administration that signed it, the Bush Administration that submitted it to Congress, and the Senate that ultimately ratified it, therefore all sought to ensure that "only acts of a certain gravity shall be considered to constitute torture."
>   The critical issue is the degree of pain and suffering that the alleged torturer intended to, and actually did, inflict

---

Dennis C. Turk, *Assess the Person, Not Just the Pain*, Pain: Clinical Updates, Sept. 1993 (emphasis added). This lack of clarity further complicates the effort to define "severe" pain or suffering.

[19] Section 3(b)(2) of the TVPA defines "mental pain or suffering" similarly to the way that section 2340(2) defines "severe mental pain or suffering."

upon the victim. The more intense, lasting, or heinous the agony, the more likely it is to be torture.

Price v. Socialist People's Libyan Arab Jamahiriya, 294 F.3d 82, 92-93 (D.C. Cir. 2002) (citations omitted). That court concluded that a complaint that alleged beatings at the hands of police but that did not provide details concerning "the severity of plaintiffs' alleged beatings, including their frequency, duration, the parts of the body at which they were aimed, and the weapons used to carry them out," did not suffice "to ensure that [it] satisf[ied] the TVPA's rigorous definition of torture." *Id.* at 93.

In *Simpson v. Socialist People's Libyan Arab Jamahiriya*, 326 F.3d 230 (D.C. Cir. 2003), the D.C. Circuit again considered the types of acts that constitute torture under the TVPA definition. The plaintiff alleged, among other things, that Libyan authorities had held her incommunicado and threatened to kill her if she tried to leave. *See id.* at 232, 234. The court acknowledged that "these alleged acts certainly reflect a bent toward cruelty on the part of their perpetrators," but, reversing the district court, went on to hold that "they are not in themselves so unusually cruel or sufficiently extreme and outrageous as to constitute torture within the meaning of the [TVPA]." *Id.* at 234. Cases in which courts have found torture suggest the nature of the extreme conduct that falls within the statutory definition. *See, e.g., Hilao v. Estate of Marcos*, 103 F.3d 789, 790-91, 795 (9th Cir. 1996) (concluding that a course of conduct that included, among other things, severe beatings of plaintiff, repeated threats of death and electric shock, sleep deprivation, extended shackling to a cot (at times with a towel over his nose and mouth and water poured down his nostrils), seven months of confinement in a "suffocatingly hot" and cramped cell, and eight years of solitary or near-solitary confinement, constituted torture); *Mehinovic v. Vuckovic*, 198 F. Supp. 2d 1322, 1332-40, 1345-46 (N.D. Ga. 2002) (concluding that a course of conduct that included, among other things, severe beatings to the genitals, head, and other parts of the body with metal pipes, brass knuckles, batons, a baseball bat, and various other items; removal of teeth with pliers; kicking in the face and ribs; breaking of bones and ribs and dislocation of fingers; cutting a figure into the victim's forehead; hanging the victim and beating him; extreme limitations of food and water; and subjection to games of "Russian roulette," constituted torture); *Daliberti v. Republic of Iraq*, 146 F. Supp. 2d 19, 22-23 (D.D.C. 2001) (entering default judgment against Iraq where plaintiffs alleged, among other things, threats of "physical torture, such as cutting off . . . fingers, pulling out . . . fingernails," and electric shocks to the testicles); *Cicippio v. Islamic Republic of Iran*, 18 F. Supp. 2d 62, 64-66

(D.D.C. 1998) (concluding that a course of conduct that included frequent beatings, pistol whipping, threats of imminent death, electric shocks, and attempts to force confessions by playing Russian roulette and pulling the trigger at each denial, constituted torture).

(2) The meaning of "severe physical pain or suffering."

The statute provides a specific definition of "severe mental pain or suffering," see 18 U.S.C. § 2340(2), but does not define the term "severe physical pain or suffering." Although we think the meaning of "severe physical pain" is relatively straightforward, the question remains whether Congress intended to prohibit a category of "severe physical suffering" distinct from "severe physical pain." We conclude that under some circumstances "severe physical suffering" may constitute torture even if it does not involve "severe physical pain." Accordingly, to the extent that the August 2002 Memorandum suggested that "severe physical suffering" under the statute could in no circumstances be distinct from "severe physical pain," id. at 6 n.3, we do not agree.

We begin with the statutory language. The inclusion of the words "or suffering" in the phrase "severe physical pain or suffering" suggests that the statutory category of physical torture is not limited to "severe physical pain." This is especially so in light of the general principle against interpreting a statute in such a manner as to render words surplusage. See, e.g., Duncan v. Walker, 533 U.S. 167, 174 (2001).

Exactly what is included in the concept of "severe physical suffering," however, is difficult to ascertain. We interpret the phrase in a statutory context where Congress expressly distinguished "physical pain or suffering" from "mental pain or suffering." Consequently, a separate category of "physical suffering" must include something other than any type of "mental pain or suffering."[20] Moreover, given that Congress precisely defined "mental pain or suffering" in the statute, it is unlikely to have intended to undermine that careful definition by including a broad range of mental sensations in a "physical suffering" component of "physical pain

---

[20] Common dictionary definitions of "physical" confirm that "physical suffering" does not include mental sensations. See, e.g., American Heritage Dictionary of the English Language at 1366 ("Of or relating to the body as distinguished from the mind or spirit"); Oxford American Dictionary and Language Guide at 748 ("of or concerning the body (physical exercise; physical education)").

or suffering."[21] Consequently, "physical suffering" must be limited to adverse "physical" rather than adverse "mental" sensations.

The text of the statute and the CAT, and their history, provide little concrete guidance as to what Congress intended separately to include as "severe physical suffering." Indeed, the record consistently refers to "severe physical pain or suffering" (or, more often in the ratification record, "severe physical pain *and* suffering"), apparently without ever disaggregating the concepts of "severe physical pain" and "severe physical suffering" or discussing them as separate categories with separate content. Although there is virtually no legislative history for the statute, throughout the ratification of the CAT—which also uses the disjunctive "pain or suffering" and which the statutory prohibition implements—the references were generally to "pain *and* suffering," with no indication of any difference in meaning. The *Summary and Analysis of the Convention Against Torture and Other Cruel, Inhuman or Degrading Treatment or Punishment*, which appears in S. Treaty Doc. No. 100-20 at 3, for example, repeatedly refers to "pain *and* suffering." *See also* S. Exec. Rep. No. 101-30 at 6 (three uses of "pain and suffering"); *id.* at 13 (eight uses of "pain and suffering"); *id.* at 14 (two uses of "pain and suffering"); *id.* at 35 (one

---

[21] This is particularly so given that, as Administration witnesses explained, the limiting understanding defining mental pain or suffering was considered necessary to avoid problems of vagueness. *See, e.g., CAT Hearing* at 8, 10 (prepared statement of Abraham Sofaer, Legal Adviser, Department of State: "The Convention's wording . . . is not in all respects as precise as we believe necessary . . . . [B]ecause [the Convention] requires establishment of criminal penalties under our domestic law, we must pay particular attention to the meaning and interpretation of its provisions, especially concerning the standards by which the Convention will be applied as a matter of U.S. law . . . . [W]e prepared a codified proposal which . . . clarifies the definition of mental pain and suffering."); *id.* at 15-16 (prepared statement of Mark Richard: "The basic problem with the Torture Convention—one that permeates all our concerns—is its imprecise definition of torture, especially as that term is applied to actions which result solely in mental anguish. This definitional vagueness makes it very doubtful that the United States can, consistent with Constitutional due process constraints, fulfill its obligation under the Convention to adequately engraft the definition of torture into the domestic criminal law of the United States."); *id.* at 17 (prepared statement of Mark Richard: "Accordingly, the Torture Convention's vague definition concerning the mental suffering aspect of torture cannot be resolved by reference to established principles of international law. In an effort to overcome this unacceptable element of vagueness in Article I of the Convention, we have proposed an understanding which defines severe mental pain constituting torture with sufficient specificity to . . . meet Constitutional due process requirements.").

use of "pain and suffering"). Conversely, the phrase "pain or suffering" is used less frequently in the Senate report in discussing (as opposed to quoting) the CAT and the understandings under consideration, e.g., *id.* at 5-6 (one use of "pain or suffering"), *id.* at 14 (two uses of "pain or suffering"); id. at 16 (two uses of "pain or suffering"), and, when used, it is with no suggestion that it has any different meaning.

Although we conclude that inclusion of the words "or suffering" in "severe physical pain or suffering" establishes that physical torture is not limited to "severe physical pain," we also conclude that Congress did not intend "severe physical pain or suffering" to include a category of "physical suffering" that would be so broad as to negate the limitations on the other categories of torture in the statute. Moreover, the "physical suffering" covered by the statute must be "severe" to be within the statutory prohibition. We conclude that under some circumstances "physical suffering" may be of sufficient intensity and duration to meet the statutory definition of torture even if it does not involve "severe physical pain." To constitute such torture, "*severe* physical suffering" would have to be a condition of some extended duration or persistence as well as intensity. The need to define a category of "severe physical suffering" that is different from "severe physical pain," and that also does not undermine the limited definition Congress provided for torture, along with the requirement that any such physical suffering be "severe," calls for an interpretation under which "severe physical suffering" is reserved for physical distress that is "severe" considering its intensity and duration or persistence, rather than merely mild or transitory.[22] Otherwise, the inclusion of such a category would lead to the kind of uncertainty in interpreting the statute that Congress sought to reduce both through its understanding to the CAT and in sections 2340-2340A.

---

[22] Support for concluding that there is an extended temporal element, or at least an element of persistence, in "severe physical suffering" as a category distinct from "severe physical pain" may also be found in the prevalence of concepts of "endurance" of suffering and of suffering as a "state" or "condition" in standard dictionary definitions. *See, e.g., Webster's Third New International Dictionary* at 2284 (defining "suffering" as "the endurance of or submission to affliction, pain, loss"; "a pain endured"); *Random House Dictionary of the English Language* 1901 (2d ed. 1987) ("the state of a person or thing that suffers"); *Funk & Wagnalls New Standard Dictionary of the English Language* 2416 (1946) ("A state of anguish or pain"); *American Heritage Dictionary of the English Language* at 1795 ("The condition of one who suffers").

(3) The meaning of "severe mental pain or suffering."

Section 2340 defines "severe mental pain or suffering" to mean:

the prolonged mental harm caused by or resulting from—

> (A) the intentional infliction or threatened infliction of severe physical pain or suffering;
> (B) the administration or application, or threatened administration or application, of mind-altering substances or other procedures calculated to disrupt profoundly the senses or the personality;
> (C) the threat of imminent death; or
> (D) the threat that another person will imminently be subjected to death, severe physical pain or suffering, or the administration or application of mind-altering substances or other procedures calculated to disrupt profoundly the senses or personality[.]

18 U.S.C. § 2340(2). Torture is defined under the statute to include an act specifically intended to inflict severe mental pain or suffering. *Id.* § 2340(1).

An important preliminary question with respect to this definition is whether the statutory list of the four "predicate acts" in section 2340(2) (A)-(D) is exclusive. We conclude that Congress intended the list of predicate acts to be exclusive—that is, to constitute the proscribed "severe mental pain or suffering" under the statute, the prolonged mental harm must be caused by acts falling within one of the four statutory categories of predicate acts. We reach this conclusion based on the clear language of the statute, which provides a detailed definition that includes four categories of predicate acts joined by the disjunctive and does not contain a catchall provision or any other language suggesting that additional acts might qualify (for example, language such as "including" or "such acts as").[23] Congress plainly considered very specific predicate acts, and this

---

[23] These four categories of predicate acts "are members of an 'associated group or series,' justifying the inference that items not mentioned were excluded by deliberate choice, not inadvertence." *Barnhart v. Peabody Coal Co.*, 537 U.S. 149, 168 (2003) (quoting *United States v. Vonn*, 535 U.S. 55, 65 (2002)). *See also, e.g., Leatherman v. Tarrant County Narcotics Intelligence & Coordination Unit*, 507 U.S. 163, 168 (1993); 2A Norman J. Singer, *Statutes and Statutory Construc-*

definition tracks the Senate's understanding concerning mental pain or suffering when giving its advice and consent to ratification of the CAT. The conclusion that the list of predicate acts is exclusive is consistent with both the text of the Senate's understanding, and with the fact that it was adopted out of concern that the CAT'S definition of torture did not otherwise meet the requirement for clarity in defining crimes. *See supra* note 21. Adopting an interpretation of the statute that expands the list of predicate acts for "severe mental pain or suffering" would constitute an impermissible rewriting of the statute and would introduce the very imprecision that prompted the Senate to adopt its understanding when giving its advice and consent to ratification of the CAT.

Another question is whether the requirement of "prolonged mental harm" caused by or resulting from one of the enumerated predicate acts is a separate requirement, or whether such "prolonged mental harm" is to be presumed any time one of the predicate acts occurs. Although it is possible to read the statute's reference to "*the* prolonged mental harm caused by or resulting from" the predicate acts as creating a statutory presumption that each of the predicate acts always causes prolonged mental harm, we do not believe that was Congress's intent. As noted, this language closely tracks the understanding that the Senate adopted when it gave its advice and consent to ratification of the CAT:

> in order to constitute torture, an act must be specifically intended to inflict severe physical or mental pain or suffering and that mental pain or suffering refers to prolonged mental harm caused by or resulting from (1) the intentional infliction or threatened infliction of severe physical pain or suffering; (2) the administration or application, or threatened administration or application, of mind altering substances or other procedures calculated to disrupt profoundly the senses or the personality; (3) the threat of imminent death; or (4) the threat that another person will imminently be subjected to death, severe physical pain or suffering, or the administration or application of mind altering substances or other procedures calculated to disrupt profoundly the senses or personality.

S. Exec. Rep. No. 101-30 at 36. We do not believe that simply by add-

---

tion § 47.23 (6th ed. 2000). Nor do we see any "contrary indications" that would rebut this inference. *Vonn*, 535 U.S. at 65.

ing the word "the" before "prolonged harm," Congress intended a material change in the definition of mental pain or suffering as articulated in the Senate's understanding to the CAT. The legislative history, moreover, confirms that sections 2340-2340A were intended to fulfill—but not go beyond—the United States' obligations under the CAT: "This section provides the necessary legislation to implement the [CAT] . . . . The definition of torture emanates directly from article 1 of the [CAT]. The definition for 'severe mental pain and suffering' incorporates the [above mentioned] understanding." S. Rep. No. 103-107, at 58-59 (1993). This understanding, embodied in the statute, was meant to define the obligation undertaken by the United States. Given this understanding, the legislative history, and the fact that section 2340(2) defines "severe mental pain or suffering" carefully in language very similar to the understanding, we do not believe that Congress intended the definition to create a presumption that any time one of the predicate acts occurs, prolonged mental harm is deemed to result.

Turning to the question of what constitutes "prolonged mental harm caused by or resulting from" a predicate act, we believe that Congress intended this phrase to require mental "harm" that is caused by or that results from a predicate act, and that has some lasting duration. There is little guidance to draw upon in interpreting this phrase.[24] Nevertheless, our interpretation is consistent with the ordinary meaning of the statutory terms. First, the use of the word "harm"—as opposed to simply repeating "pain or suffering"—suggests some mental damage or injury. Ordinary dictionary definitions of "harm," such as "physical or mental *damage: injury,*" *Webster's Third New International Dictionary* at 1034 (emphasis added), or "[p]hysical or psychological *injury or damage,*" *American Heritage Dictionary of the English Language* at 825 (emphasis added), support this interpretation. Second, to "prolong" means to "lengthen in time" or to "extend in duration," or to "draw out," *Webster's Third New International Dictionary* at 1815, further suggesting that to be "prolonged," the mental damage must extend for some period of time. This damage need not be

---

[24] The phrase "prolonged mental harm" does not appear in the relevant medical literature or elsewhere in the United States Code. The August 2002 Memorandum concluded that to constitute "prolonged mental harm," there must be "significant psychological harm of significant duration, e.g., lasting for months or even years." *Id.* at 1; *see also id.* at 7. Although we believe that the mental harm must be of some lasting duration to be "prolonged," to the extent that that formulation was intended to suggest that the mental harm would have to last for at least "months or even years," we do not agree.

permanent, but it must continue for a "prolonged" period of time.[25] Finally, under section 2340(2), the "prolonged mental harm" must be "caused by" or "resulting from" one of the enumerated predicate acts.[26]

Although there are few judicial opinions discussing the question of "prolonged mental harm," those cases that have addressed the issue are consistent with our view. For example, in the TVPA case of *Mehinovic*, the court explained that:

> [The defendant] also caused or participated in the plaintiffs' mental torture. Mental torture consists of "prolonged mental harm caused by or resulting from: the intentional infliction or threatened infliction of severe physical pain or suffering; . . . the threat of imminent death . . . ." As set out above, plaintiffs noted in their testimony that they feared that they would be killed by [the defendant] during the beatings he inflicted or during games of "Russian roulette." *Each plaintiff continues to suffer long-term psychological harm as a result of the ordeals they suffered at the hands of defendant and others.*

---

[25] For example, although we do not suggest that the statute is limited to such cases, development of a mental disorder—such as post-traumatic stress disorder or perhaps chronic depression—could constitute "prolonged mental harm." *See* American Psychiatric Association, *Diagnostic and Statistical Manual of Mental Disorders* 369-76, 463-68 (4th ed. 2000) ("DSM-IV-TR"). *See also, e.g., Report of the Special Rapporteur on Torture and Other Cruel, Inhuman or Degrading Treatment or Punishment*, U.N. Doc. A/59/324 , at 14 (2004) ("The most common diagnosis of psychiatric symptoms among torture survivors is said to be post-traumatic stress disorder."); *see also* Metin Basoglu et al., *Torture and Mental Health: A Research Overview, in* Ellen Gerrity et al. eds., *The Mental Health Consequences of Torture* 48-49 (2001) (referring to findings of higher rates of post-traumatic stress disorder in studies involving torture survivors); Murat Parker et al., *Psychological Effects of Torture: An Empirical Study of Tortured and Non-Tortured Non-Political Prisoners, in* Metin Basoglu ed., *Torture and Its Consequences: Current Treatment Approaches* 77 (1992) (referring to findings of post-traumatic stress disorder in torture survivors).

[26] This is not meant to suggest that, if the predicate act or acts continue for an extended period, "prolonged mental harm" cannot occur until after they are completed. Early occurrences of the predicate act could cause mental harm that could continue—and become prolonged—during the extended period the predicate acts continued to occur. For example, in *Sackie v. Ashcroft*, 270 F. Supp. 2d 596, 601-02 (E.D. Pa. 2003), the predicate acts continued over a three-to-four-year period, and the court concluded that "prolonged mental harm" had occurred during that time.

198 F. Supp. 2d at 1346 (emphasis added; first ellipsis in original). In reaching its conclusion, the court noted that the plaintiffs were continuing to suffer serious mental harm even ten years after the events in question: One plaintiff "suffers from anxiety, flashbacks, and nightmares and has difficulty sleeping. [He] continues to suffer thinking about what happened to him during this ordeal and has been unable to work as a result of the continuing effects of the torture he endured." *Id.* at 1334. Another plaintiff "suffers from anxiety, sleeps very little, and has frequent nightmares. . . . [He] has found it impossible to return to work." *Id.* at 1336. A third plaintiff "has frequent nightmares. He has had to use medication to help him sleep. His experience has made him feel depressed and reclusive, and he has not been able to work since he escaped from this ordeal." *Id.* at 1337-38. And the fourth plaintiff "has flashbacks and nightmares, suffers from nervousness, angers easily, and has difficulty trusting people. These effects directly impact and interfere with his ability to work." *Id.* at 1340. In each case, these mental effects were continuing years after the infliction of the predicate acts.

And in *Sackie v. Ashcroft*, 270 F. Supp. 2d 596 (E.D. Pa. 2003), the individual had been kidnapped and "forcibly recruited" as a child soldier at the age of 14, and over the next three to four years had been forced to take narcotics and threatened with imminent death. *Id.* at 597-98, 601-02. The court concluded that the resulting mental harm, which continued over this three-to-four-year period, qualified as "prolonged mental harm." *Id.* at 602.

Conversely, in *Villeda Aldana v. Fresh Del Monte Produce, Inc.*, 305 F. Supp. 2d 1285 (S.D. Fla. 2003), the court rejected a claim under the TVPA brought by individuals who had been held at gunpoint overnight and repeatedly threatened with death. While recognizing that the plaintiffs had experienced an "ordeal," the court concluded that they had failed to show that their experience caused lasting damage, noting that "there is simply no allegation that Plaintiffs have suffered any prolonged mental harm or physical injury as a result of their alleged intimidation." *Id.* at 1294-95.

(4) The meaning of "specifically intended."

It is well recognized that the term "specific intent" is ambiguous and that the courts do not use it consistently. *See* 1 Wayne R. LaFave, *Substantive Criminal Law* § 5.2(e), at 355 & n.79 (2d ed. 2003). "Specific intent" is most commonly understood, however, "to designate a special mental element which is required above and beyond any mental state required with respect to the *actus reus* of the crime." *Id.* at 354; *see also Carter v. United States*, 530 U.S. 255, 268 (2000) (explaining that general intent, as opposed to specific intent, requires "that the defendant possessed knowledge [only] with respect to the *actus reus* of the crime"). As one respected treatise explains:

> With crimes which require that the defendant intentionally cause a specific result, what is meant by an "intention" to cause that result? Although the theorists have not always been in agreement . . . , the traditional view is that a person who acts . . . intends a result of his act . . . under two quite different circumstances: (1) when he consciously desires that result, whatever the likelihood of that result happening from his conduct; and (2) when he knows that that result is practically certain to follow from his conduct, whatever his desire may be as to that result.

1 LaFave, *Substantive Criminal Law*, § 5.2(a), at 341 (footnote omitted).

As noted, the cases are inconsistent. Some suggest that only a conscious desire to produce the proscribed result constitutes specific intent; others suggest that even reasonable foreseeability suffices. In *United States v. Bailey*, 444 U.S. 394 (1980), for example, the Court suggested that, at least "[i]n a general sense," *id.* at 405, "specific intent" requires that one consciously desire the result. *Id.* at 403-05. The Court compared the common law's *mens rea* concepts of specific intent and general intent to the Model Penal Code's *mens rea* concepts of acting purposefully and acting knowingly. *Id.* at 404-05. "[A] person who causes a particular result is said to act purposefully," wrote the Court, "if 'he consciously desires that result, whatever the likelihood of that result happening from his conduct.'" *Id.* at 404 (internal quotation marks omitted). A person "is said to act knowingly," in contrast, "if he is aware 'that that result is practically certain to follow from his conduct, whatever his desire may be as to that result.'" *Id.* (internal quotation marks omitted). The Court then stated: "In a general sense, 'purpose' corresponds loosely with the common-law concept of specific intent, while 'knowledge' corresponds loosely with the concept of general intent." *Id.* at 405.

In contrast, cases such as *United States v. Neiswender*, 590 F.2d 1269 (4th Cir. 1979), suggest that to prove specific intent it is enough that the defendant simply have "knowledge or notice" that his act "would have likely resulted in" the proscribed outcome. *Id.* at 1273. "Notice," the court held, "is provided by the reasonable foreseeability of the natural and probable consequences of one's acts." *Id.*

We do not believe it is useful to try to define the precise meaning of "specific intent" in section 2340.[27] In light of the President's directive that the United States not engage in torture, it would not be appropriate to rely on parsing the specific intent element of the statute to approve as lawful conduct that might otherwise amount to torture. Some observations, however, are appropriate. It is clear that the specific intent element of section 2340 would be met if a defendant performed an act and "consciously desire[d]" that act to inflict severe physical or mental pain or suffering. 1 LaFave, *Substantive Criminal Law* § 5.2(a), at 341. Conversely, if an individual acted in good faith, and only after reasonable investigation establishing that his conduct would not inflict severe physical or mental pain or suffering, it appears unlikely that he would have the specific intent necessary to violate sections 2340-2340A. Such an individual could be said neither consciously to desire the proscribed result, *see, e.g., Bailey,* 444 U.S. at 405, nor to have "knowledge or notice" that his act "would likely have resulted in" the proscribed outcome, *Neiswender,* 590 F.2d at 1273.

Two final points on the issue of specific intent: First, specific intent must be distinguished from motive. There is no exception under the statute permitting torture to be used for a "good reason." Thus, a defendant's motive (to protect national security, for example) is not relevant to the question whether he has acted with the requisite specific intent under the statute. *See Cheek v. United States,* 498 U.S. 192, 200-01 (1991). Second, specific intent to take a given action can be found even if the defendant will take the action only conditionally. *Cf., e.g., Holloway v. United States,* 526 U.S. 1, 11 (1999) ("[A] defendant may not negate a proscribed intent by requiring the victim to comply with a condition the defendant has no right to impose."). *See also id.* at 10-11 & nn. 9-12; Model Penal Code § 2.02(6). Thus, for example, the fact that a victim might have avoided being tortured by cooperating with the perpetrator would not make permissible actions otherwise constituting torture under the statute. Presumably

---

[27] In the August 2002 Memorandum, this Office concluded that the specific intent element of the statute required that infliction of severe pain or suffering be the defendant's "precise objective" and that it was not enough that the defendant act with knowledge that such pain "was reasonably likely to result from his actions" (or even that that result "is certain to occur"). *Id.* at 3-4. We do not reiterate that test here.

that has frequently been the case with torture, but that fact does not make the practice of torture any less abhorrent or unlawful.[28]

Please let us know if we can be of further assistance.

Daniel Levin
Acting Assistant Attorney General

---

[28] In the August 2002 Memorandum, this Office indicated that an element of the offense of torture was that the act in question actually result in the infliction of severe physical or mental pain or suffering. *See id.* at 3. That conclusion rested on a comparison of the statute with the CAT, which has a different definition of "torture" that requires the actual infliction of pain or suffering, and we do not believe that the statute requires that the defendant actually inflict (as opposed to act with the specific intent to inflict) severe physical or mental pain or suffering. *Compare* CAT art. 1(1) ("the term 'torture' means any act by which severe pain or suffering, whether physical or mental, is *intentionally inflicted*") (emphasis added) *with* 18 U.S.C. § 2340 ("'torture' means an act . . . *specifically intended to inflict* severe physical or mental pain or suffering") (emphasis added). It is unlikely that any such requirement would make any practical difference, however, since the statute also criminalizes attempts to commit torture. *Id.* § 2340A(a).

U.S. Department of Justice

Office of Legal Counsel

Office of the Principal Deputy Assistant Attorney General · · · · · *Washington, D.C. 20530*

May 10, 2005

MEMORANDUM FOR JOHN A. RIZZO
SENIOR DEPUTY GENERAL COUNSEL,
CENTRAL INTELLIGENCE AGENCY

Re: Application of 18 U.S.C. §§ 2340-2340A to Certain Techniques That May Be Used in the Interrogation of a High Value al Qaeda Detainee

You have asked us to address whether certain specified interrogation techniques designed to be used on a high value al Qaeda detainee in the War on Terror comply with the federal prohibition on torture, codified at 18 U.S.C. §§ 2340-2340A. Our analysis of this question is controlled by this Office's recently published opinion interpreting the anti-torture statute. *See* Memorandum for James B. Comey, Deputy Attorney General, from Daniel Levin, Acting Assistant Attorney General, Office of Legal Counsel, *Re: Legal Standards Applicable Under 18 U.S.C. §§ 2340-2340A* (Dec. 30, 2004) (*"2004 Legal Standards Opinion"*), *available at* www .usdoj.gov. (We provided a copy of that opinion to you at the time it was issued.) Much of the analysis from our *2004 Legal Standards Opinion* is reproduced below; all of it is incorporated by reference herein. Because you have asked us to address the application of sections 2340-2340A to specific interrogation techniques, the present memorandum necessarily includes additional discussion of the applicable legal standards and their application to particular facts. We stress, however, that the legal standards we apply in this memorandum are fully consistent with the interpretation of the statute set forth in our *2004 Legal Standards Opinion* and constitute our authoritative view of the legal standards applicable under sections 2340-2340A. Our task is to explicate those standards in order to assist you in complying with the law.

A paramount recognition emphasized in our *2004 Legal Standards Opinion* merits re-emphasis at the outset and guides our analysis: Torture is abhorrent both to American law and values and to international norms. The universal repudiation of torture is reflected not only in our criminal law, *see, e.g.*, 18 U.S.C. §§ 2340-2340A, but also in international agreements,[1] in centuries of Anglo-American law, *see, e.g.*, John H. Langbein, *Torture and the Law of Proof: Europe and England in the Ancien Regime* (1977) (*"Torture and the Law of Proof"*), and in the longstanding policy of the United States, repeatedly and recently reaffirmed by the President.[2] Consistent with these norms, the President has directed unequivocally that the United States is not to engage in torture.[3]

The task of interpreting and applying sections 2340-2340A is complicated by the lack of precision in the statutory terms and the lack of relevant case law. In defining the federal crime of torture, Congress required that a defendant "*specifically intend*[] to inflict *severe* physical or mental pain or suffering," and Congress narrowly defined "severe mental pain or suffering" to mean "the *prolonged* mental harm caused by" enumerated predicate acts, including "the threat of *imminent* death" and "procedures *calculated* to disrupt *profoundly* the senses or personality." 18 U.S.C. § 2340 (emphasis added). These statutory requirements are consistent with U.S. obligations under the United Nations Convention Against Torture, the treaty that obligates the United States to ensure that torture is a crime under U.S. law and that is implemented by sections 2340-2340A. The requirements in sections 2340-2340A closely track the understandings and

---

[1] *See, e.g.*, United Nations Convention Against Torture and Other Cruel, Inhuman or Degrading Treatment or Punishment, Dec. 10, 1984, S. Treaty Doc. No. 100-20, 1465 U.N.T.S. 85 (entered into force for U.S. Nov. 20, 1994) ("Convention Against Torture" or "CAT"); International Covenant on Civil and Political Rights, Dec. 16, 1966, art. 7, 999 U.N.T.S. 171.

[2] *See, e.g.*, Statement on United Nations International Day in Support of Victims of Torture, 40 Weekly Comp. Pres. Doc. 1167 (July 5, 2004) ("Freedom from torture is an inalienable human right . . . ."); Statement on United Nations International Day in Support of Victims of Torture, 39 Weekly Comp. Pres. Doc. 824 (June 30, 2003) ("Torture anywhere is an affront to human dignity everywhere."); *see also Letter of Transmittal from President Ronal Reagan to the Senate* (May 20, 1988), in *Message from the President of the United States Transmitting the Convention Against Torture and Other Cruel, Inhuman or Degrading Treatment or Punishment*, S. Treaty Doc. No. 100-20, at ii (1988) ("Ratification of the Convention by the United States will clearly express United States opposition to torture, an abhorrent practice still prevalent in the world today.").

[3] *See, e.g.*, 40 Weekly Comp. Pres. Doc. at 1167-68 ("America stands against and will not tolerate torture. . . . Torture is wrong no matter where it occurs, and the United States will continue to lead the fight to eliminate it everywhere.").

reservations required by the Senate when it gave its advice and consent to ratification of the Convention Against Torture. They reflect a clear intent by Congress to limit the scope of the prohibition on torture under U.S. law. However, many of the key terms used in the statute (for example, "severe," "prolonged," "suffering") are imprecise and necessarily bring a degree of uncertainty to addressing the reach of sections 2340-2340A. Moreover, relevant judicial decisions in this area provide only limited guidance.[4] This imprecision and lack of judicial guidance, coupled with the President's clear directive that the United States does not condone or engage in torture, counsel great care in applying the statute to specific conduct. We have attempted to exercise such care throughout this memorandum.

With these considerations in mind, we turn to the particular question before us: whether certain specified interrogation techniques may be used by the Central Intelligence Agency ("CIA") on a high value al Qaeda detainee consistent with the federal statutory prohibition on torture, 18 U.S.C. §§ 2340-2340A.[5] For the reasons discussed below, and based on the representations we have received from you (or officials of your Agency) about the particular techniques in question, the circumstances in which they are authorized for use, and the physical and psychological assess-

---

[4] What judicial guidance there is comes from decisions that apply a related but separate statute (the Torture Victims Protection Act ("TVPA"), 28 U.S.C. § 1350 note (2000)). These judicial opinions generally contain little if any analysis of specific conduct or of the relevant statutory standards.

[5] We have previously advised you that the use by the CIA of the techniques of interrogation discussed herein is consistent with the Constitution and applicable statutes and treaties. In the present memorandum, you have asked us to address only the requirement of 18 U.S.C. §§ 2340-2340A. Nothing in this memorandum or in our prior advice to the CIA should be read to suggest that the use of these techniques would conform to the requirement of the Uniform Code of Military Justice that governs members of the Armed Forces or to United States obligations under the Geneva Conventions in circumstances where those Conventions would apply. We do not address the possible application of article 16 of the CAT, nor do we address any question relating to conditions of confinement or detention, as distinct from the interrogation of detainees. We stress that our advice on the application of sections 2340-2340A does not represent the policy views of the Department of Justice concerning interrogation practices. Finally, we note that section 6057(a) of H.R. 1268 (109th Cong. 1st Sess.), if it becomes law, would forbid expending or obligating funds made available by that bill "to subject any person in the custody or under the physical control of the United States to torture," but because the bill would define "torture" to have "the meaning given that term in section 2340(1) of title 18, United States Code," § 6057(b) (1), the provision (to the extent it might apply here to all) would merely reaffirm the preexisting prohibitions on torture in sections 2340-2340A.

ments made of the detainee to be interrogated, we conclude that the separate authorized use of each of the specific techniques at issue, subject to the limitations and safeguards described herein, would not violate sections 2340-2340A.[6] Our conclusion is straightforward with respect to all but two of the techniques discussed herein. As discussed below, use of sleep deprivation as an enhanced technique and use of the waterboard involve more substantial questions, with the waterboard presenting the most substantial question.

We base our conclusions on the statutory language enacted by Congress in sections 2340-2340A. We do not rely on any consideration of the President's authority as Commander in Chief under the Constitution, any application of the principle of constitutional avoidance (or any conclusion about constitutional issues), or any agreements based on possible defenses of "necessity" or self-defense.[7]

I.

A.

In asking us to consider certain specific techniques to be used in the interrogation of a particular al Qaeda operative, you have provided background information common to the use of all of the techniques. You have

---

[6] The present memorandum addresses only the separate use of each individual technique, not the combined use of techniques as part of an integrated regimen of interrogation. You have informed us that most of the CIA's authorized techniques are designed to be used with particular detainees in an interrelated or combined manner as part of an overall interrogation program, and you have provided us with a description of a typical scenario for the CIA's combined use of techniques. *See Background Paper on CIA's Combines Use of Interrogation Techniques* (Dec. 30, 2004) (*"Background Paper"*). A full assessment of whether the use of interrogation techniques is consistent with sections 2340-2340A should take into account the potential combined effects of using multiple techniques on a given detainee, either simultaneously or sequentially within a short time. We will address in a separate memorandum whether the combined us of certain techniques, as reflected in the *Background Paper*, is consistent with the legal requirements of sections 2340-2340A.

[7] In preparing the present memorandum, we have reviewed and carefully considered the report prepared by the CIA Inspector General, *Counterterrorism Detention and Interrogation Activities* (September 2001-October 2003), No. 2003-7123-IG (May 7, 2004) (*"IG Report"*) ███████████ Various aspects of the *IG Report* are addressed below.

advised that these techniques would be used only on an individual who is determined to be a "High Value Detainee," defined as:

> a detainee who, until time of capture, we have reason to believe: (1) is a senior member of al-Qai'da or an al-Qai'da associated terrorist group (Jemaah Islamiyyah, Egyptian Islamic Jihad, al-Zarqawi Group, etc.); (2) has knowledge of imminent terrorist threats against the USA, its military forces, its citizens and organizations, or its allies; or that has/had direct involvement in planning and preparing terrorist actions against the USA or its allies, or assisting the al-Qai'da leadership in planning and preparing such terrorist actions; and (3) if released, constitutes a clear and continuing threat to the USA or its allies.

Fax for Daniel Levin, Acting Assistant Attorney General, Office of Legal Counsel, from ▇▇▇▇▇▇ Assistant General Counsel, CIA, at 3 (Jan. 4, 2005) *("January 4* ▇▇▇ *Fax")*. For convenience, below we will generally refer to such individuals simply as detainees.

You have also explained that prior to interrogation, each detainee is evaluated by medical and psychological professionals from the CIA's Office of Medical Services ("OMS") to ensure that he is not likely to suffer any severe physical or mental pain or suffering as a result of interrogation.

> [T]echnique-specific advanced approval is required for all "enhanced" measures and is conditional on on-site medical and psychological personnel confirming from direct detainee examination that the enhanced technique(s) is not expected to produce "severe physical or mental pain or suffering." As a practical matter, the detainee's physical condition must be such that these interventions will not have a lasting effect, and his psychological state strong enough that no severe psychological harm will result.

OMS Guidelines on Medical and Psychological Support to Detainee Rendition, Interrogation and Detention at 9 (Dec. 2004) *("OMS Guidelines")* (footnote omitted). New detainees are also subject to a general intake examination, which includes "a thorough initial medical assessment . . . with a complete, documented history and physical addressing in depth any chronic or previous medical problems. This assessment should especially attend to cardio-vascular, pulmonary, neurological and musculoskeletal findings. . . . Vital signs and weight should be recorded, and blood work drawn. . . ." *Id.* at 6. In addition, "subsequent medical rechecks during the interrogation period should be performed on a regular basis." *Id.* As an additional precaution, and to ensure the objectivity of their medical and psychological assessments, OMS personnel do not participate in administering interrogation techniques; their function is to monitor interrogations and the health of the detainee.

The detainee is then interviewed by trained and certified interrogators to determine whether he is actively attempting to withhold or distort information. If so, the on-scene interrogation team develops an interrogation plan, which may include only those techniques for which there is no medical or psychological contraindication. You have informed us that the initial OMS assessments have ruled out the use of some—or all—of the interrogation techniques as to certain detainees. If the plan calls for the use of any of the interrogation techniques discussed herein, it is submitted to CIA Headquarters, which must review the plan and approve the use of any of these interrogation techniques before they may be applied. *See* George J. Tenet, Director of Central Intelligence, *Guidelines on Interrogations Conducted Pursuant to the* ▮▮▮▮▮▮▮▮▮▮▮ ▮ (Jan. 28, 2003) (*"Interrogation Guidelines"*). Prior written approval "from the Director, DCI Counterterrorist Center, with the concurrence of the Chief, CTC Legal Group," is required for the use of any enhanced interrogation techniques. *Id.* We understand that, as to the detainee here, this written approval has been given for each of the techniques we discuss, except the waterboard.

We understand that, when approved, interrogation techniques are generally used in an escalating fashion, with milder techniques used first. Use of the techniques is not continuous. Rather, one or more techniques may be applied—during or between interrogation sessions—based on the judgment of the interrogators and other team members and subject always to the monitoring of the on-scene medical and psychological personnel. Use of the techniques may be continued if the detainee is still believed to have and to be withholding actionable intelligence. The use of these techniques may not be continued for more than 30 days without additional approval from CIA Headquarters. *See generally Interrogation Guidelines* at 1-2 (describing approval procedures required for use of enhanced interrogational techniques). Moreover, even within that 30-day period, any further use of these interrogation techniques is discontinued if the detainee is judged to be consistently providing accurate intelligence or if he is no longer believed to have actionable intelligence. This memorandum addresses the use of these techniques during no more than one 30-day period. We do not address whether the use of these techniques beyond the initial 30-day period would violate the statute.

Medical and psychological personnel are on-scene throughout (and, as detailed below, physically present or otherwise observing during the application of many techniques, including all techniques involving physical contact with detainees), and "[d]aily physical and psychological evaluations are continued throughout the period of [enhanced interrogation technique] use." *IG Report* at 30 n.35; *see also* George J. Tenet, Director of Central Intelligence, *Guidelines on Confinement Conditions for CIA Detainees*, at 1 (Jan. 28, 2003) (*"Confinement Guidelines"*) ("Medical and, as appropriate, psychological personnel shall be physically present at, or reasonably available to, each Detention Facility. Medical personnel shall check the physical condition of each detainee at intervals appropriate to the circumstances and shall keep appropriate records."); *IG Report* at 28-29.[8] In addition, "[i]n each interrogation session in which an Enhanced Technique is employed, a contemporaneous record shall be created setting forth the nature and duration of each such technique employed." *Interrogation Guidelines* at 3. At any time, any on-scene personnel (including the medical or psychological personnel, the chief of base, substantive experts, security officers, and other interrogators) can intervene to stop the use of any technique if it appears that the technique is being used improperly, and on-scene medical personnel can intervene if the detainee has developed a condition making the use of the technique unsafe. More generally, medical personnel watch for signs of physical distress or mental harm so significant as possibly to amount to the "severe physical or mental pain or suffering" that is prohibited by sections 2340-2340A. As the *OMS Guidelines* explain, [m]edical officers must remain cognizant at all times of their obligation to prevent 'severe physical or mental pain or suffering.'" *OMS Guidelines* at 10. Additional restrictions on certain techniques are described below.

These techniques have all been interpreted from military Survival, Evasion, Resistance, Escape ("SERE") training, where they have been used for years on U.S. military personnel, although with some significant differences described below. *See IG Report* at 13-14. Although we refer to the SERE experience below, we note at the outset an important limitation

---

[8] In addition to monitoring the application and effects of enhanced interrogation techniques, OMS personnel are instructed more generally to ensure that "[a]dequate medical care shall be provided to detainees, even those undergoing enhanced interrogation." *OMS Guidelines* at 10.

on reliance on that experience. Individuals undergoing SERE training are obviously in a very different situation from detainees undergoing interrogation; SERE trainees know it is part of training program, not a real-life interrogation regime, they presumably know it will last only a short time, and they presumably have assurances that they will not be significantly harmed by the training.

B.

You have described the specific techniques at issue as follows:[9]

1. *Dietary manipulation.* This technique involves the substitution of commercial liquid meal replacements for normal food, present-

---

[9] The descriptions of these techniques are set out in a number of documents including: the *OMS Guidelines*; *Interrogations Guidelines*; *Confinement Guidelines*; *Background Paper, Letter from* ▓▓▓▓▓▓▓▓▓▓ Associate General Counsel, CIA to Dan Levin, Acting Assistant Attorney General, Office of Legal Counsel ("OLC") (July 30, 2004) ("July 30 ▓▓▓▓▓▓▓▓▓▓; Letter from John A. Rizzo, Acting General Counsel, CIA, to Daniel Levin, Acting Assistant Attorney General, OLC (Aug. 2, 2004) ("*August 2 Rizzo Letter*"); Letter from ▓▓▓▓▓▓▓▓▓▓, Associate General Counsel, CIA, to Dan Levin, Acting Assistant Attorney General, OLC (Aug. 19, 2004) ("*August 19* ▓▓▓▓ *Letter*"); Letter from ▓▓▓▓▓▓▓▓▓▓ Associate General Counsel, CIA, to Dan Levin, Acting Assistant Attorney, OLC (Aug. 25, 2004) ("*August 25* ▓▓▓▓ *Letter*"); Letter from ▓▓▓▓▓▓▓▓ Associate General Counsel, CIA, to Dan Levin, Acting Assistant Attorney, OLC (Oct.10, 2004) ("*October 12* ▓▓▓ *Letter*"); Letter from ▓▓▓▓▓▓▓▓ Associate General Counsel, CIA to Dan Levin, Acting Assistant Attorney General, OLC (Oct. 22, 2004) ("*October 22* ▓▓▓▓ *Letter*"). Several of the techniques are describes and discussed in an earlier memorandum to you. *See* Memorandum for John Rizzo, Acting General Counsel, Central Intelligence Agency, from Jay S. Byhee, Assistant Attorney General, Office of Legal Counsel, *Re: Interrogation of al Qaeda Operative (Aug.1, 2002)* ("*Interrogation Memorandum*") (TS). We have separately reanalyzed all techniques in the present memorandum, and we will note below where aspects of particular techniques differ from those addressed in the *Interrogation Memorandum*. In order to avoid any confusion in this extremely sensitive and important area, the discussions of the statute in the 2004 *Legal Standard Opinion* and this memorandum supersede that in the *Interrogation Memorandum*; however, this memorandum confirms the conclusion of *Interrogation Memorandum* that the use of these techniques on a particular high value al Qaeda detainee, subject to the limitations imposed herein, would not violate sections 2340-2340A. In some cases additional facts set forth below have been provided to us in communications with CIA personnel. The CIA has reviewed this memorandum and confirmed the accuracy of the descriptions and limitations. Our analysis assumes adherence to these descriptions and limitations.

ing detainees with a bland, unappetizing, but nutritionally complete diet. You have informed us that the CIA believes dietary manipulation makes other techniques, such as sleep deprivation, more effective. *See August 25* ████ *Letter* at 4. Detainees on dietary manipulation are permitted as much water as they want. In general, minimum daily fluid and nutritional requirements are estimated using the following formula:

- Fluid requirement: 35ml/kg/day. This may be increased depending on ambient temperature, body temperature, and level of activity. Medical officers must monitor fluid intake, and although detainees are allowed as much water as they want, monitoring of urine output may be necessary in the unlikely event that the officers suspect that the detainee is becoming dehydrated.

- Calorie requirement: The CIA generally follows as a guideline a caloric requirement of 900 kcal/day + 10 kcal/kg/day. This quantity is multiplied by 1.2 for a sedentary activity level or 1.4 for moderate activity level. Regardless of this formula, the recommended minimum calorie intake is 1500 kcal/day, and in no event is the detainee allowed to receive less than 1000 kcal/day.[10] Calories are provided using commercial liquid diets (such as Ensure Plus), which also supply other essential nutrients and make for nutritionally complete meals.[11]

Medical officers are required to ensure adequate fluid and nutritional intake, and frequent medical monitoring takes place while any detainee is undergoing dietary manipulation. All detainees are weighed weekly, and in the unlikely event that a detainee were to lose more than 10 percent of his body weight, the restricted diet would be discontinued.

---

[10] This is the calorie requirement for males; the CIA presently has no female detainees.

[11] While detainees subject to dietary manipulation are obviously situated differently from individuals who voluntarily engage in commercial weight-loss programs, we note that widely available commercial weight-loss programs in the United States employ diets of 1000 kcal/day for sustained periods of weeks or longer without requiring medical supervision. While we do not equate commercial weight loss programs and this interrogation technique, the fact that these calorie levels are used in the weight-loss programs, in our view, is instructive in evaluating the medical safety of the interrogation technique.

2. *Nudity.* This technique is used to cause psychological discomfort, particularly if a detainee, for cultural or other reasons, is especially modest. When the technique is employed, clothing can be provided as an instant reward for cooperation. During and between interrogation sessions, a detainee may be kept nude, provided that ambient temperatures and the health of the detainee permit. For this technique to be employed, ambient temperature must be at least 68°F.[12] No sexual abuse or threats of sexual abuse are permitted. Although each detention cell has full-time closed-circuit video monitoring, the detainee is not intentionally exposed to other detainees or unduly exposed to the detention facility staff. We understand that interrogators "are trained to avoid sexual innuendo or any acts of implicit or explicit sexual degradation." *October 12* ████ *Letter* at 2. Nevertheless, interrogators can exploit the detainee's fear of being seen naked. In addition, female officers involved in the interrogation process may see the detainees naked; and for purposes of our analysis, we will assume that detainees subjected to nudity as an interrogation technique are aware that they may be seen naked by females.

3. *Attention grasp.* This technique consists of grasping the individual with both hands, one hand on each side of the collar opening, in a controlled and quick motion. In the same motion as the grasp, the individual is drawn toward the interrogator.

4. *Walling.* This technique involves the use of a flexible, false wall. The individual is placed with his heels touching the flexible wall. The interrogator pulls the individual forward and then quickly and firmly pushes the individual into the wall. It is the individual's shoulder blades that hit the wall. During this motion, the head and neck are supported with a rolled hood or towel that provides a C-collar effect to help prevent whiplash. To reduce further the risk of injury, the individual is allowed to rebound from the flexible wall. You have informed us that the false wall is also constructed to create a loud noise when the individual hits it in order to increase the shock or surprise of the technique. We understand that walling may be used when the detainee is uncooperative or unresponsive to questions from interrogators. Depending on the extent of the

---

[12] You have informed us that it is very unlikely that nudity would be employed at ambient temperatures below 75°F. *See October 12* ████ *Letter* at 1. For purposes of our analysis, however, we will assume that ambient temperatures may be as low as 68°F.

detainee's lack of cooperation, he may be walled one time during an interrogation session (one impact with the wall) or many times (perhaps 20 or
30 times) consecutively. We understand that this technique is not designed
to, and does not, cause severe pain, even when used repeatedly as you
have described. Rather it is designed to wear down the detainee and to
shock or surprise the detainee and alter his expectations about the treatment he believes he will receive. In particular, we specifically understand
that the repetitive use of the walling technique is intended to contribute
to the shock and drama of the experience, to dispel a detainee's expectations that interrogators will not use increasing levels of force, and to wear
down his resistance. It is not intended to—and based on experience you
have informed us that it does not—inflict any injury or cause severe pain.
Medical and psychological personnel are physically present or otherwise
observing whenever this technique is applied (as they are with any interrogation technique involving physical contact with the detainee).

5. *Facial hold.* This technique is used to hold the head immobile
during interrogation. One open palm is placed on either side of the individual's face. The fingertips are kept well away from the individual's
eyes.

6. *Facial slap or insult slap.* With this technique, the interrogator
slaps the individual's face with fingers slightly spread. The hand makes
contact with the area directly between the tip of the individual's chin and
the bottom of the corresponding earlobe. The interrogator thus "invades"
the individual's "personal space." We understand that the goal of the facial
slap is not to inflict physical pain that is severe or lasting. Instead, the purpose of the facial slap is to induce shock, surprise, or humiliation. Medical
and psychological personnel are physically present or otherwise observing
whenever this technique is applied.

7. *Abdominal slap.* In this technique, the interrogator strikes the
abdomen of the detainee with the back of his open hand. The interrogator must have no rings or other jewelry on his hand. The interrogator is
positioned directly in front of the detainee, generally no more than 18
inches from the detainee. With his fingers held tightly together and fully
extended, and with his palm toward the interrogator's own body, using his
elbow as a fixed pivot point, the interrogator slaps the detainee in the detainee's abdomen. The interrogator may not use a fist, and the slap must be
delivered above the navel and below the sternum. This technique is used
to condition a detainee to pay attention to the interrogator's questions and

to dislodge expectations that the detainee will not be touched. It is not intended to—and based on experience you have informed us that it does not—inflict any injury or cause any significant pain. Medical and psychological personnel are physically present or otherwise observing whenever this technique is applied.

8. *Cramped confinement.* This technique involves placing the individual in a confined space, the dimensions of which restrict the individual's movement. The confined space is usually dark. The duration of confinement varies based upon the size of the container. For the larger confined space, the individual can stand up or sit down; the smaller space is large enough for the subject to sit down. Confinement in the larger space may last no more than 8 hours at a time for no more than 18 hours a day; for the smaller space, confinement may last no more than two hours. Limits on the duration of cramped confinement are based on considerations of the detainee's size and weight, how he responds to the technique, and continuing consultation between the interrogators and OMS officers.[13]

9. *Wall standing.* This technique is used only to induce temporary muscle fatigue. The individual stands about four to five feet from a wall, with his feet spread approximately to shoulder width. His arms are stretched out in front of him, with his fingers resting on the wall and supporting his body weight. The individual is not permitted to move or reposition his hands or feet.

10. *Stress positions.* There are three stress positions that may be used. You have informed us that these positions are not designed to produce the pain associated with contortions or twisting of the body. Rather, like wall standing, they are designed to produce the physical discomfort associated with temporary muscle fatigue. The three stress positions are (1) sitting on the floor with legs extended straight out in front and arms raised above the head, (2) kneeling on the floor while leaning back at a 45 degree angle, and (3) leaning against a wall generally about three feet away from the detainee's feet, with only the detainee's head touching the

---

[13] In *Interrogation Memorandum*, we also addressed the use of harmless insects placed in a confinement box and concluded that it did not violate the statute. We understand that—for reasons unrelated to any concern that it might violate the statute—the CIA never used that technique and has removed it from the list of authorized interrogation techniques; accordingly, we do not address it again here.

wall, while his wrists are handcuffed in front of him or behind his back, and while an interrogator stands next to him to prevent injury if he loses his balance. As with wall standing, we understand that these positions are used only to induce temporary muscle fatigue.

11. *Water dousing.* Cold water is poured on the detainee either from a container or from a hose without a nozzle. This technique is intended to weaken the detainee's resistance and persuade him to cooperate with interrogators. The water poured on the detainee must be potable, and the interrogators must ensure that water does not enter the detainee's nose, mouth, or eyes. A medical officer must observe and monitor the detainee throughout application of this technique, including for signs of hypothermia. Ambient temperatures must remain above 64°F. If the detainee is lying on the floor, his head is to remain vertical, and a poncho, mat, or other material must be placed between him and the floor to minimize the loss of body heat. At the conclusion of the water dousing session, the detainee must be moved to a heated room if necessary to permit his body temperature to return to normal in a safe manner. To ensure an adequate margin of safety, the maximum period of time that a detainee may be permitted to remain wet has been set at two-thirds the time at which, based on extensive medical literature and experience, hypothermia could be expected to develop in healthy individuals who are submerged in water of the same temperature. For example, in employing this technique:

- For water temperature of 41°F, total duration of exposure may not exceed 20 minutes without drying and rewarming.

- For water temperature of 50°F, total duration of exposure may not exceed 40 minutes without drying and rewarming.

- For water temperature of 59°F, total duration of exposure may not exceed 60 minutes without drying and rewarming.

The minimum permissible temperature of the water used in water dousing is 41°F, though you have informed us that in practice the water temperature is generally not below 50°F, since tap water rather than refrigerated water is generally used. We understand that a version of water dousing routinely used in SERE training is much more extreme in that it involves complete immersion of the individual in cold water (where water temperatures may be below 40°F) and is usually performed outdoors where ambient air temperatures may be as low as 10°F. Thus, the SERE training version involves a far greater impact on body temperature; SERE training also involves a situation where the water may enter the trainee's nose and mouth.[14]

You have also described a variation of water dousing involving much smaller quantities of water; this variation is known as "flicking." Flicking of water is achieved by the interrogator wetting his fingers and then flicking them at the detainee, propelling droplets at the detainee. Flicking of water is done "in an effort to create a distracting effect, to awaken, to startle, to irritate, to instill humiliation, or to cause temporary insult." *October 22* ▮▮▮▮▮▮ *Letter* at 2. The water used in the "flicking" variation of water dousing also must be potable and within the water and ambient air temperature ranges for water dousing described above. Although water may be flicked into the detainee's face with this variation, the flicking of water at all times is done in such a manner as to avoid the inhalation or ingestion of water by the detainee. *See id.*

12. *Sleep deprivation (more than 48 hours).* This technique subjects a detainee to an extended period without sleep. You have informed us that the primary purpose of this technique is to weaken the subject and wear down his resistance.

The primary method of sleep deprivation involves the use of shackling to keep the detainee awake. In this method, the detainee is standing and is handcuffed, and the handcuffs are attached by a length of chain to the ceiling. The detainee's hands arc shackled in front of his body, so that the detainee has approximately a two- to three-foot diameter of movement. The detainee's feet are shackled to a bolt in the floor. Due care is taken to ensure that the shackles are neither too loose nor too tight for physical safety. We understand from discussions with OMS that the shackling does not result in any significant physical pain for the subject. The detainee's hands are generally between the level of his heart and his chin. In some cases, the detainee's hands may be raised above the level of his head, but only for a period of up to two hours. All of the detainee's weight is borne by his legs and feet during standing sleep deprivation. You have informed us that the detainee is not allowed to hang from or support his body weight with the shackles. Rather, we understand that the shackles are only used

---

[14] *See October 12,* ▮▮▮▮▮ *Letter* at 2-3. Comparison of the time limits for water dousing with those used in SERE training is somewhat difficult as we understand that the SERE training time limits are based on the ambient air temperature rather than water temperature.

as a passive means to keep the detainee standing and thus to prevent him from falling asleep; should the detainee begin to fall asleep, he will lose his balance and awaken, either because of the sensation of losing his balance or because of the restraining tension of the shackles. The use of this passive means for keeping the detainee awake avoids the need for using means that would require interaction with the detainee and might pose a danger of physical harm.

We understand from you that no detainee subjected to this technique by the CIA has suffered any harm or injury, either by falling down and forcing the handcuffs to bear his weight or in any other way. You have assured us that detainees are continuously monitored by closed-circuit television, so that if a detainee were unable to stand, he would immediately be removed from the standing position and would not be permitted to dangle by his wrists. We understand that standing sleep deprivation may cause edema, or swelling, in the lower extremities because it forces detainees to stand for an extended period of time. OMS has advised us that this condition is not painful, and that the condition disappears quickly once the detainee is permitted to lie down. Medical personnel carefully monitor any detainee being subjected to standing sleep deprivation for indications of edema or other physical or psychological conditions. The *OMS Guidelines* include extensive discussion on medical monitoring of detainees being subjected to shackling and sleep deprivation, and they include specific instructions for medical personnel to require alternative, non-standing positions or to take other actions, including ordering the cessation of sleep deprivation, in order to relieve or avoid serious edema or other significant medical conditions. *See OMS Guidelines* at 14-16.

In lieu of standing sleep deprivation, a detainee may instead be seated on and shackled to a small stool. The stool supports the detainee's weight, but is too small to permit the subject to balance himself sufficiently to be able to go to sleep. On rare occasions, a detainee may also be restrained in a horizontal position when necessary to enable recovery from edema without interrupting the course of sleep deprivation.[15] We un-

---

[15] Specifically, you have informed us that on three occasions early in the program, the interrogation team and the attendant medical officers identified the potential for unacceptable edema in the lower limbs of detainees undergoing standing sleep deprivation, and in order to permit the limbs to recover without impairing interrogation requirements, the subjects underwent horizontal sleep deprivation. Fax for Steven G. Bradbury, Principal Deputy Assistant Attorney General, OLC, from █████████████ Assistant General Counsel, CIA, at 2 (Apr. 22, 2005) ("*April 22,* ███ *Fax*"). In horizontal sleep deprivation, the de-

derstand that these alternative restraints, although uncomfortable, are not significantly painful, according to the experience and professional judgment of OMS and other personnel.

We understand that a detainee undergoing sleep deprivation is generally fed by hand by CIA personnel so that he need not be unshackled; however, "[i]f progress is made during interrogation, the interrogators may unshackle the detainee and let him feed himself as a positive incentive." *October 12* ▆▆▆▆▆ *Letter* at 4. If the detainee is clothed, he wears an adult diaper under his pants. Detainees subject to sleep deprivation who are also subject to nudity as a separate interrogation technique will at times be nude and wearing a diaper. If the detainee is wearing a diaper, it is checked regularly and changed as necessary. The use of the diaper is for sanitary and health purposes of the detainee; it is not used for the purpose of humiliating the detainee, and it is not considered to be an interrogation technique. The detainee's skin condition is monitored, and diapers are changed as needed so that the detainee does not remain in a soiled diaper. You have informed us that to date no detainee has experienced any skin problems resulting from the use of diapers.

The maximum allowable duration for sleep deprivation authorized by the CIA is 180 hours, after which the detainee must be permitted to sleep without interruption for at least eight hours. You have informed us that to date, more than a dozen detainees have been subjected to sleep de-

---

tainee is placed prone on the floor on top of a thick towel or blanket (a precaution designed to prevent reduction of body temperature through direct contact with the cell floor). The detainee's hands are manacled together and the arms placed in an outstretched position—either extended beyond the head or extended to either side of the body—and anchored to a far point on the floor in such a manner that the arms cannot be bent or used for balance or comfort. At the same time, the ankles are shackled together and the legs are extended in a straight line with the body and also anchored to a far point on the floor in such a manner that the legs cannot be bend or used for balance or comfort. *Id.* You have specifically informed us that the manacles and shackles are anchored without additional stress or any of the arm or leg joints that might force the limbs beyond natural extension or create tension or any joint. *Id.* The position is sufficiently uncomfortable to detainees to deprive them of unbroken sleep, while allowing their lower limbs to recover from the effects of standing sleep deprivation. We understand that all standard precautions and procedures for shackling are observed for both hands and feet while in this position. *Id.* You have informed us that horizontal sleep deprivation has been used until the detainee's affected limbs have demonstrated sufficient recovery to return to sitting or standing sleep deprivation mode, as warranted by the requirement of the interrogation team, and subject to a determination by the medical officer that there is no contraindication to resuming other sleep deprivation modes. *Id.*

privation of more than 48 hours, and three detainees have been subjected to sleep deprivation of more than 96 hours; the longest period of time for which any detainee has been deprived of sleep by the CIA is 180 hours. Under the CIA's guidelines, sleep deprivation could be resumed after a period of eight hours of uninterrupted sleep, but only if OMS personnel specifically determined that there are no medical or psychological contraindications based on the detainee's condition at that time. As discussed below, however, in this memorandum we will evaluate only one application of up to 180 hours of sleep deprivation.[16]

You have informed us that detainees are closely monitored by the interrogation team at all times (either directly or by closed-circuit video camera) while being subjected to sleep deprivation, and that these personnel will intervene and the techniques will be discontinued if there are medical or psychological contraindications. Furthermore, as with all interrogation techniques used by the CIA, sleep deprivation will not be used on any detainee if the prior medical and psychological assessment reveals any contraindications.

13. *The "waterboard."* In this technique, the detainee is lying on a gurney that is inclined at an angle of 10 to 15 degrees to the horizontal, with the detainee on his back and his head toward the lower end of the gurney. A cloth is placed over the detainee's face, and cold water is poured on the cloth from a height of approximately 6 to 18 inches. The wet cloth creates a barrier through which it is difficult—or in some cases not possible—to breathe. A single "application" of water may not last for more than 40 seconds, with the duration of an "application" measured from the moment when water—of whatever quantity—is first poured onto the cloth until the moment the cloth is removed from the subject's face. *See August 19* ████████ *Letter* at 1. When the time limit is reached, the pouring of water is immediately discontinued and the cloth is removed. We understand that if the detainee makes an effort to defeat the technique (e.g., by twisting his head to the side and breathing out of the corner of his mouth), the interrogator may cup his hands around the detainee's nose and mouth to dam the runoff, in which case it would not be possible for the detainee to breathe during the application of the water. In addition, you have informed us that the technique may be applied in a manner to defeat efforts

---

[16] We express no view on whether any further use of sleep deprivation following a 180-hour application of the technique and 8 hours of sleep would violate sections 2340-2340A.

by the detainee to hold his breath by, for example, beginning an application of water as the detainee is exhaling. Either in the normal application, or where countermeasures are used, we understand that water may enter—and may accumulate in—the detainee's mouth and nasal cavity, preventing him from breathing.[17] In addition, you have indicated that the detainee as a countermeasure may swallow water, possibly in significant quantities. For that reason, based on advice of medical personnel, the CIA requires that saline solution be used instead of plain water to reduce the possibility of hyponatremia (i.e., reduced concentration of sodium in the blood) if the detainee drinks the water.

We understand that the effect of the waterboard is to induce a sensation of drowning. This sensation is based on a deeply rooted physiological response. Thus, the detainee experiences this sensation even if he is aware that he is not actually drowning. We are informed that based on extensive experience, the process is not physically painful, but that it usually does cause fear and panic. The waterboard has been used many thousands of times in SERE training provided to American military personnel, though in that context it is usually limited to one or two applications of no more than 40 seconds each.[18]

You have explained that the waterboard technique is used only if: (1) the CIA has credible intelligence that a terrorist attack is imminent; (2) there are "substantial and credible indicators the subject has actionable intelligence that can prevent, disrupt or delay this attack"; and (3) other interrogation methods have failed or are unlikely to yield actionable intelligence in time to prevent the attack. *See* Attachment to *August 2 Rizzo Letter.* You have also informed us that the waterboard may be approved for

---

[17] In most applications of this technique, including as it is used in SERE training, it appears that the individual undergoing the technique is not in fact completely prevented from breathing, but his airflow is restricted by the wet cloth, creating a sensation of drowning. *See IG Report* at 15 ("airflow is restricted . . . and the technique produces the sensation of drowning and suffocation."). For purposes of our analysis, however, we will assume that the individual is unable to breathe during the entire period of any application of water during the waterboard technique.

[18] The Inspector General was critical of the reliance on the SERE experience with the waterboard in light of these and other differences in application of the technique. We discuss the Inspector General's criticisms further below. Moreover, as noted above, the very different situations of detainees undergoing interrogation and military personnel undergoing training counsels against undue reliance on the experience in SERE training. That experience is nevertheless of some value in evaluating the technique.

use with a given detainee only during, at most, one single 30-day period, and that during that period, the waterboard technique may be used on no more than five days. We further understand that in any 24-hour period, interrogators may use no more than two "sessions" of the waterboard on a subject—with a "session" defined to mean the time that the detainee is strapped to the waterboard—and that no session may last more than two hours. Moreover, during any session, the number of individual applications of water lasting 10 seconds or longer may not exceed six. As noted above, the maximum length of any application of water is 40 seconds (you have informed us that this maximum has rarely been reached). Finally, the total cumulative time of all applications of whatever length in a 24-hour period may not exceed 12 minutes. *See August 19* ▮▮▮▮▮ *Letter* at 1-2. We understand that these limitations have been established with extensive input from OMS, based on experience to date with this technique and OMS's professional judgment that use of the waterboard on a healthy individual subject to these limitations would be "medically acceptable." *See OMS Guidelines* at 18-19.

During the use of the waterboard, a physician and a psychologist are present at all times. The detainee is monitored to ensure that he does not develop respiratory distress. If the detainee is not breathing freely after the cloth is removed from his face, he is immediately moved to a vertical position in order to clear the water from his mouth, nose, and nasopharynx. The gurney used for administering this technique is specially designed so that this can be accomplished very quickly if necessary. Your medical personnel have explained that the use of the waterboard does pose a small risk of certain potentially significant medical problems and that certain measures are taken to avoid or address such problems. First, a detainee might vomit and then aspirate the emesis. To reduce this risk, any detainee on whom this technique will be used is first placed on a liquid diet. Second, the detainee might aspirate some of the water, and the resulting water in the lungs might lead to pneumonia. To mitigate this risk, a potable saline solution is used in the procedure. Third, it is conceivable (though, we understand from OMS, highly unlikely) that a detainee could suffer spasms of the larynx that would prevent him from breathing even when the application of water is stopped and the detainee is returned to an upright position. In the event of such spasms, a qualified physician would immediately intervene to address the problem, and, if necessary, the intervening physician would perform a tracheotomy. Although the risk of such spasms is considered remote (it apparently has never occurred in thousands of instances of SERE training), we are informed that the necessary emergency medical equipment is always present—although not visible to the detainee—during any application of the waterboard. *See generally id.* at 17-20.[19]

We understand that in many years of use on thousands of participants in SERE training, the waterboard technique (although used in a substantially more limited way) has not resulted in any cases of serious physical pain or prolonged mental harm. In addition, we understand that the waterboard has been used by the CIA on three high level al Qaeda detainees, two of whom were subjected to the technique numerous times, and, according to OMS, none of these three individuals has shown any evidence of physical pain or suffering or mental harm in the more than 25 months since the technique was used on them. As noted, we understand that OMS has been involved in imposing strict limits on the use of the waterboard, limits that, when combined with careful monitoring, in their professional judgment should prevent physical pain or suffering or mental harm to a detainee. In addition, we understand that any detainee is closely monitored by medical and psychological personnel whenever the waterboard is applied, and that there are additional reporting requirements beyond the normal reporting requirements in place when other interrogation techniques are used. *See OMS Guidelines* at 20.

* * *

---

[19] OMS identified other potential risks:

> In our limited experience, extensive sustained use of the waterboard can introduce new risks. Most seriously, for reasons of physical fatigue or psychological resignation, the subject may simply give up, allowing excessive filling of the airways and loss of consciousness. An unresponsive subject should be righted immediately, and the interrogator should deliver a sub-xyphoid thrust to expel the water. If this fails to restore normal breathing, aggressive medical intervention is required. Any subject who has reached this degree of compromise is not considered an appropriate candidate for the waterboard, and the physician on the scene can not concur in the further use of the waterboard without specific [Chief, OMS] consultation and approval.

OMS Guidelines at 18. OMS has also stated that "[b]y days 3-5 of an aggressive program, cumulative effects become a potential concern. Without any hard data to quantify either this risk of the advantages of this technique, we believe that beyond this point continued intense waterboard applications may not be medically appropriate." *Id.* at 19. As noted above, based on OMS input, the CIA has adopted and imposed a number of strict limitations on the frequency and duration of use of the waterboard.

As noted, all of the interrogation techniques described above are subject to numerous restrictions, many based on input from OMS. Our advice in this memorandum is based on our understanding that there will be careful adherence to all of these guidelines, restrictions, and safeguards, and that there will be ongoing monitoring and reporting by the team, including OMS medical and psychological personnel, as well as prompt intervention by a team member, as necessary, to prevent physical distress or mental harm so significant as possibly to amount to the "severe physical or mental pain or suffering" that is prohibited by sections 2340-2340A. Our advice is also based on our understanding that all interrogators who will use these techniques are adequately trained to understand that the authorized use of the techniques is not designed or intended to cause severe physical or mental pain or suffering, and also to understand and respect the medical judgment of OMS and the important role that OMS personnel play in the program.

C.

You asked for our advice concerning these interrogation techniques in connection with their use on a specific high value al Qaeda detainee named ███████████. You informed us that the ██████████████ had information about al Qaeda's plans to launch an attack within the United States. According to ████████████ had extensive connections to various al Qaeda leaders, members of the Taliban, and the al-Zarqawi network, and had arranged meetings between an associate and ████████ ██████to discuss such an attack. *August 25* ████████ *Letter* at 2-3. You advised us that medical and psychological assessments ████████were completed by a CIA physician and psychologist, and that based on this examination, the physician concluded "████████████ medically stable and has no medical contraindications to interrogation, including the use of interrogation techniques" addressed in this memorandum.[20] *Medical and Psychological Assessment of* ████████████████*attached to August 2 Rizzo Letter* at 1.[21] The psychological assessment found ████████

---

[20] You have advised us that the waterboard has not been used ██████████. We understand that there may have been medical reasons against using that technique in his case. Of course, our advise assumes that the waterboard could be used only in the absence of medical contraindications.

[21] The medical examination reported ████████ was obese, and that he reported a "5-6 year history of non-exertional chest pressures, which are intermit-

was alert and oriented and his concentration and attention were appropriate." *Id.* at 2. The psychologist further found ███████████ "thought processes were clear and logical; there was no evidence of a thought disorder, delusions, or hallucinations[, and t]here were no significant signs of depression, anxiety, or other "mental disturbance." *Id.* The psychologist evaluated ████████ "psychologically stable, reserved and defensive," and "opined that there was no evidence that the use of the approved interrogation methods would cause any severe or prolonged psychological disturbance ████████ . *Id.* at 2. Our conclusions depend on these assessments. Before using the techniques on other detainees, the CIA would need to ensure, in each case, that all medical and psychological assessments indicate that the detainee is fit to undergo the use of the interrogation techniques.

II.

[Deleted. This section incorporates almost verbatim sections I and II of the December 30, 2004 Memorandum for James B. Comey.]

III.

In the discussion that follows, we will address each of the specific interrogation techniques you have described. Subject to the understandings, limitations, and safeguards discussed herein, including ongoing medical and psychological monitoring and team intervention as necessary, we conclude that the authorized use of each of these techniques, considered individually, would not violate the prohibition that Congress has adopted in sections 2340-2340A. This conclusion is straightforward with respect

---

tent, at times accompanied by nausea and depression and shortness of breath." *Medical and Psychological Assessment of* ████████ at 1, attached to *August 2 Rizzo Letter.* ████████████ he has never consulted a physician for this problem," and was "unable or unwilling to be more specific about the frequency or intensity of the aforementioned symptoms." *Id.* He also reported suffering "long-term medical and mental problems" from a motor vehicle accident "many years ago," and stated that he took medication as a result of that accident until ten years ago. *Id.* He stated that he was not currently taking any medication. He also reported seeing a physician for kidney problems that caused him to urinate frequently and complained of a toothache. *Id.* The medical examination ████████ showed a rash on his chest and shoulders and that "his nose and chest were clear, [and] his heart sounds were normal with no murmurs or gallops." *Id.* The physician opined ████████ "likely has some reflux esophagitis and mild check folliculitis, but doubt[ed] that he has any coronary pathology." *Id.*

to all but two of the techniques. Use of sleep deprivation as an enhanced technique and use of the waterboard, however, involve more substantial questions, with the waterboard presenting the most substantial question. Although we conclude that the use of these techniques—as we understand them and subject to the limitations you have described—would not violate the statute, the issues raised by these two techniques counsel great caution of their use, including both careful adherence to the limitations and restrictions you have described and also close and continuing medical and psychological monitoring.

Before addressing the application of sections 2340-2340A to the specific techniques in question, we note certain overall features of the CIA's approach that are significant to our conclusions. Interrogators are trained and certified in a course that you have informed us currently lasts approximately four weeks. Interrogators (and other personnel deployed as part of this program) are required to review and acknowledge the applicable interrogation guidelines. *See Confinement Guidelines* at 2; *Interrogation Guidelines* at 2 ("The Director, DCI Counterterrorist Center shall ensure that all personnel directly engaged in the interrogation of persons detained pursuant to the authorities set forth in ███████████ have been appropriately screened (from the medical, psychological and security standpoints), have reviewed these Guidelines, have received appropriate training in their implementation, and have completed the attached Acknowledgement."). We assume that all interrogators are adequately trained, that they understand the design and purpose of the interrogation techniques, and that they will apply the techniques in accordance with their authorized and intended use.

In addition, the involvement of medical and psychological personnel in the adaptation and application of the established SERE techniques is particularly noteworthy for purposes of our analysis.[33] Medical personnel

---

[33] As noted above, each of these techniques has been adapted (although in some cases with significant modifications) from SERE training. Through your consultation with various individuals responsible for such training, you have learned facts relating to experience with them, which you have reported to us. Again, fully recognizing the limitations of reliance on this experience, you have advised us that these techniques have been used as elements of a course of training without any reported incidents of prolonged mental harm or of any severe physical pain, injury, or suffering. With respect to the psychological impact, ████████████████████████ of the SERE school advised that during his three and a half years in that position, he trained 10,000 students, only two of whom dropped out following use of the techniques. Although on rare occa-

have been involved in imposing limitations on—and requiring changes to—certain procedures, particularly the use of the waterboard.[34] We have had extensive meetings with the medical personnel involved in monitoring the use of these techniques. It is clear that they have carefully worked to ensure that the techniques do not result in severe physical or mental pain or suffering to the detainees.[35] Medical and psychological personnel

---

sions students temporarily postponed the remainder of the training and received psychological counseling, we understand that those students were able to finish the program without any indication of subsequent mental health effects. ██████████ ███████████who has had over ten years experience with SERE training, told you that he was not aware of any individuals who completed the program suffering any adverse mental health effects (though he advised of one person who did not complete the training who had an adverse mental health reaction that lasted two hours and spontaneously dissipated without requiring treatment and with no further symptoms reported). In addition, the ████████████ ███████████████████who has had experience with all of the techniques discussed herein, had advised that the use of these procedures has not resulted in any reported instances of prolonged mental harm and very few instances of immediate and temporary adverse psychological responses to the training. Of 26,829 students in Air Force SERE training from 1992 through 2001, only 0.14% were pulled from the program for psychological reasons (specifically, although 4.3% had some contact with psychology services, only 3% of those individuals with such contact in fact withdrew from the program). We understand that the ████████████████████████ expressed confidence—based on debriefing of students and other information—that the training did not cause any long-term psychological harm and that if there are any long-term psychological effects of the training at all, they "are certainly minimal."

[34] We note that this involvement of medical personal in designing safeguards for, and in monitoring implementation of, the procedures is a significant difference from earlier uses of the techniques catalogued in the Inspector General's Report. *See IG Report* at 21 n.26 ("OMS was neither consulted nor involved in the initial analysis of the risk and benefits of [enhanced interrogation techniques], nor provided with the OTS report cited in the OLC opinion [the *Interrogation Memorandum*].''). Since that time, based on comments from OMS, additional constraints have been imposed on use of the techniques.

[35] We are mindful that, historically, medical personnel have sometimes been used to enhance, not prevent, torture—for example, by keeping a torture victim alive and conscious so as to extend his suffering. It is absolutely clear, as you have informed us and as our own dealings with OMS personnel have confirmed, that the involvement of OMS is intended to prevent harm to the detainees and not to extend or increase pain or suffering. As the *OMS Guidelines* explain, "OMS is responsible for assessing and monitoring the health of all Agency detainees subject to 'enhanced' interrogation techniques, and for determining that the authorized administration of these techniques would not be expected to cause

evaluate each detainee before the use of these techniques on the detainee is approved, and they continue to monitor each detainee throughout his interrogation and detention. Moreover, medical personnel are physically present throughout application of the waterboard (and present or otherwise observing the use of all techniques that involve physical contact, as discussed more fully above), and they carefully monitor detainees who are undergoing sleep deprivation or dietary manipulation. In addition, they regularly assess both the medical literature and the experience with detainees.[36] OMS has specifically declared that "[m]edical officers must remain cognizant at all times of their obligation to prevent 'severe physical or mental pain or suffering.'" *OMS Guidelines* at 10. In fact, we understand that medical and psychological personnel have discontinued the use of techniques as to a particular detainee when they believed he might suffer such pain or suffering, and in certain instances, OMS medical personnel have not cleared certain detainees for some—or any—techniques based on the initial medical and psychological assessments. They have also imposed additional restrictions on the use of techniques (such as the waterboard) in order to protect the safety of detainees, thus reducing further the risk of severe pain or suffering. You have informed us that they will continue to have this role and authority. We assume that all interrogators understand the important role and authority of OMS personnel and will cooperate with OMS in the exercise of these duties.

Finally, in sharp contrast to those practices universally condemned as torture over the centuries, the techniques we consider here have been carefully evaluated to avoid causing severe pain or suffering to the detainees. As OMS has described these techniques as a group:

> In all instances, the general goal of these techniques is a psychological impact, and not some physical effect, with a specific goal of "dislocat[ing] [the detainee's] expectations regarding the treatment he believes he will receive. . . ." The more physical techniques are delivered in a manner carefully limited to avoid serious pain. The slaps, for example, are de-

---

serious or permanent harm." *OMS Guidelines* at 9 (footnote omitted).

[36] To assist in monitoring experience with the detainees, we understand that there is regular reporting on medical and psychological experience with the use of these techniques on detainees and that there are special instructions on documenting experience with sleep deprivation and the waterboard. *See OMS Guidelines* at 6-7, 16, 20.

signed "to induce shock, surprise, and/or humiliation" and "not to inflict physical pain that is severe or lasting."

Id. at 8-9.

With this background, we turn to the application of sections 2340-2340A to each of the specific interrogation techniques.

1. *Dietary manipulation.* Based on experience, it is evident that this technique is not expected to cause any physical pain, let alone pain that is extreme in intensity. The detainee is carefully monitored to ensure that he does not suffer acute weight loss or any dehydration. Further, there is nothing in the experience of caloric intake at this level that could be expected to cause physical pain. Although we do not equate a person who voluntarily enters a weight-loss program with a detainee subjected to dietary manipulation as an interrogation technique, we believe that it is relevant that several commercial weight-loss programs available in the United States involve similar or even greater reductions in caloric intake. Nor could this technique reasonably be thought to induce "severe physical suffering." Although dietary manipulation may cause some degree of hunger, such an experience is far from extreme hunger (let alone starvation) and cannot be expected to amount to "severe physical suffering" under the statute. The caloric levels are set based on the detainee's weight, so as to ensure that the detainee does not experience extreme hunger. As noted, many people participate in weight-loss programs that involve similar or more stringent caloric limitations, and, while such participation cannot be equated with the use of dietary manipulation as an interrogation technique, we believe that the existence of such programs is relevant to whether dietary manipulation would cause "severe physical suffering" within the meaning of sections 2340-2340A. Because there is no prospect that the technique would cause severe physical pain or suffering, we conclude that the authorized use of this technique by an adequately trained interrogator could not reasonably be considered specifically intended to do so.

This technique presents no issue of "severe mental pain or suffering" within the meaning of sections 2340-2340A, because the use of the technique would involve no qualifying predicate act. The technique does not, for example, involve "the intentional infliction or threatened infliction of severe physical pain or suffering," 18 U.S.C. § 2340(2)(A), or the "application . . . of . . . procedures calculated to disrupt profoundly the senses or the personality," *id.* § 2340(2)(B). Moreover, there is no basis to believe that dietary manipulation could cause "prolonged mental harm." Therefore, we conclude that the authorized use of this technique by an adequately trained interrogator could not reasonably be considered specifically intended to cause such harm.[37]

2. *Nudity.* We understand that nudity is used as a technique to create psychological discomfort, not to inflict any physical pain or suffering. You have informed us that during the use of this technique, detainees are kept in locations with ambient temperatures that ensure there is no threat to their health. Specifically, this technique would not be employed at temperatures below 68°F (and is unlikely to be employed below 75°F). Even if this technique involves some physical discomfort, it cannot be said to cause "suffering" (as we have explained the term above), let alone "severe physical pain or suffering," and we therefore conclude that its authorized use by an adequately trained interrogator could not reasonably be considered specifically intended to do so. Although some detainees might be humiliated by this technique, especially given possible cultural sensitivities and the possibility of being seen by female officers, it cannot constitute "severe mental pain or suffering" under the statute because it does not involve any of the predicate acts specified by Congress.

3. *Attention grasp.* The attention grasp involves no physical pain or suffering for the detainee and does not involve any predicate act for purposes of severe mental pain or suffering under the statute. Accordingly, because this technique cannot be expected to cause severe physical or mental pain or suffering, we conclude that its authorized use by an adequately trained interrogator could not reasonably be considered specifically intended to do so.

4. *Walling.* Although the walling technique involves the use of considerable force to push the detainee against the wall and may involve a large number of repetitions in certain cases, we understand that the false wall that is used is flexible and that this technique is not designed to, and does not, cause severe physical pain to the detainee. We understand that there may be some pain or irritation associated with the collar, which is

---

[37] In *Ireland v. United Kingdom*, 25 Eur. Ct. H.R. (ser. A)(1978), the European Court of Human Rights concluded by a vote of 13-4 that a reduced diet, even in conjunction with a number of other techniques, did not amount to "torture," as defined in the European Convention on Human Rights. The reduced diet there consisted of one "round" of bread and a pint of water every six hours, *see id.*, separate opinion of Judge Zekia, Part A. The duration of the reduced diet in that case is not clear.

used to help avoid injury such as whiplash to the detainee, but that any physical pain associated with the use of the collar would not approach the level of intensity needed to constitute severe physical pain. Similarly, we do not believe that the physical distress caused by this technique or the duration of its use, even with multiple repetitions, could amount to severe physical suffering within the meaning of sections 2340-2340A. We understand that medical and psychological personnel are present or observing during the use of this technique (as with all techniques involving physical contact with a detainee), and that any member of the team or the medical staff may intercede to stop the use of the technique if it is being used improperly or if it appears that it may cause injury to the detainee. We also do not believe that the use of this technique would involve a threat of infliction of severe physical pain or suffering or other predicate act for purposes of severe mental pain or suffering under the statute. Rather, this technique is designed to shock the detainee and disrupt his expectations that he will not be treated forcefully and to wear down his resistance to interrogation. Based on these understandings, we conclude that the authorized use of this technique by adequately trained interrogators could not reasonably be considered specifically intended to cause severe physical or mental pain or suffering in violation of sections 2340-2340A.[38]

5. *Facial hold.* Like the attention grasp, this technique involves no physical pain or suffering and does not involve any predicate act for purposes of severe mental pain or suffering. Accordingly, we conclude that its authorized use by adequately trained interrogators could not reasonably be considered specifically intended to cause severe physical or mental pain or suffering.

6. *Facial slap or insult slap.* Although this technique involves a degree of physical pain, the pain associated with a slap to the face, as you have described it to us, could not be expected to constitute severe physical

---

[38] *In Interrogation Memorandum*, we did not describe the walling technique as involving the number of repetitions that we understand may be applied; Our advice with respect to walling in the present memorandum is specifically based on the understanding that the repetitive use of walling is intended only to increase the drama and shock of the technique, to wear down the detainee's resistance, and to disrupt expectations that he will not be treated with force, and that such use is not intended to, and does not in fact, cause severe physical pain to the detainee. Moreover, our advice specifically assumes that the use of walling will be stopped if there is any indication that the use of the technique is or may be causing severe physical pain to a detainee.

pain. We understand that the purpose of this technique is to cause shock, surprise, or humiliation, not to inflict physical pain that is severe or lasting; we assume it will be used accordingly. Similarly, the physical distress that may be caused by an abrupt slap to the face, even if repeated several times, would not constitute an extended state or condition of physical suffering and also would not likely involve the level of intensity required for severe physical suffering under the statute. Finally, a facial slap would not involve a predicate act for purposes of severe mental pain or suffering. Therefore, the authorized use of this technique by adequately trained interrogators could not reasonably be considered specifically intended to cause severe physical or mental pain or suffering in violation of sections 2340-2340A.[39]

7. *Abdominal slap.* Although the abdominal slap technique might involve some minor physical pain, it cannot, as you have described it to us, be said to involve even moderate, let alone *severe*, physical pain or suffering. Again, because the technique cannot be expected to cause severe physical pain or suffering, we conclude that its authorized use by an adequately trained interrogator could not reasonably be considered specifically intended to do so. Nor could it be considered specifically intended to cause severe mental pain or suffering within the meaning of sections 2340-2340A, as none of the statutory predicate acts would be present.

8. *Cramped confinement.* This technique does not involve any significant physical pain or suffering. It also does not involve a predicate act for purposes of severe mental pain or suffering. Specifically, we do not believe that placing a detainee in a dark, cramped space for the limited period of time involved here could reasonably be considered a procedure calculated to disrupt profoundly the senses so as to cause prolonged mental harm. Accordingly, we conclude that its authorized use by adequately trained interrogators could not reasonably be considered specifically intended to cause severe physical or mental pain or suffering in violation of sections 2340-2340A.

---

[39] Our advice about both the facial slap and the abdominal slap assumes that the interrogators will apply those techniques as designed and will not strike the detainee with excessive force or repetition in a manner that might result in severe physical pain.

9. *Wall standing.* The wall standing technique, as you have described it, would not involve severe physical pain within the meaning of the statute. It also cannot be expected to cause severe physical suffering. Even if the physical discomfort of muscle fatigue associated with wall standing might be substantial, we understand that the duration of the technique is self-limited by the individual detainee's ability to sustain the position; thus, the short duration of the discomfort means that this technique would not be expected to cause, and could not reasonably be considered specifically intended to cause, severe physical suffering. Our advice also assumes that the detainee's position is not designed to produce severe pain that might result from contortions or twisting of the body, but only temporary muscle fatigue. Nor does wall standing involve any predicate act for purposes of severe mental pain or suffering. Accordingly, we conclude that the authorized use of this technique by adequately trained interrogators could not reasonably be considered specifically intended to cause severe physical or mental pain or suffering in violation of the statute.

10. *Stress positions.* For the same reasons that the use of wall standing would not violate the statute, we conclude that the authorized use of stress positions such as those described in *Interrogation Memorandum,* if employed by adequately trained interrogators, could not reasonably be considered specifically intended to cause severe physical or mental pain or suffering in violation of sections 2340-2340A. As with wall standing, we understand that the duration of the technique is self-limited by the individual detainee's ability to sustain the position; thus, the short duration of the discomfort means that this technique would not be expected to cause, and could not reasonably be considered specifically intended to cause, severe physical suffering. Our advice also assumes that stress positions are not designed to produce severe pain that might result from contortions or twisting of the body, but only temporary muscle fatigue.[40]

---

[40] A stress position that involves such contortion or twisting, as well as one held for so long that it could not be aimed only at producing temporary muscle fatigue, might raise more substantial questions under the statute. *Cf. Army Field Manual 34-52: Intelligence Interrogation* at 1-8 (1992) (indicating that "[f]orcing an individual to stand, sit, or kneel in abnormal positions for prolonged periods of time" may constitute "torture" within the meaning of the Third Geneva Convention's requirement that " [n]o physical or mental torture, nor any other form of coercion, may be inflicted on prisoners of war," but not addressing 18 U.S.C. §§ 2340-2340A); United Nations General Assembly *Report of the Special Rapporieur on Torture and Other Cruel, Inhuman or Degrading Treatment or Punishment,* U.N. Doc. A/59/150 at 6 (Sept. 1, 2004) (suggesting that "holding

11. *Water dousing.* As you have described it to us, water dousing involves dousing the detainee with water from a container or a hose without a nozzle, and is intended to wear him down both physically and psychologically. You have informed us that the water might be as cold as 41°F, though you have further advised us that the water generally is not refrigerated and therefore is unlikely to be less than 50°F. (Nevertheless, for purposes of our analysis, we will assume that water as cold as 4I°F might be used.) OMS has advised that, based on the extensive experience in SERE training, the medical literature, and the experience with detainees to date, water dousing as authorized is not designed or expected to cause significant physical pain, and certainly not severe physical pain. Although we understand that prolonged *immersion* in very cold water may be physically painful, as noted above, this interrogation technique does not involve immersion and a substantial margin of safety is built into the time limitation on the use of the CIA's water dousing technique—use of the technique with water of a given temperature must be limited to no more than two-thirds of the time in which hypothermia could be expected to occur from *total immersion* in water of the same temperature.[41] While being cold can involve physical discomfort, OMS also advises that in their professional judgment any resulting discomfort is not expected to be intense, and the duration is limited by specific times tied to water temperature. Any discomfort caused by this technique, therefore, would not qualify as "severe physical suffering" within the meaning of sections 2340-2340A. Consequently, given that there is no expectation that the technique will cause severe physical pain or suffering when properly used, we conclude that the authorized use of this technique by an adequately trained interrogator could not reasonably be considered specifically intended to cause these results.

With respect to mental pain or suffering, as you have described the procedure, we do not believe that any of the four statutory predicate acts necessary for a possible finding of severe mental pain or suffering under the statute would be present. Nothing, for example, leads us to believe that the detainee would understand the procedure to constitute a threat

---

detainees in painful and/or stressful positions" might in certain circumstances be characterized as torture).

[41] Moreover, even in the extremely unlikely event that hypothermia set in, under the circumstances in which this technique is used—including close medical supervision and, if necessary, medical attention—we understand that the detainee would be expected to recover fully and rapidly.

of imminent death, especially given that care is taken to ensure that no water will get into the detainee's mouth or nose. Nor would a detainee reasonably understand the prospect of being doused with cold water as the threatened infliction of severe pain. Furthermore, even if we were to conclude that there could be a qualifying predicate act, nothing suggests that the detainee would be expected to suffer any prolonged mental harm as a result of the procedure. OMS advises that there has been no evidence of such harm in the SERE training, which utilizes a much more extreme technique involving total immersion. The presence of psychologists who monitor the detainee's mental condition makes such harm even more unlikely. Consequently, we conclude that the authorized use of the technique by adequately trained interrogators could not reasonably be considered specifically intended to cause severe mental pain or suffering within the meaning of the statute.

The flicking technique, which is subject to the same temperature limitations as water dousing but would involve substantially less water, *a fortiori* would not violate the statute.

12. *Sleep deprivation.* In the *Interrogation Memorandum*, we concluded that sleep deprivation did not violate sections 2340-2340A. *See id.* at 10, 14-15. This question warrants further analysis for two reasons. First, we did not consider the potential for physical pain or suffering resulting from the shackling used to keep detainees awake or any impact from the diapering of the detainee. Second, we did not address the possibility of severe physical suffering that does not involve severe physical pain.

Under the limitations adopted by the CIA, sleep deprivation may not exceed 180 hours, which we understand is approximately two-thirds of the maximum recorded time that humans have gone without sleep for purposes of medical study, as discussed below.[42] Furthermore, any detainee who has undergone 180 hours of sleep deprivation must then be allowed to sleep without interruption for at least eight straight hours. Although we understand that the CIA's guidelines would allow another session of sleep deprivation to begin after the detainee has gotten at least eight hours

---

[42] The *IG Report* described the maximum allowable period of sleep deprivation at that time as 264 hours or 11 days. *See IG Report* at 15. You have informed us that you have since established a limit of 180 hours, that in fact no detainee has been subjected to more than 180 hours of sleep deprivation, and that sleep deprivation will rarely exceed 120 hours. To date, only three detainees have been subjected to sleep deprivation for more than 96 hours.

of uninterrupted sleep following 180 hours of sleep deprivation, we will evaluate only one application of up to 180 hours of sleep deprivation.[43]

We understand from OMS, and from our review of the literature on the physiology of sleep, that even very extended sleep deprivation does not cause physical pain, let alone severe physical pain.[44] "The longest studies of sleep deprivation in humans . . . [involved] volunteers [who] were deprived of sleep for 8 to 11 days. . . . Surprisingly, little seemed to go wrong with the subjects physically. The main effects lay with sleepiness and impaired brain functioning, but even these were no great cause for concern." James Horne, *Why We Sleep: The Functions of Sleep in Humans and Other Mammals* [at] 23-24 (1988) (*"Why We Sleep"*) (footnote omitted). We note that there are important differences between sleep deprivation as an interrogation technique used by the CIA and the controlled experiments documented in the literature. The subjects of the experiments were free to move about and engage in normal activities and often led a "tranquil existence" with "plenty of time for relaxation," *see id.* at 24, whereas a detainee in CIA custody would be shackled and prevented from moving freely. Moreover, the subjects in the experiments often increased their food consumption during periods of extended sleep loss, *see id.* at 38, whereas the detainee undergoing interrogation may be placed on a reduced-calorie diet, as discussed above. Nevertheless, we understand that experts who have studied sleep deprivation have concluded that "[t]he most plausible reason for the uneventful physical findings with these hu-

---

[43] As noted above, we are not concluding that additional use of sleep deprivation, subject to close and careful medical supervision, would violate the statute, but at the present time we express no opinion on whether additional sleep deprivation would be consistent with sections 2340-2340A.

[44] Although sleep deprivation is not itself physically painful, we understand that some studies have noted that extended total sleep deprivation may have the effect of reducing tolerance to some forms of pain in some subjects. *See, e.g.*, B. Kundermann, et al., *Sleep Deprivation Affects Thermal Pain Threshold but not Somatosensory Thresholds in Healthy Volunteers*, 66 Psychosomatic Med. 932 (2004) (finding a significant decrease in heat pain thresholds and some decrease in cold pain thresholds after one night without sleep); S., Hakki Onen, et al, *The Effects of Total Sleep Deprivation, Selective Sleep Interruption and Sleep Recovery on Pain Tolerance Thresholds in Healthy Subjects*, 10 J. Sleep Research 35, 41 (2001) (finding a statistically significant drop of 8-9% in tolerance thresholds for mechanical or pressure pain after 40 hours); *id.* at 35-36 (discussing other studies), We will discuss the potential interactions between sleep deprivation and other interrogation techniques in the separate memorandum, to which we referred in footnote 6, addressing whether the combined use of certain techniques is consistent with the legal requirements of 2340-2340A.

man beings is that . . . sleep loss is not particularly harmful." *Id.* at 24. We understand that this conclusion does not depend on the extent of physical movement or exercise by the subject or whether the subject increases his food consumption. OMS medical staff members have also informed us, based on their experience with detainees who have undergone extended sleep deprivation and their review of the relevant medical literature, that extended sleep deprivation does not cause physical pain. Although edema, or swelling, of the lower legs may sometimes develop as a result of the long periods of standing associated with sleep deprivation, we understand from OMS that such edema is not painful and will quickly dissipate once the subject is removed from the standing position. We also understand that if any case of significant edema develops, the team will intercede to ensure that the detainee is moved from the standing position and that he receives any medical attention necessary to relieve the swelling and allow the edema to dissipate. For these reasons, we conclude that the authorized use of extended sleep deprivation by adequately trained interrogators would not be expected to cause and could not reasonably be considered specifically intended to cause severe physical pain.

In addition, OMS personnel have informed us that the shackling of detainees is not designed to and does not result in significant physical pain. A detainee subject to sleep deprivation would not be allowed to hang by his wrists, and we understand that no detainee subjected to sleep deprivation to date has been allowed to hang by his wrists or has otherwise suffered injury.[45] If necessary, we understand that medical personnel will intercede to prevent any such injury and would require either that interrogators use a different method to keep the detainee awake (such as through the use of sitting or horizontal positions), or that the use of the technique be stopped altogether. When the sitting position is used, the detainee is seated on a small stool to which he is shackled; the stool supports his weight but is too small to let the detainee balance himself and fall asleep. We also specifically understand that the use of shackling with horizontal sleep deprivation, which has only been used rarely, is done in such a way as to ensure that there is no additional stress on the detainee's arm or leg joints that might force the limbs beyond natural extension or create tension on any joint. Thus, shackling cannot be expected to result in severe physical pain, and we conclude that its authorized use by adequately trained interrogators could not reasonably be considered specifically intended to do

---

[45] This includes a total of more than 24 detainees subjected to at least some period of sleep deprivation. *See January 4* ▮▮▮ *Fax* at 1-3.

so. Finally, we believe that the use of a diaper cannot be expected to—and could not reasonably be considered intended to—result in any physical pain, let alone severe physical pain.

Although it is a more substantial question, particularly given the imprecision in the statutory standard and the lack of guidance from the courts, we also conclude that extended sleep deprivation, subject to the limitations and conditions described herein, would not be expected to cause "severe physical suffering." We understand that some individuals who undergo extended sleep deprivation would likely at some point experience physical discomfort and distress. We assume that some individuals would eventually feel weak physically and may experience other unpleasant physical sensations from prolonged fatigue, including such symptoms as impairment to coordinated body movement, difficulty with speech, nausea, and blurred vision. *See Why We Sleep* at 30. In addition, we understand that extended sleep deprivation will often cause a small drop in body temperature, *see id.* at 31, and we assume that such a drop in body temperature may also be associated with unpleasant physical sensations. We also assume that any physical discomfort that might be associated with sleep deprivation would likely increase, at least to a point, the longer the subject goes without sleep. Thus, on these assumptions, it may be the case that at some point, for some individuals, the degree of physical distress experienced in sleep deprivation might be substantial.[46]

On the other hand, we understand from OMS, and from the literature we have reviewed on the physiology of sleep, that many individuals may tolerate extended sleep deprivation well and with little apparent distress, and that this has been the CIA's experience.[47] Furthermore, the principal physical problem associated with standing is edema, and in any instance of significant edema, the interrogation team will remove the detainee from the standing position and will seek medical assistance. The shackling is used only as a passive means of keeping the detainee awake and, in both the tightness of the shackles and the positioning of the hands, is not intended to cause pain. A detainee, for example, will not be allowed

---

[46] The possibility noted above that sleep deprivation might heighten susceptibility to pain, *see supra* note 44, magnifies this concern.

[47] Indeed, although it may seem surprising to those not familiar with the extensive medical literature relating to sleep deprivation, based on that literature and its experience with the technique, in its Guidelines, OMS lists sleep deprivation as less intense than water dousing, stress positions, walling cramped confinement, and the waterboard. *See OMS Guidelines* at 8.

to hang by his wrists. Shackling in the sitting position involves a stool that is adequate to support the detainee's weight. In the rare instances when horizontal sleep deprivation may be used, a thick towel or blanket is placed under the detainee to protect against reduction of body temperature from contact with the floor, and the manacles and shackles are anchored so as not to cause pain or create tension on any joint. If the detainee is nude and is using an adult diaper, the diaper is checked regularly to prevent skin irritation. The conditions of sleep deprivation are thus aimed at preventing severe physical suffering. Because sleep deprivation does not involve physical pain and would not be expected to cause extreme physical distress to the detainee, the extended duration of sleep deprivation, within the 180-hour limit imposed by the CIA, is not a sufficient factor alone to constitute severe physical suffering within the meaning of sections 2340-2340A. We therefore believe that the use of this technique, under the specified limits and conditions, is not "extreme and outrageous" and does not reach the high bar set by Congress for a violation of sections 2340-2340A. *See Price v. Socialist People's Libyan Arab Jamahiriya,* 294 F.3d at 92 (to be torture under the TVPA, conduct must be "extreme and outrageous"); *cf. Mehinovic v. Vuckovic,* 198 F. Supp. 2d at 1332-40, 1345-46 (standard met under the TVPA by a course of conduct that included severe beatings to the genitals, head, and other parts of the body with metal pipes and various other items; removal of teeth with pliers; kicking in the face and ribs; breaking of bones and ribs and dislocation of fingers; cutting a figure into the victim's forehead; hanging the victim and beating him; extreme limitations of food and water; and subjection to games of "Russian roulette").

Nevertheless, because extended sleep deprivation could in some cases result in substantial physical distress, the safeguards adopted by the CIA, including ongoing medical monitoring and intervention by the team if needed, are important to ensure that the CIA's use of extended sleep deprivation will not run afoul of the statute. Different individual detainees may react physically to sleep deprivation in different ways. We assume, therefore, that the team will separately monitor each individual detainee who is undergoing sleep deprivation, and that the application of this technique will be sensitive to the individualized physical condition and reactions of each detainee. Moreover, we emphasize our understanding that OMS will intervene to alter or stop the course of sleep deprivation for a detainee if OMS concludes in its medical judgment that the detainee is or may be experiencing extreme physical distress.[48] The team, we under-

---

[48] For example, any physical pain or suffering associated with standing or

stand, will intervene not only if the sleep deprivation itself may be having such effects, but also if the shackling or other conditions attendant to the technique appear to be causing severe physical suffering. With these precautions in place, and based on the assumption that they will be followed, we conclude that the authorized use of extended sleep deprivation by adequately trained interrogators would not be expected to and could not reasonably be considered specifically intended to cause severe physical suffering in violation of 18 U.S.C. §§ 2340-2340A.

Finally, we also conclude that extended sleep deprivation cannot be expected to cause "severe mental pain or suffering" as defined in sections 2340-2340A, and that its authorized use by adequately trained interrogators could not reasonably be considered specifically intended to do so. First, we do not believe that use of the sleep deprivation technique, subject to the conditions in place, would involve one of the predicate acts necessary for "severe mental pain or suffering" under the statute. There would be no infliction or threatened infliction of severe physical pain or suffering, within the meaning of the statute, and there would be no threat of imminent death. It may be questioned whether sleep deprivation could be characterized as a "procedure[] calculated to disrupt profoundly the senses or the personality" within the meaning of section 2340(2)(B), since we understand from OMS and from the scientific literature that extended sleep deprivation might induce hallucinations in some cases. Physicians from OMS have informed us, however, that they are of the view that, in general, no "profound" disruption would result from the length of sleep deprivation contemplated by the CIA, and again the scientific literature we have reviewed appears to support this conclusion. Moreover, we understand that any team member would direct that the technique be immediately discontinued if there were any sign that the detainee is experiencing hallucinations. Thus, it appears that the authorized use of sleep deprivation by the CIA would not be expected to result in a profound disruption of the senses, and if it did, it would be discontinued. Even assuming, however, that the extended use of sleep deprivation may result in hallucinations that

---

with shackles might become more intense with an extended use of the technique on a particular detainee whose condition and strength do not permit him to tolerate it. And we understand that personnel monitoring the detainee will take this possibility into account and, if necessary, will ensure that the detainee is placed into a sitting or horizontal position or will direct that sleep deprivation be discontinued altogether. *See OMS Guidelines* at 14-16.

could fairly be characterized as a "profound" disruption of the subject's senses, we do not believe it tenable to conclude that in such circumstances the use of sleep deprivation could be said to be "calculated" to cause such profound disruption to the senses, as required by the statute. The term "calculated" denotes something that is planned or thought out beforehand: "Calculate," as used in the statute, is defined to mean "to plan the nature of beforehand: think out"; "to design, prepare, or adapt by forethought or careful plan: fit or prepare by appropriate means." *Webster's Third New International Dictionary* at 315 (defining "calculate"—"used chiefly [as it is in section 2340(2)(B)] as [a] past part[iciple] with complementary infinitive <*calculated* to succeed>"). Here, it is evident that the potential for any hallucinations on the part of a detainee undergoing sleep deprivation is not something that would be a "calculated" result of the use of this technique, particularly given that the team would intervene immediately to stop the technique if there were signs the subject was experiencing hallucinations.

Second, even if we were to assume, out of an abundance of caution, that extended sleep deprivation could be said to be a "procedure[] calculated to disrupt profoundly the senses or the personality" of the subject within the meaning of section 2340-2340(2)(B), we do not believe that this technique would be expected to—or that its authorized use by adequately trained interrogators could reasonably be considered specifically intended to—cause "*prolonged* mental harm" as required by the statute, because, as we understand it, any hallucinatory effects of sleep deprivation would dissipate rapidly. OMS has informed us, based on the scientific literature and on its own experience with detainees who have been sleep deprived, that any such hallucinatory effects would not be prolonged. We understand from OMS that *Why We Sleep* provides an accurate summary of the scientific literature on this point. As discussed there, the longest documented period of time for which any human has gone without sleep is 264 hours. *See id.* at 29-34. The longest study with more than one subject involved 205 hours of sleep deprivation. *See id.* at 37-42. We understand that these and other studies constituting a significant body of scientific literature indicate that sleep deprivation temporarily affects the functioning of the brain but does not otherwise have significant physiological effects. *See id.* at 100. Sleep deprivation's effects on the brain are generally not severe but can include impaired cognitive performance and visual hallucinations; however, these effects dissipate rapidly, often with as little as one night's sleep. *See id.* at 31-32, 34-37, 40, 47-53. Thus, we conclude, any temporary hallucinations that might result from extended sleep deprivation could not reasonably be considered "prolonged mental harm" for purposes of sections 2340-2340A.[49]

In light of these observations, although in its extended uses it may present a substantial question under sections 2340-2340A, we conclude that the authorized use of sleep deprivation by adequately trained interrogators, subject to the limitations and monitoring in place, could not reasonably be considered specifically intended to cause severe mental pain or suffering. Finally, the use of a diaper for sanitary purposes on an individual subjected to sleep deprivation, while potentially humiliating, could not be considered specifically intended to inflict severe mental pain or suffering within the meaning of the statute, because there would be no statutory predicate act and no reason to expect "prolonged mental harm" to result.[50]

---

[49] Without determining the minimum time for mental harm to be considered "prolonged," we do not believe that "prolonged mental harm" would occur during the sleep deprivation itself. As noted, OMS would order that the technique be discontinued if hallucinations occurred. Moreover, even if OMS personnel were not aware of any such hallucinations, whatever time would remain between the onset of such hallucinations, which presumably would be well into the period of sleep deprivation, and the 180-hour maximum for sleep deprivation would not constitute "prolonged" mental harm within the meaning of the statute. Nevertheless, we note that this aspect of the technique calls for great care in monitoring by OMS personnel, including psychologists, especially as the length of the period of sleep deprivation increases.

[50] We note that the court of appeals in *Hilao v. Estate of Marcos*, 103 F.3d. 789 (9th Cir. 1996), stated that a variety of techniques taken together, one of which was sleep deprivation, amounted to torture. The court, however, did not specifically discuss sleep deprivation apart from the other conduct at issue, and it did not conclude that sleep deprivation alone amounted to torture. In *Ireland v. United Kingdom*, the European Court of Human Rights concluded by a vote of 13-4 that sleep deprivation, even in conjunction with a number of other techniques, did not amount to torture under the European Charter. The duration of the sleep deprivation at issue was not clear. *See* separate opinion of Judge Fitzmaurice at ¶ 19, but may have been 96-120 hours, see majority opinion at ¶ 104. Finally, we note that the Committee Against Torture of the Office of the High Commissioner for Human Rights, in *Concluding Observations of the Committee Against Torture: Israel*, U.N. Doc A/52/44, at ¶ 257 (May 9, 1997), concluded that a variety of practices taken together, including "sleep deprivation for prolonged periods," "constitute torture as defined in article 1 of the [CAT]." *See also* United Nations General Assembly, *Report of the Committee Against Torture*, U.N. Doc. A/52/44 at ¶ 56 (Sept. 10, 1997) ("sleep deprivation practiced on suspects . . . may in some cases constitute torture"). The committee provided no details on the length of the sleep deprivation or how it was implemented and no

13. *Waterboard.* We previously concluded that the use of the waterboard did not constitute torture under sections 2340-2340A. *See Interrogation Memorandum* at 11, 15. We must reexamine the issue, however, because the technique, as it would be used, could involve more applications in longer sessions (and possibly using different methods) than we earlier considered.[51]

We understand that in the escalating regimen of interrogation techniques, the waterboard is considered to be the most serious, requires a separate approval that may be sought only after other techniques have not worked (or are considered unlikely to work in the time available), and in fact has been—and is expected to be—used on very few detainees. We accept the assessment of OMS that the waterboard "is by far the most

---

analysis to support its conclusion. These precedents provide little or no helpful guidance in our review of the CIA's use of sleep deprivation under sections 2340-2340A. While we do not rely on this fact in interpreting sections 2340-2340A, we note that we are aware of no decision of any foreign court or international tribunal finding that the techniques analyzed here, if subject to the limitations and conditions set out, would amount to torture.

[51] The *IG Report* noted that in some cases the waterboard was used with far grater frequency than initially indicated, *see IG Report* at 5, 44, 46, 103-04, and also that it was used in a different manner. *See id.* at 37 ("[T]he waterboard technique . . . was different from the technique described in the DoJ opinion and used in the SERE training. The difference was in the manner in which the detainee's breathing was obstructed. At the SERE school and in the DoJ opinion, the subject's airflow is disrupted by the firm application of a damp cloth over the air passages; the interrogator applies a small amount of water to the cloth in a controlled manner. By contrast, the Agency interrogator . . . applied large volumes of water to a cloth that covered the detainee's mouth and nose. One of the psychologists/interrogators acknowledged that the Agency's use of the technique is different from that used in SERE training because it is 'for real' and is more poignant and convincing."); *see also id.* at 14 n.14. The Inspector General further reported that "OMS contends that the expertise of the SERE psychologist/ interrogators on the waterboard was probably misrepresented at the time, as the SERE waterboard experience is so different from the subsequent Agency usage as to make it almost irrelevant. Consequently, according to OMS, there was no *a priori* reason to believe that applying the waterboard with the frequency and intensity with which it was used by the psychologist/interrogators was either efficacious or medically safe." *Id.* at 21 n.26. We have carefully considered the *IG Report* and discussed it with OMS personnel. As noted, OMS input has resulted in a number of changes in the application of the waterboard, including limits on the frequency and cumulative use of the technique. Moreover, OMS personnel are carefully instructed in monitoring this technique and are personally present whenever it is used. *See OMS Guidelines* at 17-20. Indeed, although physician assistants can be present when other enhanced techniques are applied, "use of the waterboard requires the presence of a physician." *Id.* at 9 n.2.

traumatic of the enhanced interrogation techniques." *OMS Guidelines* at 15. This technique could subject a detainee to a high degree of distress. A detainee to whom the technique is applied will experience the physiological sensation of drowning, which likely will lead to panic. We understand that even a detainee who knows he is not going to drown is likely to have this response. Indeed, we are informed that even individuals very familiar with the technique experience this sensation when subjected to the waterboard.

Nevertheless, although this technique presents the most substantial question under the statute, we conclude for the reasons discussed below that the authorized use of the waterboard by adequately trained interrogators, subject to the limitations and conditions adopted by the CIA and in the absence of any medical contraindications, would not violate sections 2340-2340A. (We understand that a medical contraindication may have precluded the use of this particular technique on ███████████. In reaching this conclusion, we do not in any way minimize the experience. The panic associated with the feeling of drowning could undoubtedly be significant. There may be few more frightening experiences than feeling that one is unable to breathe.[52]

However frightening the experience may be, OMS personnel have informed us that the waterboard technique is not physically painful. This conclusion, as we understand the facts, accords with the experience in SERE training, where the waterboard has been administered to several thousand members of the United States Armed Forces.[53] To be sure, in

---

[52] As noted above, in most uses of the technique, the individual is in fact able to breathe, though his breathing is restricted. Because in some uses breathing would not be possible, for purposes of our analysis we assume that the detainee is unable to breath during applications of water.

[53] We understand that the waterboard is currently used only in Navy SERE training. As noted in the *IG Report*, "[a]ccording to individuals with authoritative knowledge of the SERE program, . . . [e]xcept for Navy SERE training, use of the waterboard was discontinued because of its dramatic effect on the students who were subjects." *IG Report* at 14 n.14. We understand that use of the waterboard was discontinued by the other services not because of any concerns about possible physical or mental harm, but because students were not successful at resisting the technique and, as such, it was not considered to be a useful training technique. We note that OMS has concluded that "[w]hile SERE trainees believe that trainees are unable to maintain psychological resistance to the waterboard, our experience was otherwise. Some subjects unquestionably can withstand a large number of applications, with no immediately discernible cumulative impact beyond their strong aversion to the experience." *OMS Guidelines* at

SERE training, the technique is confined to at most two applications (and usually only one) of no more than 40 seconds each. Here, there may be two sessions of up to two hours each, during a 24-hour period, and each session may include multiple applications, of which six may last 10 seconds or longer (but none more than 40 seconds), for a total time of application of as much as 12 minutes in a 24-hour period. Furthermore, the waterboard may be used on up to five days during the 30-day period for which it is approved. *See August 19* ███████████ *Letter* at 1-2. As you have informed us, the CIA has previously used the waterboard repeatedly on two detainees, and, as far as can be determined, these detainees did not experience physical pain [n]or, in the professional judgment of doctors, is there any medical reason to believe they would have done so. Therefore, we conclude that the authorized use of the waterboard by adequately trained interrogators could not reasonably be considered specifically intended to cause "severe physical pain."

We also conclude that the use of the waterboard, under the strict limits and conditions imposed, would not be expected to cause "severe physical suffering" under the statute. As noted above, the difficulty of specifying a category of physical suffering apart from both physical pain and mental pain or suffering, along with the requirement that any such suffering be "severe," calls for an interpretation under which "severe physical suffering" is reserved for physical distress that is severe considering both its intensity and duration. To the extent that in some applications the use of the waterboard could cause choking or similar physical—as opposed to mental—sensations, those physical sensations might well have an intensity approaching the degree contemplated by the statute. However, we understand that any such physical—as opposed to mental—sensations caused by the use of the waterboard end when the application ends. Given the time limits imposed, and the fact that any physical distress (as opposed to possible mental suffering, which is discussed below) would occur only during the actual application of water, the physical distress caused by the waterboard would not be expected to have the duration required

---

17. We are aware that at a recent Senate Judiciary Committee hearing, Douglas Johnson, Executive Director of the Center for Victims of Torture, testified that some U.S. military personnel who have undergone waterboard training have apparently stated "that it's taken them 15 years to get over it." You have informed us that, in 2002 the CIA made inquiries to Department of Defense personnel involved in SERE training and that the Department of Defense was not aware of any information that would substantiate such statements, nor is the CIA aware of any such information.

to amount to severe physical suffering.[54] Applications are strictly limited to at most 40 seconds, and a total of at most 12 minutes in any 24-hour period, and use of the technique is limited to at most five days during the 30-day period we consider. Consequently, under these conditions, use of the waterboard cannot be expected to cause "severe physical suffering" within the meaning of the statute, and we conclude that its authorized use by adequately trained interrogators could not reasonably be considered specifically intended to cause "severe physical suffering."[55] Again, however, we caution that great care should be used in adhering to the limitations imposed and in monitoring any detainee subjected to it to prevent the detainee from experiencing severe physical suffering.

The most substantial question raised by the waterboard relates to the statutory definition of "severe mental pain or suffering." The sensation of drowning that we understand accompanies the use of the waterboard arguably could qualify as a "threat of imminent death" within the meaning of section 2340(2)(C) and thus might constitute a predicate act for "severe mental pain or suffering" under the statute.[56] Although the waterboard is used with safeguards that make actual harm quite unlikely, the detainee may not know about these safeguards, and even if he does learn of them, the technique is still likely to create panic in the form of acute instinctual fear arising from the physiological sensation of drowning.

Nevertheless, the statutory definition of "severe mental pain or suffering" also requires that the predicate act produce "prolonged mental harm." 18 U.S.C. § 2340(2). As we understand from OMS personnel fa-

---

[54] We emphasize that physical suffering differs from physical pain in this respect. Physical pain may be "severe" even if lasting only seconds; whereas, by contrast, physical distress may amount to "severe physical suffering" only if it is severe both in intensity and duration.

[55] As with sleep deprivation, the particular condition of the individual detainee must be monitored so that, with extended or repeated use of the technique, the detainee's experience does not depart from these expectations.

[56] It is unclear whether a detainee being subjected to the waterboard in fact experiences it as a "threat of imminent death." We understand that the CIA may inform a detainee on whom this technique is used that he would not be allowed to drown. Moreover, after multiple applications of the waterboard, it may become apparent to the detainee that, however frightening the experience may be, it will not result in death. Nevertheless, for purposes of our analysis, we will assume that the physiological sensation of drowning associated with the use of the waterboard may constitute a "threat of imminent death" within the meaning of sections 2340-2340A.

miliar with the history of the waterboard technique, as used both in SERE training (though in a substantially different manner) and in the previous CIA interrogations, there is no medical basis to believe that the technique would produce any mental effect beyond the distress that directly accompanies its use and the prospect that it will be used again. We understand from the CIA that to date none of the thousands of persons who have undergone the more limited use of the technique in SERE training has suffered prolonged mental harm as a result. The CIA's use of the technique could far exceed the one or two applications to which SERE training is limited, and the participant in SERE training presumably understands that the technique is part of a training program that is not intended to hurt him and will end at some foreseeable time. But the physicians and psychologists at the CIA familiar with the facts have informed us that in the case of the two detainees who have been subjected to more extensive use of the waterboard technique, no evidence of prolonged mental harm has appeared in the period since the use of the waterboard on those detainees, a period which now spans at least 25 months for each of these detainees. Moreover, in their professional judgment based on this experience and the admittedly different SERE experience, OMS officials inform us that they would not expect the waterboard to cause such harm. Nor do we believe that the distress accompanying use of the technique on five days in a 30-day period, in itself, could be the "prolonged mental harm" to which the statute refers. The technique may be designed to create fear at the time it is used on the detainee, so that the detainee will cooperate to avoid future sessions. Furthermore, we acknowledge that the term "prolonged" is imprecise. Nonetheless, without in any way minimizing the distress caused by this technique, we believe that the panic brought on by the waterboard during the very limited time it is actually administered, combined with any residual fear that may be experienced over a somewhat longer period, could not be said to amount to the "prolonged mental harm" that the statute covers.[57] For these reasons, we conclude that the authorized use of

---

[57] In *Hilao v. Estate of Marcos*, the Ninth Circuit stated that a course of conduct involving a number of techniques, one of which has similarities to the waterboard, constituted torture. The court described the course of conduct as follows:

> He was then interrogated by members of the military, who blindfolded and severely beat him while he was handcuffed and fettered; they also threatened him with death. When this round of interrogation ended, he was denied sleep and repeatedly threatened with death. In the next round of interrogation, all of his limbs were

the waterboard by adequately trained interrogators could not reasonably be considered specifically intended to cause "prolonged mental harm." Again, however, we caution that the use of this technique calls for the most careful adherence to the limitations and safeguards imposed, including constant monitoring by both medical and psychological personnel of any detainee who is subjected to the waterboard.

Even if the occurrence of one of the predicate acts could, depending on the circumstances of a particular case, give rise to an inference of intent to cause "prolonged mental harm," no such circumstances exist here. On the contrary, experience with the use of the waterboard indicates that prolonged mental harm would not be expected to occur, and CIA's use of the technique is subject to a variety of safeguards, discussed above, designed to ensure that prolonged mental harm does not result. Therefore,

---

shackled to a cot and a towel was placed over his nose and mouth; his interrogators then poured water down his nostrils so that he felt as though he were drowning. This lasted for approximately six hours, during which time interrogators threatened [him] with electric shock and death. At the end of this water torture, [he] was left shackled to the cot for the following three days, during which time he was repeatedly interrogated. He was then imprisoned for seven month in a suffocatingly hot and unlit cell, measuring 2.5 meters square; during this time he was shackled to his cot, at first by all his limbs and later by one hand and one foot, for all but the briefest periods (in which he was allowed to eat or use the toilet). The handcuffs were often so tight that the slightest movement . . . made them cut into his flesh. During this period, he felt 'extreme pain, almost undescribable, the boredom' and 'the feeling that tons of lead . . . were falling on [his] brain. [He] was never told how long the treatment inflicted upon him would last. After his seven months shackled to his cot, [he] spent more than eight years in detention, approximately five of the in solitary confinement and the rest in near-solitary confinement.

103 F.3d at 790-91. The court then concluded, "it seems clear that all the abuses to which [a plaintiff] testified—including the eight years during which he was held in solitary or near-solitary confinement—constituted a single course of conduct of torture." *Id.* at 795. In addition to the obvious differences between the technique in *Hilao* and the CIA's use of the waterboard subject to the careful limits described above (among other things, in *Hilao* the session lasted six hours and followed explicit threats of death and severe physical beatings), the court reached no conclusion that the technique by itself constituted torture. However, the fact that a federal appellate court would even colloquially describe a technique that may share some of the characteristics of the waterboard as "water torture" counsels continued care and careful monitoring in the use of this technique.

the circumstances here would negate any potential inference of specific intent to cause such harm.

Assuming adherence to the strict limitations discussed herein, including the careful medical monitoring and available intervention by the team as necessary, we conclude that although the question is substantial and difficult, the authorized use of the waterboard by adequately trained interrogators and other team members could not reasonably be considered specifically intended to cause severe physical or mental pain or suffering and thus would not violate sections 2340-2340A.[58]

*   *   *

In sum, based on the information you have provided and the limitations, procedures, and safeguards that would be in place, we conclude that—although extended sleep deprivation and use of the waterboard present more substantial questions in certain respects under the statute and the use of the waterboard raises the most substantial issue—none of these specific techniques, considered individually, would violate the prohibition in sections 2340-2340A. The universal rejection of torture and the President's unequivocal directive that the United States not engage in torture warrant great care in analyzing whether particular interrogation techniques are consistent with the requirements of sections 2340-2340A, and we have attempted to employ such care throughout our analysis. We emphasize that these are issues about which reasonable persons may disagree. Our task has been made more difficult by the imprecision of the statute and the relative absence of judicial guidance, but we have applied our best reading of the law to the specific facts that you have provided. As is apparent, our conclusion is based on the assumption that close observation, including medical and psychological monitoring of the detainees, will continue during the period when these techniques are used; that the personnel present are authorized to, and will, stop the use of a technique

---

[58] As noted, medical personnel are instructed to exercise special care in monitoring and reporting on use of the waterboard. *See OMS Guidelines* at 20 ("NOTE: In order to best inform future medical judgments and recommendations, it is important that every application of the waterboard be thoroughly documented: how long each application (and the entire procedure) lasted, how much water was used in the process (realizing that much splashes off), how exactly the water was applied, if a seal was achieved, if the naso- or oropharynx was filled, what sort of volume was expelled, how long was the break between applications, and how the subject looked between each treatment." (emphasis omitted).

at any time if they believe it is being used improperly or threatens a detainee's safety or that a detainee may be at risk of suffering severe physical
or mental pain or suffering; that the medical and psychological personnel
are continually assessing the available literature and ongoing experience
with detainees, and that, as they have done to date, they will make adjust-
ments to techniques to ensure that they do not cause severe physical or
mental pain or suffering to the detainees; and that all interrogators and
other team members understand the proper use of the techniques, that the
techniques are not designed or intended to cause severe physical or mental
pain or suffering, and that they must cooperate with OMS personnel in the
exercise of their important duties.

Please let us know if we may be of further assistance.

Steven G. Bradbury
Principal Deputy
Assistant Attorney General

U.S. Department of Justice

Office of Legal Counsel

Office of the Principal Deputy Assistant Attorney General   *Washington, D.C. 20530*

May 10, 2005

MEMORANDUM FOR JOHN A. RIZZO
SENIOR DEPUTY GENERAL COUNSEL,
CENTRAL INTELLIGENCE AGENCY

Re: Application of 18 U.S.C. §§ 2340-2340A to the Combined Use of Certain Techniques in the Interrogation of High Value al Qaeda Detainees

In our Memorandum for John A. Rizzo, Senior Deputy General Counsel, Central Intelligence Agency, from Steven G. Bradbury, Principal Deputy Assistant Attorney General, Office of Legal Counsel, *Re: Application of 18 U.S.C. §§ 2340-2340A to Certain Techniques That May Be Used in the Interrogation of a High Value al Qaeda Detainee* (May 10, 2005) (*"Techniques"*), we addressed the application of the anti-torture statute, 18 U.S.C. §§ 2340-2340A, to certain interrogation techniques that the CIA might use in the questioning of a specific al Qaeda operative. There, we considered each technique individually. We now consider the application of the statute to the use of these same techniques in combination. Subject to the conditions and limitations set out here and in *Techniques*, we conclude that the authorized combined use of these specific techniques by adequately trained interrogators would not violate sections 2340-2340A.

Techniques, which set out our general interpretation of the statutory elements, guides us here.[1] While referring to the analysis provided in that

---

[1] As noted in *Techniques*, the Criminal Division of the Department of Justice is satisfied that our general interpretation of the legal Standards under sections 1240-2340A, found in *Techniques*. is consistent with its concurrences in our Memorandum for James B. Comey, Deputy Attorney General, from Daniel Levin, Acting Assistant Attorney General, Office of Legal Counsel, *Re: Legal Standards Applicable Under 18 U.S.C. §§ 2340-2340A (Dec. 30, 2004)*. In the present memorandum, we address only the application of 18 U.S.C.§§ 2340-2340A to combinations of interrogation techniques. Nothing in this memoran-

opinion, we do not repeat it, but instead presume a familiarity with it. Furthermore, in referring to the individual interrogation techniques whose combined use is our present subject, we mean those techniques as we described them in *Techniques*, including all of the limitations, presumptions, and safeguards described there.

One overarching point from *Techniques* bears repeating: Torture is abhorrent and universally repudiated, *see Techniques* at 1, and the President has stated that the United States will not tolerate it. *Id.* at 1-2 & n.2 (citing Statement on United Nations International Day in Support of Victims of Torture, 40 Weekly Comp. Pres. Doc. 1167-68 (July 5, 2004)). In *Techniques*, we accordingly exercised great care in applying sections 2340-2340A to the individual techniques at issue; we apply the same degree of care in considering the combined use of these techniques.

I.

Under 18 U.S.C. § 2340A, it is a crime to commit, attempt to commit, or conspire to commit torture outside the United States. "Torture" is defined as "an act committed by a person acting under color of law specifically intended to inflict severe physical or mental pain or suffering (other than pain or suffering incidental to lawful sanctions) upon another person within his custody or physical control." 18 U.S.C. § 2340(1). "Severe mental pain or suffering" is defined as "the prolonged mental harm caused by

---

dum or in our prior advice to the CIA should be read to suggest that the use of these techniques would conform to the requirement of the Uniform Code of Military Justice that governs members of the Armed Forces or to United States obligations under the Geneva Conventions in circumstances where those Conventions would apply. We do not address the possible application of article 16 of the United Nations Convention Against Torture and Other Cruel, Inhuman or Degrading Treatment or Punishment, Dec. 10, 1984, S. Treaty Doc. No. 100-20, 1465 U.N.T.S. 85 (entered into force for U.S. Nov. 20, 1994), nor do we address any question relating to conditions of confinement or detention, as distinct from the interrogation of detainees. We stress that our advice on the application of sections 2340-2340A does not represent the policy views of the Department of Justice concerning interrogation practices. Finally, we note that section 6057(a) of H.R. 1268 (109th Cong. 1st Sess.), if it becomes law, would forbid expending or obligating funds made available by that bill "to subject any person in the custody or under the physical control of the United States to torture," but because the bill would define "torture" to have "the meaning given that term in section 2340(1) of title 18, United States Code," § 6057(b)(1), the provision (to the extent it might apply here at all) would merely reaffirm the preexisting prohibitions on torture in sections 2340-2340A.

or resulting from" any of four predicate acts. *Id.* § 2340(2). These acts are (1) "the intentional infliction or threatened infliction of severe physical pain or suffering"; (2) "the administration or application, or threatened administration or application, of mind-altering substances or other procedures calculated to disrupt profoundly the senses or the personality"; (3) "the threat of imminent death"; and (4) "the threat that another person will imminently be subjected to death, severe physical pain or suffering, or the administration or application of mind-altering substances or other procedures calculated to disrupt profoundly the senses or personality."

In *Techniques*, we concluded that the individual authorized use of several specific interrogation techniques, subject to a variety of limitations and safeguards, would not violate the statute when employed in the interrogation of a specific member of al Qaeda, though we concluded that at least in certain respects two of the techniques presented substantial questions under sections 2340-2340A. The techniques that we analyzed were dietary manipulation, nudity, the attention grasp, walling, the facial hold, the facial slap or insult slap, the abdominal slap, cramped confinement, wall standing, stress positions, water dousing, extended sleep deprivation, and the "waterboard." *Techniques* at 7-15.

Techniques analyzed only the use of these techniques individually. As we have previously advised, however, "courts tend to take a totality-of-the-circumstances approach and consider an entire course of conduct to determine whether torture has occurred." Memorandum for John Rizzo, Acting General Counsel, Central Intelligence Agency, from Jay S. Bybee, Assistant Attorney General, Office of Legal Counsel, *Re: Interrogation of al Qaeda Operative* at 9 (Aug. 1, 2002) (*"Interrogation Memorandum"*) (TS). A complete analysis under sections 2340-2340A thus entails an examination of the combined effects of any techniques that might be used.

In conducting this analysis, there are two additional areas of general concern. First, it is possible that the application of certain techniques might render the detainee unusually susceptible to physical or mental pain or suffering. If that were the case, use of a second technique that would not ordinarily be expected to—and could not reasonably be considered specifically intended to—cause severe physical or mental pain or suffering by itself might in fact cause severe physical or mental pain or suffering because of the enhanced susceptibility created by the first technique. Depending on the circumstances, and the knowledge and mental state of the interrogator, one might conclude that severe pain or suffering was specifically intended by the application of the second technique to a detainee who was particularly vulnerable because of the application of the first technique. Because the use of these techniques in combination is intended to, and in fact can be expected to, physically wear down a detainee, because it is difficult to assess as to a particular individual whether the application of multiple techniques renders that individual more susceptible to physical pain or suffering, and because sleep deprivation, in particular, has a number of documented physiological effects that, in some circumstances, could be problematic, it is important that all participating CIA personnel, particularly interrogators and personnel of the CIA Office of Medical Services ("OMS"), be aware of the potential for enhanced susceptibility to pain and suffering from each interrogation technique. We also assume that there will be active and ongoing monitoring by medical and psychological personnel of each detainee who is undergoing a regimen of interrogation, and active intervention by a member of the team or medical staff as necessary, so as to avoid the possibility of severe physical or mental pain or suffering within the meaning of 18 U.S.C. §§ 2340-2340A as a result of such combined effects.

Second, it is possible that certain techniques that do not themselves cause severe physical or mental pain or suffering might do so in combination, particularly when used over the 30-day interrogation period with which we deal here. Again, depending on the circumstances, and the mental state of the interrogator, their use might be considered to be specifically intended to cause such severe pain or suffering. This concern calls for an inquiry into the totality of the circumstances, looking at which techniques are combined and how they are combined.

Your office has outlined the manner in which many of the individual techniques we previously considered could be combined in *Background Paper on CIA's Combined Use of Interrogation Techniques* (undated, but transmitted Dec. 30, 2004) (*"Background Paper"*). The *Background Paper*, which provides the principal basis for our analysis, first divides the process of interrogation into three phases: "Initial Conditions," "Transition to Interrogation," and "Interrogation." *Id.* at 1. After describing these three phases, *see id.* at 1-9, the *Background Paper* "provides a look at a prototypical interrogation with an emphasis on the application of interrogation techniques, in combination and separately," *id.* at 9-18. The *Background Paper* does not include any discussion of the waterboard; however, you have separately provided to us a description of how the waterboard may be used in combination with other techniques, particularly dietary manipulation and sleep deprivation. *See* Fax for Steven G. Bradbury, Principal Deputy Assistant Attorney General, Office of Legal Counsel, from ███████████ Assistant General Counsel, CIA, at 3-4 (Apr. 22, 2005) (*"April 22* ███████ *Fax"*).

Phases of the Interrogation Process

The first phase of the interrogation process, "Initial Conditions," does not involve interrogation techniques, and you have not asked us to consider any legal question regarding the CIA's practices during this phase. The "Initial Conditions" nonetheless set the stage for use of the interrogation techniques, which come later.[2]

According to the *Background Paper*, before being flown to the site of interrogation, a detainee is given a medical examination. He then is "securely shackled and is deprived of sight and sound through the use of blindfolds, earmuffs, and hoods" during the flight. *Id.* at 2. An on-board medical officer monitors his condition. Security personnel also monitor the detainee for signs of distress. Upon arrival at the site, the detainee "finds himself in complete control of Americans" and is subjected to "precise, quiet, and almost clinical" procedures designed to underscore "the enormity and suddenness of the change in environment, the uncertainty about what will happen next, and the potential dread [a detainee] may have of US custody." *Id.* His head and face are shaved; his physical condition is documented through photographs taken while he is nude; and he is given medical and psychological interviews to assess his condition and to make sure there are no contraindications to the use of any particular interrogation techniques. *See id.* at 2-3.

The detainee then enters the next phase, the "Transition to Interrogation." The interrogators conduct an initial interview, "in a relatively benign environment," to ascertain whether the detainee is willing to cooperate. The detainee is "normally clothed but seated and shackled for security purposes." *Id.* at 3. The interrogators take "an open, non-threatening

---

[2] Although the *OMS Guidelines on Medical and Psychological Support to Detainee Rendition, Interrogation and Detention* (Dec. 2004) ("*OMS Guidelines*") refer to the administration of sedatives during transport if necessary to protect the detainees or the rendition team, *id.* at 4-5, the *OMS Guidelines* do not provide for the use of sedatives for interrogation. The *Background Paper* does not mention the administration of any drugs during the detainee's transportation to the site of the interrogation or at any other time, and we do not address any such administration. OMS, we understand, is unaware of any use of sedation during the transport of a detainee in the last two years and states that the interrogation program does not use sedation or medication for the purpose of interrogation. We caution that any use of sedatives should be carefully evaluated, including under 18 U.S.C.§ 2340(2)(B). For purposes of our analysis, we assume that no drugs are administered during the relevant period or that there are no ongoing effects from any administration of any drugs; if that assumption does not hold, our analysis and conclusions could change.

approach," but the detainee "would have to provide information on action-able threats and location information on High-Value Targets at large—not lower-level information—for interrogators to continue with [this] neutral approach." *Id.* If the detainee does not meet this "very high" standard, the interrogators submit a detailed interrogation plan to CIA headquarters for approval. If the medical and psychological assessments find no contrain-dications to the proposed plan, and if senior CIA officers at headquarters approve some or all of the plan through a cable transmitted to the site of the interrogation, the interrogation moves to the next phase. *Id.*[3]

Three interrogation techniques are typically used to bring the de-tainee to a "baseline, dependent state," "demonstrat[ing] to the [detainee] that he has no control over basic human needs" and helping to make him "perceive and value his personal welfare, comfort, and immediate needs more than the information he is protecting." *Id.* at 4. The three techniques used to establish this "baseline" are nudity, sleep deprivation (with shack-ling and, at least at times, with use of a diaper), and dietary manipulation. These techniques, which *Techniques* described in some detail, "require little to no physical interaction between the detainee and interrogator." *Background Paper* at 5.

Other techniques, which "require physical interaction between the interrogator and detainee," are characterized as "corrective" and "are used principally to correct, startle, or . . . achieve another enabling objective with the detainee." *Id.* These techniques "are not used simultaneously but

---

[3] The CIA maintains certain "detention conditions" at all of its detention facilities. (These conditions "are not interrogation techniques," *id.* at 4, and you have not asked us to assess their lawfulness under the statute.) The detainee is "exposed to white noise/loud sounds (not to exceed 79 decibels) and constant light during portions of the interrogation process." *Id.* These conditions enhance security. The noise prevents the detainee from overhearing conversations of staff members, precludes him from picking up "auditory clues" about his sur-roundings, and disrupts any efforts to communicate with other detainees. *Id.* The light provides better conditions for security and for monitoring by the medical and psychological staff and the interrogators. Although we do not address the lawfulness of using white noise (not to exceed 79 decibels) and constant light, we note that according to materials you have furnished to us, (1) the Occupa-tional Safety and Health Administration has determined that there is no risk of permanent hearing loss from continuous, 24-hour per day exposure to noise of up to 82 decibels, and (2) detainees typically adapt fairly quickly to the con-stant light and it does not interfere unduly with their ability to sleep. *See* Fax for Dan Levin, Acting Assistant Attorney General, Office of Legal Counsel, from ████████████████████ Assistant General Counsel, Central Intelligence Agency at 3 (Jan. 4, 2005) ("████ *Fax*").

are often used interchangeably during an individual interrogation session." *Id.* The insult slap is used "periodically throughout the interrogation process when the interrogator needs to immediately correct the detainee or provide a consequence to a detainee's response or non-response." *Id.* at 5-6. The insult slap "can be used in combination with water dousing or kneeling stress positions"—techniques that are not characterized as "corrective." *Id.* at 6. Another corrective technique, the abdominal slap, "is similar to the insult slap in application and desired result" and "provides the variation necessary to keep a high level of unpredictability in the interrogation process." *Id.* The abdominal slap may be simultaneously combined with water dousing, stress positions, and wall standing. A third corrective technique, the facial hold, "is used sparingly throughout interrogation." *Id.* It is not painful, but "demonstrates the interrogator's control over the [detainee]." *Id.* It too may be simultaneously combined with water dousing, stress positions, and wall standing. *Id.* Finally, the attention grasp "may be used several times in the same interrogation" and may be simultaneously combined with water dousing or kneeling stress positions. *Id.*

Some techniques are characterized as "coercive." These techniques "place the detainee in more physical and psychological stress." *Id* at 7. Coercive techniques "are typically not used in combination, although some combined use is possible." *Id.* Walling "is one of the most effective interrogation techniques because it wears down the [detainee] physically, heightens uncertainty in the detainee about what the interrogator may do to him, and creates a sense of dread when the [detainee] knows he is about to be walled again." *Id.*[4] A detainee "may be walled one time (one impact with the wall) to make a point or twenty to thirty times consecutively when the interrogator requires a more significant response to a question," and "will be walled multiple times" during a session designed to be

---

[4] Although walling "wears down the [detainee] physically," *Background Paper* at 7, and undoubtedly may startle him, we understand that it is not significantly painful. The detainee hits "a flexible false wall," designed "to create a loud sound when the individual hits it" and thus to cause "shock and surprise." *Interrogation Memorandum* at 2. But the detainee's "head and neck are supported with a rolled hood or towel that provides a c-collar effect to help prevent whiplash"; it is the detainee's shoulder blades that hit the wall; and the detainee is allowed to rebound from the flexible wall in order to reduce the chances of any injury. *See Id.* You have informed us that a detainee is expected to feel "dread" at the prospect of walling because of the shock and surprise caused by the technique and because of the sense of powerlessness that comes from being roughly handled by the interrogators, not because the technique causes significant pain.

intense. *Id.* Walling cannot practically be used at the same time as other interrogation techniques.

Water temperature and other considerations of safety established by OMS limit the use of another coercive technique, water dousing. *See id.* at 7-8. The technique "may be used frequently within those guidelines." *Id.* at 8. As suggested above, interrogators may combine water dousing with other techniques, such as stress positions, wall standing, the insult slap, or the abdominal slap. *See id.* at 8.

The use of stress positions is "usually self-limiting in that temporary muscle fatigue usually leads to the [detainee's] being unable to maintain the stress position after a period of time." *Id.* Depending on the particular position, stress positions may be combined with water dousing, the insult slap, the facial hold, arid the attention grasp. *See id.* Another coercive technique, wall standing, is "usually self-limiting" in the same way as stress positions. *Id.* It may be combined with water dousing and the abdominal slap. *See id.* OMS guidelines limit the technique of cramped confinement to no more than eight hours at a time and 18 hours a day, and confinement in the "small box" is limited to two hours. *Id.* Cramped confinement cannot be used in simultaneous combination with corrective or other coercive techniques.

We understand that the CIA's use of all these interrogation techniques is subject to ongoing monitoring by interrogation team members who will direct that techniques be discontinued if there is a deviation from prescribed procedures and by medical and psychological personnel from OMS who will direct that any or all techniques be discontinued if in their professional judgment the detainee may otherwise suffer severe physical or mental pain or suffering. *See Techniques* at 6-7.

A Prototypical Interrogation

In a "prototypical interrogation," the detainee begins his first interrogation session stripped of his clothes, shackled, and hooded, with the walling collar over his head and around his neck. *Background Paper* at 9-10. The interrogators remove the hood and explain that the detainee can improve his situation by cooperating and may say that the interrogators "will do what it takes to get important information." *Id.*[5] As soon as the detainee does anything inconsistent with the interrogators' instructions, the interrogators use an insult slap or abdominal slap. They employ wall-

---

[5] We address the effects of this statement below [. . .].

ing if it becomes clear that the detainee is not cooperating in the interrogation. This consequence "may continue for several more iterations as the interrogators continue to measure the [detainee's] resistance posture and apply a negative sequence to [his] resistance efforts." *Id.* The interrogators and security officers then put the detainee into position for standing sleep deprivation, begin dietary manipulation through a liquid diet, and keep the detainee nude (except for a diaper). *See id.* at 10-11. The first interrogation session, which could have lasted from 30 minutes to several hours, would then be at an end. *See id.* at 11.

If the interrogation team determines there is a need to continue, and if the medical and psychological personnel advise that there are no contraindications, a second session may begin. *See id.* at 12. The interval between sessions could be as short as an hour or as long as 24 hours. *See id.* at 11. At the start of the second session, the detainee is released from the position for standing sleep deprivation, is hooded, and is positioned against the walling wall, with the walling collar over his head and around his neck. *See id.* Even before removing the hood, the interrogators use the attention grasp to startle the detainee. The interrogators take off the hood and begin questioning. If the detainee does not give appropriate answers to the first questions, the interrogators use an insult slap or abdominal slap. *See id.* They employ walling if they determine that the detainee "is intent on maintaining his resistance posture." *Id.* at 13. This sequence "may continue for multiple iterations as the interrogators continue to measure the [detainee's] resistance posture." *Id.* The interrogators then increase the pressure on the detainee by using a hose to douse the detainee with water for several minutes. They stop and start the dousing as they continue the interrogation. *See id.* They then end the session by placing the detainee into the same circumstances as at the end of the first session: the detainee is in the standing position for sleep deprivation, is nude (except for a diaper), and is subjected to dietary manipulation. Once again, the session could have lasted from 30 minutes to several hours. *See id.*

Again, if the interrogation team determines there is a need to continue, and if the medical and psychological personnel find no contraindications, a third session may follow. The session begins with the detainee positioned as at the beginning of the second. *See id.* at 14. If the detainee continues to resist, the interrogators continue to use walling and water dousing. The corrective techniques—the insult slap, the abdominal slap, the facial hold, the attention grasp—may be used several times during this session based on the responses and actions of the [detainee]." *Id.* The interrogators integrate stress positions and wall standing into the session. Furthermore, "[i]ntense questioning and walling would be repeated multiple times." *Id.* Interrogators "use one technique to support another." *Id.* For example, they threaten the use of walling unless the detainee holds a stress position, thus inducing the detainee to remain in the position longer than he otherwise would. At the end of the session, the interrogators and security personnel place the detainee into the same circumstances as at the end of the first two sessions, with the detainee subject to sleep deprivation, nudity, and dietary manipulation. *Id.*

In later sessions, the interrogators use those techniques that are proving most effective and drop the others. Sleep deprivation "may continue to the 70 to 120 hour range, or possibly beyond for the hardest resisters, but in no case exceed the 180-hour time limit." *Id.* at 15.[6] If the medical or psychological personnel find contraindications, sleep deprivation will end earlier. *See id.* at 15-16. While continuing the use of sleep deprivation, nudity, and dietary manipulation, the interrogators may add cramped confinement. As the detainee begins to cooperate, the interrogators "begin gradually to decrease the use of interrogation techniques." *Id.* at 16. They may permit the detainee to sit, supply clothes, and provide more appetizing food. *See id.*

The entire process in this "prototypical interrogation" may last 30 days. If additional time is required and a new approval is obtained from headquarters, interrogation may go longer than 30 days. Nevertheless, "[o]n average, the actual use of interrogation techniques covers a period of three to seven days, but can vary upwards to fifteen days based on the resilience of the [detainee]." *Id.* As in *Techniques*, our advice here is limited to an interrogation process lasting no more than 30 days. *See Techniques* at 5.

Use of the Waterboard in Combination with Other Techniques

We understand that for a small number of detainees in very limited circumstances, the CIA may wish to use the waterboard technique. You have previously explained that the waterboard technique would be used only if: (1) the CIA has credible intelligence that a terrorist attack is imminent; (2) there are "substantial and credible indicators the subject has actionable intelligence that can prevent, disrupt or delay this attack"; and (3) other interrogation methods have failed or are unlikely to yield actionable intelligence in time to prevent the attack. *See* Attachment to Letter

---

[6] As in *Techniques*, our advice here is restricted to one application of no more than 180 hours of sleep deprivation.

from John A. Rizzo, Acting General Counsel, CIA, to Daniel Levin, Acting Assistant Attorney General, Office of Legal Counsel (Aug. 2, 2004). You have also informed us that the waterboard may be approved for use with a given detainee only during, at most, one single 30-day period, and that during that period, the waterboard technique may be used on no more than five days. We further understand that in any 24-hour period, interrogators may use no more than two "sessions" of the waterboard on a subject—with a "session" defined to mean the time that the detainee is strapped to the waterboard—and that no session may last more than two hours. Moreover, during any session, the number of individual applications of water lasting 10 seconds or longer may not exceed six. The maximum length of any application of water is 40 seconds (you have informed us that this maximum has rarely been reached). Finally, the total cumulative time of all applications of whatever length in a 24-hour period may not exceed 12 minutes. *See* Letter from ▮▮▮▮▮▮▮ Associate General Counsel, CIA, to Dan Levin, Acting Assistant Attorney General, Office of Legal Counsel, at 1-2 (Aug. 19, 2004).

You have advised us that in those limited cases where the waterboard would be used, it would be used only in direct combination with two other techniques, dietary manipulation and sleep deprivation. *See April 22* ▮▮▮ *Fax* at 3-4. While an individual is physically on the waterboard, the CIA does not use the attention grasp, walling, the facial hold, the facial or insult slap, the abdominal slap, cramped confinement, wall standing, stress positions, or water dousing, though some or all of these techniques may be used with the individual before the CIA needs to resort to the waterboard, and we understand it is possible that one or more of these techniques might be used on the same day as a waterboard session, but separately from that session and not in conjunction with the waterboard. *See id.* at 3.

As we discussed in *Techniques*, you have informed us that an individual undergoing the waterboard is always placed on a fluid diet before he may be subjected to the waterboard in order to avoid aspiration of food matter. The individual is kept on the fluid diet throughout the period the waterboard is used. For this reason, and in this way, the waterboard is used in combination with dietary manipulation. *See April 22* ▮▮▮ *Fax* at 3.

You have also described how sleep deprivation may be used prior to and during the waterboard session. *Id.* at 4. We understand that the time limitation on use of sleep deprivation, as set forth in *Techniques*, continues to be strictly monitored and enforced when sleep deprivation is used in combination with the waterboard (as it is when used in combination with other techniques). *See April 22* ▮▮▮ *Fax* at 4. You have also informed us that there is no evidence in literature or experience that sleep deprivation exacerbates any harmful effects of the waterboard, though it does reduce the detainee's will to resist and thereby contributes to the effectiveness of the waterboard as an interrogation technique. *Id.* As in *Techniques*, we understand that in the event the detainee were [*sic*] perceived to be unable to withstand the effects of the waterboard for any reason, any member of the interrogation team has the obligation to intervene and, if necessary, to halt the use of the waterboard. *See April 22* ████ *Fax* at 4.

II.

The issue of the combined effects of interrogation techniques raises complex and difficult questions and comes to us in a less precisely defined form than the questions treated in our earlier opinions about individual techniques. In evaluating individual techniques, we turned to a body of experience developed in the use of analogous techniques in military train-ing by the United States, to medical literature, and to the judgment of medical personnel. Because there is less certainty and definition about the use of techniques in combination, it is necessary to draw more inferences in assessing what may be expected. You have informed us that, although "the exemplar [that is, the prototypical interrogation] is a fair representa-tion of how these techniques are actually employed," "there is no tem-plate or script that states with certainty when and how these techniques will be used in combination during interrogation." *Background Paper* at 17. Whether any other combination of techniques would, in the relevant senses, be like the ones presented—whether the combination would be no more likely to cause severe physical or mental pain or suffering within the meaning of sections 2340-2340A—would be a question that cannot be assessed in the context of the present legal opinion. For that reason, our advice does not extend to combinations of techniques unlike the ones dis-cussed here. For the same reason, it is especially important that the CIA use great care in applying these various techniques in combination in a real-world scenario, and that the members of the interrogation team, and the attendant medical staff, remain watchful for indications that the use of techniques in combination may be having unintended effects, so that the interrogation regimen may be altered or halted, if necessary, to ensure that it will not result in severe physical or mental pain or suffering to any detainee in violation of 18 U.S.C. §§ 2340-2340A.

Finally, in both of our previous opinions about specific techniques, we evaluated the use of those techniques on particular identified individu-als. Here, we are asked to address the combinations without reference to any particular detainee. As is relevant here, we know only that an enhanced interrogation technique, such as most of the techniques at issue in *Techniques*, may be used on a detainee only if medical and psychological personnel have determined that he is not likely, as a result, to experience severe physical or mental pain or suffering. *Techniques* at 5. Once again, whether other detainees would, in the relevant ways, be like the ones previously at issue would be a factual question we cannot now decide. Our advice, therefore, does not extend to the use of techniques on detainees unlike those we have previously considered. Moreover, in this regard, it is also especially important, as we pointed out in *Techniques* with respect to certain techniques, *see, e.g., id.* at 37 (discussing sleep deprivation), that the CIA will carefully assess the condition of each individual detainee and that the CIA's use of these techniques in combination will be sensitive to the individualized physical condition and reactions of each detainee, so that the regimen of interrogation would be altered or halted, if necessary, in the event of unanticipated effects on a particular detainee.

Subject to these cautions and to the conditions, limitations, and safeguards set out below and in *Techniques*, we nonetheless can reach some conclusions about the combined use of these techniques. Although this is a difficult question that will depend on the particular detainee, we do not believe that the use of the techniques in combination as you have described them would be expected to inflict "severe physical or mental pain or suffering" within the meaning of the statute. 18 U.S.C. § 2340(1). Although the combination of interrogation techniques will wear a detainee down physically, we understand that the principal effect, as well as the primary goal, of interrogation using these techniques is psychological—"to create a state of learned helplessness and dependence conducive to the collection of intelligence in a predictable, reliable, and sustainable manner," *Background Paper* at 1—and numerous precautions are designed to avoid inflicting "severe physical or mental pain or suffering."

For present purposes, we may divide "severe physical or mental pain or suffering" into three categories: "severe physical . . . pain," "severe physical . . . suffering," and "severe . . . mental pain or suffering" (the last being a defined term under the statute). *See Techniques* at 22-26, Memorandum for James B. Comey, Deputy Attorney General, from Daniel Levin, Acting Assistant Attorney General, Office of Legal Counsel, *Re: Legal Standards Applicable Under 18 U.S.C. §§ 2340-2340A* (Dec. 30, 2004).

As explained below, any physical pain resulting from the use of these techniques, even in combination, cannot reasonably be expected to meet the level of "severe physical pain" contemplated by the statute. We conclude, therefore, that the authorized use in combination of these techniques by adequately trained interrogators, as described in the *Background Paper* and the *April 22* ███ *Fax*, could not reasonably be considered specifically intended to do so. Moreover, although it presents a closer question under sections 2340-2340A, we conclude that the combined use of these techniques also cannot reasonably be expected to—and their combined use in the authorized manner by adequately trained interrogators could not reasonably be considered specifically intended to—cause severe physical suffering. Although two techniques, extended sleep deprivation and the waterboard, may involve a more substantial risk of physical distress, nothing in the other specific techniques discussed in the *Background Paper* and the *April 22* ███ *Fax*, or, as we understand it, in the CIA's experience to date with the interrogations of more than two dozen detainees (three of whose interrogations involved the use of the waterboard), would lead to the expectation that any physical discomfort from the combination of sleep deprivation or the waterboard and other techniques would involve the degree of intensity and duration of physical distress sufficient to constitute severe physical suffering under the statute. Therefore, the use of the technique could not reasonably be viewed as specifically intended to cause severe physical suffering. We stress again, however, that these questions concerning whether the combined effects of different techniques may rise to the level of physical suffering within the meaning of sections 2340-2340A are difficult ones, and they reinforce the need for close and ongoing monitoring by medical and psychological personnel and by all members of the interrogation team and active intervention if necessary.

Analyzing the combined techniques in terms of severe mental pain or suffering raises two questions under the statute. The first is whether the risk of hallucinations from sleep deprivation may become exacerbated when combined with other techniques, such that a detainee might be expected to experience "prolonged mental harm" from the combination of techniques. Second, the description in the *Background Paper* that detainees may be specifically told that interrogators will "do what it takes" to elicit information, *id.* at 10, raises the question whether this statement might qualify as a threat of infliction of severe physical pain or suffering or another of the predicate acts required for "severe mental pain or suffering" under the statute. After discussing both of those possibilities below, however, we conclude that the authorized use by adequately trained interrogators of the techniques in combination, as you have described them, would not reasonably be expected to cause prolonged mental harm and could not reasonably be considered specifically intended to cause severe mental pain or suffering. We stress that these possible questions about the combined use of the techniques under the statutory category of severe mental pain or suffering are difficult ones and they serve to reinforce the need for close and ongoing monitoring and active intervention if necessary.

Severe Physical Pain

Our two previous opinions have not identified any techniques that would inflict pain that approaches the "sever[ity]" required to violate the statute. A number of the techniques—dietary manipulation, nudity, sleep deprivation, the facial hold, and the attention grasp—are not expected to cause physical pain at all. *See Techniques* at 30-36. Others might cause some pain, but the level of pain would not approach that which would be considered "severe." These techniques are the abdominal slap, water dousing, various stress positions, wall standing, cramped confinement, walling, and the facial slap. *See id.* We also understand that the waterboard is not physically painful. *Id.* at 41. In part because none of these techniques would individually cause pain that even approaches the "severe" level required to violate the statute, the combined use of the techniques under the conditions outlined here would not be expected to—and we conclude that their authorized use by adequately trained interrogators could not reasonably be considered specifically intended to—reach that level.[7]

---

[7] We are not suggesting that combinations or repetitions of acts that do not individually cause severe physical pain could not result in severe physical pain. Other than the repeated use of the "walling" technique, however, nothing in the *Background Paper* suggests the kind of repetition that might raise an issue about severe physical pain; and, in the case of walling, we understand that this technique involves a false, flexible wall and is not significantly painful, even with repetition. Our advice with respect to walling in the present memorandum is based on the understanding that the repetitive use of walling is intended only to increase the shock and drama of the technique, to tear down the detainee's resistance, and to disrupt expectations that he will not be treated with force, and that such use is not intended to, and does not in fact, cause severe physical pain to the detainee. Along these lines, we understand that the repeated use of the insult slap and the abdominal slap gradually reduces their effectiveness and that their use is therefore limited to times when the detainee's overt disrespect for the question or questioner requires immediate correction, when the detainee displays obvious efforts to misdirect or ignore the question or questioner, or when the detainee attempts to provide an obvious lie in response to a specific question. Our advice assumes that the interrogators will apply those techniques as designed and will

We recognize the theoretical possibility that the use of one or more techniques would make a detainee more susceptible to severe pain or that the techniques, in combination, would operate differently from the way they would individually and thus cause severe pain. But as we understand the experience involving the combination of various techniques, the OMS medical and psychological personnel have not observed any such increase in susceptibility. Other than the waterboard, the specific techniques under consideration in this memorandum—including sleep deprivation—have been applied to more than 25 detainees. *See* ▮ *Fax* at 1-3. No apparent increase in susceptibility to severe pain has been observed either when techniques are used sequentially or when they are used simultaneously—for example, when an insult slap is simultaneously combined with water dousing or a kneeling stress position, or when wall standing is simultaneously combined with an abdominal slap and water dousing. Nor does experience show that, even apart from changes in susceptibility to pain, combinations of these techniques cause the techniques to operate differently so as to cause severe pain. OMS doctors and psychologists, moreover, confirm that they expect that the techniques, when combined as described in the *Background Paper* and in the *April 22* ▮ *Fax*, would not operate in a different manner from the way they do individually, so as to cause severe pain.

We understand that experience supports these conclusions even though the *Background Paper* does give examples where the distress caused by one technique would be increased by use of another. The "conditioning techniques"—nudity, sleep deprivation, and dietary manipulation—appear designed to wear down the detainee, physically and psychologically, and to allow other techniques to be more effective, *see Background Paper* at 5, 12; *April 22* ▮ *Fax* at 4; and "these [conditioning] techniques are used in combination in almost all cases," *Background Paper* at 17. And, in another example, the threat of walling is used to cause a detainee to hold a stress position longer than he otherwise would. *See id.* at 14. The issue raised by the statute, however, is whether the techniques would be specifically intended to cause the detainee to experience "severe . . . pain." 18 U.S.C. § 2340(1). In the case of the conditioning techniques, the principal effect, as you have described it, is on the detainee's will to resist other

---

not strike the detainee with excessive force or repetition in a manner that might result in severe physical pain. As to all techniques, our advice assumes that the use of the technique will be stopped if there is any indication that it is or may be causing severe physical pain to the detainee.

techniques, rather than on the pain that the other techniques cause. *See Background Paper* at 5, 12; *April 22* ▮ *Fax* at 4. Moreover, the stress positions and wall standing, while inducing muscle fatigue, do not cause "severe physical . . . pain," and there is no reason to believe that a position held somewhat longer than otherwise, would create such pain. *See Techniques* at 33-34.[8]

In any particular case, a combination of techniques might have unexpected results, just as an individual technique could produce surprising effects. But the *Background Paper* and the *April 22* ▮ *Fax*, as well as *Techniques*, describe a system of medical and psychological monitoring of the detainee that would very likely identify any such unexpected results as they begin to occur and would require an interrogation to be modified or stopped if a detainee is in danger of severe physical pain. Medical and psychological personnel assess the detainee before any interrogation starts. *See, e.g., Techniques* at 5. Physical and psychological evaluations are completed daily during any period in which the interrogators use enhanced techniques, including those at issue in *Techniques* (leaving aside dietary manipulation and sleep deprivation of less than 48 hours). *See id.* at 5-7. Medical and psychological personnel are on scene throughout the interrogation, and are physically present or are otherwise observing during many of the techniques. *See id.* at 6-7. These safeguards, which were critically important to our conclusions about individual techniques, are even more significant when techniques are combined.

In one specific context, monitoring the effects on detainees appears particularly important. The *Background Paper* and the *April 22* ▮ *Fax* illustrate that sleep deprivation is a central part of the "prototypical interrogation." We noted in *Techniques* that extended sleep deprivation may cause a small decline in body temperature and increased food consumption. *See Techniques* at 33-34. Water dousing and dietary manipulation and perhaps even nudity may thus raise dangers of enhanced susceptibility to hypothermia or other medical conditions for a detainee undergoing sleep deprivation. As in *Techniques*, we assume that medical personnel will be aware of these possible interactions and will monitor detainees closely for any signs that such interactions are developing. *See id.* at 33-35. This monitoring, along with quick intervention if any signs

---

[8] Our advice about wall standing and stress positions assumes that the positions used in each technique are not designed to produce severe pain that might result from contortions or twisting of the body, but only temporary muscle fatigue.

of problematic symptoms develop, can be expected to prevent a detainee from experiencing severe physical pain.

We also understand that some studies suggest that extended sleep deprivation may be associated with a reduced tolerance for some forms of pain.[9] Several of the techniques used by the CIA may involve a degree of physical pain, as we have previously noted, including facial and abdominal slaps, walling, stress positions, and water dousing. Nevertheless, none of these techniques would cause anything approaching severe physical pain. Because sleep deprivation appears to cause at most only relatively moderate decreases in pain tolerance, the use of these techniques in combination with extended sleep deprivation would not be expected to cause severe physical pain.

Therefore, the combined use of techniques, as set out in the *Background Paper* and the *April 22* ██████ *Fax*, would not reasonably be expected by the interrogators to result in severe physical pain. We conclude that the authorized use of these techniques in combination by adequately trained interrogators, as you have described it, could not reasonably be considered specifically intended to cause such pain for purposes of sections 2340-2340A. The close monitoring of each detainee for any signs that he is at risk of experiencing severe physical pain reinforces the conclusion that the combined use of interrogation techniques is not intended to inflict such pain. OMS has directed that "[m]edical officers must remain cognizant at all times of their obligation to prevent 'severe physical or mental pain or suffering.'" *OMS Guidelines* at 10. The obligation of interrogation team members and medical staff to intercede if their observations indicate a detainee is at risk of experiencing severe physical pain, and the expectation that all interrogators understand the important role played by OMS and will cooperate with them in the exercise of this duty, are here, as in *Techniques*, essential to our advice. *See Techniques* at 14.

---

[9] For example, one study found a statistically significant drop of 8-9% in subjects' tolerance thresholds for mechanical or pressure pain after 40 hours of total sleep deprivation. *See* S. Hakki Onen, et al., *The Effects of Total Sleep Deprivation, Selective Sleep Interruption and Sleep Recovery on Pain Tolerance Thresholds in Healthy Subjects.* 10 J. Sleep Research 35, 41 (2001); *see also id.* at 35-36 (discussing other studies). Another study of extended total sleep deprivation found a significant decrease in the threshold for heat pain and some decrease in the cold pain threshold. *See* B. Kundermann, et al., *Sleep Deprivation Affects Thermal Pain Thresholds but not Somotosensory Thresholds in Healthy Volunteers.* 66 Psychosomatic Med. 932 (2004).

Severe Physical Suffering

We noted in *Techniques* that, although the statute covers a category of "severe physical . . . suffering" distinct from "severe physical pain," this category encompasses only "physical distress that is 'severe' considering its intensity and duration or persistence, rather than merely mild or transitory." *Id.* at 23 (internal quotation marks omitted). Severe physical suffering for purposes of sections 2340-2340A, we have concluded, means a state or condition of physical distress, misery, affliction, or torment, usually involving physical pain, that is both extreme in intensity and significantly protracted in duration or persistent over time. *Id.* Severe physical suffering is distinguished from suffering that is purely mental or psychological in nature, since mental suffering is encompassed by the separately defined statutory category of "severe mental pain or suffering," discussed below. To amount to torture, conduct must be "sufficiently extreme and outrageous to warrant the universal condemnation that the term 'torture' both connotes and invokes." *See Price v. Socialist People's Libyan Arab Jamahiriya*, 294 F.3d 82, 92 (D.C. Cir. 2002) (interpreting the TVPA); *cf. Mehinovic v. Vuckovic*, 198 F. Supp. 2d 1322, 1332-40, 1345-46 (N.D. Ga. 2002) (standard met under the TVPA by a course of conduct that included severe beatings to the genitals, head, and other parts of the body with metal pipes and various other items; removal of teeth with pliers; kicking in the face and ribs; breaking of bones and ribs and dislocation of fingers; cutting a figure into the victim's forehead; hanging the victim and beating him; extreme limitations of food and water; and subjection to games of "Russian roulette").

In *Techniques*, we recognized that, depending on the physical condition and reactions of a given individual, extended sleep deprivation might cause physical distress in some cases. *Id.* at 34. Accordingly, we advised that the strict limitations and safeguards adopted by the CIA are important to ensure that the use of extended sleep deprivation would not cause severe physical suffering. *Id.* at 34-35. We pointed to the close medical monitoring by OMS of each detainee subjected to sleep deprivation, as well as to the power of any member of the interrogation team or detention facility staff to intervene and, in particular, to intervention by OMS if OMS concludes in its medical judgment that the detainee may be experiencing extreme physical distress. With those safeguards in place, and based on the assumption that they would be strictly followed, we concluded that the authorized use of sleep deprivation by adequately trained interrogators could not reasonably be considered specifically intended to cause such severe physical suffering. *Id.* at 34. We pointed out that "[d]ifferent individual detainees may react physically to sleep deprivation in different ways," *id.*, and we assumed that the interrogation team and medical staff "will separately monitor each individual detainee who is undergoing sleep deprivation, and that the application of this technique will be sensitive to the individualized physical condition and reactions of each detainee." *Id.*

Although it is difficult to calculate the additional effect of combining other techniques with sleep deprivation, we do not believe that the addition of the other techniques as described in the *Background Paper* would result in "severe physical . . . suffering." The other techniques do not themselves inflict severe physical pain. They are not of the intensity and duration that are necessary for "severe physical suffering"; instead, they only increase, over a short time, the discomfort that a detainee subjected to sleep deprivation experiences. They do not extend the time at which sleep deprivation would end, and although it is possible that the other techniques increase the physical discomfort associated with sleep deprivation itself, we cannot say that the effect would be so significant as to cause "physical distress that is 'severe' considering its intensity and duration or persistence." *Techniques* at 23 (internal quotation marks omitted). We emphasize that the question of "severe physical suffering" in the context of a combination of techniques is a substantial and difficult one, particularly in light of the imprecision in the statutory standard and the relative lack of guidance in the case law. Nevertheless, we believe that the combination of techniques in question here would not be "extreme and outrageous" and thus would not reach the high bar established by Congress in sections 2340-2340A, which is reserved for actions that "warrant the universal condemnation that the term 'torture' both connotes and invokes." *See Price v. Socialist People's Libyan Arab Jamahiriya,* 294 F.3d at 92 (interpreting the TVPA).

As we explained in *Techniques,* experience with extended sleep deprivation shows that " '[s]urprisingly, little seemed to go wrong with the subjects physically. The main effects lay with sleepiness and impaired brain functioning, but even these were no great cause for concern.' " *Id.* at 36 (quoting James Horne, *Why We Sleep: The Functions of Sleep in Humans and Other Mammals* 23-24 (1988)). The aspects of sleep deprivation that might result in substantial physical discomfort, therefore, are limited in scope; and although the degree of distress associated with sleepiness, as noted above, may differ from person to person, the CIA has found that many of the at least 25 detainees subjected to sleep deprivation have tolerated it well. The general conditions in which sleep deprivation takes place would not change this conclusion. Shackling is employed as a passive means of keeping a detainee awake and is used in a way designed to prevent causing significant pain. A detainee is not allowed to hang by his wrists. When the detainee is shackled in a sitting position, he is on a stool adequate to bear his weight; and if a horizontal position is used, there is no additional stress on the detainee's arm or leg joints that might force his limbs beyond their natural extension or create tension on any joint. Furthermore, team members, as well as medical staff, watch for the development of edema and will act to relieve that condition, should significant edema develop. If a detainee subject to sleep deprivation is using an adult diaper, the diaper is checked regularly and changed as needed to prevent skin irritation.

Nevertheless, we recognize, as noted above, the possibility that sleep deprivation might lower a detainee's tolerance for pain. *See supra* p. 13 & n.9. This possibility suggests that use of extended sleep deprivation in combination with other techniques might be more likely than the separate use of the techniques to place the detainee in a state of severe physical distress and, therefore, that the detainee might be more likely to experience severe physical suffering. However, you have informed us that the interrogation techniques at issue would not be used during a course of extended sleep deprivation with such frequency and intensity as to induce in the detainee a persistent condition of extreme physical distress such as may constitute "severe physical suffering" within the meaning of sections 2340-2340A. We understand that the combined use of these techniques with extended sleep deprivation is not designed or expected to cause that result. Even assuming there could be such an effect, members of the interrogation team and medical staff from OMS monitor detainees and would intercede if there were indications that the combined use of the techniques may be having that result, and the use of the techniques would be reduced in frequency or intensity or halted altogether, as necessary. In this regard, we assume that if a detainee started to show an atypical, adverse reaction during sleep deprivation, the system for monitoring would identify this development.

These considerations underscore that the combination of other techniques with sleep deprivation magnifies the importance of adhering strictly to the limits and safeguards applicable to sleep deprivation as an individual technique, as well as the understanding that team personnel, as well as OMS medical personnel, would intervene to alter or stop the use of an interrogation technique if they conclude that a detainee is or may be experiencing extreme physical distress.

The waterboard may be used simultaneously with two other techniques: it may be used during a course of sleep deprivation, and as explained above, a detainee subjected to the waterboard must be under dietary manipulation, because a fluid diet reduces the risks of the technique. Furthermore, although the insult slap, abdominal slap, attention grasp, facial hold, walling, water dousing, stress positions, and cramped confinement cannot be employed during the actual session when the waterboard is being employed, they may be used at a point in time close to the waterboard, including on the same day. *See April 22* ███ *Fax* at 3.

In *Techniques*, we explained why neither sleep deprivation nor the waterboard would impose distress of such intensity and duration as to amount to "severe physical suffering," and, depending on the circumstances and the individual detainee, we do not believe the combination of the techniques, even if close in time with other techniques, would change that conclusion. The physical distress of the waterboard, as explained in *Techniques*, lasts only during the relatively short periods during a session when the technique is actually being used. Sleep deprivation would not extend that period. Moreover, we understand that there is nothing in the literature or experience to suggest that sleep deprivation would exacerbate any harmful effects of the waterboard. *See supra* p. 9. Similarly, the use of the waterboard would not extend the time of sleep deprivation or increase its distress, except during the relatively brief times that the technique is actually being used. And the use of other techniques that do not involve the intensity and duration required for "severe physical suffering" would not lengthen the time during which the waterboard would be used or increase, in any apparent way, the intensity of the distress it would cause. Nevertheless, because both the waterboard and sleep deprivation raise substantial questions, the combination of the techniques only heightens the difficulty of the issues. Furthermore, particularly because the waterboard is so different from other techniques in its effects, its use in combination with other techniques is particularly difficult to judge in the abstract and calls for the utmost vigilance and care.

Based on these assumptions, and those described at length in *Techniques*, we conclude that the combination of techniques, as described in the *Background Paper* and the *April 22* ███ *Fax*, would not be expected by the interrogators to cause "severe physical . . . suffering," and that the authorized use of these techniques in combination by adequately trained interrogators could not reasonably be considered specifically intended to cause severe physical suffering within the meaning of sections 2340-2340A.

Severe Mental Pain or Suffering

As we explained in *Techniques*, the statutory definition of "severe mental pain or suffering" requires that one of four specified predicate acts cause "prolonged mental harm." 18 U.S.C. § 2340(2); *see Techniques* at 24-25. In *Techniques*, we concluded that only two of the techniques at issue here—sleep deprivation and the waterboard—could even arguably involve a predicate act. The statute provides that "the administration or application . . . of . . . procedures calculated to disrupt profoundly the senses or the personality" can be a predicate act. 18 U.S.C. § 2340(2)(B). Although sleep deprivation may cause hallucinations, OMS, supported by the scientific literature of which we are aware, would not expect a profound disruption of the senses and would order sleep deprivation discontinued if hallucinations occurred. We nonetheless assumed in *Techniques* that any hallucinations resulting from sleep deprivation would amount to a profound disruption of the senses. Even on this assumption, we concluded that sleep deprivation should not be deemed "calculated" to have that effect. *Techniques* at 35-36. Furthermore, even if sleep deprivation could be said to be "calculated" to disrupt the senses profoundly and thus to qualify as a predicate act, we expressed the understanding in *Techniques* that, as demonstrated by the scientific literature about which we knew and by relevant experience in CIA interrogations, the effects of sleep deprivation, including the effects of any associated hallucinations, would rapidly dissipate. Based on that understanding, sleep deprivation therefore would not cause "prolonged mental harm" and would not meet the statutory definition for "severe mental pain or suffering." *Id.* at 36.

We noted in *Techniques* that the use of the waterboard might involve a predicate act. A detainee subjected to the waterboard experiences a sensation of drowning, which arguably qualifies as a "threat of imminent death." 18 U.S.C. § 2340(2)(C). We noted, however, that there is no medical basis for believing that the technique would produce any prolonged mental harm. As explained in *Techniques*, there is no evidence for such prolonged mental harm in the CIA's experience with the technique, and we understand that it has been used thousands of times (albeit in a somewhat different way) during the military training of United States personnel, without producing any evidence of such harm.

There is no evidence that combining other techniques with sleep deprivation or the waterboard would change these conclusions. We understand that none of the detainees subjected to sleep deprivation has exhibited any lasting mental harm, and that, in all but one case, these detainees have been subjected to at least some other interrogation technique besides the sleep deprivation itself. Nor does this experience give any reason to believe that, should sleep deprivation cause hallucinations, the use of these other techniques in combination with sleep deprivation would change the expected result that, once a person subjected to sleep deprivation is allowed to sleep, the effects of the sleep deprivation, and of any associated hallucinations, would rapidly dissipate.

Once again, our advice assumes continuous, diligent monitoring of the detainee during sleep deprivation and prompt intervention at the first signs of hallucinatory experiences. The absence of any atypical, adverse reaction during sleep deprivation would buttress the inference that, like others deprived of sleep for long periods, the detainee would fit within the norm established by experience with sleep deprivation, both the general experience reflected in the medical literature and the CIA's specific experience with other detainees. We understand that, based on these experiences, the detainee would be expected to return quickly to his normal mental state once he has been allowed to sleep and would suffer no "prolonged mental harm."

Similarly, the CIA's experience has produced no evidence that combining the waterboard and other techniques causes prolonged mental harm, and the same is true of the military training in which the technique was used. We assume, again, continuous and diligent monitoring during the use of the technique, with a view toward quickly identifying any atypical, adverse reactions and intervening as necessary.

The *Background Paper* raises one other issue about "severe mental pain or suffering." According to the *Background Paper*, the interrogators may tell detainees that they "will do what it takes to get important information." *Background Paper* at 10. (We understand that interrogators may instead use other statements that might be taken to have a similar import.) Conceivably, a detainee might understand such a statement as a threat that, if necessary, the interrogators will imminently subject him to "severe physical pain or suffering" or to "the administration or application of mind-altering substances or other procedures calculated to disrupt profoundly the senses or the personality," or he perhaps even could interpret the statement as a threat of imminent death (although, as the detainee himself would possibly realize, killing a detainee would end the flow of information). 18 U.S.C. § 2340(2)(A)-(C).

We doubt that this statement is sufficiently specific to qualify as a predicate act under section 2340(2). Nevertheless, we do not have sufficient information to judge whether, in context, detainees understand the statement in any of these ways. If they do, this statement at the beginning of the interrogation arguably requires considering whether it alters the detainee's perception of the interrogation techniques and whether, in light of this perception, prolonged mental harm would be expected to result from the combination throughout the interrogation process of all of the techniques used. We do not have any body of experience, beyond the CIA's own experience with detainees, on which to base an answer to this question. SERE training, for example, or other experience with sleep deprivation, does not involve its use with the standing position used here, extended nudity, extended dietary manipulation, and the other techniques which are intended "to create a state of learned helplessness," *Background Paper* at 1, and SERE training does not involve repeated applications of the waterboard. A statement that the interrogators "will do what it takes to get important information" moves the interrogations at issue here even further from this body of experience.

Although it may raise a question, we do not believe that, under the careful limitations and monitoring in place, the combined use outlined in the *Background Paper*, together with a statement of this kind, would violate the statute. We are informed that, in the opinion of OMS, none of the detainees who have heard such a statement in their interrogations has experienced "prolonged mental harm," such as post-traumatic stress disorder, *see Techniques* at 26 n.31, as a result of it or the various techniques utilized on them. This body of experience supports the conclusion that the use of the statement does not alter the effects that would be expected to follow from the combined use of the techniques. Nevertheless, in light of these uncertainties, you may wish to evaluate whether such a statement is a necessary part of the interrogation regimen or whether a different statement might be adequate to convey to the detainee the seriousness of his situation.

*   *   *

In view of the experience from past interrogations, the judgment of medical and psychological personnel, and the interrogation team's diligent monitoring of the effects of combining interrogation techniques, interrogators would not reasonably expect that the combined use of the interrogation methods under consideration, subject to the conditions and safeguards set forth here and in *Techniques*, would result in severe physical or mental pain or suffering within the meaning of sections 2340-2340A. Accordingly, we conclude that the authorized use, as prescribed in the *Background Paper* and the *April 22* ▮▮▮ *Fax*, of these techniques in combination by adequately trained interrogators could not reasonably be considered specifically intended to cause severe physical or mental pain or suffering, and thus would not violate sections 2340-2340A. We nonetheless underscore that when these techniques are combined in a real-world scenario, the members of the interrogation team and the attendant medical staff must be vigilant in watching for unintended effects, so that the individual characteristics of each detainee are constantly taken into account and the interrogation may be modified or halted, if necessary, to avoid causing severe physical or mental pain or suffering to any detainee. Furthermore, as noted above, our advice does not extend to combinations of techniques unlike the ones discussed here, and whether any other combination of techniques would be more likely to cause severe physical or mental pain or suffering within the meaning of sections 2340-2340A would be a question that we cannot assess here. Similarly, our advice does not extend to the use of techniques on detainees unlike those we have previously considered, and whether other detainees would, in the relevant ways, be like the ones at issue in our previous advice would be a factual question we cannot now decide. Finally, we emphasize that these are issues about which reasonable persons may disagree. Our task has been made more difficult by the imprecision of the statute and the relative absence of judicial guidance, but we have applied our best reading of the law to the specific facts that you have provided.

Please let us know if we may be of further assistance.

Steven G. Bradbury
Principal Deputy
Assistant Attorney General

U.S. Department of Justice

Office of Legal Counsel

Office of the Principal Deputy Assistant Attorney General   *Washington, D.C. 20530*

May 30, 2005

MEMORANDUM FOR JOHN A. RIZZO
SENIOR DEPUTY GENERAL COUNSEL,
CENTRAL INTELLIGENCE AGENCY

*Re: Application of United States Obligations Under Article 16
of the Convention Against Torture to Certain Techniques That May
Be Used in the Interrogation of High Value al Qaeda Detainees*

You have asked us to address whether certain "enhanced interrogation techniques" employed by the Central Intelligence Agency ("CIA") in the interrogation of high value al Qaeda detainees are consistent with United States obligations under Article 16 of the United Nations Convention Against Torture and Other Cruel, Inhuman or Degrading Treatment or Punishment, Dec. 10, 1984, S. Treaty Doc. No. 100-20, 1465 U.N.T.S. 85 (entered into force for U.S. Nov 20, 1994) ("CAT"). We conclude that use of these techniques, subject to the CIA's careful screening criteria and limitations and its medical safeguards, is consistent with United States obligations under Article 16.[1]

---

[1] Our analysis and conclusions are limited to the specific legal issues we address in this memorandum. We note that we have previously concluded that use of these techniques, subject to the limits and safeguards required by the interrogation program, does not violate the federal prohibition on torture, codified at 18 U.S.C. §§ 2340-2340A. *See* Memorandum for John A. Rizzo, Senior Deputy General Counsel, Central Intelligence Agency, from Steven G. Bradbury, Principal Deputy Assistant Attorney General, Office of Legal Counsel, *Re: Application of 18 U.S.C. §§ 2340-2340A to Certain Techniques that May Be Used in the Interrogation of a High Value al Qaeda Detainee* (May 10, 2005); *see also* Memorandum for John A. Rizzo, Senior Deputy General Counsel, Central Intelligence Agency, from Steven G. Bradbury, Principal Deputy Assistant Attorney General, Office of Legal Counsel, *Re: Application of 18 U.S.C. §§ 2340-2340A to the Combined Use of Certain Techniques in the Interrogation of a High Value al*

By its terms, Article 16 is limited to conduct within "territory under [United States] jurisdiction." We conclude that territory under United States jurisdiction includes, at most, areas over which the United States exercises at least de facto authority as the government. Based on CIA assurances, we understand that the interrogations do not take place in any such areas. We therefore conclude that Article 16 is inapplicable to the CIA's interrogation practices and that those practices thus cannot violate Article 16. Further, the United States undertook its obligations under Article 16 subject to a Senate reservation, which, as relevant here, explicitly limits those obligations to "the cruel, unusual and inhumane treatment . . . prohibited by the Fifth Amendment . . . to the Constitution of the United States."[2] There is a strong argument that through this reservation the Senate intended to limit the scope of United States obligations under Article 16 to those imposed by the relevant provisions of the Constitution. As construed by the courts, the Fifth Amendment does not apply to aliens outside the United States. The CIA has assured us that the interrogation techniques are not used within the United States or against United States persons, including both United States citizens and lawful permanent residents. Because the geographic limitation on the face of Article 16 renders it inapplicable to the CIA interrogation program in any event, we need not decide in this memorandum the precise effect, if any, of the Senate reservation on the geographic reach of United States obligations under Article 16. For these reasons, we conclude in Part II that the interrogation techniques where and as used by the CIA are not subject to, and therefore do not violate, Article 16.

Qaeda Detainees (May, 10, 2005) (concluding that the anticipated combined) the use of these techniques would not violate the federal prohibition on torture). The legal advice provided in this memorandum does not represent the policy views of the Department of Justice concerning the use of any interrogation methods.

[2] The reservation provides in full:

That the United States considers itself bound by the obligation under Article 16 to prevent "cruel, inhuman or degrading treatment or punishment," only insofar as the term "cruel, inhuman or degrading treatment or punishment" means the cruel, unusual and inhumane treatment or punishment prohibited by the Fifth, Eighth, and/or Fourteenth Amendments to the Constitution of the United States.

136 Cong. Rec. 36198 [*sic*] (1990). As we explain below, the Eight and Fourteenth Amendments are not applicable in this context.

Notwithstanding these conclusions, you have also asked whether the interrogation techniques at issue would violate the substantive standards applicable to the United States under Article 16 if, contrary to our conclusion in Part II, those standards did extend to the CIA interrogation program. As detailed below in Part III, the relevant constraint here, assuming Article 16 did apply, would be the Fifth Amendment's prohibition of executive conduct that "shocks the conscience." The Supreme Court has emphasized that whether conduct "shocks the conscience" is a highly context-specific and fact-dependent question. The Court, however, has not set forth with precision a specific test for ascertaining whether conduct can be said to "shock the conscience" and has disclaimed the ability to do so. Moreover, there are few Supreme Court cases addressing whether conduct "shocks the conscience," and the few cases there are have all arisen in very different contexts from that which we consider here.

For these reasons, we cannot set forth or apply a precise test for ascertaining whether conduct can be said to "shock the conscience." Nevertheless, the Court's "shocks the conscience" cases do provide some signposts that can guide our inquiry. In particular, on balance the cases are best read to require a determination whether the conduct is "'arbitrary in the constitutional sense,'" *County of Sacramento v. Lewis,* 523 U.S. 833, 846 (1998) (citation omitted); that is, whether it involves the "exercise of power without any reasonable justification in the service of a legitimate governmental objective," *id.* "[C]onduct intended to injure in some way unjustifiable by any government interest is the sort of official action most likely to rise to the conscience-shocking level." *Id.* at 849. Far from being constitutionally arbitrary, the interrogation techniques at issue here are employed by the CIA only as reasonably deemed necessary to protect against grave threats to United States interests, a determination that is made at CIA Headquarters, with input from the on-scene interrogation team, pursuant to careful screening procedures that ensure that the technique will be used as little as possible on as few detainees as possible. Moreover, the techniques have been carefully designed to minimize the risk of suffering or injury and to avoid inflicting any serious or lasting physical or psychological harm. Medical screening, monitoring, and ongoing evaluations further lower such risk. Significantly, you have informed us that the CIA believes that this program is largely responsible for preventing a subsequent attack within the United States. Because the CIA interrogation program is carefully limited to further a vital government interest and designed to avoid unnecessary or serious harm, we conclude that it cannot be said to be constitutionally arbitrary.

The Supreme Court's decisions also suggest that it is appropriate to consider whether, in light of "traditional executive behavior, of contemporary practice, and the standards of blame generally applied to them," use of techniques in the CIA interrogation program "is so egregious, so outrageous, that it may fairly be said to shock the contemporary conscience." *Id.* at 847 n 8. We have not found evidence of traditional executive behavior or contemporary practice either condemning or condoning an interrogation program carefully limited to further a vital government interest and designed to avoid unnecessary or serious harm. We recognize, however, that use of coercive interrogation. techniques in other contexts—in different settings, for other purposes, or absent the CIA's safeguards—might be thought to "shock the conscience." *Cf., e.g., Rochin v. California,* 342 U.S. 165, 172 (1952) (finding that pumping the stomach of a criminal defendant to obtain evidence "shocks the conscience"); *U.S. Army Field Manual 34-52: Intelligence Interrogation* (1992) (*"Field Manual 34-52"*) (detailing guidelines for interrogations in the context of traditional warfare); Department of State, Country Reports on Human Rights Practices (describing human-rights abuses condemned by the United States). We believe, however, that each of these other contexts, which we describe more fully below, differs critically from the CIA interrogation program in ways that would be unreasonable to ignore in examining whether the conduct involved in the CIA program "shock[s] the contemporary conscience." Ordinary criminal investigations within the United States, for example, involve fundamentally different government interests and implicate specific constitutional guarantees, such as the privilege against self-incrimination, that are not at issue here. Furthermore, the CIA interrogation techniques have all been adapted from military Survival, Evasion, Resistance, Escape ("SERE") training. Although there are obvious differences between training exercises and actual interrogations, the fact that the United States uses similar techniques on its own troops for training purposes strongly suggests that these techniques are not categorically beyond the pale.

Given that the CIA interrogation program is carefully limited to further the Government's paramount interest in protecting the Nation while avoiding unnecessary or serious harm, we conclude that the interrogation program cannot "be said to shock the contemporary conscience" when considered in light of "traditional executive behavior" and "contemporary practice." *Lewis,* 523 U.S. at 847 n.8.

I.

Elsewhere, we have described the CIA interrogation program in great detail. *See* Memorandum for John A. Rizzo, Senior Deputy General Counsel, Central Intelligence Agency, from Steven G. Bradbury, Principal Deputy Assistant Attorney General, Office of Legal Counsel, *Re: Application of 18 U.S.C. §§2340-2340A to Certain Techniques that May Be Used in the Interrogation of a High Value al Qaeda Detainee* at 4-15, 28-45 (May 10, 2005) (*"Techniques"*); Memorandum for John A. Rizzo, Senior Deputy General Counsel, Central Intelligence Agency, from Steven G.

Bradbury, Principal Deputy Assistant Attorney General, Office of Legal Counsel, *Re: Application of 18 U.S.C. §§ 2340-2340A to the Combined Use of Certain Techniques in the Interrogation of High Value al Qaeda Detainees* at 3-9 (May 10, 2005) (*"Combined Use"*). The descriptions of the techniques, including all limitations and safeguards applicable to their use, set forth in *Techniques* and *Combined Use* are incorporated by reference herein, and we assume familiarity with those descriptions. Here, we highlight those aspects of the program that are most important to the question under consideration. Where appropriate, throughout this opinion we also provide more detailed background information regarding specific high value detainees who are representative of the individuals on whom the techniques might be used.[3]

A.

Under the CIA's guidelines, several conditions must be satisfied before the CIA considers employing enhanced techniques in the interrogation of any detainee. The CIA must, based on available intelligence, conclude that the detainee is an important and dangerous member of an al Qaeda-affiliated group. The CIA must then determine, at the Headquarters level and on a case-by-case basis with input from the on-scene interrogation team, that enhanced interrogation methods are needed in a particular interrogation, Finally, the enhanced techniques, which have been designed and implemented to minimize the potential for serious or unnecessary harm to the detainees, may be used only if there are no medical or psychological contraindications.

I.

---

[3] The CIA has reviewed and confirmed the accuracy of our description of the interrogation program, including its purposes, methods, limitations, and results.

████████████████████████████████ the CIA
uses enhanced interrogation techniques only if the CIA's Counterterrorist
Center ("CTC") determines an individual to be a "High Value Detainee,"
which the CIA defines as:

> a detainee who, until time of capture, we have reason to be-
> lieve: (1) is a senior member of al-Qai'da or an al-Qai'da asso-
> ciated terrorist group (Jemaah Islamiyyah, Egyptian Islamic
> Jihad, al-Zarqawi Group, etc,); (2) has knowledge of immi-
> nent terrorist threats against the USA, its military forces, its
> citizens and organizations, or its allies; or that has/had di-
> rect involvement in planning and preparing terrorist actions
> against the USA or its allies, or assisting the al-Qai'da leader-
> ship in planning and preparing such terrorist actions; and (3)
> if released, constitutes a clear and continuing threat to the
> USA or its allies.

Fax for Daniel Levin, Acting Assistant Attorney General, Office of Legal
Counsel, from ███████████████ Assistant General Counsel, Central
Intelligence Agency at 4 (Jan. 4, 2005) (*January 4* ██ *Fax*"). The CIA,
therefore, must have reason to believe that the detainee is a senior member
(rather than a mere "foot soldier") of al Qaeda or an associated terrorist
organization, who likely has actionable intelligence concerning terrorist
threats, and who poses a significant threat to United States interests.

The "waterboard," which is the most intense of the CIA interrogation techniques, is subject to additional limits. It may be used on a High
Value Detainee only if the CIA has "credible intelligence that a terrorist
attack is imminent"; "substantial and credible indicators that the subject
has actionable intelligence that can prevent, disrupt or delay this attack";
and "[o]ther interrogation methods have failed to elicit this information
[or] CIA has clear indications that other . . . methods are unlikely to elicit
this information *within the perceived time limit for preventing the attack*."
Letter from John A. Rizzo, Acting General Counsel, Central Intelligence
Agency, to Daniel Levin, Acting Assistant Attorney General, Office of
Legal Counsel at 5 (Aug. 2, 2004) ("*August 2 Rizzo Letter*") (attachment).
To date, the CIA has taken custody of 94 detainees ████████
████████████████████████████████
████████████ and has employed enhanced techniques to varying de-
grees in the interrogations of 28 of these detainees. We understand that

two individuals ███████████████████████ are representative of the high value detainees on whom enhanced techniques have been, or might be, used. On ██████████ the CIA took custody of █████ whom the CIA believed had actionable intelligence concerning the pre-election threat to the United States. *See* Letter from ████████████████, Associate General Counsel, Central Intelligence Agency, to Daniel Levin, Acting Assistant Attorney General, Office of Legal Counsel at 2 (Aug. 25, 2004) (*"August 25* ███████████ *Letter"*). ████████ extensive connections to various al Qaeda leaders, members of the Taliban, and the al-Zarqawi network, and intelligence indicated ███████████ arranged a . . . meeting between ████████████████████████ and ████████ ████████████████████ at which elements of the pre-election threat were discussed." *Id* at 2-3; *see also* Undated CIA Memo. ████████ ████████████████

Intelligence indicated that prior to his capture, ██████████ "perform[ed] critical facilitation and finance activities for al-Qa'ida," including "transporting people, funds, and documents." Fax for Jack L. Goldsmith, III, Assistant Attorney General, Office of Legal Counsel, from ████████████████ Assistant General Counsel, Central Intelligence Agency (March 12, 2004). The CIA also suspected ██████████ played an active part in planning attacks against United States forces ███████ ████████████ had extensive contacts with key members of al Qaeda, including, prior to their captures, Khalid Shaykh Muhammad ("KSM") and Abu Zubaydah. *See id.* ████████████ ████ was captured while on a mission from ████████████ to establish contact" with al-Zarqawi. *See* CIA Directorate of Intelligence, *US Efforts Grinding Down al-Qa'ida* 2 (Feb. 21, 2004).

Consistent with its heightened standard for use of the waterboard, the CIA has used this technique in the interrogations of only three detainees to date (KSM, Zubaydah, and 'Abd Al-Rahim Al-Nashiri) and has not used it since the March 2003 interrogation of KSM. *See* Letter from Scott W. Muller, General Counsel, Central Intelligence Agency, to Jack L. Goldsmith III, Assistant Attorney General, Office of Legal Counsel at 1 (June 14, 2004).

We understand that Abu Zubaydah and KSM are representative of the types of detainees on whom the waterboard has been, or might be, used. Prior to his capture, Zubaydah was "one of Usama Bin Laden's key lieutenants." CIA, *Zayn al-Abidin Muhammad Husayn ABU ZUBAYDAH* at 1 (Jan. 7, 2002) (*"Zubaydah Biography"*). Indeed, Zubaydah was al Qaeda's third or fourth highest ranking member and had been involved "in every major terrorist operation carried out by al Qaeda." Memorandum for

John Rizzo, Acting General Counsel, Central Intelligence Agency, from Jay S. Bybee, Assistant Attorney General, Office of Legal Counsel, *Re: Interrogation of al Qaeda Operative* at 7 (Aug. 1, 2002) (*"Interrogation Memorandum"*); Zubaydah Biography (noting Zubaydah's involvement in the September 11 attacks). Upon his capture on March 27, 2002, Zubaydah became the most senior member of al Qaeda in United States custody. *See IG Report* at 12.

KSM, "a mastermind" of the September 11, 2001, attacks, was regarded as "one of al-Qa'ida's most dangerous and resourceful operatives." CIA Khalid Sheikh ███████████ (Nov. 1, 2002) (*"CIA KSM Biography"*) ███████████████████████████████ Prior to his capture, the CIA considered KSM to be one of al Qaeda's "most important operational leaders . . . based on his close relationship with Usama Bin Laden and his reputation among the al-Qa'ida rank and file." *Id.* After the September 11 attacks, KSM assumed "the role of operations chief for al-Qa'ida around the world." CIA Directorate of Intelligence, *Khalid Shaykh Muhammad: Preeminent Source on Al-Qa'ida* 7 (July 13, 2004) (*"Preeminent Source"*). KSM also planned additional attacks within the United States both before and after September 11. *See id.* at 7-8; *see also The 9/11 Commission Report: Final Report of the National Commission on Terrorist Attacks Upon the United States* 150 (official gov't ed. 2004) (*"9/11 Commission Report"*).[4]

2.

Even with regard to detainees who satisfy these threshold requirements, enhanced techniques are considered only if the on-scene interrogation team determines that the detainee is withholding or manipulating information. In order to make this assessment, interrogators conduct an initial interview "in a relatively benign environment." Fax for Daniel Levin, Acting Assistant Attorney General, Office of Legal Counsel, from ████████████████████ Associate General Counsel, Central Intelligence Agency, *Re: Background Paper on CIA's Combined Use of Interrogation Techniques* at 3 (Dec. 30, 2004) (*"Background Paper"*). At

---

[4] Al-Nashiri, the only other detainee to be subjected to the waterboard, planned the bombing of the U.S.S. Cole and was subsequently "recognized as the chief of al Qaeda operations in and around the Arabian Peninsula." *9/11 Commission Report* at 153.

this stage, the detainee is "normally clothed but seated and shackled for security purposes," and the interrogators take "an open, non-threatening approach." *Id.* In order to be judged participatory, however, a high value detainee "would have to willingly provide information on actionable threats and location information on High-Value Targets at large—not lower level information." *Id.* If the detainee fails to meet this "very high" standard, the interrogation team develops an interrogation plan, which generally calls for the use of enhanced techniques only as necessary and in escalating fashion. *See id.* at 3·4; *Techniques* at 5.

Any interrogation plan that involves the use of enhanced techniques must be reviewed and approved by "the Director, DCI Counterterrorist Center, with the concurrence of the Chief, CTC Legal Group." George J. Tenet, Director of Central Intelligence, *Guidelines on Interrogations Conducted Pursuant to the* ███████████████████████ at 3 (Jan. 28, 2003) ("*Interrogation Guidelines*").[5] Each approval lasts for a period of at most 30 days, *see id.* at 1-2, although enhanced interrogation techniques are generally not used for more than seven days, see *Background Paper* at 17.

For example, after medical and psychological examinations found no contraindications, ████████████ s interrogation team sought and obtained approval to use the following techniques: attention grasp, walling, facial hold, facial slap, wall standing, stress positions, and sleep deprivation. *See August 25* ████████████ *Letter* at 2. The interrogation team "carefully analyzed Gul's responsiveness to different areas of inquiry" during this time and noted that his resistance increased as questioning moved to his "knowledge of operational terrorist activities." *Id.* at 3. ████████████████████ feigned memory problems (which CIA psychologists ruled out through intelligence and memory tests) in order to avoid answering questions. *Id.*

At that point, the interrogation team believed ████████ "maintains a tough, Mujahidin fighter mentality and has conditioned himself for a physical interrogation." *Id.* The team therefore concluded that "more subtle interrogation measures designed more to weaken ████████ physical ability and mental desire to resist interrogation over the long run are likely to be more effective." *Id.* For these reasons, the team sought authorization to use dietary manipulation, nudity, water dousing, and abdominal slap. *Id.* at 4-5. In the team's view, adding these techniques would be especially

---

[5] You have informed us that the current practice is for the Director of the Central Intelligence Agency to make this determination personally.

helpful ███████████ because he appeared to have a particular weakness for food and also seemed especially modest. *See id.* at 4.

The CIA used the waterboard extensively in the interrogations of KSM and Zubaydah, but did so only after it became clear that standard interrogation techniques were not working. Interrogators used enhanced techniques in the interrogation of al-Nashiri with notable results as early as the first day. *See 1G Report* at 35-36. Twelve days into the interrogation, the CIA subjected al-Nashiri to one session of the waterboard during which water was applied two times. *See id.* at 36.

3.

Medical and psychological professionals from the CIA's Office of Medical Services ("OMS") carefully evaluate detainees before any enhanced technique is authorized in order to ensure that the detainee "is not likely to suffer any severe physical or mental pain or suffering as a result of interrogation." *Techniques* at 4; *see OMS Guidelines on Medical and Psychological Support to Detainee Rendition, Interrogation and Detention* at 9 (Dec. 2004) (*"OMS Guidelines"*). In addition, OMS officials continuously monitor the detainee's condition throughout any interrogation using enhanced techniques, and the interrogation team will stop the use of particular techniques or the interrogation altogether if the detainee's medical or psychological condition indicates that the detainee might suffer significant physical or mental harm. *See Techniques* at 5-6. OMS has, in fact, prohibited the use of certain techniques in the interrogations of certain detainees. *See id.* at 5. Thus, no technique is used in the interrogation of any detainee—no matter how valuable the information the CIA believes the detainee has—if medical and psychological evaluations or ongoing monitoring suggest that the detainee is likely to suffer serious harm. Careful records are kept of each interrogation, which ensures accountability and allows for ongoing evaluation of the efficacy of each technique and its potential for any unintended or inappropriate results. *See id.*

B.

Your office has informed us that the CIA believes that "the intelligence acquired from these interrogations has been a key reason why al-Qa'ida has failed to launch a spectacular attack in the West since 11 September 2001." Memorandum for Steven G. Bradbury, Principal Deputy Assistant Attorney General, Office of Legal Counsel, from ████████ ███████████████████████████████████ DCI Counterterrorist Center, *Re: Effectiveness of the CIA Counterintelligence Interrogation Techniques* at 2 (Mar. 2 2005) (*"Effectiveness Memo"*). In particular, the CIA believes that it would have been unable to obtain critical information from numerous detainees, including KSM and Abu Zubaydah, without these enhanced techniques. Both KSM and Zubaydah had "expressed their belief that the general US population was 'weak,' lacked resilience, and would be unable to 'do what was necessary' to prevent the terrorists from succeeding in their goals." *Id.* at 1. Indeed, before the CIA used enhanced techniques in its interrogation of KSM, KSM resisted giving any answers to questions about future attacks, simply noting, "Soon, you will know." *Id.* We understand that the use of enhanced techniques in the interrogations of KSM, Zubaydah, and others, by contrast, has yielded critical information. *See IG Report* at 86, 90-91 (describing increase in intelligence reports attributable to use of enhanced techniques). As Zubaydah himself explained with respect to enhanced techniques, "brothers who are captured and interrogated are permitted by Allah to provide information when they believe they have 'reached the limit of their ability to withhold it' in the face of psychological and physical hardships." *Effectiveness Memo* at 2. And, indeed, we understand that since the use of enhanced techniques, "KSM and Abu Zubaydah have been pivotal sources because of their ability and willingness to provide their analysis and speculation about the capabilities, methodologies, and mindsets of terrorists," *Preeminent Source* at 4.

Nevertheless, current CIA threat reporting indicates that, despite substantial setbacks over the last year, al Qaeda continues to pose a grave threat to the United States and its interests. *See CIA*

██ You have
informed us that the CIA believes that enhanced interrogation techniques
remain essential to obtaining vital intelligence necessary to detect and
disrupt such emerging threats.

In understanding the effectiveness of the interrogation program, it
is important to keep two related points in mind. First, the total value of the
program cannot be appreciated solely by focusing on individual pieces of
information. According to the CIA Inspector General:

> CTC frequently uses the information from one detainee as
> well as other sources, to vet the information of another de-
> tainee. Although lower-level detainees provide less informa-
> tion than the high value detainees, information from these
> detainees has, on many occasions, supplied the information
> needed to probe the high value detainees further . . . [T]he
> triangulation of intelligence provides a fuller knowledge of
> Al-Qa'ida activities than would be possible from a single
> detainee.

IG Report at 86. As illustrated below, we understand that even interrogations of comparatively lower-tier high value detainees supply information
that the CIA uses to validate and assess information elicited in other interrogations and through other methods. Intelligence acquired from the
interrogation program also enhances other intelligence methods and has
helped to build the CIA's overall understanding of al Qaeda and its affiliates. Second, it is difficult to quantify with confidence and precision
the effectiveness of the program. As the *IG Report* notes, it is difficult
to determine conclusively whether interrogations have provided information critical to interdicting specific imminent attacks *See id.* at 88. And,
because the CIA has used enhanced techniques sparingly, "there is limited data on which to assess their individual effectiveness." *Id.* at 89. As
discussed below, however, we understand that interrogations have led to
specific, actionable intelligence as well as a general increase in the amount
of intelligence regarding al Qaeda and its affiliates. *See id* at 85-91.

With these caveats, we turn to specific examples that you have provided to us. You have informed us that the interrogation of KSM—once
enhanced techniques were employed—led to the discovery of a KSM plot,
the "Second Wave," "to use East Asian operatives to crash a hijacked airliner into" a building in Los Angeles. *Effectiveness Memo* at 3. You have
informed us that information obtained from KSM also led to the capture
of Riduan bin Isomuddin, better known as Hambali, and the discovery of

the Guraba Cell, a 17-member Jemaah Islamiyah cell tasked with executing the "Second Wave." *See id.* at 3-4; CIA Directorate of Intelligence, *Al Qa'ida's Ties to Other Key Terror Groups: Terrorists Links in a Chain* 2 (Aug. 28, 2003). More specifically, we understand that KSM admitted that he had tasked Maiid Khan with delivering a large sum of money to an al Qaeda associate, *See* Fax from ███████████████████████ ██████████████ DCI Counterterrorist Center, *Briefing Notes on the Value of Detainee Reporting* at 1 (Apr. 15, 2005) (*"Briefing Notes"*). Khan subsequently identified the associate (Zubair), who was then captured. Zubair, in turn, provided information that led to the arrest of Hambali. *See id.* The information acquired from these captures allowed CIA interrogators to pose more specific questions to KSM, which led the CIA to Hambali's brother, al-Hadi. Using information obtained from multiple sources, al-Hadi was captured, and he subsequently identified the Guraba cell. *See id* at 1-2. With the aid of this additional information, interrogations of Hambali confirmed much of what was learned from KSM.[6]

Interrogations of Zubaydah—again, once enhanced techniques were employed—furnished detailed information regarding al Qaeda's "organizational structure, key operatives, and modus operandi" and identified KSM as the mastermind of the September 11 attacks. *See Briefing Notes* at 4. You have informed us that Zubaydah also "provided significant information on two operatives, [including] Jose Padilla[,] who planned to build and detonate a 'dirty bomb' in the Washington DC area." *Effectiveness Memo* at 4. Zubaydah and KSM have also supplied important information about al-Zarqawi and his network. *See* Fax for Jack L. Goldsmith III, Assistant Attorney General, Office of Legal Counsel, from ████████████████████ Office of General Counsel, CIA, ██

---

[6] We discuss only a small fraction of the important intelligence CIA interrogators have obtained from KSM. ███████████████████████

---

[7] As with KMS we discuss only a portion of the intelligence obtained through interrogations of Zubaydah.

More generally, the CIA has informed us that, since March 2002, the intelligence derived from CIA detainees has resulted in more than 6,000 intelligence reports and, in 2004, accounted for approximately half of CTC's reporting on al Qaeda. *See Briefing Notes* at 1; *see also IG Report* at 86 (noting that from September 11, 2001, through April 2003, the CIA "produced over 3,000 intelligence reports from" a few high value detainees). You have informed us that the substantial majority of this intelligence has come from detainees subjected to enhanced interrogation techniques. In addition, the CIA advises us that the program has been virtually indispensable to the task of deriving actionable intelligence from other forms of collection.

C.

[Deleted. This section duplicates description of techniques in the May 10, 2005 Memorandum to John Rizzo *Re: Application of 18 U.S.C. 2340-2340A to Certain Techniques That May Be Used in the Interrogation of a High Value al Qaeda Detainee.*]

II.

We conclude, first, that the CIA interrogation program does not implicate United States obligations under Article 16 of the CAT because Article 16 has limited geographic scope. By its terms, Article 16 places no obligations on a State Party outside "territory under its jurisdiction." The ordinary meaning of the phrase, the use of the phrase elsewhere in the CAT, and the negotiating history of the CAT demonstrate that the phrase "territory under its jurisdiction" is best understood as including, at most, areas where a State exercises territory-based jurisdiction; that is, areas over which the State exercises at least de facto authority as the government. As we explain below, based on CIA assurances, we understand that the interrogations conducted by the CIA do not take place in any "territory under [United States] jurisdiction" within the meaning of Article 16. We therefore conclude that the CIA interrogation program does not violate the obligations set forth in Article 16.

Apart from the terms of Article 16 as stated in the CAT, the United States undertook its obligations under the CAT subject to a Senate reservation that provides: "[T]he United States considers itself bound by the obligation under Article 16 . . . only insofar as the term 'cruel, inhuman or degrading treatment or punishment' means the cruel, unusual and inhumane treatment or punishment prohibited by the Fifth, Eighth, and/or Fourteenth Amendments to the Constitution of the United States." There is a strong argument that in requiring this reservation, the Senate intended to limit United States obligations under Article 16 to the existing obligations already imposed by these Amendments. These Amendments have been construed by the courts not to extend protections to aliens outside the United States. The CIA has also assured us that the interrogation techniques are not used within the United States or against United States persons, including both U.S. citizens and lawful permanent resident aliens.

A.

"[W]e begin with the text of the treaty and the context in which the written words are used." *Eastern Airlines, Inc. v. Floyd,* 499 U.S. 530, 534 (1991) (quotation marks omitted). *See also* Vienna Convention on the Law of Treaties, May 23, 1969, art. 31(1), 1155 U.N.T.S. 331, 340 (1980) ("A treaty shall be interpreted in good faith in accordance with the ordinary meaning to be given to the terms of the treaty in their context and in light of its object and purpose.").[12] Article 16 states that "[e]ach State Party shall undertake to prevent *in any territory under its jurisdiction* other acts of cruel, inhuman or degrading treatment or punishment which do not amount to torture." CAT Art. 16(1) (emphasis added).[13] This territorial limitation is confirmed by Article 16's explication of this basic obligation: "In particular, the obligations contained in articles 10, 11, 12 and 13 shall apply with the substitution for references to torture of references to other forms of cruel, inhuman or degrading treatment or punishment." *Id.* Articles 11 through 13 impose on each State Party certain specific obligations, each of which is expressly limited to "territory under its jurisdiction." *See infra* pp. 18-19 (describing requirements). Although Article 10, which as incorporated in Article 16 requires each State Party to "ensure that education and information regarding the prohibition" against cruel, inhuman, or degrading treatment or punishment is given to specified government personnel, does not expressly limit its obligation to "territory under [each State's] jurisdiction," Article 10's reference to the "prohibition"

---

[12] The United States is not a party to the Vienna Convention and is therefore not bound by it. Nevertheless, Article 31(1)'s emphasis on textual analysis reflects international interpretive practice. *See, e.g.,* Rudolf Bernhardt, "Interpretation in International Law," in *2 Encyclopedia of Public International Law* 1416, 1420 (1995) ("According to the prevailing opinion, the starting point in any treaty interpretation is the treaty text and the normal or ordinary meaning of its forms.")

[13] Article 16(1) provides in full:

Each State Party undertakes to prevent in any territory under its jurisdiction other acts or cruel, inhuman or degrading treatment or punishment which do not amount to torture as defined in article 1, when such acts are committed by or at the instigation or with the consent or acquiescence of a public official or other person acting in an official capacity. In particular, the obligations contained in articles 10, 11, 12, and 13 shall apply with the substitution for references to torture of references to other forms of cruel, inhuman or degrading treatment or punishment.

against such treatment or punishment can only be understood to refer to the territorially limited obligation set forth in Article 16.

The obligations imposed by the CAT are thus more limited with respect to cruel, inhuman, or degrading treatment or punishment than with respect to torture. To be sure, Article 2, like Article 16, imposes an obligation on each State Party to prevent torture "in any territory under its jurisdiction." Article 4(1), however, separately requires each State Party to "ensure that *all* acts of torture are offenses under its criminal law." (Emphasis added.) The CAT imposes no analogous requirement with respect to cruel, inhuman, or degrading treatment or punishment.[14]

Because the CAT does not define the phrase "territory under its jurisdiction," we turn to the dictionary definitions of the relevant terms. *See Olympic Airways v Husain,* 540 U.S. 644, 654-55 (2004) (drawing on dictionary definitions in interpreting a treaty); *Sale v. Haitian Centers Council, Inc.,* 509 U.S. 155, 180-81 (1993) (same). Common dictionary definitions of "jurisdiction" include "[t]he right and power to interpret and apply the law[; a]uthority or control[; and t]he territorial range of authority or control." *American Heritage Dictionary* 711 (1973); *American Heritage Dictionary* 978 (3d ed. 1992) (same definitions); *see also Black's Law Dictionary* 766 (5th ed. 1979) ("[a]reas of authority"). Common dictionary definitions of "territory" include "[a]n area of land[; or t]he land and waters under the jurisdiction of a state, nation, or sovereign." *American Heritage Dictionary* at 1329 (1973); *American Heritage Dictionary* at 1854 (3d ed. 1992) (same); *see also Black's Law Dictionary* at 1321 ("A part of a country separated from the rest, and subject to a particular jurisdiction. Geographical area under the jurisdiction of another country or sovereign power."); *Black's Law Dictionary* at 1512 (8th ed. 2004) ("[a] geographical area included within a particular government's jurisdiction; the portion of the earth's surface that is in a state's exclusive possession and control"). Taking these definitions together, we conclude that the most plausible meaning of the term "territory under its jurisdiction" is the land

---

[14] In addition, although Article 2(2) emphasizes that "[n]o exceptional circumstances whatsoever, whether a state of war or a threat of war, internal political instability or any other public emergency, may be invoked as a justification of torture," the CAT has no analogous provision with respect to cruel, inhuman, or degrading treatment or punishment. Because we conclude that the CIA interrogation program does not implicate United States obligations under Article 16 and that the program would conform to United States obligations under Article 16 even if that provision did apply, we need not consider whether the absence of a provision analogous to Article 2(2) implies that State Parties could derogate from their obligations under Article 16 in extraordinary circumstances.

over which a State exercises authority and control as the government. *Cf. Rasul v. Bush,* 124 S. Ct. 2686, 2696 (2004) (concluding that "the territorial jurisdiction of the United States" subsumes areas over which "the United States exercises complete jurisdiction and control") (internal quotation marks omitted); *Cunard S.S. Co. v. Mellon,* 262 U.S. 100, 123 (1923) ("It now is settled in the United States and recognized elsewhere that the territory subject to its jurisdiction includes the land areas under its dominion and control[.]").

This understanding of the phrase "territory under its jurisdiction" is confirmed by the way the phrase is used in various provisions throughout the CAT. *See Air France v. Saks,* 470 U.S. 392, 398 (1985) (treaty drafters "logically would . . . use [] the same word in each article" when they intend to convey the same meaning throughout); J. Herman Burgers & Hans Danelius, *The United Nations Convention Against Torture: A Handbook on the Convention Against Torture and Other Cruel, Inhuman or Degrading Treatment or Punishment* 53 (1988) (*"CAT Handbook"*) (noting that "it was agreed that the phrase 'territory under its jurisdiction' had the same meaning" in different articles of the CAT).

For example, Article 5 provides:

> Each State Party shall take such measures as may be necessary to establish its jurisdiction over the offences referred to in article 4 [requiring each State Party to criminalize all acts of torture] in the following cases:
>
> (a) When the offences are committed in any *territory under its jurisdiction* or on board a ship or aircraft registered in that State;
>
> (b) When the alleged offender is a national of that State;
>
> (c) When the victim is a national of that State if that State considers it appropriate.

CAT art. 5(1) (emphasis added). The CAT thereby distinguishes jurisdiction based on territory from jurisdiction based on the nationality of either the victim or the perpetrator. Paragraph (a) also distinguishes jurisdiction based on territory from jurisdiction based on registry of ships and aircraft. To read the phrase "territory under its jurisdiction" to subsume these other types of jurisdiction would eliminate these distinctions and render most of Article 5 surplusage. Each of Article 5's provisions, however, "like all the other words of the treaty, is to be given a meaning, if reasonably possible, and rules of construction may not be resorted to to render it meaningless or inoperative." *Factor v. Laubenheimer,* 290 U.S. 276, 303-04 (1933).

Articles 11 through 13, moreover, use the phrase "territory under its jurisdiction" in ways that presuppose that the relevant State exercises the traditional authorities of the government in such areas. Article 11 requires each State to "keep under systematic review . . . arrangements for the custody and treatment of persons subjected to any form of arrest, detention or imprisonment in any territory under its jurisdiction" Article 12 mandates that "[e]ach State Party shall ensure that its competent authorities proceed to a prompt and impartial investigation, wherever there is reasonable ground to believe that an act of torture has been committed in any territory under its jurisdiction." Similarly, Article 13 requires "[e]ach State Party [to] ensure that any individual who alleges he has been subjected to torture in any territory under its jurisdiction has the right to complain to, and to have his case promptly and impartially examined by, its competent authorities." These provisions assume that the relevant State exercises traditional governmental authority—including the authority to arrest, detain, imprison, and investigate crime—within any "territory under its jurisdiction."

Three other provisions underscore this point. Article 2(1) requires each State Party to "take effective legislative, administrative, judicial or other measures to prevent such acts of torture in any territory under its jurisdiction." "Territory under its jurisdiction," therefore, is most reasonably read to refer to areas over which States exercise broad governmental authority—the areas over which States could take legislative, administrative, or judicial action. Article 5(2), moreover, enjoins "[e]ach State Party . . . to establish its jurisdiction over such offences in cases where the alleged offender is present in any territory under its jurisdiction and it does not extradite him." Article 7(1) similarly requires State Parties to extradite suspects or refer them to "competent authorities for the purpose of prosecution." These provisions evidently contemplate that each State Party has authority to extradite and prosecute those suspected of torture in any "territory under its jurisdiction." That is, each State Party is expected to operate as the government in "territory under its jurisdiction."[15]

---

[15] Article 6 may suggest an interpretation of the phrase "territory under its jurisdiction" that is potentially broader than the traditional notion of "territory." Article 6(1) directs a State Party "in whose territory a person alleged to have committed [certain offenses] is present" to take the suspected offender into custody. (Emphases added.) The use of the word "territory" in Article 6 rather

This understanding is supported by the negotiating record. *See Zi-cherman v. Korean Air Lines Co.,* 516 U.S. 217, 226 (1996) ("Because a treaty ratified by the United States is not only the law of this land, see U.S. Const., Art. II, § 2, but also an agreement among sovereign powers, we have traditionally considered as aids to its interpretation the negotiating and drafting history . . ."); Vienna Convention on the Law of Treaties, art. 32 (permitting recourse to "the preparatory work and the circumstances of its conclusion" *inter alia* "to confirm" the ordinary meaning of the text). The original Swedish proposal, which was the basis for the first draft of the CAT, contained a predecessor to Article 16 that would have required that "[e]ach State Party undertake[] to ensure that [a proscribed act] does not take place *within its jurisdiction.*" Draft International Convention Against Torture and Other Cruel, Inhuman or Degrading Treatment or Punishment, submitted by Sweden on January 18, 1978, arts. 2-3, E/CN.4/1285, *in CAT Handbook* app. 6, at 203 (emphasis added); *CAT Handbook* at 47. France objected that the phrase "within its jurisdiction" was too broad. For example, it was concerned that the phrase might extend to signatories' citizens located in territory belonging to other nations. *See* Report of the Pre-Sessional Working Group, E/CN.4/L.1470 (1979), *reprinted in* Report of the United Nations Commission on Human Rights, E/CN.4/1347 35, 40 (1979); *CAT Handbook* at 48. Although France suggested replacing "within its jurisdiction" with "in its territory," the phrase "any territory under its jurisdiction" was chosen instead. *See CAT Handbook* at 48.

There is some evidence that the United States understood these phrases to mean essentially the same thing. *See, e.g.,* Exec. Report 101-30, 101st Cong. 2d Sess., 23-24 (Aug. 30, 1990) (Senate Foreign Relations Committee Report) (suggesting that the phrase "in any territory under its jurisdiction" would impose obligations on a State Party with respect to conduct committed "in its territory" but not with respect to conduct "occurring abroad"); *Convention Against Torture: Hearing Before the Committee on Foreign Relations, United States Senate,* S. Hrg. 101-718 at 7 (Jan. 30, 1990) (prepared statement of Hon. Abraham D. Sofaer, Legal

---

than the phrase "territory under its jurisdiction" suggests that the terms have distinct meanings. *See Factor,* 290 U.S. at 303-04 (stating that treaty language should not be construed to render certain phrases "meaningless or inoperative"). Article 6 may thus support the position, discussed below, that "territory under its jurisdiction" may extend beyond sovereign territory to encompass areas where a State exercises de facto authority as the government, such as occupied territory. *See infra* p. 20. Article 20, which refers to "the territory of a State Party" may support the same inference.

Adviser, Department of State) (stating that under Article 2, State Parties would be obligated "to take administrative, judicial or other measures to prevent torture *within their territory*") (emphasis added). Other evidence, however, suggests that the phrase "territory under its jurisdiction" has a somewhat broader meaning than "in its territory." According to the record of the negotiation relating to Articles 12 and 13 of the CAT, "[i]n response to the question on the scope of the phrase 'territory under its jurisdiction' as contained in these articles, it was said that it was intended to cover, *inter alia*, territories still under colonial rule and occupied territory." U.N. Doc. E/CN.4/1367, Mar. 5, 1980, at 13. And one commentator has stated that the negotiating record suggests that the phrase "territory under its jurisdiction" is not limited to a State's land territory, its territorial sea and the airspace over its land and sea territory, but it also applies to territories under military occupation, to colonial territories and to any other territories over which a State has factual control." *Id.* at 131. Others have suggested that the phrase would also reach conduct occurring on ships and aircraft registered in a State. *See CAT Handbook* at 48; Message from the President of the United States Transmitting the Convention Against Torture and Other Cruel, Inhuman or Degrading Treatment or Punishment, S. Treaty Doc. No. 100-20, at 5 (1988) (Secretary of State Schultz) (asserting that "territory under its jurisdiction" "refers to all places that the State Party controls as a governmental authority, including ships and aircraft registered in that State").[16]

Thus, although portions of the negotiating record of the CAT may support reading the phrase "any territory under its jurisdiction" to include not only sovereign territory but also areas subject to de facto government authority (and perhaps registered ships and aircraft), the negotiating record as a whole tends to confirm that the phrase does not extend to places where a State does not exercise authority as the government.

The CIA has assured us that the interrogations at issue here do not take place within the sovereign territory or special maritime and territorial jurisdiction ("SMTJ") of the United States. *See* 18 U.S.C. § 5 (defin-

---

[16] This suggestion is in tension with the text of Article 5(1)(a), which seems to distinguish "territory under [a State's] jurisdiction" from "ship[s] or aircraft registered in that State." *See Chan v. Korean Airlines, Ltd.*, 490 U.S. 122, 134 n.5 (1989) noting that where treaty text is not perfectly clear, the "natural meaning" of the text "could properly be contradicted only by clear drafting history"). Because the CIA has assured us that its interrogations do not take place on ships or aircraft registered in the United States, we need not resolve this issue here.

ing "United States"); *id* § 7 (defining SMTJ). As relevant here, we believe that the phrase "any territory under its jurisdiction" certainly reaches no further than the sovereign territory and the SMTJ of the United States.[17] Indeed, in many respects, it probably does not reach this far. Although many provisions of the SMTJ invoke territorial bases of jurisdiction, other provisions assert jurisdiction on other grounds, including, for example, sections 7(5) through 7(9), which assert jurisdiction over certain offenses committed by or against United States citizens. Accordingly, we conclude that the interrogation program does not take place within "territory under [United States] jurisdiction" and therefore does not violate Article 16— even absent the Senate's reservation limiting United States obligations under Article 16, which we discuss in the next section.

B.

As a condition to its advice and consent to the ratification of the CAT, the Senate required a reservation that provides that the United States is

> bound by the obligation under Article 16 to prevent "cruel, inhuman or degrading treatment or punishment," only insofar as the term "cruel, inhuman or degrading treatment or punishment" means the cruel, unusual and inhumane treatment or punishment prohibited by the Fifth, Eighth, and/or Fourteenth Amendments to the Constitution of the United States.

Cong. Rec. 36,198 (1990). This reservation, which the United States deposited with its instrument of ratification, is legally binding and defines the scope of United States obligations under Article 16 of the CAT. *See Relevance of Senate Ratification History to Treaty Interpretation,* 11 Op. O.L.C 28, 33 (1987) (Reservations deposited with the instrument of ratification "are generally binding . . . both internationally and domestically . . . in . . . subsequent interpretation of the treaty.").[18]

---

[17] As we have explained, there is an argument that "territory under [a State's] jurisdiction" might also include occupied territory. Accordingly, at least absent the Senate's reservation, Article 16's obligations might extend to occupied territory. Because the United States is not currently an occupying power within the meaning or the laws of war anywhere in the world, we need not decide whether occupied territory is "territory under [United States] jurisdiction."

[18] "The Senate's right to qualify its consent to ratification by reservations,

Under the terms of the reservation, the United States is obligated to prevent "cruel, inhuman or degrading treatment" only to the extent that such treatment amounts to "the cruel, unusual and inhumane treatment or punishment prohibited by the Fifth, Eighth, and/or Fourteenth Amendments." Giving force to the terms of this reservation, treatment that is not "prohibited by" these amendments would not violate United States obligations as limited by the reservation.

Conceivably, one might read the text of the reservation as limiting only the substantive (as opposed to the territorial) reach of United States obligations under Article 16. That would not be an unreasonable reading of the text. Under this view, the reservation replaced only the phrase "cruel, inhuman or degrading treatment or punishment" and left untouched the phrase "in any territory under its jurisdiction," which defines the geographic scope of the Article. The text of the reservation, however, is susceptible to another reasonable reading—one suggesting that the Senate intended to ensure that the United States would, with respect to Article 16, undertake no obligations not already imposed by the Constitution itself. Under this reading, the reference to the treatment or punishment prohibited by the constitutional provisions does not distinguish between the substantive scope of the constitutional prohibitions and their geographic scope. As we discuss below, this second reading is strongly supported by the Senate's ratification history of the CAT.

The Summary and Analysis of the CAT submitted by the President to the Senate in 1988 expressed concern that "Article 16 is arguably broader than existing U.S. law." Summary and Analysis of the Convention Against Torture and Other Cruel, Inhuman or Degrading Treatment or Punishment, *in* S. Treaty Doc. No, 100-20, at 15. "In view of the ambiguity of the terms," the Executive Branch suggested "that U.S. obligations under this article [Article 16] should be limited to *conduct prohibited by the U.S. Constitution.*" S. Exec. Rep. No. 101-30, at 8 (1990) (emphasis added); *see also id.* at 25-26. Accordingly, it proposed what became the Senate's reser-

---

amendments and interpretations was established, through a reservation to the lay treaty of 1794," Quincy Wright, *The Control of American Foreign Relations* 253 (1922), and has been frequently exercised since then. The Supreme Court has indicated its acceptance of this practice. *See Haver v. Yoker*, 76 U.S. (9 Wall.) 32, 35 (1869); *United States v. Schooner Peggy*, 5 U.S. (1 Cranch) 103, 107 (1801). *See also Constitutionality of Proposed Conditions to Senate Consent to the Interim Convention on the Conservation of North Pacific Fur Seals*, 10 Op. O.L.C. 12, 16 (1986) ("[T]he Senate's practice of conditioning its consent to particular treaties is well-established.").

vation in order "[t]o make clear that the United States construes the phrase
["cruel, inhuman or degrading treatment or punishment"] to be coexten-
sive with its constitutional guarantees against cruel, unusual, and inhumane treatment." *Id.* at 25-26; S. Treaty Doc. No. 100-20, at 15 (same). As
State Department Legal Adviser Abraham D. Sofaer explained, "because
the Constitution of the United States directly addresses this area of the
law . . . [the reservation] would limit our obligations under this Convention to the proscriptions already covered in our Constitution." *Convention
Against Torture: Hearing Before the Senate Comm. on Foreign Relations,*
101st Cong. 11 (1990) (prepared statement). The Senate Foreign Relations
Committee expressed the same concern about the potential scope of Article 16 and recommended the same reservation to the Senate. *See* S. Exec.
Rep. No. 101-30, at 8, 25-26.

Furthermore, the Senate declared that Articles 1 through 16 of the
CAT are not self-executing, *see* Cong. Rec. 36,198 (1990), and the discussions surrounding this declaration in the ratification history also indicate
that the United States did not intend to undertake any obligations under
Article 16 that extended beyond those already imposed by the Constitution.
The Administration expressed the view that "as indicated in the original
Presidential transmittal, existing Federal and State law appears sufficient
to implement the Convention, except that new Federal legislation would be
required *only to establish criminal jurisdiction under Article 5.*" Letter for
Senator Pressler, from Janet Mullins, Assistant Secretary, Legislative Affairs, Department of State (April 4, 1990), *in* S. Exec. Rep. No. 10-30, at 41
(emphasis added). It was understood that the "majority of the obligations
to be undertaken by the United States pursuant to the Convention [were]
already covered by existing law" and that "additional implementing legislation [would] be needed *only with respect to article 5.*" S. Exec. Rep. No.
101-30, at 10 (emphasis added). Congress then enacted 18 U.S.C, §§ 2340-
2349A, the only "necessary legislation to implement" United States obligations under the CAT, noting that the United States would "not become
a party to the convention until the necessary implementing legislation is
enacted." S. Rep. No. 103-107, at 366 (1993). Reading Article 16 to extend
the substantive standards of the Constitution in contexts where they did
not already apply would be difficult to square with the evident understanding of the United States that existing law would satisfy its obligations under the CAT except with respect to Article 5. The ratification history thus
strongly supports the view that United States obligations under Article 16
were intended to reach no further—substantively, territorially, or in any
other respect—than its obligations under the Fifth, Eighth, and Fourteenth
Amendments.

The Supreme Court has repeatedly suggested in various contexts that the Constitution docs not apply to aliens outside the United States, *See, e.g., United States v. Belmont,* 301 U.S, 324, 332 (1937) ("[O]ur Constitution, laws, and policies have no extraterritorial operation, unless in respect of our own citizens."]; *United States v. Curtiss-Wright Export Corp.,* 299 U.S, 304, 318 (1936) ("Neither the Constitution nor the laws passed in pursuance of it have any force in foreign territory unless in respect of our own citizens . . . "); *see also United States v. Verdugo-Urquidez,* 494 U.S. 259, 271 (1990) (noting that cases relied upon by an alien asserting constitutional rights "establish only that aliens receive constitutional protections when they have come within the territory of the United States and developed substantial connections with this country"). Federal courts of appeals, in turn, have held that "[t]he Constitution does not extend its guarantees to nonresident aliens living outside the United States," *Vancouver Women's Health Collective Soc'y v. A.H. Robins Co.,* 820 F.2nd 1359, 1363 (4th Cir. 1987); that "non-resident aliens . . . plainly cannot appeal to the protection of the Constitution or laws of the United States," *Pauling v. McElroy,* 278 F.2d 252, 254 n.3 (D.C. Cir. 1960) (per curiam); and that a "foreign entity without property or presence in this country has no constitutional rights, under the due process clause or otherwise," *32 County Sovereignty Comm. v. Dep't of State,* 292 F.3d 797, 799 (D.C. Cir. 2002) (quoting *People's Mojahedin Org. of Iran v. Dep't of State,* 182 F.3d 17, 22 (D.C. Cir. 1999)).[19]

As we explain below, it is the Fifth Amendment that is potentially relevant in the present context. With respect to that Amendment, the Supreme Court has "rejected the claim that aliens are entitled to Fifth Amendment rights outside the sovereign territory of the United States." *Verdugo-Urquidez,* 494 U.S. at 269. In *Verdugo-Urquidez,* 494 U.S. at 269, the Court noted its "emphatic" "rejection of extraterritorial application of the Fifth Amendment" in *Johnson v. Eisentrager,* 339 U.S. 763 (1950), which rejected "[t]he doctrine that the term 'any person' in the Fifth Amendment spreads its protection over alien enemies anywhere in the world engaged in hostilities against us," *id* at 782. *Accord Zadvydas v. Davis,* 533 U.S. 678, 693 (2001) (citing *Verdugo-Urquidez* and *Eisentrager* and noting that "[i]t is well established that" Fifth Amendment pro-

---

[19] The Restatement (Third) of Foreign Relations Law asserts that "[a]lthough the matter has not been authoritatively adjudicated, at least some actions by the United States in respect to foreign nationals outside the country are also subject to constitutional limitations." *Id. § 722,* cmt. m. This statement is contrary to the authorities cited in the text.

tections are "unavailable to aliens outside of our geographic borders"). Federal courts of appeals have similarly held that "non-resident aliens who have insufficient contacts with the United States are not entitled to Fifth Amendment protections." *Jifry v. F.A.A.*, 370 F.3d 1174, 1182 (D.C. Cir. 2004]; *see also Harbury v. Deutch,* 233 F.3d 596, 604 (D.C. Cir. 2000) (relying on *Eisentrager* and *Verdugo-Urquidez* to conclude that an alien could not state a due process claim for torture allegedly inflicted by United States agents abroad), *rev'd on other grounds sub nom. Christopher v. Harbury,* 536 U.S. 403 (2002); *Cuban Am. Bar Ass'n, Inc. v. Christopher,* 43 F.3d 1412, 1428-29 (11th Cir. 1995) (relying on *Eisentrager* and *Verdugo-Urquidez* to conclude that aliens held at Guantanamo Bay lack Fifth Amendment rights).[20]

---

[20] The Court's decision in *Rasul v. Bush*, 124 S. Ct. 2686 (2004), is not to the contrary. To be sure, the Court stated in a footnote that:

Petitioners' allegations—that, although they have engaged neither in combat nor in acts of terrorism against the United States, they have been held in Executive detention for more than two years in territory subject to the long-term, exclusive jurisdiction and control of the United States, without access to counsel and without being charged with any wrongdoing—unquestionably describe "custody in violation of the Constitution or laws or treaties of the United States."

Id. at 2698 n.15. We believe this footnote is best understood to leave intact the Court's settled understanding of the Fifth Amendment. First, the Court limited its holding to the issue before it: whether the federal courts have *statutory jurisdiction* over habeas petitions brought by such aliens held at Guantanamo as enemy combatants. *See id.* at 2699 ("Whether and what further proceedings may become necessary . . . are matters that we need not address now. What is presently at stake is only whether the federal courts have jurisdiction to determine the legality of the Executive's potentially indefinite detention of individuals who claim to be wholly innocent of wrongdoing."). Indeed, the Court granted the petition for writ of certiorari "limited to the following Question: Whether United States courts lack jurisdiction to consider challenges to the legality of the detention of foreign nationals captured abroad in connection with hostilities and incarcerated at the Guantanamo Bay Naval Base, Cuba." *Rasul v. Bush*, 540 U.S. 1003 (2003).

Second, the footnote relies on a portion of Justice Kennedy's concurrence in *Verdugo-Urquidez* "and the cases cited therein," *Rasul*, 124 S. Ct. at 2698 n.15. In this portion of Justice Kennedy's *Verdugo-Urquidez* concurrence, Justice Kennedy discusses the *Insular Cases*. These cases stand for the proposition that although not every provision of the Constitution applies in United States territory overseas, certain core constitutional protections may apply in certain insular territories of the United States. *See also, e.g., Reid v. Covert*, 354 U.S. 1, 74-75 (1957) (Harlan, J., concurring in judgment) (discussing *Insular Cases*), *Balzac v.*

The reservation required by the Senate as a condition of its advice and consent to the ratification of the CAT thus tends to confirm the territorially limited reach of U.S. obligations under Article 16. Indeed, there is a strong argument that, by limiting United States obligations under Article 16 to those that certain provisions of the Constitution already impose, the Senate's reservation limits territorial reach of Article 16 even more sharply than does the text of Article 16 standing alone. Under this view, Article 16 would impose no obligations with respect to aliens outside the United States.[21] And because the CIA has informed us that these techniques are not for authorized use against United States persons, or within the United States, they would not, under this view, violate Article 16. Even if the reservation is read only to confirm the territorial in Article 16, however, or even if it is read not to bear on this question at all, the program would still not violate Article 16 for the reasons discussed in Part IIA. Accordingly, we need not decide here the precise effect, if any, of the Senate reservation on the geographic scope of U.S. obligations under Article 16.[22]

Porto Rico, 258 U.S. 298 (1922). Given that the Court in *Rasul* stressed GTMO's unique status as "territory subject to the long-term, exclusive jurisdiction and control of the United States," *Rasul*, 124 S. Ct. at 2698 n.15, in every sentence that cited Justice Kennedy's concurrence, it is conceivable that footnote 15 might reflect at most, a willingness to consider whether GTMO is similar in significant respects to the territories at issue in the *Insular Cases*. *See also id.* at 2696 (noting that under the agreement with Cuba "the United States exercises complete jurisdiction and control over the Guantanamo Bay Navel [sic] Base") (internal quotation marks omitted); *id.* at 2700 *(*Kennedy, J., concurring) (asserting that "Guantanamo Bay is in every practical respect a United States territory" and explaining that "[w]hat matters is the unchallenged and indefinite control that the United States has long exercised over Guantanamo Bay").

[21] Additional analysis may be required in the case of aliens entitled to lawful permanent resident status. *Compare Kwong Hai Chew v. Colding*, 344 U.S. 590 (1953), *with Shaughnessy v. United States ex. rel. Mezei*, 345 U.S. 206 (1953). You have informed us that the CIA does not use these techniques on any United States persons, including lawful permanent residents, and we do not here address United States obligations under Article 16 with respect to such aliens.

[22] Our analysis is not affected by the recent enactment of the Emergency Supplemental Appropriations Act for Defense, the Global War on Terror, and Tsunami Relief, 2005, Pub. L. No. 109-13, 119 Stat. 231 (2005). Section 1031(a)(1) of that law provides that:

> [n]one of the funds appropriated or otherwise made available by this Act shall be obligated or expended to subject any person in the custody or under the physical control of the United States to torture or cruel, inhuman, or degrading treatment or punishment that is

III.

You have also asked us to consider whether the CIA interrogation program would violate the substantive standards applicable to the United States under Article 16 if, contrary to the conclusions reached in Part II above, those standards did extend to the CIA interrogation program. Pursuant to the Senate's reservation, the United States is bound by Article 16 to prevent "the cruel, unusual and inhumane treatment or punishment prohibited by the Fifth, Eighth, and/or Fourteenth Amendments to the Constitution of the United States." As we explain, the relevant test is whether use of the CIA's enhanced interrogation techniques constitutes government conduct that "shocks the conscience." Based on our understanding of the relevant case law and the CIA's descriptions of the interrogation program, we conclude that use of the enhanced interrogation techniques, subject to all applicable conditions, limitations, and safeguards, does not "shock the conscience." We emphasize, however, that this analysis calls for the application of a somewhat subjective test with only limited guidance from the Court. We therefore cannot predict with confidence whether a court would agree with our conclusions, though, as discussed more fully below, we believe the interpretation of Article 16's substantive standard is unlikely to be subject to judicial inquiry.

A.

Although, pursuant the Senate's reservation, United States obligations under Article 16 extend to "the cruel, unusual and inhumane treatment or punishment prohibited by the Fifth, Eighth, and/or Fourteenth Amendments to the Constitution of the United States," only the Fifth Amendment is potentially relevant here. The Fourteenth Amendment provides, in relevant part: "No *State* shall . . . deprive any person of life,

---

prohibited by the Constitution, laws or treaties of the United States.

119 Stat. at 256. Because the Senate reservation, as deposited with the United States instrument of ratification, defines United States obligations under Article 16 of the CAT, this statute does not prohibit the expenditure of funds for conduct that does not violate United States obligations under Article 16, as limited by the Senate reservation. Furthermore, this statute itself defines "cruel, inhuman, or degrading treatment or punishment" as "the cruel, unusual, and inhumane treatment or punishment prohibited by the fifth amendment, eighth amendment, or fourteenth amendment to the Constitution of the United States." *Id.* § 1031(b)(2).

liberty, or property, without due process of law." (Emphasis added.) This Amendment does not apply to actions taken by the federal Government. *See, e.g., San Francisco Arts & Athletics, Inc. v. United States Olympic Comm.*, 483 U.S. 522, 542 n.21 (1987) (explaining that the Fourteenth Amendment "does not apply" to the federal Government); *Bolling v. Sharpe*, 347 U.S. 497, 498-99 (1954) (noting that the Fifth Amendment rather than the Fourteenth Amendment applies to actions taken by the District of Columbia). The Eighth Amendment prohibits the infliction of "cruel and unusual *punishments.*" (Emphasis added.) As the Supreme Court has repeatedly held, the Eighth Amendment does not apply until there has been a formal adjudication of guilt. *E.g., Bell v. Wolfish*, 441 U.S. 520, 535 n.16 (1979); *Ingraham v. Wright*, 430 U.S. 651, 671 n.40 (1977). *See also In re Guantanamo Detainee Cases*, 355 F. Supp. 2d 443, 480 (D.D.C. 2005*)* (dismissing detainees' claims based on Eighth Amendment because "the Eighth Amendment applies only after an individual is convicted of a crime") (stayed pending appeal). The same conclusion concerning the limited applicability of the Eighth Amendment under Article 16 was expressly recognized by the Senate and the Executive Branch during the CAT ratification deliberations:

> The Eighth Amendment prohibition of cruel and unusual punishment is, of the three [constitutional provisions cited in the Senate reservation], the most limited in scope, as this amendment has consistently been interpreted as protecting only "those convicted of crimes." *Ingraham v. Wright*, 430 U.S. 651, 664 (1977). The Eighth Amendment does, however, afford protection against torture and ill-treatment of persons in prison and similar situations of *criminal punishment.*

Summary and Analysis of the Convention Against Torture and Other Cruel, Inhuman or Degrading Treatment or Punishment, *in* S. Treaty Doc. No. 100-20, at 9 (emphasis added). Because the high value detainees on whom the CIA might use enhanced interrogation techniques have not been convicted of any crime, the substantive requirements of the Eighth Amendment would not be relevant here, if we assume that Article 16 has application to the CIA's interrogation program.[23]

---

[23] To be sure, treatment amounting to punishment (let alone, cruel and unusual punishment) generally cannot be imposed on individuals who have not been convicted of crimes. But this prohibition flows from the Fifth Amendment

The Fifth Amendment however, is not subject to these same limitations. As potentially relevant here, the substantive due process component of the Fifth Amendment protects against executive action that "shocks the conscience." *Rochin v. California,* 342 U.S. 165, 172 (1952); *see also County of Sacramento v. Lewis,* 523 U.S. 833, 846 (1998) ("To this end, for half a century now we have spoken of the cognizable level of executive abuse of power as that which shocks the conscience.").[24]

B.

We must therefore determine whether the CIA interrogation program involves conduct that "shocks the conscience." The Court has indicated that whether government conduct can be said to "shock the conscience" depends primarily on whether the conduct is "arbitrary in the constitutional sense," *Lewis,* 523 U.S. at 846 (internal quotation marks omitted); that is, whether it amounts to the "exercise of power without any reasonable justification in the service of a legitimate governmental objective," *id.* "[C]onduct intended to injure in some way unjustifiable by any government interest is the sort of official action most likely to rise to the conscience-shocking level," *id.* at 849, although, in some cases, deliberate indifference to the risk of inflicting such unjustifiable injury might also "shock the conscience," *id.* at 850-51. The Court has also suggested that it is appropriate to consider whether, in light of "traditional executive behavior, of contemporary practice, and of the standards of blame generally ap-

---

rather than the Eighth. *See Wolfish,* 441 U.S. at 535 n.16, *United States v. Salerno,* 481 U. S. 739, 746-47 (1987). *See also infra* note 26.

[24] Because what is at issue under the text of the Senate reservation is the subset of "cruel, inhuman or degrading treatment" that is "the cruel, unusual and inhumane treatment . . . prohibited by the Fifth . . . Amendment[]," we do not believe that the procedural aspects of the Fifth Amendment are relevant, at least in the context of interrogation techniques unrelated to the criminal justice system. Nor, given the language of Article 16 and the reservation, do we believe that United States obligations under this Article include other aspects of the Fifth Amendment, such as the Takings Clause or the various privacy rights that the Supreme Court has found to be protected by the Due Process Clause.

plied to them," conduct "is so egregious, so outrageous, that it may fairly be said to shock the contemporary conscience." *Id.* at 847 n.8.[25]

Several considerations complicate our analysis. First, there are relatively few cases in which the Court has analyzed whether conduct "shocks the conscience," and these cases involve contexts that differ dramatically from the CIA interrogation program. Further, the Court has emphasized that there is "no calibrated yard stick" with which to determine whether conduct "shocks the conscience." *Id* at 847. To the contrary: "Rules of due process are not . . . subject to mechanical application in unfamiliar territory." *Id.* at 850. A claim that government conduct "shocks the conscience," therefore, requires "an exact analysis of circumstances." *Id.* The Court has explained:

> The phrase [due process of law] formulates a concept less rigid and more fluid than those envisaged in other specific and particular provisions of the Bill of Rights. Its application is less a matter of rule. Asserted denial is to be tested by an appraisal of the totality of facts in a given case. That which may, in one setting, constitute a denial of fundamental fairness, shocking to the universal sense of justice, may, in other circumstances, and in light of other considerations, fall short of such a denial.

Id. at 850 (quoting *Betts v. Brady*, 316 U.S. 455, 462 (1942)) (alteration in

---

[25] It appears that conscience-shocking conduct is a necessary but perhaps not sufficient condition to establishing that executive conduct violates substantive due process. *See Lewis*, 523 U. S. at 847 n.8 ("Only if the necessary condition of egregious behavior were satisfied would there be a possibility of recognizing a substantive due process right to be free of such executive action, and only then might there be a debate about the sufficiency of enforcement of the right claimed, or its recognition in other ways.") (emphases added); *see also, e.g.*, *Terrell v. Larson*, 396 F.3d 975, 978 n.1 (8th Cir. 2005) ("To violate substantive due process, the conduct of an executive official must be conscience shocking *and* must violate" a fundamental right.); *Slusarchuck v. Hoff*, 346 F.3d 1178, 1181 (8th Cir. 2003). It is therefore arguable that conscience-shocking behavior would not violate the Constitution if it did not violate a fundamental right or if it were narrowly tailored to serve a compelling state interest. *See, e.g., Washington v. Glucksbert*, 521 U. S. 702, 721 (1997). Because we conclude that the CIA interrogation program does not "shock the conscience," we need not address these issues here.

Lewis) Our task, therefore, is to apply in a novel context a highly fact-dependent test with little guidance from the Supreme Court.

1.

We first consider whether the CIA interrogation involves conduct that is "constitutionally arbitrary." We conclude that it does not. Indeed, we find no evidence of "conduct intended to injure in some way unjustifiable by any government interest," *id.* at 849, or of deliberate indifference to the possibility of such unjustifiable injury, *see id.* at 853.

As an initial matter, the Court has made clear that whether conduct can be considered to be constitutionally arbitrary depends vitally on whether it furthers a government interest, and, if it does, the nature and importance of that interest. The test is not merely whether the conduct is "intended to injure," but rather whether it is "intended to injure *in some way unjustifiable by any government interest.*" *Id.* at 849 (emphasis added). It is the "exercise of power *without any reasonable justification in the service of a legitimate governmental objective*" that can be said to "shock the conscience." *Id* at 846 (emphasis added). In *United States v. Salerno,* 481 U.S. 739, 748 (1987), for example, the Court explained that the Due Process Clause "lays down [no] . . . categorical imperative," and emphasized that the Court has "repeatedly held that the Government's regulatory interest in community safety can, in appropriate circumstances, outweigh an individual's liberty interest." *See also Hamdi v. Rumsfeld,* 124 S. Ct. 2633, 2646 (2004) (plurality opinion) (explaining that the individual's interests must be weighed against the government's). The government's interest is thus an important part of the context that must be carefully considered in evaluating an asserted violation of due process.[26]

---

[26] The pretrial detention context is informative. Analysis of the government's interest and purpose in imposing a condition of confinement is essential to determining whether there is a violation of due process in this context. *See Salerno,* 481 U.S. at 747-50. The government has a legitimate interest in "effectuat[ing] th[e] detention," *Wolfish,* 441 U. S. at 537, which supports government action that "may rationally be connected" to the detention, *Salerno,* 481 U. S. at 747 (internal quotation marks omitted). By contrast, inflicting cruel and unusual punishment on such detainee would violate due process because the government has no legitimate interest in inflicting punishment prior to conviction. *See Wolfish,* 441 U. S. at 535 & n.16.

In addition, *Lewis* suggests that the Court's Eighth Amendment jurisprudence sheds at least some light on the due process inquiry. *See* 523 U. S. at 852-53 (analogizing the due process inquiry to the Eighth Amendment context and

Al Qaeda's demonstrated ability to launch sophisticated attacks causing mass casualties within the United States and against United States interests worldwide, as well as its continuing efforts to plan and to execute such attacks, *see supra* p. 9, indisputably pose a grave and continuing threat. "It is 'obvious and unarguable' that no governmental interest is more compelling than the security of the Nation." *Haig v. Agee,* 453 U.S. 280, 307 (1981) (citations omitted); *see also Salerno,* 481 U.S. at 748 (noting that "society's interest is at its peak" "in times of war or insurrection"). It is this paramount interest that the Government seeks to vindicate through the interrogation program. Indeed, the program, which the CIA believes "has been a key reason why al-Qa'ida has failed to launch a spectacular attack in the West since 11 September 2001," *Effectiveness Memo* at 2, directly furthers that interest, producing substantial quantities of otherwise unavailable actionable intelligence. As detailed above, ordinary interrogation techniques had little effect on either KSM or Zubaydah. Use of enhanced techniques, however, led to critical, actionable intelligence such as the discovery of the Guraba Cell, which was tasked with executing KSM's planned Second Wave attacks against Los Angeles. Interrogations of these most valuable detainees and comparatively lower-tier high value detainees ███████████████████████████████ have also greatly increased the CIA's understanding of our enemy and its plans.

As evidenced by our discussion in Part I, the CIA goes to great lengths to ensure that the techniques are applied only as reasonably necessary to protect this paramount interest in "the security of the Nation." Various aspects of the program ensure that enhanced techniques will be used only in the interrogations of the detainees who are most likely to have critical, actionable intelligence. The CIA screening procedures, which the CIA imposes in addition to the standards applicable to activities conducted pursuant to paragraph four of the Memorandum of Notification, ensure that the techniques are not used unless the CIA reasonably believes that the detainee is a "senior member of al-Qai'da or [its affiliates],"

---

noting that in both cases "liability should turn on 'whether force was applied in a good faith effort to maintain or restore discipline or maliciously and sadistically for the very purpose of causing harm'") (quoting *Whitley v. Albers,* 475 U. S. 312, 320-21 (1986)). The interrogation program we consider does not involve or allow the malicious or sadistic infliction of harm. Rather, as discussed in the text, interrogation techniques are used only as reasonably deemed necessary to further a government interest of the highest order, and have been carefully designed to avoid inflicting severe pain or suffering or any other lasting or significant harm and to minimize the risk of any harm that does not further this government interest. *See infra* pp. 29-31.

and the detainee has "knowledge of imminent terrorist threats against the USA" or has been directly involved in the planning of attacks. *January 4* ▮▮▮▮▮▮ *Fax* at 5; *supra* p. 5. The fact that enhanced techniques have been used to date in the interrogations of only 28 high value detainees out of the 94 detainees in CIA custody demonstrates this selectivity.

Use of the waterboard is limited still further, requiring "credible intelligence that a terrorist attack is imminent; . . . substantial and credible indicators that the subject has actionable intelligence that can prevent, disrupt or delay this attack; and [a determination that o]ther interrogation methods have failed to elicit the information [and that] . . . other . . . methods are unlikely to elicit this information *within the perceived time limit for preventing the attack.*" *August 2 Rizzo Letter* (attachment). Once again, the CIA's practice confirms the program's selectivity. CIA interrogators have used the waterboard on only three detainees to date—KSM, Zubaydah, and Al-Nashiri—and have not used it at all since March 2003.

Moreover, enhanced techniques are considered only when the on-scene interrogation team considers them necessary because a detainee is withholding or manipulating important, actionable intelligence or there is insufficient time to try other techniques. For example, as recounted above, the CIA used enhanced techniques in the interrogations of KSM and Zubaydah only after ordinary interrogation tactics had failed. Even then, CIA Headquarters must make the decision whether to use enhanced techniques in any interrogation. Officials at CIA Headquarters can assess the situation based on the interrogation team's reports and intelligence from a variety of other sources and are therefore well positioned to assess the importance of the information sought.

Once approved, techniques are used only in escalating fashion so that it is unlikely that a detainee would be subjected to more duress than is reasonably necessary to elicit the information sought. Thus, no technique is used on a detainee unless use of that technique at that time appears necessary to obtaining the intelligence. And use of enhanced techniques ceases "if the detainee is judged to be consistently providing accurate intelligence or if he is no longer believed to have actionable intelligence." *Techniques* at 5. Indeed, use of the techniques usually ends after just a few days when the detainee begins participating. Enhanced techniques, therefore, would not be used on a detainee not reasonably thought to possess important, actionable intelligence that could not be obtained otherwise.

Not only is the interrogation program closely tied to a government interest of the highest order, it is also designed, through its careful limitations and screening criteria, to avoid causing any severe pain or suffering or inflicting significant or lasting harm. As the *OMS Guidelines* explain, "[i]n all instances the general goal of these techniques is a psychological impact, and not some physical effect, with a specific goal of 'dislocate[ing] [the detainee's] expectations regarding the treatment he believes he will receive.'" *OMS Guidelines* at 8-9 (second alteration in original). Furthermore, techniques can be used only if there are no medical or psychological contraindications. Thus, no technique is ever used if there is reason to believe it will cause the detainee significant mental or physical harm. When enhanced techniques are used, OMS closely monitors the detainee's condition to ensure that he does not, in fact, experience severe pain or suffering or sustain any significant or lasting harm.

This facet of our analysis bears emphasis. We do not conclude that any conduct, no matter how extreme, could be justified by a sufficiently weighty government interest coupled with appropriate tailoring. Rather, our inquiry is limited to the program under consideration, in which the techniques do not amount to torture considered independently or in combination. *See Techniques* at 28-45; *Combined Use* at 9-19. Torture is categorically prohibited both by the CAT, *see* art. 2(2) ("No exceptional circumstances whatsoever . . . may be invoked as a justification of torture."), and by implementing legislation, *see* 18 U.S.C. §§ 2340-2340A.

The program, moreover, is designed to minimize the risk of injury or any suffering that is unintended or does not advance the purpose of the program. For example, in dietary manipulation, the minimum caloric intake is set at or above levels used in commercial weight-loss programs, thereby avoiding the possibility of significant weight loss. In nudity and water dousing, interrogators set ambient temperatures high enough to guard against hypothermia. The walling technique employs a false wall and a C-collar (or similar device) to help avoid whiplash. *See Techniques* at 8. With respect to sleep deprivation, constant monitoring protects against the possibility that detainees might injure themselves by hanging from their wrists, suffer from acute edema, or even experience non-transient hallucinations. *See Techniques* at 11-13. With the waterboard, interrogators use potable saline rather than plain water so that detainees will not suffer from hyponatremia and to minimize the risk of pneumonia. *See id.* at 13-14. The board is also designed to allow interrogators to place the detainee in a head-up position so that water may be cleared very quickly, and medical personnel and equipment are on hand should any unlikely problems actually develop. *See id.* 14. All enhanced techniques are conducted only as authorized and pursuant to medical guidelines and supervision.[27]

---

[27] The CIA's CTC generally consults with the CIA's Office of General

As is clear from these descriptions and the discussion above, the CIA uses enhanced techniques only as necessary to obtain information that it reasonably views as vital to protecting the United States and its interests from further terrorist attacks. The techniques are used only in the interrogation of those who are reasonably believed to be closely associated with al Qaeda and senior enough to have actionable intelligence concerning terrorist threats. Even then, the techniques are used only to the extent reasonably believed to be necessary to obtain otherwise unavailable intelligence. In addition, the techniques are designed to avoid inflicting severe pain or suffering, and no technique will be used if there is reason to believe it will cause significant harm. Indeed, the techniques have been designed to minimize the risk of injury or any suffering that does not further the Government's interest in obtaining actionable intelligence. The program is clearly not intended "to injure in some way unjustifiable by any government interest." *Lewis,* 523 U.S. at 849. Nor can it be said to reflect "deliberate indifference" to a substantial risk of such unjustifiable injury. *Id.* at 851.[28]

Counsel (which in turn may consult with this Office) when presented with novel circumstances. This consultation further reduces any possibility that CIA interrogators could be thought to be "abusing [their] power, or employing it as an instrument of oppression," *Lewis*, 523 U. S. at 840 (citation and quotation marks omitted; alteration in *Lewis*) *see also Chavez*, 538 U. S. at 774 (opinion of Thomas, J.), so as to render their conduct constitutionally arbitrary.

[28] This is not to say that the interrogation program has worked perfectly. According to the *IG Report*, the CIA, at least initially, could not always distinguish detainees who had information but were successfully resisting interrogation from those who did not actually have the information. *See IG Report* at 83-85. On at least one occasion, this may have resulted in what might be deemed in retrospect to have been the unnecessary use of enhanced techniques. On that occasion, although the on-scene interrogation team judged Zubaydah to be compliant elements with CIA Headquarters still believed he was withholding information. ████████████████████████████████████. *See id.* at 84. At the direction of CIA headquarters interrogators therefore used the waterboard one more time on Zubaydah. ████████████████ *See id.* at 84-85.

This example, however, does not show CIA "conduct [that is] intended to injure in some way unjustifiable by any government interest," or "deliberate indifference" to the possibility of such unjustifiable injury. *Lewis*, 523 U.S. at 849. As long as the CIA reasonably believed that Zubaydah continued to withhold sufficiently important information, use of the waterboard was supported by the Government's interest in protecting the Nation from subsequent terrorist attacks. The existence of a reasonable, good faith belief is not negated because the factual

2.

We next address whether, considered in light of "an understanding of traditional executive behavior, of contemporary practice, and of the standards of blame generally applied to them," use of the enhanced interrogation techniques constitutes government behavior that "is so egregious, so outrageous, that it may fairly be said to shock the contemporary conscience." *Id.* at 847 n.8. We have not evidence of traditional executive behavior or contemporary practice either condemning or condoning an interrogation program carefully limited to further a vital government interest and designed to avoid unnecessary or serious harm.[29] However, in many contexts, there is a strong tradition against the use of coercive interrogation techniques. Accordingly, this aspect of the analysis poses a more difficult question. We examine the traditions surrounding ordinary criminal investigations within the United States, the military's tradition of not employing coercive techniques in intelligence interrogations, and the fact that the United States regularly condemns conduct undertaken by other countries that bears at least some resemblance to the techniques at issue.

These traditions provide significant evidence that the use of enhanced interrogation techniques might "shock the contemporary conscience" in at least some contexts. *Id.* As we have explained, however, the

---

predicates for that belief are subsequently determined to be false. Moreover, in the Zubaydah example, CIA Headquarters dispatched officials to observe the last waterboard session. These officials reported that enhanced techniques were no longer needed. *See IG Report* at 85. Thus, the CIA did not simply rely on what appeared to be credible intelligence but rather ceased using enhanced techniques despite this intelligence.

[29] CIA interrogation practice appears to have varied over time. The *IG Report* explains that the CIA "has had intermittent involvement in the interrogation of individuals whose interests are opposed to those of the United States." *IG Report* at 9. In the early 1980s, for example, the CIA initiated the Human Resource Exploitation ("HRE") training program, "designed to train foreign liaison services on Interrogation techniques." *Id.* The CIA terminated the HRE program in 1986 because of allegations of human right abuses in Latin America. *See id.* at 10.

due process inquiry depends critically on setting and circumstance, *see, e.g., id* at 847, *850,* and each of these contexts differs in important ways from the one we consider here. Careful consideration of the underpinnings of the standards of conduct expected in these other contexts, moreover, demonstrates that those standards are not controlling here. Further, as explained below, these enhanced techniques are all adapted from techniques used by the United States on its own troops, albeit under significantly different conditions. At a minimum, this confirms that use of these techniques cannot be considered to be categorically impermissible; that is, in some circumstances, use of these techniques is consistent with "traditional executive behavior" and "contemporary practice." *Id* at 847 n.8. As explained below, we believe such circumstances are present here.

Domestic Criminal Investigations. Use of interrogation practices like those we consider here in ordinary criminal investigations might well "shock the conscience." In *Rochin v. California,* 342 U.S. 165 (1952), the Supreme Court reversed a criminal conviction where the prosecution introduced evidence against the defendant that had been obtained by the forcible pumping of the defendant's stomach. The Court concluded that the conduct at issue "shocks the conscience" and was "too close to the rack and the screw." *Id.* at 172. Likewise, in *Williams v. United States,* 341 U.S. 97 (1951), the Court considered a conviction under a statute that criminalized depriving an individual·of a constitutional right under color of law. The defendant suspected several persons of committing a particular crime. He then

> over a period of three days took four men to a paint shack . . .
> and used brutal methods to obtain a confession from each of
> them. A rubber hose, a pistol, a blunt instrument, a sash cord
> and other implement [*sic*] were used in the project . . . Each
> was beaten, threatened, and unmercifully punished for sev-
> eral hours until he confessed.

Id. at 98-99. The Court characterized this as "the classic use of force to make a man testify against himself," which would render the confessions inadmissible. *Id* at 101. The Court concluded:

> But where police take matters in their own hands, seize vic-
> tims, beat and pound them until they confess, there cannot be
> the slightest doubt that the police have deprived the victim of
> a right under the Constitution. It is the right of the accused

to be tried by a legally constituted court, not by a kangaroo court.

Id. at 101.

More recently, in *Chavez v. Martinez,* 538 U.S. 760 (2003), the police had questioned the plaintiff, a gunshot wound victim who was in severe pain and believed he was dying, At issue was whether a section 1983 suit could be maintained by the plaintiff against the police despite the fact that no charges had ever been brought against the plaintiff. The Court rejected the plaintiff's Fifth Amendment Self-Incrimination Clause claim, *see id* at 773 (opinion of Thomas, J.); *id.* at 778-79 (Souter, J., concurring in judgment), but remanded for consideration of whether the questioning violated the plaintiff's substantive due process rights, *see id.* at 779-80. Some of the justices expressed the view that the Constitution categorically prohibits such coercive interrogations. *See id.* at 783, 788 (Stevens, J., concurring in part and dissenting in part) (describing the interrogation at issue as "torturous" and asserting that such interrogation "is a classic example of a violation of a constitutional right implicit in the concept of ordered liberty") (internal quotation marks omitted); *id.* at 796 (Kennedy, J., concurring in part and dissenting in part) ("The Constitution does not countenance the official imposition of severe pain or pressure for purposes of interrogation. This is true whether the protection is found in the Self-Incrimination Clause, the broader guarantees of the Due Process Clause, or both.").

The CIA program is considerably less invasive or extreme than much of the conduct at issue in these cases. In addition, the government interest at issue in each of these cases was the general interest in ordinary law enforcement (and, in *Williams,* even that was doubtful). That government interest is strikingly different from what is at stake here: the national security—in particular, the protection of the United States and its interests against attacks that may result in massive civilian casualties. Specific constitutional constraints, such as the Fifth Amendment's Self-Incrimination Clause, which provides that "[n]o person . . . shall be compelled *in any criminal case* to be a witness against himself," (emphasis added), apply when the government acts to further its general interest in law enforcement and reflect explicit fundamental limitations on how the government may further that interest. Indeed, most of the Court's police interrogation cases appear to be rooted in the policies behind the Self-Incrimination Clause and concern for the fairness and integrity of the trial process. In *Rochin,* for example, the Court was concerned with the use of evidence obtained by coercion to bring about a criminal conviction. *See, e.g.,* 342

U.S. at 173 ("Due process of law, as a historic and generative principle, precludes defining, and thereby confining, these standards of conduct more precisely than to say that convictions cannot be brought about by methods that offend 'a sense of justice.'") (citation omitted); *id.* (refusing to hold that "in order to convict a man the police cannot extract by force what is in his mind but can extract what is in his stomach"). *See also Jackson v. Denno,* 378 U.S. 368, 377 (1964) (characterizing the interest at stake in police interrogation cases as the "right to be free of a conviction based upon a coerced confession"); *Lyons v. Oklahoma,* 322 U.S. 596, 605 (1944) (explaining that "[a] coerced confession is offensive to basic standards of justice, not because the victim has a legal grievance against the police, but because declarations procured by torture are not premises from which a civilized forum will infer guilt"). Even *Chavez,* which might indicate the Court's receptiveness to a substantive due process claim based on coercive police interrogation practices irrespective of whether the evidence obtained was ever used against the individual interrogated, involved an interrogation implicating ordinary law enforcement interests.

Courts have long distinguished the government's interest in ordinary law enforcement from other government interests such as national security. The Foreign Intelligence Surveillance Court of Review recently explained that, with respect to the Fourth Amendment, "the [Supreme] Court distinguishe[s] general crime control programs and those that have another particular purpose, such as protection of citizens against special hazards or protection of our borders." *In re Sealed Case,* 310 F.3d 717, 747-46 (For. Intel. Surv. Ct Rev. 2002) (discussing the Court's "special needs" cases and distinguishing "FISA's general programmatic purpose" of "protect[ing] the nation against terrorists and espionage threats directed by foreign powers" from general crime control). Under the "special needs" doctrine, the Supreme Court has approved of warantless [*sic*] and even suspicionless searches that serve "special needs, beyond the normal. need for law enforcement." *Vernonia Schol* [*sic*] *Dist. 47J v. Acton,* 515 U.S. 646, 653 (1995) (quotation marks and citation omitted). Thus, although the Court has explained that it "cannot sanction [automobile] stops justified only by the" "general interest in crime control," *Indianapolis v. Edmond,* 531 U.S. 32, 44 (2000) (quotation marks and citation omitted), it suggested that it might approve of a "roadblock set up to thwart an imminent terrorist attack," *id. See also* Memorandum for James B. Comey, Deputy Attorney General, from Noel J. Francisco, Deputy Assistant Attorney General, Office of Legal Counsel, *Re: Whether OFAC May Without Obtaining A Judicial Warrant Enter the Commercial Premises of a Designated Entity To Secure Property That Has Been Blocked Pursuant to IEEPA* (April 11,

2005). Notably, in the due process context, the Court has distinguished the Government's interest in detaining illegal aliens generally from its interest in detaining suspected terrorists. *See Zadvydas,* 533 U.S. at 691. Although the Court concluded that a statute permitting the indefinite detention of aliens subject to a final order of removal but who could not be removed to other countries would raise substantial constitutional questions, it suggested that its reasoning might not apply to a statute that "appl[ied] narrowly to a small segment of particularly dangerous individuals, say, suspected terrorists." *Id.* at 691 (quotation marks and citation omitted).

Accordingly, for these reasons, we do not believe that the tradition that emerges from the police interrogation context provides controlling evidence of a relevant executive tradition prohibiting use of these techniques in the quite different context of interrogations undertaken solely to prevent foreign terrorist attacks against the United States and its interests.

United States Military Doctrine. Army Field Manual 34-52 sets forth the military's basic approach to intelligence interrogations. It lists a variety of interrogation techniques that generally involve only verbal and emotional tactics. In the "emotional love approach," for example, the interrogator might exploit the love a detainee feels for his fellow soldiers, and use this to motivate the detainee to cooperate. *Id.* at 3-15. In the "fear-up (harsh) approach," "the interrogator behaves in an overpowering manner with a loud and threatening voice [and] may even feel the need to throw objects across the room to heighten the [detainee's] implanted feelings of fear." *Id.* at 3-16. The *Field Manual* counsels that "[g]reat care must be taken when [using this technique] so any actions would not violate the prohibition on coercion and threats contained in the GPW, Article 17." *Id.* Indeed, from the outset, the *Field Manual* explains that the Geneva Conventions "and US policy expressly prohibit acts of violence or intimidation, including physical or mental torture, threats, insults, or exposure to inhumane treatment as a means of or aid to interrogation." *Id.* at I-8. As prohibited acts of physical and mental torture, the *Field Manual* lists "[f]ood deprivation" and "[a]bnormal sleep deprivation" respectively. *Id.*

The *Field Manual* provides evidence "of traditional executive behavior [and] of contemporary practice," *Lewis,* 523 U.S. at 847 n.8, but we do not find it dispositive for several reasons. Most obviously, as the *Field Manual* makes clear, the approach it embodies is designed for traditional armed conflicts, in particular, conflicts governed by the Geneva Conventions. *See Field Manual 34-52* at 1-7 to 1-8; *see also id.* at iv-v (noting that interrogations must comply with the Geneva Conventions and the Uniform Code of Military Justice). The United States, however, has

long resisted efforts to extend the protections of the Geneva Conventions
to terrorists and other unlawful combatants. As President Reagan stated
when the United States rejected Protocol I to the Geneva Conventions,
the position of the United States is that it "must not, and need not, give
recognition and protection to terrorist groups as a price for progress in
humanitarian law." President Ronald Reagan, Letter of Transmittal to the
Senate of Protocol II additional to the Geneva Conventions of 12 August
1949, concluded at Geneva on June 10, 1977 (Jan. 29, 1987). President
Bush, moreover, has expressly determined that the Geneva Convention
Relative to the Treatment of Prisoners of War ("GPW") does not apply
to the conflict with al Qaeda. *See* Memorandum from the President, *Re:
Humane Treatment of al Qaeda and Taliban Detainees* at 1 (Feb. 7, 2002);
see also Memorandum for Alberto R. Gonzales, Counsel to the President
and William J. Haynes II, General Counsel, Department of Defense, from
Jay S. Bybee, Assistant Attorney General, Office of Legal Counsel, *Re:
Application of Treaties and Laws to al Qaeda and Taliban Detainees* at
9-10 (Jan. 22, 2002) (explaining that GPW does not apply to non-state actors such as al Qaeda).

We think that a policy premised on the applicability of the Geneva
Conventions and not purporting to bind the CIA does not constitute controlling evidence of executive tradition and contemporary practice with
respect to untraditional armed conflict where those treaties do not apply,
where the enemy flagrantly violates the laws of war by secretly attacking
civilians, and where the United States cannot identify the enemy or prevent its attacks absent accurate intelligence.

State Department Reports. Each year, in the State Department's
Country Reports on Human Rights Practices, the United States condemns
coercive interrogation techniques and other practices employed by other
countries. Certain of the techniques the United States has condemned appear to bear some resemblance to some of the CIA interrogation techniques. In their discussion of Indonesia, for example, the reports list as
"[p]sychological torture" conduct that involves "food and sleep deprivation," but give no specific information as to what these techniques involve. In their discussion of Egypt, the reports list as "methods of torture"
"stripping and suspending victims; suspending victims from a ceiling or
doorframe with feet just touching the floor; beating victims [with various
objects]; . . . and dousing victims with cold water." *See also, e.g.,* Algeria
(describing the "chiffon" method, which involves "placing a rag drenched
in dirty water in someone's mouth"); Iran (counting sleep deprivation as
either torture or severe prisoner abuse); Syria (discussing sleep depriva-

tion and "having cold water thrown on detainees as either torture or "ill-treatment"). The State Department's inclusion of nudity, water dousing, sleep deprivation, and food deprivation among the conduct it condemns is significant and provides some indication of an executive foreign relations tradition condemning the use of these techniques.[30]

To the extent that they may be relevant, however, we do not believe that the reports provide evidence that the CIA interrogation program "shocks the contemporary conscience." The reports do not generally focus on or provide precise interrogation techniques. Nor do the reports discuss in any detail the contexts in which the techniques are used. From what we glean from the report, however, it appears that the condemned techniques are often part of a course of conduct that involves techniques and is undertaken in ways that bear no resemblance to the CIA program. Much of the condemned conduct goes far beyond the CIA techniques and would almost certainly constitute torture under United States law. *See, e.g.,* Egypt (discussing "suspending victims from a ceiling or doorframe with feet just touching the floor" and "beating victims [with various objects]"); Syria (discussing finger crushing and severe beatings); Pakistan (beatings, burning with cigarettes, electric shock); Uzbekistan (electric shock, rape, sexual abuse, beatings). The condemned conduct, moreover, is often undertaken for reasons totally unlike the CIA's. For example, Indonesia security forces apparently use their techniques in order to obtain confessions, to punish, and to extort money. Egypt "employ[s] torture to extract information, coerce opposition figures to cease their political activities, and to deter others from similar activities." There is no indication that techniques are used only as necessary to protect against grave terrorist threats or for any similarly vital government interests (or indeed for any legitimate government interest). On the contrary, much of the alleged abuses discussed in the reports appears [*sic*] to involve either the indiscriminate use of force, *see, e.g.,* Kenya, or the targeting of critics of the government, *see., e.g.,* Liberia, Rwanda. And there is certainly no indication that these countries apply careful screening procedures, medical monitoring, or any of the other safeguards required by the CIA interrogation program.

---

[30] We recognize that as a matter of diplomacy, the United States may for various reasons in various circumstances call another nation to account for practices that may in some respects resemble conduct in which the United States might in some circumstances engage, covertly or otherwise. Diplomatic relations with regard to foreign countries are not reliable evidence of United States executive practice and thus may be of only limited relevance here.

A United States foreign relations tradition of condemning torture, the indiscriminate use of force, the use of force against the government's political opponents, or the use of force to obtain confessions in ordinary criminal cases says little about the propriety of the CIA's interrogation practices. The CIA's careful screening procedures are designed to ensure that enhanced techniques are used in the relatively few interrogations of terrorists who are believed to possess vital, actionable intelligence that might avert an attack against the United States or its interests. The CIA uses enhanced techniques only to the extent reasonably believed necessary to obtain the information and takes great care to avoid inflicting severe pain or suffering or any lasting or unnecessary harm. In short, the CIA program is designed to subject detainees to no more duress than is justified by the Government's interest in protecting the United States from further terrorist attacks. In these essential respects, it differs from the conduct condemned in the State Department reports.

SERE Training. There is also evidence that use of these techniques is in some circumstances consistent with executive tradition and practice. Each of the CIA's enhanced interrogation techniques has been adapted from military SERE training, where the techniques have long been used on our own troops. *See Techniques* at 6; *IG Report* at 13-14. In some instances, the CIA uses a milder form of the technique than SERE. Water dousing, as done in SERE training, involves complete immersion in water that may be below 40°F. *See Techniques* at 10. This aspect of SERE training is done outside with ambient air temperatures as low as 10°F. *See id.* In the CIA technique, by contrast, the detainee is splashed with water that is never below 41°F and is usually warmer. *See id.* Further, ambient air temperatures are never below 64°F. *See id.* Other techniques, however, are undeniably more extreme as applied in the CIA interrogation program. Most notably, the waterboard is used quite sparingly in SERE training—at most two times on a trainee for at most 40 seconds each time. *See id.* at 13, 42. Although the CIA program authorizes waterboard use only in narrow circumstances (to date, the CIA has used the waterboard on only three detainees), where authorized, it may be used for two "sessions" per day of up to two hours. During a session, water may be applied up to six times for ten seconds or longer (but never more than 40 seconds). In a 24-hour period, a detainee may be subjected to up to twelve minutes of water application. *See id.* at 42. Additionally, the waterboard may be used on as many as five days during a 30-day approval period. *See August 19* ███████ *Letter* at 1-2. The CIA used the waterboard "at least 83 times during August

2002" in the interrogation of Zubaydah, *IG Report* at 90, and 183 times during March 2003 in the interrogation of KSM, *see id.* at 91.

In addition, as we have explained before:

> Individuals undergoing SERE training are obviously in a very different situation from detainees undergoing interrogation; SERE trainees know it is part of a training program, not a real-life interrogation regime, they presumably know it will last only a short time, and they presumably have assurances that they will not be significantly harmed by the training.

Techniques at 6. On the other hand, the interrogation program we consider here furthers the paramount interest of the United States in the security of the Nation more immediately and directly than SERE training, which seeks to reduce the possibility that United States military personnel might reveal information that could harm the national security in the event they are captured. Again, analysis of the due process question must pay careful attention to these differences. But we can draw at least one conclusion from the existence of SERE training. Use of the techniques involved in the CIA's interrogation program (or at least the similar techniques from which these have been adapted) cannot be considered to be *categorically* inconsistent with "traditional executive behavior" and "contemporary practice" regardless of context.[31] It follows that use of these techniques will not shock the conscience in at least some circumstances. We believe that such circumstances exist here, where the techniques are used against unlawful combatants who deliberately and secretly attack civilians in an untraditional armed conflict in which intelligence is difficult or impossible to collect by other means and is essential to the protection of the United States and its interests, where the techniques are used only when necessary and only in the interrogations of key terrorist leaders reasonably thought to have actionable intelligence and where every effort is made to minimize unnecessary suffering and to avoid inflicting significant or lasting harm.

---

[31] In addition, the fact that individuals voluntarily undergo the techniques in SERE training is probative. *See Breithaupt v. Abram*, 352 U. S. 432, 436-37 (1957) (noting that people regularly voluntarily allow their blood to be drawn and concluding that involuntary blood testing does not "shock the conscience").

Accordingly, we conclude that, in light of "an understanding of traditional executive behavior, of contemporary practice, and of the standards of blame generally applied to them," the use of the enhanced interrogation techniques in the CIA interrogation program as we understand it, does not constitute government behavior that "is so egregious, so outrageous, that it may fairly be said to shock the contemporary conscience." *Lewis*, 523 U.S. at 847 n.8.

C.

For the reasons stated, we conclude that the CIA interrogation techniques, with their careful screening procedures and medical monitoring, do not "shock the conscience." Given the relative paucity of Supreme Court precedent applying this test at all, let alone in anything resembling this setting, as well as the context-specific, fact-dependent, and somewhat subjective nature of the inquiry, however, we cannot predict with confidence that a court would agree with our conclusion. We believe, however, that the question whether the CIA's enhanced interrogation techniques violate the substantive standard of United States obligations under Article 16 is unlikely to be subject to judicial inquiry.

As discussed above, Article 16 imposes no legal obligations on the United States that implicate the CIA interrogation program in view of the language of Article 16 itself and, independently, the Senate's reservation. But even if this were less clear (indeed, even if it were false), Article 16 itself has no domestic legal effect because the Senate attached a non-self-execution declaration to its resolution of ratification. *See* Cong. Rec. 36,198 (1990) ("the United States declares that the provisions of Articles 1 through 16 of the Convention are not self-executing"). It is well settled that non-self-executing treaty provisions "can only be enforced pursuant to legislation to carry them into effect." *Whitney v. Robertson,* 124 U.S. 190, 194 (1888*); see also Foster v. Neilson,* 27 U.S. (2 Pet.) 253, 314 (1829) ("A treaty is in its nature a contract between two nations, not a legislative act. It does not generally effect, of itself, the object to be accomplished, . . . but is carried into execution by the sovereign power of the respective parties to the instrument."). One implication of the fact that Article 16 is non-self-executing is that, with respect to Article 16, "the courts have nothing to do and can give no redress." *Head Money Cases,* 112 U.S. 580, 598 (1884). As one court recently explained in the context of the CAT itself, "Treaties that are not self-executing do not create judicially-enforceable rights unless they are first given effect by implementing legislation." *Auguste v. Ridge,* 395 F.3d 123, 132 n.7 (3d Cir. 2005) (citations omitted). Because (with perhaps one narrow exception[32]) Article 16 has not been legislatively implemented, the interpretation of its substantive standard is unlikely to be subject to judicial inquiry.[33]

*   *   *

Based on CIA assurances, we understand that the CIA interrogation program is not conducted in the United States or "territory under [United States] jurisdiction" and that it is not authorized for use against United States persons. Accordingly, we conclude that the program does not implicate Article 16. We also conclude that the CIA interrogation program, subject to its careful screening, limits, and medical monitoring, would not violate the substantive standards applicable to the United States under Article 16 even if those standards extended to the CIA interrogation pro-

---

[32] As noted above, Section 1031 of Public Law 109-13 provides that "[n]one of the funds appropriated or otherwise made available by this Act shall be obligated or expended to subject any person in the custody or under the physical control of the United States to . . . cruel, inhuman, or degrading treatment or punishment that is prohibited by the Constitution, laws, or treaties of the United States." To the extent this appropriations rider implements Article 16, it creates a narrow domestic law obligation not to expand funds appropriated under Public Law 109-13 for conduct that violates Article 16. This appropriations rider, however, is unlikely to result in judicial interpretation of Article 16's substantive standards since it does not create a private right of action. *See, e.g., Alexander v. Sandoval*, 532 U. S. 275, 286 (2001) ("Like substantive federal law itself, private rights of action to enforce federal law must be created by Congress."); *Resident Counsel Allen Parkway VIII v. Dep't of Hous. & Urban Dev.*, 980 F.2d 1043, 1052 (5th *Cir.* 1993) ("courts have been reluctant to infer congressional intent to create private rights under appropriations measures") (citing *California v. Sierra Club*, 451 U.S. 287 (1981)).

It is possible that a court could address the scope of Article 16 if a prosecution were brought under the Antideficiency Act, 31 U.S.C. § 1341 (2000), for a violation of section 1031's spending restriction. Section 1341(a)(1)(A) of title 31 provides that officers or employees of the United States may not "make or authorize an expenditure or obligation exceeding an amount available in an appropriation or fund for the expenditure or obligation." "[K]nowing[] and willful[] violati[ons]" of section 1341(a) are subject to criminal penalties. *Id* § 1350.

[33] Although the interpretation of Article 16 is unlikely to be subject to judicial inquiry, it is conceivable that a court might attempt to address substantive questions under the Fifth Amendment if, for example the United States sought a criminal conviction of a high value detainee in an Article III court in the United States using evidence that had been obtained from the detainee through the use of enhanced interrogation techniques.

gram. Given the paucity of relevant precedent and the subjective nature of this inquiry, however, we cannot predict with confidence whether a court would agree with this conclusion, though, for the reasons explained, the question is unlikely to be subject to judicial inquiry.

Please let us know if we may be of further assistance.

Steven G. Bradbury
Principal Deputy Assistant Attorney General

RELEASE OF DECLASSIFIED NARRATIVE DESCRIBING THE DEPARTMENT OF JUSTICE OFFICE OF LEGAL COUNSEL'S OPINIONS ON THE CIA'S DETENTION AND INTERROGATION PROGRAM

SENATOR JOHN D. ROCKEFELLER IV
APRIL 22, 2009

PREFACE

The release of the following declassified narrative completes an effort that I began last year as Chairman of the Select Committee on Intelligence. The document is an effort to provide to the public an initial narrative of the history of the opinions of the Department of Justice's Office of Legal Counsel (OLC), from 2002 to 2007, on the legality of the Central Intelligence Agency's detention and interrogation program.

In August 2008, I asked Attorney General Michael B. Mukasey to join the effort to create such an unclassified narrative. The Attorney General committed himself to the endeavor, saying that if we failed it would not be for want of effort. Over the next months, Committee counsel and representatives of the Department of Justice, CIA, Office of the Director of National Intelligence, and the office of the Counsel to the President discussed potential text. The shared objective was to produce a text that, putting aside debate about the merits of the OLC opinions, describes key elements of the opinions and sets forth facts that provide a useful context for those opinions, within the boundaries of what the Department of Justice (DOJ) and the Intelligence Community would recommend in 2008 for declassification.

The understanding of the participants was that while the final product would be a Legislative Branch document, the collaborative nature of this process would provide the Executive Branch participants with the opportunity to ensure its accuracy. Before the end of the year, this process produced a narrative whose declassification DOJ, the DNI and the CIA supported. However, the prior Administration's National Security Council did not agree to declassify the narrative.

I renewed this effort in early February as soon as Attorney General Eric H. Holder, Jr., took office. Except for this preface, some minor edits, and the addition of a final paragraph to bring the narrative up to date as of President Obama's Executive Orders of January 22, 2009, this document is the same as the one that secured support for declassification last year. This declassification, which National Security Adviser James L.

Jones effected on April 16, 2009 and Attorney General Holder transmitted to the Committee on April 17, 2009, is supported again by the DOJ, the DNI, and the CIA. Because the text of the narrative was settled prior to the release on April 16, 2009 of the declassified OLC opinions from August 2002 and May 2005, the narrative does not include additional information from those opinions that is now in the public domain.

JOHN D. ROCKEFELLER IV

OLC OPINIONS ON THE CIA DETENTION
AND INTERROGATION PROGRAM

Submitted by Senator John D. Rockefeller IV
for Classification Review

On May 19, 2008, the Department of Justice and the Central Intelligence Agency (CIA) provided the Committee with access to all opinions and a number of other documents prepared by the Office of Legal Counsel of the Department of Justice (OLC) concerning the legality of the CIA's detention and interrogation program. Five of the documents provided addressed the use of water boarding. Committee Members and staff reviewed these documents over the course of several weeks; however, the Committee was not allowed to retain copies of the OLC documents about the CIA's interrogation and detention program.

The Committee had previously received one classified OLC opinion—an August 1, 2002, OLC opinion—in May 2004 as an attachment to a special review issued by the CIA's Inspector General on the CIA's detention and interrogation program. The opinion is marked as "Top Secret." The Executive Branch initially provided access to this review and its attachments to the Committee Chairman and Vice Chairman and staff directors. On September 6, 2006, all Members of the Committee obtained access to the Inspector General's review. The August 1, 2002, opinion is currently the only classified OLC opinion in the Committee's possession as to the legality of the CIA's interrogation techniques.

The capture of Abu Zubaydah and the initiation of the CIA detention and interrogation program

In late March 2002, senior Al-Qa'ida operative Abu Zubaydah was captured. Abu Zubaydah was badly injured during the firefight that brought him into custody. The CIA arranged for his medical care, and, in conjunction with two FBI agents, began interrogating him. At that time, the CIA assessed that Abu Zubaydah had specific information concerning future Al-Qa'ida attacks against the United States.

CIA records indicate that members of the National Security Council (NSC) and other senior Administration officials were briefed on the CIA's detention and interrogation program throughout the course of the program.[1] In April 2002, attorneys from the CIA's Office of General Counsel began discussions with the Legal Adviser to the National Security Council and OLC concerning the CIA's proposed interrogation plan for Abu Zubaydah and legal restrictions on that interrogation. CIA records indicate that the Legal Adviser to the National Security Council briefed the National Security Adviser, Deputy National Security Adviser, and Counsel to the President, as well as the Attorney General and the head of the Criminal Division of the Department of Justice.

According to CIA records, because the CIA believed that Abu Zubaydah was withholding imminent threat information during the initial interrogation sessions, attorneys from the CIA's Office of General Counsel met with the Attorney General, the National Security Adviser, the Deputy National Security Adviser, the Legal Adviser to the National Security Council, and the Counsel to the President in mid-May 2002 to discuss the possible use of alternative interrogation methods that differed from the traditional methods used by the U.S. military and intelligence community. At this meeting, the CIA proposed particular alternative interrogation methods, including waterboarding.

The CIA's Office of General Counsel subsequently asked OLC to prepare an opinion about the legality of its proposed techniques. To enable OLC to review the legality of the techniques, the CIA provided OLC with written and oral descriptions of the proposed techniques. The CIA also provided OLC with information about any medical and psychological effects of DoD's Survival, Evasion, Resistance and Escape (SERE) School, which is a military training program during which military personnel receive counter-interrogation training.

On July 13, 2002, according to CIA records, attorneys from the CIA's Office of General Counsel met with the Legal Adviser to the National Security Council, a Deputy Assistant Attorney General from OLC, the head of the Criminal Division of the Department of Justice, the chief of staff to the Director of the Federal Bureau of Investigation, and the Counsel to the President to provide an overview of the proposed interrogation plan for Abu Zubaydah.

On July 17, 2002, according to CIA records, the Director of Central Intelligence (DCI) met with the National Security Adviser, who ad-

---

[1] Descriptions of these meetings are based on contemporaneous CIA records that Committee staff has reviewed. The Committee has not conducted a complete search of Executive Branch records, nor has it requested records or testimony from all of the individuals whom CIA records included as having participated in these meetings.

vised that the CIA could proceed with its proposed interrogation of Abu Zubaydah. This advice, which authorized CIA to proceed as a policy matter, was subject to a determination of legality by OLC.

On July 24, 2002, according to CIA records, OLC orally advised the CIA that the Attorney General had concluded that certain proposed interrogation techniques were lawful and, on July 26, that the use of waterboarding was lawful. OLC issued two written opinions and a letter memorializing those conclusions on August 1, 2002.

August 1, 2002 OLC opinions

On August 1, 2002, OLC issued three documents analyzing U.S. obligations with respect to the treatment of detainees. Two of these three documents were unclassified: an unclassified opinion interpreting the federal criminal prohibition on torture, and a letter concerning U.S. obligations under the Convention Against Torture and the Rome Statute. Those two documents were released in 2004 and are publicly available.

The third document issued by OLC was a classified legal opinion to the CIA's Acting General Counsel analyzing whether the use of the interrogation techniques proposed by the CIA on Abu Zubaydah was consistent with federal law. OLC had determined that the only federal law governing the interrogation of an alien detained outside the United States was the federal anti-torture statute. The opinion thus assessed whether the use of the proposed interrogation techniques on Abu Zubaydah would violate the criminal prohibition against torture found at Section 2340A of title 18 of the United States Code. The Department of Justice released a highly redacted version of this opinion in July 2008 in response to a Freedom of Information Act lawsuit.

The classified opinion described the interrogation techniques proposed by the CIA. Only one of these techniques—waterboarding—has been publicly acknowledged. In addition to describing the form of waterboarding that the CIA proposed to use, the opinion discusses procedures the CIA identified as limitations as well as procedures to stop the use of interrogation techniques if deemed necessary to prevent severe mental or physical harm. Although a form of "waterboarding" has been employed on U.S. military personnel as part of the SERE training program, the Executive Branch considers classified the precise operational details concerning the CIA's form of the technique.

The opinion also outlined the factual predicates for the legal analysis, including the CIA's background research on the proposed techniques and their possible effect on the mental health of Abu Zubaydah.

The opinion described the information provided by the CIA concerning whether "prolonged mental harm" would be likely to result from the use of those proposed procedures. Because the military's SERE training program, like the CIA program, involved a series of stressful interrogation techniques (including a form of waterboarding) the opinion discussed inquiries and statistics relating to possible adverse psychological reactions to SERE training.

The anti-torture statute prohibits an act "specifically intended" to inflict "severe physical or mental pain or suffering." The opinion separately considered whether each of the proposed interrogation techniques, individually or in combination, would inflict "severe physical pain or suffering" or "severe mental pain or suffering." The opinion also considered whether individuals using the techniques would have the mental state necessary to violate the statute.

The opinion concluded that none of the techniques individually was likely to cause "severe physical pain or suffering" under the statute. With respect to waterboarding, the OLC opinion concluded that the technique would not inflict "severe physical pain or suffering" because it does not inflict actual physical harm or physical pain. The opinion concluded that, although OLC did not then believe physical suffering to be a concept under the statute distinct from physical pain, waterboarding would not inflict severe suffering, because any physical effects of waterboarding did not extend for the protracted period of time generally required by the term "suffering."

The OLC opinion also concluded that none of the techniques would constitute "severe mental pain or suffering" as that term is defined under the anti-torture statute. The opinion concluded that under the anti-torture statute, "severe mental pain or suffering" requires the occurrence of one of four specified predicate acts, as well as "prolonged mental harm." The opinion interpreted "prolonged mental harm" to require harm of some lasting duration, such as mental harm lasting months or years.

With respect to waterboarding, based on information provided by the CIA, the OLC opinion assessed whether it constituted, as a legal matter, one of the four predicate acts under the mental harm component of the anti-torture statute. The opinion concluded that the technique would not cause "severe mental pain or suffering" because, based on the U.S. military's experience with the form of waterboarding used in its SERE program, the CIA did not anticipate that waterboarding would cause prolonged mental harm.

After evaluating the proposed techniques individually, the OLC opinion considered whether the combined use of the proposed interrogation techniques would cause "severe physical pain or suffering" or "severe mental pain or suffering." OLC concluded that the combined use of the interrogation techniques would not constitute severe physical pain or suffering, because individually the techniques fell short of and would not be combined in such a way as to reach that threshold. The opinion concluded that OLC lacked sufficient information concerning the proposed use of the techniques to assess whether their combined use might inflict one of the predicate conditions for severe mental pain or suffering. The opinion concluded, however, that even if a predicate condition would be satisfied, it would not violate the prohibition because there was no evidence that the proposed course of conduct would produce any prolonged mental harm.

Finally, the opinion addressed whether an individual carrying out the proposed interrogation procedures would have the specific intent to inflict severe physical or mental pain or suffering required by the statute. It concluded that the interrogator would not have the requisite intent because of the circumstances surrounding the use of the techniques, including the interrogator's expectation that the techniques would not cause severe physical or mental pain or suffering, and the CIA's intent to include specific precautions to prevent serious physical harm.

For those reasons, the classified opinion concluded that none of the proposed interrogation techniques, used individually or in combination, would violate the criminal prohibition against torture found at section 2340A of title 18 of the United States Code.

Events after issuance of August 1, 2002 OLC opinion

According to CIA records, after receiving the legal approval of the Department of Justice and approval from the National Security Adviser, the CIA went forward with the interrogation of Abu Zubaydah and with the interrogation of other high-value Al-Qa'ida detainees who were then in, or later came into, U.S. custody. Waterboarding was used on three detainees: Abu Zubaydah, Abd al-Rahim al-Nashiri, and Khalid Sheikh Muhammad. The application of waterboarding to these detainees occurred during the 2002 and 2003 timeframe.

In the fall of 2002, after the use of interrogation techniques on Abu Zubaydah, CIA records indicate that the CIA briefed the Chairman and Vice Chairman of the Committee on the interrogation.[2] After the

---

[2] Just as the statement does not purport to identify all Executive Branch meetings and documents on the CIA detention and interrogation program, the state-

change in leadership of the Committee in January of 2003, CIA records indicate that the new Chairman of the Committee was briefed on the CIA's program in early 2003. Although the new Vice-Chairman did not attend that briefing, it was attended by both the staff director and minority staff director of the Committee. According to CIA records, the Chairman and Vice Chairman of the Committee were also briefed on aspects of the program later in 2003, after the use of interrogation techniques on Khalid Sheikh Muhammad.

In the spring of 2003, the DCI asked for a reaffirmation of the policies and practices in the interrogation program. In July 2003, according to CIA records, the NSC Principals met to discuss the interrogation techniques employed in the CIA program. According to CIA records, the DCI and the CIA's General Counsel attended a meeting with the Vice President, the National Security Adviser, the Attorney General, the Acting Assistant Attorney General for the Office of Legal Counsel, a Deputy Assistant Attorney General, the Counsel to the President, and the Legal Adviser to the National Security Council to describe the CIA's interrogation techniques, including waterboarding. According to CIA records, at the conclusion of that meeting, the Principals reaffirmed that the CIA program was lawful and reflected administration policy.

According to CIA records, pursuant to a request from the National Security Adviser, the Director of Central Intelligence subsequently briefed the Secretary of State and the Secretary of Defense on the CIA's interrogation techniques on September 16, 2003.

In May 2004, the CIA's Inspector General issued a classified special review of the CIA's detention and interrogation program, a copy of which was provided to the Committee Chairman and Vice Chairman and staff directors in June of 2004. The classified August 1, 2002, OLC opinion was included as an attachment to the Inspector General's review. That review included information about the CIA's use of waterboarding on the three detainees.

After the issuance of that review, the CIA requested that OLC prepare an updated legal opinion that incorporated actual CIA experiences and practice in the use of the techniques to date included in the Inspector General review, as well as legal analysis as to whether the interrogation

ment does not purport to describe either all Executive Branch communications or briefings to the Committee about, or the limitations on the Committee's use of and access to information about, the CIA's program.

techniques were consistent with the substantive standards contained in the Senate reservation to Article 16 of the Convention Against Torture.

Article 16 of the Convention Against Torture requires signatories to "undertake to prevent in any territory under its jurisdiction other acts of cruel, inhuman and degrading treatment which do not amount to torture." The Senate reservation to that treaty defines the phrase "cruel, inhuman and degrading treatment" as the treatment prohibited by the Fifth, Eighth, and Fourteenth Amendments to the Constitution. Thus, the CIA requested that OLC assess whether the interrogation techniques were consistent with the substantive provisions of the due process clause, as well as the constitutional requirement that the government not inflict cruel or unusual punishment.

In May 2004, after the issuance of the Inspector General review, CIA records indicate that the CIA's General Counsel met with the Counsel to the President, the Counsel to the Vice President, the NSC Legal Adviser, and senior Department of Justice officials about the CIA's program and the Inspector General review.

In June 2004, OLC withdrew its unclassified August 1, 2002, opinion on the anti-torture statute. OLC did not, however, withdraw the classified August 1, 2002 opinion, because it concluded that the classified opinion was narrower in scope than the unclassified opinion that was withdrawn. The classified opinion applied the anti-torture statute to the CIA's specific interrogation methods, but, unlike the unclassified August 1, 2002, opinion, it did not rely on or interpret the President's Commander in Chief power or consider whether torture could be lawful under any circumstances.

In July 2004, the CIA briefed the Chairman and Vice Chairman of the Committee on the facts and conclusions of the Inspector General special review. The CIA indicated at that time that it was seeking OLC's legal analysis on whether the program was consistent with the substantive provisions of Article 16 of the Convention Against Torture.

According to CIA records, subsequent to the meeting with the Committee Chairman and Vice Chairman in July 2004, the CIA met with the NSC Principals to discuss the CIA's program. At the conclusion of that meeting, it was agreed that the CIA would formally request that OLC prepare a written opinion addressing whether the CIA's proposed interrogation techniques would violate substantive constitutional standards, including those of the Fifth, Eighth and Fourteenth Amendments regardless of whether or not those standards were deemed applicable to aliens detained abroad.

DOJ advice from June 2004 to May 2005

Following the withdrawal of the unclassified August 1, 2002, opinion in June 2004, OLC began work on preparing an unclassified opinion concerning its interpretation of the anti-torture statute. At the same time, in accord with the request described above, OLC worked on classified opinions that would evaluate the specific techniques of the CIA program, individually and in combination, under its revised interpretation of the anti-torture statute, as well as an opinion that would evaluate whether the program was consistent with the substantive provisions of Article 16 of the Convention Against Torture.

On July 14, 2004, in unclassified written testimony before the House Permanent Select Committee on Intelligence, an Associate Deputy Attorney General explained the Department of Justice's understanding of the substantive constitutional standards embodied in the Senate reservation to Article 16 of the Convention Against Torture. The official's written testimony stated that under Supreme Court precedent, the substantive due process component of the Fifth Amendment protects against treatment that "shocks the conscience." In addition, his testimony stated that under Supreme Court precedent, the Eighth Amendment protection against Cruel and Unusual Punishment has no application to the treatment of detainees where there has been no formal adjudication of guilt.

While OLC worked on drafting new opinions with respect to the CIA program, the CIA continued its interrogation of high-value Al-Qa'ida detainees in U.S. custody. On July 22, 2004, the Attorney General confirmed in writing to the Acting Director of Central Intelligence that the use of the interrogation techniques addressed by the August 1, 2002, classified opinion, other than waterboarding, would not violate the U.S. Constitution or any statute or treaty obligation of the United States, including Article 16 of the Convention Against Torture. On August 6, 2004, the Acting Assistant Attorney General for OLC advised in writing that, subject to the CIA's proposed limitations, conditions and safeguards, the CIA's use of waterboarding would not violate any of those legal restrictions. The letter noted that a formal written opinion would follow explaining the basis for those conclusions. According to the CIA, the CIA nonetheless chose not to use waterboarding in 2004. Waterboarding was not subsequently used on any detainee, and was removed from CIA's authorized list of techniques sometime after 2005.

On December 30, 2004, the Office of Legal Counsel issued an unclassified opinion interpreting the federal criminal prohibition against torture, 18 USC 2340- 2340A, superseding in its entirety the withdrawn August 1, 2002, unclassified opinion. That December 30, 2004, opinion included a footnote stating "While we have identified various disagreements with the August 2002 Memorandum, we have reviewed this Office's prior opinions addressing issues involving treatment of detainees and do not believe that any of their conclusions would be different under the standards set forth in this memorandum."

In January of 2005, in response to a question for the record following his confirmation hearing, Attorney General Gonzales indicated that "the Administration . . . wants to be in compliance with the relevant substantive constitutional standard incorporated in Article 16 [of the Convention Against Torture], even if such compliance is not legally required." Attorney General Gonzales further indicated that "the Administration has undertaken a comprehensive legal review of all interrogation practices. . . . The analysis of practices under the standards of Article 16 is still under way."

The CIA briefed the Chairman and Vice Chairman of the Committee on the CIA's interrogation program again in March 2005. At that time, the CIA indicated that it was waiting for a revised opinion from OLC.

May 2005 opinions

In May 2005, OLC issued three classified legal opinions analyzing the legality of particular interrogation techniques. The first legal opinion analyzed the legality of particular interrogation techniques, including waterboarding, under the interpretation of the federal criminal prohibition against torture set forth in the December 30, 2004, unclassified opinion. The May 2005 opinion includes additional facts about the proposed techniques and a more extensive description of the applicable legal standards than the August 1, 2002, opinion.

With respect to waterboarding, the opinion concluded that while the technique presented a substantial question under the statute, the authorized use of waterboarding, when conducted with measures identified by the CIA as safeguards and limitations, would not violate the federal criminal prohibition against torture. To understand the possible effects of waterboarding, the May 2005 opinion relied on the military's experience in the administration of its form of the technique on American military personnel who had undergone SERE training, while recognizing some limitations with that reliance, such as the expectations of the individual going through the practice. The opinion also relied on the CIA's experience with the use of its form of waterboarding on the three detainees in 2002 and 2003.

The opinion concluded that waterboarding does not cause "severe physical pain" because it is not physically painful. It further reasoned that the CIA's form of waterboarding could not reasonably be considered specifically intended to cause "severe physical pain." The opinion also concluded that under the limitations and conditions adopted by the CIA, the technique would not be expected to cause distress of a sufficient intensity and duration to constitute "severe physical suffering," which the December 30, 2004 unclassified opinion had recognized to be a separate element under the federal anti-torture statute. The opinion concluded that waterboarding would not cause "severe mental pain or suffering" because OLC understood from the CIA that any mental harm from waterboarding would not be "prolonged," even if it met a predicate condition under the statute.

OLC's second legal opinion issued in May 2005 addressed the legality of the combined use of particular techniques, including waterboarding, under the criminal prohibition against torture. That opinion relied on information provided by the CIA concerning the manner in which the individual techniques were proposed to be combined in the CIA program. After considering the combined use of techniques as described by the CIA, OLC concluded that the combined use of the proposed techniques by trained interrogators would not be expected to cause the severe mental or physical pain or suffering required by the criminal prohibition against torture.

OLC's third legal opinion in May 2005 assessed the legality of particular interrogation techniques under Article 16 of the Convention Against Torture. The Executive Branch had previously concluded that Article 16 does not apply to detainees, such as those in CIA custody, who were held outside territory under U.S. jurisdiction. Nonetheless, as articulated in the January 2005 testimony of the Attorney General, the Executive Branch had decided to comply, as a matter of policy, with the relevant substantive constitutional standards incorporated in Article 16. Because of that policy determination, and because of the CIA's request that OLC address the substantive "cruel, inhuman or degrading" standard, OLC analyzed whether a number of interrogation techniques, including waterboarding, would violate the substantive constitutional standards contained in the Senate reservation to CAT.

The May 2005 opinion on Article 16 concluded that the CIA's use of interrogation techniques, including waterboarding, on senior members of al-Qa'ida with knowledge of, or involvement in, terrorist threats would not be prohibited by the Fifth, Eighth or Fourteenth Amendments under the particular circumstances of the CIA program. OLC concluded that with respect to the treatment of detainees in U.S. custody, who had not been convicted of any crime, the relevant constitutional prohibition was the "shocks the conscience" standard of the substantive due process component of the Fifth Amendment. Under the "shocks the conscience" standard, OLC concluded that Supreme Court precedent requires consideration as to whether the conduct is "arbitrary in the constitutional sense" and whether it is objectively "egregious" or "outrageous" in light of traditional executive behavior and contemporary practices.

To assess whether the CIA's interrogation program was "arbitrary in the constitutional sense," OLC asked whether the CIA's conduct of its interrogation program was proportionate to the governmental interests involved. Applying that test, OLC concluded that the CIA's interrogation program was not "arbitrary in the constitutional sense" because of the CIA's proposed use of measures that it deemed to be "safeguards" and because the techniques were to be used only as necessary to obtain information that the CIA reasonably viewed as vital to protecting the United States and its interests from further terrorist attacks.

OLC also concluded that the techniques in the CIA program were not objectively "egregious" or "outrageous" in light of traditional executive behavior and contemporary practice. In reaching that conclusion, OLC reviewed U.S. judicial precedent, public military doctrine, the use of stressful techniques in SERE training, public State Department reports on the practices of other countries, and public domestic criminal practices. OLC concluded that these sources demonstrated that, in some circumstances (such as domestic criminal investigations) there was a strong tradition against the use of coercive interrogation practices, while in others (such as with SERE training) stressful interrogation techniques were deemed constitutionally permissible. OLC therefore determined that use of such techniques was not categorically inconsistent with traditional executive behavior, and concluded that under the facts and circumstances concerning the program, the use of the techniques did not constitute government behavior so egregious or outrageous as to shock the conscience in violation of the Fifth Amendment.

Before the passage of the Detainee Treatment Act, in October of 2005, the Principal Deputy Assistant Attorney General for OLC noted in response to questions for the record: "[I]t is our policy to abide by the substantive constitutional standard incorporated into Article 16 even if such compliance is not legally required, regardless of whether the detainee in question is held in the United States or overseas." Similarly, in December of 2005, both the Secretary of State and the National Security Adviser stated publicly that U.S. policy was to treat detainees abroad in accordance with the prohibition on cruel, inhuman and degrading treatment contained in Article 16.

Subsequent Developments in the Law

In December 2005, Congress passed the Detainee Treatment Act (DTA), and the President subsequently signed it into law on December 30, 2005. That Act applied the substantive legal standards contained in the Senate reservation to Article 16 to the treatment of all detainees in U.S. custody, including those held by the CIA. At the time of the passage of the DTA, the Administration had concluded, based on the May 2005 OLC opinion, that the CIA's interrogation practices, including waterboarding, were consistent with the substantive constitutional standards embodied in the DTA.

In June 2006, in *Hamdan v. Rumsfeld*, the Supreme Court held that Common Article 3 of the Geneva Convention applied to the conflict with Al-Qa'ida, contrary to the position previously adopted by the President. Common Article 3 of the Geneva Conventions requires that detainees "shall in all circumstances be treated humanely," and prohibits "outrages upon personal dignity, in particular, humiliating and degrading treatment" and "violence to life and person, in particular murder of all kinds, mutilation, cruel treatment and torture." At the time of the *Hamdan* decision, the War Crimes Act defined the term "war crime" to include "a violation of Common Article 3."

In August 2006, OLC issued two documents considering the legality of the conditions of confinement in CIA facilities. One of the documents was an opinion interpreting the Detainee Treatment Act; the other document was a letter interpreting Common Article 3 of the Geneva Conventions, as enforced by the War Crimes Act. These documents included consideration of U.S. constitutional law and the legal decisions of international tribunals and other countries.

On September 6, 2006, the President publicly disclosed the existence of the CIA's detention and interrogation program. On the same day, the CIA briefed all Committee Members about the CIA's detention and interrogation program, including the CIA's use of enhanced interrogation techniques.

In October 2006, Congress passed the Military Commissions Act (MCA) to set forth particular violations of Common Article 3 subject to criminal prosecution under the War Crimes Act. Specifically, the MCA amended the War Crimes Act to designate nine actions as grave breaches of Common Article 3, punishable under criminal law. Although only these nine violations of Common Article 3 are subject to criminal prosecution, Congress recognized that Common Article 3 imposes additional legal obligations on the United States. The MCA provided that the President has the authority "to interpret the meaning and application of the Geneva Conventions and to promulgate higher standards and administrative regulations for violations of treaty obligations which are not grave breaches of the Geneva Conventions."

In July 2007, the President issued Executive Order 13440, which interpreted the additional obligations of the United States imposed by Common Article 3 of the Geneva Conventions. In conjunction with release of that Executive Order, OLC issued a legal opinion analyzing the legality of the interrogation techniques currently authorized for use in the CIA program under Common Article 3 of the Geneva Conventions, the Detainee Treatment Act, and the War Crimes Act.

The July 2007 opinion includes extensive legal analysis of the war crimes added by the MCA, U.S. constitutional law, the treaty obligations of the United States, and the legal decisions of foreign and international tribunals. The July 2007 opinion does not include analysis of the anti-torture statute but rather incorporates by reference the analysis of the May 2005 opinions that certain proposed techniques do not violate the anti-torture statute, either individually or combined.

In considering "traditional executive behavior and contemporary practices" under the substantive due process standard embodied in the Detainee Treatment Act, OLC considered similar sources to those considered in the May 2005 opinion on Article 16. In addition, OLC examined the legislative history of the MCA, which the President had sought, in part, to ensure that the CIA program could go forward following *Hamdan*, consistent with Common Article 3 and the War Crimes Act. OLC observed that, in considering the MCA, Congress was confronted with the question of whether the CIA should operate an interrogation program for high value detainees that employed techniques exceeding those used by the U.S. military but that remained lawful under the anti-torture statute and the War Crimes Act. OLC concluded that while the passage of the MCA was not conclusive on the constitutional question as to whether the program "shocked the conscience," the legislation did provide a "relevant measure of contemporary standards" concerning the CIA program and suggested that Congress had endorsed the view that the CIA's interrogation program was consistent with contemporary practice.

Because waterboarding was not among the authorized list of techniques, the 2007 OLC opinion did not address the legality of waterboarding. OLC therefore has not considered the legality of waterboarding under either of the two provisions that have been applied to the CIA's treatment of detainees since the passage of the Detainee Treatment Act in December of 2005: Common Article 3 of the Geneva Conventions and the War Crimes Act, as amended by the MCA.

Present Circumstances

On January 30, 2008, at a hearing of the Senate Judiciary Committee on Oversight of the Department of Justice, the Attorney General disclosed that waterboarding was not among the techniques currently authorized for use in the CIA program. He therefore declined to express a view as to the technique's legality. The Attorney General also stated that for waterboarding to be authorized in the future, the CIA would have to request its use, the CIA Director "would have to ask me, or any successor of mine, if its use would be lawful, taking into account the particular facts and circumstances at issue, including how and why it is to be used, the limits of its use and the safeguards that are in place for its use," and the President would have to address the issue.

In February 2008, in testimony before this Committee, the CIA Director publicly disclosed that waterboarding had been used on three detainees, as previously described. At that same hearing, the Director of National Intelligence (DNI) testified that waterboarding was not currently a part of the CIA's program, and that if there was a reason to use such a technique, the Director of the CIA and the Director of National Intelligence would have to agree whether to move forward and ask the Attorney General for a ruling on the legality of the specifics of the situation. The Committee also discussed the CIA's interrogation program with those two officials in closed session.

Although waterboarding was no longer a technique authorized for use in the CIA program, and the Attorney General and DNI testified in 2008 that a new legal opinion based on current law would be required before it could be used again, the May 2005 opinions on the legality of waterboarding under the anti-torture statute and Article 16 of the Convention Against Torture (the legal standards subsequently embodied in the DTA) remained precedents of the Office of Legal Counsel at the time of the Attorney General's and DNI's 2008 testimony.

On January 22, 2009, the President issued Executive Order 13491 on "Ensuring Lawful Interrogations." The Executive Order revoked

Executive Order 13440, limited the interrogation techniques that may be used by officers, employees, or other agents of the United States Government, and established a Special Interagency Task Force on Interrogation and Transfer Policies to report recommendations to the President. With respect to prior interpretations of law governing interrogation, section 3(c) of Executive Order 13491 directed that, unless the Attorney General provides further guidance, officers, employees, and other agents of the United States Government may not rely on interpretations of the law governing interrogations issued by the Department of Justice between September 11, 2001, and January 20, 2009.